The Flower of Kings

The Flower of Kings

A STUDY OF
THE ARTHURIAN LEGEND
IN ENGLAND
BETWEEN 1485 AND 1835

by

JAMES DOUGLAS MERRIMAN

THE UNIVERSITY PRESS OF KANSAS

Lawrence/Manhattan/Wichita

© Copyright 1973 by The University Press of Kansas
Standard Book Number 7006–0102–3
Library of Congress Catalog Card Number 72–92904
Printed in the United States of America

To

Helen Lenore Merriman

Mother, Teacher,
and Friend

Preface

In contrast to the vast array of scholarly work devoted to the medieval versions of the Arthurian legend, little more than a handful of studies concern themselves comprehensively with the latter-day treatments of Arthur and the knights of his Round Table.[1] Of these, the earliest, M. W. MacCallum's *Tennyson's Idylls of the King and Arthurian Story from the XVIth Century* (1894), still remains the only inclusive, critically intelligent, dependable book in the field.[2] Nevertheless, the work has its limitations today. A large number of minor treatments of Arthurian story find no place in MacCallum's account, and even his study of the more important modern versions is surprisingly incomplete in various ways. Moreover, the nearly eighty years that have elapsed since the book appeared have seen an accumulation of scholarly materials and a refinement of critical techniques unknown to MacCallum's time. Later attempts at inclusive study of the Arthurian tradition in modern times are considerably less useful. Howard Maynadier's *The Arthur of the English Poets* (1907), a rapid, descriptive survey of the field, affords no more than the briefest indications of the intellectual and aesthetic bearings of the material.[3] A more ambitious work, Margaret J. C. Reid's *The Arthurian Legend: Comparison of Treatment in Modern and Medieval Literature; A Study in the Literary Value of Myth and Legend* (1938), is, as Vinaver has described it, "obviously a beginner's thesis, not a work of research."[4] Something of the same observation might be made of R. W. Barber's *Arthur of Albion* (1961), which devotes its final quarter to the period after Malory.[5]

In addition to these books, which aim at more or less comprehensive and detailed surveys of the later uses of Arthurian material, a variety of other studies include more specialized or less elaborate examinations. Roberta Florence Brinkley's *Arthurian Legend in the Seventeenth Century* (1932)[6] and Nathan Comfort Starr's *King Arthur Today: The*

Arthurian Legend in English and American Literature 1901–1953 (1954) give generally reliable surveys of the uses of the tradition in their respective periods. The most thorough and the most useful of the studies restricted to the nineteenth century is Meier Schüler's *Sir Thomas Malorys 'Le Morte D'Arthur' und die englische Arthurdichtung des XIX. Jahrhunderts* (1900).[7] Of specific Arthurian themes, the most popular has been the Tristram story, which has inspired a respectable array of monographs.[8] A number of writers have also traced the varying metamorphoses of individual Arthurian figures: Gawain, Lancelot, Galahad, Merlin, and Arthur himself.[9] Finally, there is a considerable body of essays dealing with particular later Arthurian works.

Thus, although there is a substantial body of scholarship devoted to the subject, there is also much wanting to our understanding of the later uses of Arthurian story in England. The contribution made by many of the specialized studies to our knowledge is great; still, it is no injustice to say that by the limited nature of their aims, they give, both individually and collectively, a fragmented image. The more general studies are now either out-dated or marred by other inadequacies. The fact is that there is no place today for the student to turn for a single, up-to-date, systematic, and comprehensive account of the later fortunes of Arthurian legend in English literature. When I first began my own researches, it was my fond hope to provide such an account in one book. In the event, I have discovered that this undertaking was far from practicable. The material in the period between Malory and the Victorians—a period which I had innocently assumed to be largely a blank for the Arthurian story—surprised me both by its richness and by the interest of the critical and historical questions that it raised. As for the Victorian age, it soon became obvious that there alone was material for a large volume. I have accordingly felt myself compelled to realize my earlier ambition not in one book, but in two. Of these, the reader now holds the first in his hands.

In preparing this study, I have had several closely related purposes in mind. The first was to provide a reliable, thorough, and continuous survey of the British uses of Arthurian story between 1485 and 1835. As far as has been possible, this account takes advantage of the relevant scholarship that has accumulated since MacCallum first undertook a similar though more extensive task in the late nineteenth century. Beyond chronicling the later fortunes of the legend, I have tried to explain what the requirements for a fully successful handling of the old materials were, and how the intellectual, aesthetic, and cultural attitudes of various times have either militated against such a handling or made it increasingly possible. I have been particularly concerned to find answers to a number of questions of considerable scholarly and critical interest raised by the later history of Arthurian story. Why did a subject that had inspired some of the greatest works of medieval literature fall into comparative disuse for so long? Why did a story capable of continuing to excite the imaginations of the greatest poets repeatedly fail to achieve adequate expression in their work? What necessary combination of intellectual and poetic attitudes was missing during a period of some three centuries? What made it possible for the Romantics to come closer and closer to genuinely successful use of Arthurian story? In my efforts to provide answers to these questions resides a large part of this book's claim to novelty. Its usefulness as a reference work extends, I hope, beyond my answers.

Within the range that I have chosen, my effort has been to be reasonably thorough, but it would be folly to claim to be exhaustive in so large a field. The emphasis of this study, as will be seen, falls on the history of Arthurian story from the middle of the eighteenth century to the beginning of the Victorian era. For this choice, there are several reasons. For one, the uses of Arthurian legend and tradition from Tudor times through the seventeenth century have been dealt with previously in works that are still generally reliable. But the emphasis has been determined especially by my conviction that the most interesting and significant developments in the later history of the legend occur from 1750 on, and are closely related to that large general movement, still not exhausted, that we call Romanticism. I have stopped short of the Victorians because with the end of the first third of the nineteenth century, my narrative finally reached one point that, in Aristotelian terms, might be called an end or, perhaps, the beginning of yet another story. But within the period 1750–1835, I think I can justly say that I have tried to examine and appraise every British Arthurian work available, including several that have not been considered in any previous study of the field.

For the length of this book, I offer my sincerest apologies—and a defense. In order to accomplish the purpose of providing a detailed survey of the British uses of Arthurian story over a period of some three and a half centuries, I have been obliged to trench upon the reader's patience beyond the limits I should like to have set. Many of the minor works that I have touched upon or even analyzed at length cannot possibly be described as "good" or even "important" in any but the most relative terms. But literary history like political history cannot be a mere record of the work of heroes. This is especially so in a book that attempts to trace the history of a legend, a history which is written not only in the occasional great monuments that it has produced, but also in a host of lesser productions, which, perhaps, indicate even more clearly than the greater works the extent and quality of a culture's attitudes toward that legend. I must beg special pardon for the summaries and extensive notes. Despite the unavoidable tedium of both, it has seemed necessary to me in a book that to a large degree traces the history of a story *as story* to outline in some detail the actual shape of the forms that the story has taken at various times. And this has seemed all the more imperative in dealing with a large number of unfamiliar works, many of which are ordinarily unobtainable. As for the notes, I offer something of the same defense; in a book intended as a reference work, I have been anxious to provide the reader with a precise indication of the evidence on which I have based my assertions, and to point him to the minor byways of the subject.

But now, lest I exhaust my reader in prospect before I do so in fact, let me conclude with words whose conventionality will not, I trust, obscure their sincerity. Like most researchers, I owe my truest, largest, and deepest debt to the many preceding scholars whose labors, patient and impatient, have furnished me with much of the foundation of the present book; the extent of my indebtedness to them will be evident from my notes. It is less easy to indicate my obligation to the librarians of the New York Public Library, the Columbia University Libraries, and the Ablah Library of Wichita State University, who have assisted me in obtaining sight of many scarce, out-of-the-way books. I am also indebted to Columbia University and to the Council for Research in the Humanities for generous grants that provided me with free time when my studies stood most in need of it. Thanks are due also to the Research Committee of Wichita State University for a grant to cover typing expenses. To all my many teachers throughout nearly two decades of undergraduate and graduate study, I owe a debt no less great than it is general for the curiosity and the shaping of the mind that has produced this book. To Professors Marjorie Hope Nicolson, Jerome H. Buckley, A. Kent Hieatt, William Nelson, David Robertson, and Carl Woodring, I am particularly grateful for generous assistance, advice, and encouragement given me during the earlier stages of the writing of this study. I am also grateful to Professors Charles Moorman and Nathan Comfort Starr, whose detailed comments at a later stage showed me the way to a variety of improvements as well as saving me from a number of mistakes. I am thankful to Dean Thomas C. Rumble, who kindly supplied me with information I could obtain nowhere else. To my good friends Dean Morgan Schmitter and Louis T. Milic, I owe much for sympathetic support and patient listening. To John Langley, Director of the University Press of Kansas, and to his predecessor, John Dessauer, I am grateful for generous and unstinting willingness to produce what is—at least in its detail and its notes—a deliberately old-fashioned work of scholarship. I am especially obligated to Yvonne Willingham of the Press for patience with many delays and for extraordinary editorial care and helpfulness. I am indebted to Karen Kelly for her admirably accurate typing of a difficult manuscript, to Robin Eversole for her compilation of the index, and to my student Mary Bigane for her cheerful endurance of the tedium of proofreading. Finally, my parents and my wife, Mira, who bore with me and cheered me on during the long task of making this book, deserve a gratitude quite beyond my abilities to express.

J. D. M.

Wichita State University
November 1972

Contents

The Flower of Kings

Nothing in human nature, my dear friend, is without its reasons. The modes and fashions of different times may appear, at first sight, fantastic and unaccountable. But they, who look nearly into them, discover some latent cause of their production.

Bishop Hurd, *Letters on Chivalry and Romance*

Introduction

Today the Arthurian legend seems one of the most permanent fixtures of the imagination of the English-speaking peoples. A successful Broadway musical, comic strips, movies, and boys' books by the dozens, all draw at least a part of their substance from the tales of Arthur and his Round Table. In our language the name of the chastest knight, Galahad, has become a synonym for utter purity. Scarcely a year passes without a new edition or adaptation of Malory's *Morte Darthur*, whether announced by the sedate advertisements of a university press or blazoned abroad with a prominently displayed "Unexpurgated!" by less respectable sources. Poets and novelists in our century have turned with persistent frequency to the theme, and an independent scholarly specialty has developed in academic circles around Arthurian literature in its medieval forms.

Yet, as the most casual student of the subject knows, such widespread interest, such interpenetration of the popular and literary imagination has not always existed. During the Middle Ages, of course, for several centuries the Arthurian legend came as close to dominating imaginative literature as any story or body of story could have done. But after this splendid development, which produced some of the supreme glories of medieval literature, the legend fell upon increasingly hard times, and no wholly satisfactory treatment of the tragic career of Arthur emerged in England for a very long time—some three hundred and fifty years in all.

That is not to say that the subject was forgotten between Malory and the Victorians. On the contrary, for the better part of that time, it exercised a continuing fascination over men of the most diverse talents, among them some of the most illustrious figures in English literature. Yet none of them translated this fascination into an altogether worthy successor to the medieval tradition. Spenser appropriated names and a certain amount of atmosphere from the old legend, but the story itself was not apposite to his purposes in the *Faerie Queene*. In Milton's mind, the Arthurian theme long vied for attention with such high subjects as the story of Job and the justification of God's ways to men, but in the end he abandoned it. Dryden, having projected a mighty epic on the legend, finally settled for a trivial and debased treatment. Many lesser men, like Blackmore, fell in unequal combat with the legend's difficulties, leaving behind them works known only, if known at all, to ridicule—and specialists. By the middle of the eighteenth century, when Fielding used Arthur's association with a hero of the nursery, Tom Thumb, for the purposes of literary burlesque, the old story appeared to have lost all viability.

But, as we shall see, at the very moment of the Arthurian legend's lowest ebb, the conditions for a revival of the *matière de Bretagne* were already developing. Eighteenth-century antiquarianism, the Gothic revival, Medievalism, the New History, and indeed the whole nexus of ideas, attitudes, and interests that go under the name of Romanticism were preparing the soil for another great flowering of the Arthurian cycle. In the second half of the eighteenth century, Hurd, Percy, and Warton labored to revalidate chivalric romance, and in their wake such obscure figures as William Hilton and Richard Hole sought to call Arthur back in song. In the next century Frere and Peacock continued the older program of using Arthurian legend for burlesque or satire, but Scott and Wordsworth along with a number of lesser writers turned to the old story for serious purposes. While most of the Pre-Romantic and Romantic versions were relatively pale blooms, they are clearly harbingers of the great and long-delayed second blossoming of the legend in the work of Tennyson, Morris, Arnold, Swinburne, and a small army of their followers.

To a large degree the growing receptivity of the Romantics, both as poets and as readers, to the Arthurian story rests on the Romantic revaluation of the Middle Ages and a resultant awakening of sympathy for nearly every aspect of that period. While a part of this sympathy was doubtless purely emotional and even sentimental, a large part was also the response of men who sought (and often thought they found) in the Middle Ages solutions to their own age's grave social, intellectual, and aesthetic problems. That the Victorians to come would find one of the major symbolic expressions of their conception of life in Arthurian story is not surprising. The medieval triumph of the matter of Britain owes much, as will be seen, to its unequalled capability for expressing the ideals of Christian chivalry—ideals which represent at least in part an uneasy compromise in a strongly polarized conflict between the demands of spiritual and secular life, the Church's way and the world's way. The nineteenth century shows a similarly sharp cleavage between the calls of moral aspiration and secular actualities. What the moral life was in ideal was clearly established and its imperatives were categorical; what the demands of secular life were in an age of Benthamite economics and power politics were equally clear and sometimes equally categorical. If, in a manner of speaking, the compromise between the spiritual life and the robber baron of the Middle Ages had been the Christian knight, the compromise between the moral life and the robber baron of the nineteenth century was the Christian gentleman. Arthur and his men, once archetypes of chivalry, became at last splendid symbols of the gentlemanly code, an ideal historically rooted in chivalry. It is no accident that the speaker in Tennyson's "The Epic" would dream of Arthur's appearing to him "like a modern gentleman."

While this reasoning goes far to explain the enthusiasm of writers and their readers in the nineteenth century for Arthurian story, it does not tell us what secret the Romantics began to understand in the old legend—a secret which enabled them to use it seriously and which would allow the Victorians at last to exploit the old material to the full. And the consonance of Arthurian story with nineteenth-century expressive needs is of even less assistance to an understanding of the curious fatality that dogged most of the plans or attempts to use the legend during the period between Malory and the Victorians. Actually, as we shall see, a great many factors conspired against the production of a truly successful treatment of Arthurian story in those years. Antagonism toward the Middle Ages and medieval romance, the involvement of Arthur's career in dynastic politics and in a long struggle between patriotic enthusiasts and humanist scholars, classicist literary theories and rationalist notions of truth, all contributed to discourage any adequate use of the legend.

But of all the difficulties that baffled writers from the Renaissance through the eighteenth century in their attempts to deal with Arthur and his knights, perhaps the most crucial was one of which they appear to have been least aware. For if there is any one thing that most of these authors share, it is a uniform conviction that the story may be limitlessly altered or manipulated to suit any individual whim or aim. It is not hard to understand such a belief. From the Middle Ages, they had inherited a vast body of immensely varied materials: romances in verse and prose, popular ballads, folk tales, and pseudohistorical chronicles. The surface contradictions between these various versions of Arthur's reign, or even within the versions themselves doubtless suggested a hopeless confusion, a barbaric lack of order to the new age. Yet—as the Romantics began to discover, thereby opening the way to successful re-creation of the legend—behind these shifting, Protean appearances there was a fixed core, an essential story that no individual genius could successfully alter any more than any individual genius could have created it. To see what the nature of this fixed core is, to comprehend how categorical its requirements were, we must now cast far back, though briefly, into the origins and medieval development of Arthurian story.

PART I

*From Heroic Myth
to Farce and Nursery Tale*

1 ❧ The Growth of a Legend

ARTHUR IN THE MIDDLE AGES

MYTHIC ORIGINS

The beginnings of Arthurian story are lost in the dim prehistory of the peoples of Western Europe. Yet by piecing together scattered bits of evidence, scholars have been able to suggest that its first traces are to be found in the mythologies of the eastern Mediterranean peoples, which over a period of hundreds, perhaps even thousands, of years were carried to Southern Ireland. Here the stories and rituals slowly mingled with native Irish mythology and, as this growing body of legend moved into Wales, with various Brythonic and Romano-British religious elements.[1] Whatever the processes of this diffusion and accretion were, it seems clear that long before the conversion of the Celtic peoples to Christianity (and therefore long before the existence of the historical Arthur, if he existed at all), there had developed among them an extensive literature of gods and heroes among whom nearly all of the chief figures around Arthur had their first recognizable forms. Such mythic origins were recognized even in the Middle Ages, as occasional references make clear,[2] but it was not until the nineteenth century that these origins became the object of serious study. Matthew Arnold was quick to note of the characters of the *Mabinogion*:

> These are no mediaeval personages; they belong to an older, pagan, mythological world. The very first thing that strikes one . . . is how evidently the mediaeval story-teller is pillaging an antiquity of which he does not fully possess the secret; he is like a peasant building his hut on the site of Helicarnassus or Ephesus; he builds, but what he builds is full of materials of which he knows not the history, or knows by a glimmering tradition merely;—stones "not of this building," but of an older architecture, greater, cunninger, more majestical.[3]

Later studies show clearly that in many of the characters and incidents of

9

medieval Arthurian romance and "history" we have survivals of ancient solar and lunar myths, seasonal and vegetation myths, fertility cults, and initiation rites. The Gawain of later story whose strength waxes before noon and wanes afterward, the Guenevere whose abduction is related to the changing seasons, the Grail King whose wounded "thighs" leave his land sterile and waste—these are not arbitrary creations of individual imaginations.

While the antiquity of these knights and ladies of the Round Table is thus clear, Arthur himself presents, curiously enough, a very different problem. His name, unlike those of his companions, cannot properly be derived from any of the Celtic deities. Instead it appears to have the Roman proper name *Artorius* as its source.[4] And when we first meet him in the early ninth-century *Historia Brittonum* of Nennius, he is not a god, but a man, a *dux bellorum* or "battle chief" who is said to have led the Britons successfully in twelve battles against the Saxons at a time some three hundred years previously—that is, around the end of the fifth and beginning of the sixth centuries. At the same time, obviously fabulous elements were already gathering around the name and figure of Arthur. In one of the twelve battles, he is said to have slain 960 men single-handed, and in the *Mirabilia* attached to the *Historia*, we learn of marvels associated with the tomb of Arthur's son, Amir, and with a footprint left by Arthur's hound, Cabal, during the great chase of the boar Troynt. But Arthur is also clearly a Christian hero; in at least one of his battles he bore the image of the Virgin on his shoulders, an act which appears to have assisted his routing of the pagans.[5]

Arthur's success against the pagan warriors was evidently matched by his victories over the pagan deities, and here too the symbol of the new religion no doubt played its part. A variety of evidence shows clearly that in the eleventh century, the legendary king was already the center to which were drawn a number of originally independent heroes.[6] Arthur and tales about him are mentioned frequently in the Welsh triads, and Cei (Kay) and Bedwyr (Bedivere) are among the first gods to be demoted to subordinates of the new king.[7] In the *Spoils of Annwfn* Arthur and his men engage in what is clearly an expedition to the Celtic Other World, obtaining there a magical cauldron that will not cook for a coward.[8] This cauldron, as well as the chase of the fabulous monster boar, Twrch Trwyth, alluded to in the Nennian *Mirabilia*, makes another appearance in the Welsh tale of Culhwch and Olwen in which Arthur and a numerous body of his knights are active in many adventures of a fabulous sort, some of them involving the execution of various agricultural tasks. Mere battle chief no more, Arthur has become a king ruling over an extensive

area and a band of wondrous heroes, many of whom are clearly mythological figures.[9] Together they accomplish marvelous feats of land cleans-
ing and such culture activities as plowing and bringing back to their
people the advantages of the Other World. How much of the tragic
ending of Arthur's story had developed by this time is unclear; possibly
his mortal wounding at the hands of his treacherous nephew was already
known,[10] and certainly his mystic survival either in Avalon or some other
place was widely believed in from an early time.[11]

The much belabored question of whether Arthur ever "really" existed
is of no great consequence here; after all, it is not as an actual ruler, but as
a king of romance that Arthur made a realm and ruled in literature.[12]
But it is of the greatest consequence that there was a *belief*, very likely
widespread, in the historical existence of such a hero. It was just this
belief, including as it did Arthur's championing of the cause of Christ
against the pagan, that permitted the survival in the Christian society of
the Middle Ages of elements that would otherwise have been all too
clearly recognizable as pagan. Like the Celtic cross with its Christian
cross superimposed on the elder solar circle, Arthur was an acceptable
fusion of antithetical elements: Christian and pagan, cryptohistorical and
mythological. And just as the early Church had grown in strength by
absorbing the energies of the old religions, the extraordinary vitality of
Arthurian story may in part result from its progressive synthesis of these
elements.

GEOFFREY'S *HISTORIA*

The vitality of the story of Arthur is already clear in the first really
impressive treatment of the legend by an Englishman. Geoffrey of Monmouth's *Historia Regum Britanniae* (*ca.* 1136) purports, as its title indicates, to be a comprehensive history. But for Geoffrey's readers in the
twelfth century as well as for those in the twentieth, the story of Arthur
was certainly the most impressive part of the book, and it seems likely
that Geoffrey intended it to be so received.[13] In the shaping heat of his
imagination, history and tradition fused into a continuous narrative of
tragic dignity and significance.[14] Begotten on Igrayne by Uther Pendragon through Merlin's magic ruse, Arthur succeeds to the throne despite
his clouded title, drives the Saxons from his realm, and takes Ganhumara
as his queen. Abroad he extends his conquests, and at home maintains a
court to which come the greatest knights of the world to live in gallantry
and honor under his liberal reign. On his last great campaign against
Lucius of Rome, he is triumphant until he learns that his nephew Modred,

to whom he had entrusted his queen and realm, has gathered together an army of rebels, usurped the throne, and taken Ganhumara as his wife. Arthur returns, fights Modred's forces, kills Modred in a last great battle, is mortally wounded himself, and carried to Avalon to be healed.[15]

The underlying motifs of much of this story were, as we have seen, already present in the core of the legend, but there are also important additions: the mysterious circumstances surrounding Arthur's parentage, conception, and birth; his marriage to the fatally attractive Ganhumara; and his betrayal and the consequent destruction of his realm and life through the treachery of his nephew Modred. If these motifs, so clearly mythological in origin as they are, cannot be credited to Geoffrey's originality, a very significant shift in atmosphere and emphasis can be. In the *Historia*, the vague culture hero of Celtic tradition has become an actualized Christian king, a champion of women, and a righter of wrongs. His court has become at the same time an idealized gathering place for the noblest knights and ladies of his time[16]—a time which is neither that of sixth-century Britain nor that of twelfth-century Norman England, but rather the time of heroic legend and romance, which is never a definite past and never the present, but always "long, long ago." It is this strange combination of actualized characters with romantic or heroic time and place that is Geoffrey's signal contribution to Arthurian story.

The importance of Geoffrey in the evolution of Arthurian story is, however, difficult to assess. The two-hundred-odd extant manuscripts[17] along with various translations and abridgements and the denunciations of subsequent historians attest to the popularity of his work. There can be no doubt at all that he is the source and originator of the long line of chronicles that for centuries maintained Arthur's place in what passed for serious and exact history.[18] Through them or directly, his influence from the Renaissance on into the eighteenth century was to be, as we shall see, enormous. Nor is there any reason to doubt that his presentation of Arthur as a historical figure produced a more serious attitude toward the legend and thereby assisted at least indirectly the success of imaginative Arthurian literature.[19] But his direct influence on early romances on the Continent appears to be very doubtful.

ARTHUR AMONG THE ROMANCERS

It is to the Breton *conteurs* or professional storytellers, as Loomis has noted, that we must assign "the preponderant share . . . in popularizing the Arthurian legend in the courts and baronial halls of France and England during the twelfth century."[20] From such oral sources a vast body of metrical and prose romances proliferated in the following centuries, spreading over all of Western Europe, and in the process profoundly affecting the nature of the story itself.[21] The taste of the age lay in the direction of the fantastic, and accordingly the stories became an endless and frequently tedious succession of meaningless marvels, extravagant and unmotivated incidents. Since "Arthur's warlike exploits and his achievements on a large public scale naturally did not furnish the medieval romancers with such attractive material as the private adventures of love and knight-errantry which his followers undertook,"[22] the emphasis tended to shift from Arthur himself to the exploits of his knights—Gawain, Tristram, Lancelot, and others—or to adventures such as the Quest of the Grail in which he had little if any part. But if Arthur was reduced in the metrical versions to a mere nucleus about which the biographical romances of his heroes accreted, in the later prose romances his fame, at least as the faultless king of the romantic historians, was blackened by the addition of the mythological motif of an unwitting incestuous relationship with his half-sister from which sprang the instrument of his fate, Modred. MacCallum's contention that Arthur was thus made "the author of his own ruin,"[23] may explain the intentions, dimly realized if at all, of the romancers, but it ignores the fact that such an accidental, essentially unwilled sin, no matter how satisfactory it might be for classical tragedy (e.g., *Oedipus*), was radically inadequate for a Christian society. That some of the romancers themselves perceived its inadequacy may be gathered from their steady emphasis on another of their additions, the adultery between Lancelot and Guinevere, a sin of the will which has as its consequences the deterioration of the Round Table and the destruction of Arthur and his realm. This emphasis on adultery was, of course, a reaction to more than abstract theological or moral requirements; it was a reflection of the intellectual and emotional tensions generated by the doctrines of courtly love, which pervaded the secular thought of the Middle Ages and not a little of its religious speculation. It is in this responsiveness, this adaptability of Arthurian story to the tastes and imaginative needs of the age that one clue to its popularity is to be found.

THE VOGUE OF ARTHURIAN ROMANCE

The enormous popularity of Arthurian story is clearly such as to justify the epithet "miraculous."[24] In the rapidity of its diffusion through Western Europe and even as far as Iceland and Jerusalem, in its ascendancy over the earlier matters even to the extent of markedly influencing them, and in its absorption of many of the greatest imaginative talents of the Middle Ages, Arthurian story obviously dominated medieval romance.[25] The reasons for this vogue are not, however, so obvious. The view that a "perfect explanation for the miraculous spread of the Arthurian legend" is to be found in the Breton *conteurs'* recounting of these tales "with such verve that they were able to fascinate counts and kings,"[26] while it may explain *how* the story became popular, is, as far as explaining *why*, little more than a perpetuation of one of the more ubiquitous latter-day Celtic myths: the supernatural storytelling abilities of the Celtic people.[27] Nor is the solution materially advanced by such explanations of "the chief causes" as this:

> The search for the strange and exotic which found satisfaction in the marvels of the Alexander legend took delight also in the wonders which had once abounded in the land of Logres, the Out Isles, and the fay-haunted forest of Broceliande—turning castles, testing horns, enchanted springs. . . . So, too, the new interest in the various manifestations of love, which was first exploited by the authors of *Enéas* and the *Roman de Troie*, found larger scope in the amorous adventures of Gawain, the tragic fate of Tristan and Isolt, the imperious whims and the jealousy of Guenevere, and the agonies of Lancelot. The Grail quest, so tantalizing in its contradictions and obscurity, led to ponderings on the mysteries of religion, while profound lessons of morality could be extracted from the history of Parzival.[28]

But surely this is to say little more than that when one puts rabbits in a hat one may draw out rabbits. After all, the "amorous adventures" of Gawain were what the medieval authors added to the original solar god; the Christian symbolism and moral truths of the Grail story were what they had grafted onto the stock of a Celtic fertility myth. The problem, in short, is why was this particular hat chosen? why did the matter of Arthur rather than that of, say Charlemagne or Alexander, become one of the most comprehensive expressions of medieval sensibility?

In a very general way, these questions are to be answered, as MacCallum suggested, "by supposing that the new matter was exceptionally suitable to the spirit of the time. It must have met a deep-felt want, and shown itself capable of receiving the stamp of the medieval spirit and expressing the medieval modes of life and thought more perfectly, than any previous theme."[29] If we are to understand this "deep-felt want," we must consider the situation from which it arose. The efforts of historical reconstructionists have been so far successful that we tend to overlook the fact that in the medieval governing and military classes among which romance found its natural audience, barbarism, primitive violence, and unbridled passions survived well into the later Middle Ages.[30] Earlier these savage energies had been well employed in fighting off the incursions of heathen invaders, but by the end of the first Christian millennium this work had been done, and the feudal knights had become what Hearnshaw has called "dangerously unemployed anachronisms," hated by king, clergy, and people alike for their greediness and defiance of civil and religious authority.[31] Out of the various attempts to convert their energies into socially useful, religiously acceptable activities grew, at least in part, the institution of Christian chivalry. There were, to be sure, other factors that contributed to the rise of chivalry as an institution. On the part of the lesser knightly class itself, chivalry was an attempt to justify through a code of high aspiration its climb from a mere horse soldiery to a position of social eminence in the increasingly prosperous and civilized courts of later feudal society.[32] Again, as Huizinga has suggested, chivalry, along with all the rigid formality and ceremony of medieval upper-class society, represents an effort of an emotionally primitive and savage military caste to control its violence and pride.[33] As the Middle Ages wore on, the attendant ritual of chivalry increasingly became, it is true, a mere device by which a strong but progressively less important noble class would evade the facts of political and social reality.[34] But in its origin, chivalry was above all a serious attempt to effect "a kind of compromise between the ascetic theology of the medieval church and the unsanctified life of the world which the church rejected as wholly bad."[35]

The chivalric code that was thus evolved, though it nowhere reaches any fixed or formal uniformity, demanded of its adherents virtues essentially Christian, but with emphasis on those which were particularly proper for the fighting man: "To defend the church, attack unbelief, venerate the priesthood, protect the poor from injury, keep peace in the state, pour out their blood for their brothers," as John of Salisbury defined its duties.[36] From such general obligations there developed an elaborate and minutely particularized code governing every aspect of the ideal knight's life.[37] In its very beginnings the oath of the chivalric knight had enjoined along with martial service of church and king, the protection of women, and chivalry thus easily absorbed into its blend of war and religion[38] the theories of courtly love, which from the end of the eleventh century had begun to take the ascendant in medieval erotic thought.[39] While the knightly code that thus evolved inevitably permitted a concentration on essentially anti-Christian ideals of personal honor and glory and the passionate service of woman rather than God,[40] nevertheless, even as late as the fifteenth century, "chivalry was still, after religion, the strongest of all the ethical conceptions which dominated the mind and the heart."[41] And like other widely held theories of conduct, chivalry doubtless early created a very large demand for artistic expression, which in all times and places has been the layman's philosophy.

That the Arthurian story was hit upon for that expression is no doubt partly due to the simple coincidence that the new story material was becoming available on the Continent at almost the same moment in time in which the new chivalric ideal was arising.[42] But a more compelling explanation is to be seen in the fact that the other great matters available to the poets were radically unsuitable as embodiments of chivalry. The matter of Charlemagne leaned too far in the direction of ecclesiastical heroism;[43] the matter of Alexander and other heroes of classical tradition obviously could not be bent far enough in the direction of Christianity. And, as MacCallum puts it, "In each case the hero . . . had a character too obstinately representative of another age and another code of life, thoroughly to submit to a change that would make him merely a chivalrous knight, neither more nor less."[44] Arthur, on the other hand, suffered from none of these disabilities. From the beginning, as we have seen, he had been a fusion of Christian warrior and purely secular hero. Nor had he any of the recalcitrance of genuine historical figures to artistic manipulation in terms of manners or the atmosphere in which he moved. And finally, by right of the band of heroes already grouped about him from early times, his story was capable of expressing the whole gamut of variations which develop in any widely held theory of social and spiritual relationships. Added to these qualifications were the Arthurian legend's inherent tragic dignity and its richness in the marvels so dear to the medieval mind. The combination, then, so well suited to the interests of the age, awaited only the touch of genius to flower into a great expression of that age and its ideals. On the Continent it received that touch from Chrétien de Troyes, Gottfried von Strassburg, Robert de Boron, to mention only a few. In time the ensuing multiplication of individual romances resulted in a huge and appallingly heterogeneous mass of stories. The duplications, contradictions, and discrepancies between the various versions must early have attracted attention, and from the late thirteenth century on, more or less ambitious compilations involving varying degrees of systematization begin to make their appearance.

MALORY AND *LE MORTE DARTHUR*

The popularity of various *rifacimenti* of Arthurian story doubtless played its part in William Caxton's decision to "enprynte a book of the noble hystoryes of the sayd kynge Arthur and of certeyn of his knyghtes, after a copye unto me delyverd, whyche copye syr Thomas Malorye dyd

take oute of certeyn bookes of Frensshe and reduced it into Englysshe."[45]
The importance of Malory's *Le Morte Darthur*, as Caxton refers to it in
his colophon, would be difficult to exaggerate.[46] Appearing in 1485 at the
very end of the Middle Ages and culminating the medieval Arthurian
tradition, "thys noble and Ioyous book" has been the seminal source of
nearly every worthwhile subsequent artistic treatment of the legend in
English. Nevertheless, it is peculiarly difficult to arrive at a just estimate
of the work. Influenced by the alterations, additions, representations, and
implications supplied by the "symple connynge" of Caxton, readers and
critics for four-and-a-half centuries took the book to be intended as a
single, continuous whole and praised and blamed it accordingly. Lang
noted that the adventures in Malory are, "unlike the Homeric adventures,
without an end or aim,"[47] but Strachey was led to assert that "the plan of
the book is properly epic," and that it has an "epic unity and harmony,
'a beginning, a middle, and an end.' "[48] And Saintsbury, with customary
orotundity, declared: "What is certain is that [Malory], and he only in
any language, makes of this vast assemblage of stories one story, and one
book."[49] Yet the discovery in 1934 and subsequent editing of the Winchester manuscript, the only known manuscript of Malory, led Eugène
Vinaver to assert that "one book" is just what Malory had neither attempted nor produced. On the contrary, Vinaver, in his significantly titled
edition of the manuscript, *The Works of Sir Thomas Malory*, declared
that the work, which the "knight-prisoner" completed in 1469, was a series
or set of eight distinct and quite separate romances, individually more or
less consistent, but exhibiting noticeable contradictions from one to
another.[50]

The question of unity in the *Morte Darthur* thus raised by Vinaver
has all but dominated Malory studies for more than two decades. One
group of scholars has argued with considerable ingenuity—and some heat
—that Malory produced a single book manifesting a very high degree of
unity—both "critical" and "historical" (i.e., intentional).[51] Nor has Vinaver's hypothesis had any very active support among scholars.[52] Nevertheless, the claims of his opponents have often struck more detached observ-
ers as excessive and their arguments as overly ingenious and occasionally
even willful.[53]

The fact that the question of unity could arise at all and that it could
be argued so plausibly or, at any rate, so extensively, and, finally, so incon-
clusively, suggests that the question has not always been properly posed.
To begin with, it has been put in terms, C. S. Lewis points out, that
Malory, as a medieval writer, would not have understood:

> I do not for a moment believe that Malory had any intention either of
> writing a single "work" or of writing many "works" as we should
> understand the expressions. He was telling us about Arthur and the
> knights. Of course his matter was one—the same king, the same court.
> Of course his matter was many—they had had many adventures.
>
> The choice we try to force upon Malory is really a choice for us. It
> is our imagination, not his, that makes the work one or eight or fifty.
> We can read it either way. We can read it now one way, now another.
> We partly make what we read.[54]

Moreover, insofar as *unity* is regarded as an absolute feature of a literary
work rather than as what it always is in practice—a feature present to some
degree in any work, the use of the term has predictably confused the
issue.[55] And finally, the claims for an *intentional* unity raise questions
that probably need not be resolved and in any event certainly cannot be
resolved by the methods adopted.[56]

Perhaps the right way, then, to put the question of Malory's unity is
in other terms. What kind of unity is it probable for Malory to have had
in mind? What degree of unity did he achieve? Clearly he could not
have intended the kind of detailed integration and scrupulous economy
that is the aim of much modern novelistic technique; he could not for the
simple reason that neither the novel form nor Jamesian theories about it
existed in Malory's time.[57] Nor is it likely that he even intended, as
Helaine Newstead points out, a "tightly unified structure, like the *Divine
Comedy*."[58] Dante's work was a conscious, autonomous fiction in a way
that Malory's could not be. Malory and other medieval writers engaged
in handing on a traditional matter, C. S. Lewis reminds us, "proceed as if
they were more or less historians; unscholarly, decorating, and emotional
historians to be sure, like Livy or Plutarch, but (by and large) historians
still."[59] Thus some material that a modern novelist would surely have
eliminated or drastically curtailed had to be included at inconvenient
length simply because it was part of the matter. Nevertheless, the *Morte
Darthur* could have—and it does have—the unity of its subject matter. If
the subject is a great one—and Malory's is—then it will go a long way
toward generating a sense of significant unity by itself, no matter how
unfortunate this may be for the more delicate aesthetic speculations of our
day. Moreover, it was possible within the framework of the more or less
familiar, traditional material to achieve a certain kind of "connectedness"
or "cohesion," to use the terms advocated by D. S. Brewer.[60] Various
kinds of links, references to what was to come or what had already taken
place, some degree of consistency of characterization, even (though less
clearly and surely) some degree of consistency in thematic emphasis and

attitude—all these contribute toward our feeling that the *Morte Darthur* is more one thing than it is eight separate things, that its sections or parts or tales are to be read in a "particular order," and that so read they have a "cumulative effect."[61]

What the older critics referred to as Malory's "failure" to unify completely his materials may very well have been due to his artistic tact. To talk, as MacCallum does, of a need for gathering "the loose threads . . . together" and assigning "each of the adventures . . . its proper place in one grand scheme," is to fall into the trap of confusing fiction with history, and is to suggest not "a task that might engross the best powers of the loftiest genius,"[62] but rather an undertaking as absurdly impossible as, say, attempting to assign a chronological place in Lincoln's biography to all the anecdotes he is supposed to have told. Nevertheless, Malory's accomplishments in the direction of simplification were not inconsiderable. The narrative method of the various English and French romances in verse and prose on which he drew was excessively complicated; no matter how consciously chosen the method by which "each episode appeared to be a digression from the previous one and at the same time a sequel to some earlier unfinished story,"[63] it has generally struck modern readers, as it did Southey, as highly "inartificial":

> Adventure produces adventure in infinite series; not like a tree, whose boughs and branches bearing a necessary relation and due proportion to each other, combine into one beautiful form, but resembling such plants as the prickly pear, where one joint grows upon another, all equal in size and alike in shape, and the whole making a formless and misshaped mass. Even this clumsy mode of transition is often disregarded, and the author passes from adventure to adventure without the slightest connection, introducing you without prologue or prelude of any kind to a new scene, and bringing forward a new set of personages.[64]

Malory must have felt a similar dissatisfaction with the older method; at any rate, he clearly labors in all of his work to disentangle the various stories and by a variety of alterations including condensation, combination, and rearrangement to achieve a simplified, single line of narration. He thus anticipated modern fictional structure. The resultant gain in unity of effect might well have been sufficient in itself to have guaranteed the survival of Malory's version of the Arthurian cycle.[65]

That survival also owes a great deal to other remarkable qualities of the work and the man. Malory's prose style is, to use the conventional adjectives, concise, vigorous, and straightforward. It would probably be more precise to speak of styles, for Malory is master of many tones from the most matter-of-fact narrative summary to the most impassioned rhetoric. He is, in short, nearly always capable of suiting the words to the action. And here too, in his directness and lucidity, he anticipates modern notions of narrative writing. The same can also be said for his achievement, considerably more limited, in shifting his emphasis from mere action to character with its attendant interests of emotion, conscience, and motivation. While some of the earlier romances contain a great deal of overt psychological analysis, Malory's presentation of character is consistently dramatic.[66] This objective approach to character is but one aspect of a pervasive matter-of-factness in his treatment of the stories. Generally skeptical of the nonmaterial and the nonrational, Malory characteristically deemphasizes not only the more fanciful extremes of chivalry and *amour courtois*, but also the supernatural elements and doctrinal elucidations which had come to bulk so large in many of the Continental romances.[67] The same sturdy, commonsense bias seems to mark Malory's moral sensibility insofar as it is to be detected in a book that is remarkably free of moralizing. "Malory is," as Andrew Lang puts it, "throughout strong on the side of goodness."[68] In such alterations of emphasis from mannered artificiality to vigorous simplicity, from subjectivity to objectivity, from doctrinal subtlety to practical ethics may well lie a large share of Malory's greatness. For it was by these alterations that the great story of the British hero was reacclimated to the land of its origin.

Recognition of Malory's achievement ought not, however, to obscure the fact that the work has many faults, many failures of consistency:

> variations in political or religious or narrative emphasis in the different tales; differences in proportions, selectiveness, technique, and even style; the belated mention of vital episodes which are not even narrated; inconsistencies in the biographical and historical timing; the institution of motifs and the apparent forgetting of them for great stretches; the extraordinary differences in the character of some knights between one tale and another; the many episodes that seem to have no more connection with the rest than that they take place in Arthur's realm.[69]

For all his compression and combination, there remains in Malory a plethora of foolish and meaningless incidents, successions of monotonously similar tournaments and adventures. Knights errant encounter, challenge, and tilt at each other like so many brainless automata without a hint of motivation. The dearest friends, even brothers, are incapable of recognizing each other except by name, and this information they regularly refuse to supply. Hermits appear with relentless regularity to offer interpretations only a trifle more incomprehensible than the dreams or events they profess to explain. Despite Malory's efforts at simplification, the narrative line splits and resplits in a way that sometimes defies comprehension.[70] These faults are particularly obvious in his treatment of the Tristram story and the legend of the Grail Quest. In the former he not only unhappily chose the inferior version in which Tristram meets his death at Mark's hands, but at the same time failed to complete the story, leaving that death to be reported later by a mere casual allusion.[71] In the Grail adventures, Malory himself appears to have been as thoroughly mystified as his reader. Contradiction and inconsequence give the effect of dreamlike unreality and, at times, insupportable tedium to the narrative.[72]

Nevertheless, the *Morte Darthur*, taken as a whole, remains incomparably the greatest of the earlier English treatments of the central story of Arthur and his knights; to it indeed, as Vinaver says, "Arthurian romance owes its survival in the English-speaking world."[73] There is no exaggeration even in saying that interest in Arthurian matter closely parallels interest in Malory. The century and a half between Caxton's first publication and Stansby's edition (1634), which saw the appearance of Spenser's *Faerie Queene* and the evolution in young John Milton's mind of a plan for an epic treatment of Arthurian story, also saw the publication of six separate editions of Malory. In the succeeding period of nearly two centuries there was not a single edition of the *Morte Darthur*, and artistic interest in Arthurian story correspondingly reached its nadir.[74] Then, in a matter of only two years (1816–1817) three competing editions came into the market in quick succession just before the second great flowering of the legend began.

THE ESSENTIAL ARTHURIAN STORY

The unmistakable correlation between the fortunes of Malory's book and the fortunes of the Arthurian legend itself suggests that the *Morte Darthur* contains within itself virtually all that is truly significant in Arthurian story as story. Such long popularity and such influence on later poets are not wholly explained by merely formal literary excellences— "noble prose," "limpid narrative," "vivid characterization"—even if Malory had actually manifested these qualities to the degree claimed by his editors. Nor does his importance rest on invention. Translator, abridger, adapter, rearranger, condenser—Malory was all of these, but it is unlikely that he added a single important narrative element to the Arthurian story.[75] Quite the contrary; his real triumph—a partial one, to be sure— lay in the fact that beneath all the tangled accretions, he discerned, consciously or unconsciously, the indispensable elements in the legend. This is not to say, of course, either that he isolated these essential elements and ignored the rest, or that he achieved a completely successful artistic subordination of the multifarious episodes of the adventures of Arthur's other knights to the story of the king's tragic career. The former course would have been repugnant to his uninhibited enthusiasm for the whole range of Arthurian romance; the latter would doubtless have been far beyond his shaping powers. Nevertheless, as he proceeded in his work, he clearly emphasized more and more and at the same time purified of irrelevant elements that core or central story.[76] It is this essential story, its events and its spirit, that abides and even strengthens in the reader's mind long after he has closed the book, long after he has forgotten the book's other virtues and, for that matter, its *longueurs*. And it is this story that accounts for much of the sense of unity that critics have felt in the book.

The essential Arthurian story or, in Platonic terms, the ideal story, as it manifests itself in Malory combines a number of elements which go back to Nennius and Geoffrey with a variety of additions which entered the story during its centuries of popularity on the Continent. Through Merlin's magic, Uther Pendragon begets Arthur on Igrayne, Duchess of Cornwall, during the very night that the Duke, as it happens, is killed. At his birth, in accord with a promise exacted of Uther by Merlin, Arthur is handed to the mage, who secretly gives him to Sir Ector to rear. Years later, after Uther's death and when the land is being ravaged by civil discord, Arthur unwittingly reveals his right to the kingship by removing a sword from a stone, and hence is crowned by the people. But many struggles with petty kings must be gone through before his throne is secure. In one of these wars he succours Lodegreaunce, father of Gwenyvere. Despite Merlin's prediction of tragic consequences, he marries her and founds his Round Table of many knights. With them he cleanses his land, rights old wrongs, and conquers an empire. But at the same time that the strength of his realm increases, so also the sinful love of Gwenyvere and Lancelot, Arthur's greatest knight and dearest friend, grows steadily stronger. The Grail makes a temporary appearance among his knights and leads them all to vow its quest, a quest which, as Arthur foresees, weakens the Round Table and from which many fail to return. Of those who go, only three, Bors, Percival, and Galahad, are successful; Lancelot, held back by his sin, is only partially successful. The court becomes increasingly filled with dissension over the adulterous couple, and finally when he kills Gawain's brothers in his attempts to protect Gwenyvere, Lancelot is forced to flee, and the unity and fellowship of Arthur's Round Table are irrevocably destroyed. While Arthur is abroad besieging Lancelot, his nephew Mordred treacherously seizes the kingdom. Arthur, returning without the help of Lancelot and his knights, is mortally wounded and nearly all his knights are killed in a great battle with the dissident factions under Mordred. His final end is not certainly known, whether he is buried or goes to Avalon to heal himself of his wounds. Gwenyvere and Lancelot, separated from each other, die afterwards in bitterest remorse and contrition. Such, with one omission, is the outline of the central story in Malory.

That omission is the sequence of events before Arthur's marriage to Gwenyvere in which Arthur, unaware that Margawze is his half-sister, incestuously begets upon her Mordred, who is thus both his son and his nephew. In an effort to avert the dire consequences of this offense, Arthur unsuccessfully tries to kill Mordred by having all the children born on May Day set adrift. Yet despite the prominence given to this episode by some of the critics, especially in the nineteenth century, it seems clear that the incest motif is not essential to the story. It does not appear in the earlier versions, e.g., Geoffrey's, but is instead a later romance addition, and its relevance to the central conflict is so slight that even Malory, who follows the Continental versions in including it, puts little emphasis on it. After the barest recital of the events and a few allusions to Mordred's incestuous begetting in the first two books, Malory appears to forget the matter altogether. Though Mordred is mentioned a number of times in the next seventeen books he is regularly identified only as Gawain's brother and never as Arthur's son; a weak, mean-spirited, evil-tongued knight, he is of little importance until he begins to work against Lancelot, mostly through the latter's adulterous relationship with Gwenyvere. Not until late in the twentieth book after Arthur goes to make war against Lancelot and leaves Mordred in charge of the kingdom, is Mordred again identified as Arthur's son, and even here Malory makes nothing but the most noncommital allusions to the relation.[77] Whether from a lack of interest in the motif or from a consciousness of the danger of diverting attention from the tragic conflict involved in the adultery motif, Malory makes no attempt to develop the pathos so imminent in the father-son relationship. Mordred is nowhere presented as embittered by or even concerned with his origins, and Arthur's reaction to his treason is not the grief of a father at a child's betrayal but the anger of a king at the threat to his throne. The incest motif, clearly, remained a mere attachment to the story, never assimilated into its spirit or emotional structure.[78]

The essential conflict on which that emotional structure is based is the adulterous love of Gwenyvere and Lancelot.[79] From this tragic betrayal of the king springs all the pathos of the story, and, significantly, it is for this betrayal that Arthur grieves. Out of this unsanctified love comes the breakup of the Round Table and the destruction of Arthur's weakened forces in the last great battle. The fatal attractiveness of the queen may be traced back to the earliest Celtic versions of Arthurian story, and is doubtless, in her remarkable susceptibility to abduction, ultimately related to ancient culture myths of a solar or vegetation goddess being carried off by the powers of darkness.[80] So persistent in the later versions is the motif of Guinevere's adultery, either freely chosen or forced, that, as Miss Bensel has put it, "whether Arthur is the brave world-conqueror of the chronicles, the courteous, affable king of romance, or the world-reformer of later times, the queen's infidelity marks the fatal end of his glorious career and entails the final destruction of his kingdom."[81] What in pagan times had been a symbolization of primitive man's conception of natural processes became increasingly in a Christian society a matter of moral concern and a question of sexual ethics. Even in Geoffrey's *Historia*, untouched by erotic speculation, that concern was already felt; as a result of Arthur's governance of his court, Geoffrey tells us, the women "became more chaste and better, and the knights for love of them more brave."[82] But the erotic problem did not receive suitable narrative formulation until Continental romancers, impelled to find artistic expression for the doctrines of courtly love and seizing on hints in the tales recited by the Breton *conteurs*, elevated Lancelot, a figure scarcely mentioned before Chrétien's *Le Chevalier de la Charrette*, to a position of paramount importance. By the first quarter of the thirteenth century, Lancelot's love for Guinevere had become, as Professor App says, "the pivotal point of the whole story."[83]

The danger in this rapid elevation of Lancelot was, of course, that the queen's lover might come to overshadow the queen's husband, the king. And indeed that is just what often happened in the French romances. Arthur's court became only "the conventional starting point of knightly quests and Arthur himself a fantastic character, a king of Fairyland."[84] Malory must have perceived that such a weakening of the third side of the triangle inevitably weakened the tension of the conflict. If Arthur was a mere *roi fainéant*, a complaisant cuckold, where was the tragedy? Thus Malory labored to restore Arthur's grandeur, and, as Professor Vinaver points out, he makes his Arthur in the early books "the true embodiment of heroic chivalry," not "a mere abstract centre of the fellowship of the Round Table, but . . . a political and military leader, conscious of his responsibility for the welfare and prestige of his kingdom," a brave and generous leader.[85] Not only in his actions, but also in his moral rectitude, he is an influence for the better on his knights.[86] Only on such an exalted foundation could the sin of Lancelot and Guinevere attain dignity and significance. Only on such a foundation could Malory have built the tragedy with which his story closes, a tragedy in which "the clash of loyalties, the exuberance of the noble passions that once made Arthurian chivalry great, causes the downfall of Arthur's kingdom."[87]

In his restoration of heroic dignity to the figure of Arthur and in his emphasis on the adultery motif, Malory shows something beyond an awareness of the indispensable events or actions of the essential Arthurian story. He reveals a profound sensitivity to that story's spirit or inherent nature of which the events are but the concrete form. While that spirit is as necessary as the form, it is obviously less easy to describe. Yet if we are to understand the later history of the Arthurian legend, we shall have to understand its essential nature.

To begin with, the story of Arthur is not historical. As we have seen, the historical Arthur, if he existed at all, was no more than the grain of sand about which a pre-existing body of mythic materials accreted and thereby survived into Christian times. What little we may guess about the Arthur of history is almost wholly lacking in poetic interest or significance; the mere chieftain of battles lacks the royal éclat of a king. His story has no details outside the battles and no dramatic conflict—in short, it is not a story at all.[88] The writers of the Middle Ages, untroubled by any notions of exact history, rejected the *dux bellorum* as, for that matter, the folk and the *conteurs* had already done. The Arthurian story that counts—the story found in the romances—is not even a result of the magnification of the achievements of such a petty warlord. Nor is it to be comprehended simply as an ordinary fiction or folktale.

On the contrary, the Arthurian legend is distinguished from the other *matières* by a mysteriousness that is not a simple matter of the "magical elements of folklore."[89] And it is further distinguished by the enduring fascination that it has exercised over men's minds. Both that mysteriousness and that persistency derive from the fact that its basic materials had been evolved, as has been noted, out of the mythopoeic impulses of primitive peoples.[90] The essential Arthurian story is no arbitrary, excogitated creation of individual imagination; instead it is, in the fullest anthropological and literary sense of the word, a myth.[91] In the mysterious circumstances of Arthur's begetting, the concealment of his parentage, his rearing by comparatively humble persons, and the revelation of his royal origins by a magical feat, the similarities to the myths of the births of such heroes as Oedipus and Perseus are obvious.[92] The parallels in the later careers, betrayals, and final ends of Arthur and a wide variety of mythic heroes are equally conspicuous.[93] In earlier times these myths were probably closely related to the religious activities of the community; it is likely, even, that they grew directly out of primitive religious rituals.[94] The attachment of the myths to natural phenomena such as solar, lunar, or vegetative cycles was perhaps an early response to man's desire to "understand" his universe, or perhaps a reflection of his anxiety to conceal from himself the psychic content of the myths.[95] But when men ceased to believe that fertility could be restored to the land only by a ritual mating of the king with a goddess, or that the disappearance of the sun was to be "explained" by a story of a god killed in a great battle in the west, the myths should, logically speaking, have withered away. The fact is that they did not.

That such mythic elements persisted in the stories of Arthur and his knights and survived into the Christian Middle Ages, that they remained perceptible here and there beneath the romancers' occasional and more or less perfunctory attempts at rationalization, suggests that we are dealing with a legend capable of exercising a lasting and all but universal fascination. At its heart lay some of the deepest intuitions of the race. Whether or not we accept Jung's explanation of the mechanism by which these "archetypal patterns" exert their influence on the human mind is of little significance here.[96] What is important to see is that such a legend is from the beginning relatively fixed both in form and spirit. Growing out of the unconscious or nonrational mind, its configuration will reject any significant alteration in events. And it is equally resistant to any change in its spirit.

That spirit in the central story of Arthur is profoundly tragic.[97] That is to say, the story's significance, whether we think of Arthur as a culture hero or as a heroic rebel against elder authority, is intimately bound up with its tragic outcome. It can no more have a "happy ending" than could the stories of Oedipus or Orestes or Hamlet. Merely to state the matter is to make apparent the ridiculousness of such an alteration—the tragedy *is* the story. Nor can the early "happy" parts of the central story when Arthur and his Round Table are still increasing in glory be used successfully apart from the tragic denouement.[98] They are as insignificant by themselves as would be, let us say, a play dealing with Hamlet's student days in Wittenberg.

But if the Arthurian legend is, as are other myths, relatively fixed in form and spirit, it is at the same time—again like other myths—remarkably responsive to changes in its symbolic content. It is this flexibility that Ernest Rhys referred to when he wrote: "The power of romance is that it fits itself anew to every period. Each one takes up again the undying legend of Arthur, and more or less deludes itself with the notion that its latest version is the truest. But every century must still read its own emotion and its own colours into the past."[99] From the beginning the story's characters and events had carried concealed meanings, had expressed in symbolic terms the fears, aspirations, and intuitions of men. Arthur especially "has always figured as an ideal king," Miss Bensel observes; "he is not representative of his age, strictly speaking, but far better and nobler than the best people of that time. Hence he embodies their strongly idealized morals and social views."[100]

In its absorption of the social views of the Christian Middle Ages, Arthurian legend underwent—without any violation of its essential form or spirit—an alteration that almost amounts to a qualitative change. This change distinguishes the legend sharply from classical myth, and consequently, as we shall see, from classical epic or tragedy. Like other myths, the Arthurian story in its earlier forms depends for its interest almost wholly on the actions and fate of a single hero. But unlike the classical myths, Arthurian legend in its serious artistic handlings was deeply influenced by a secular ideal—that is, the chivalric ideal—that was markedly social rather than individual in its implications. In absorbing this ideal, the story became no longer an individual tragedy, but instead the tragedy of a society.[101] The result was a number of slight adjustments necessary to give full expression to the new ideal or content.

The most important of these adjustments was, as we have seen, the increasingly heavy emphasis laid on the socially significant sin of the betrayal of trust involved in the adulterous relationship of Lancelot and Guinevere. In this sin the romancers saw the conflict of the story, the moral evil that brought on the collapse of the society founded by Arthur. It is no accident that in the conflict between Lancelot's duty to his king as defined by the chivalric ideal and his duty to the queen as defined by the doctrines of courtly love lay the point of extreme contradiction in the social ideal that the myth had been made to symbolize. The sin also represents symbolically the highest tension between the calls of the flesh and the spirit. The paradox of chivalry was, of course, only a shadow of the basically paradoxical nature of Christianity itself with its impossible and still categorical commands. Out of the need to give expression in the story to this absolute ideal grew a further adjustment of the legend—the development of the Grail story. Only from this quest could the society receive its final test and reveal its failure in terms of a comparison with absolute standards.

Both of these elements, the adultery motif and the Grail Quest, had been built up on foundations, or at least suggestions, already present in the body of stories that had gathered around Arthur in the dim times before the cycle was carried to the Continent. It was also in these stories with their extensive cast of characters that the romancers found the other element necessary to give full expression to the social ideal. As we have already noted, the fact that the cycle contained many heroes rather than a single one allowed the presentation of the whole range of variations of which the chivalric ideal was capable. But from an artistic standpoint it is more important that the essentially social chivalric ideal could thus find expressive form in the growth, flowering, decay, and destruction not of an individual, but of a society. In this assimilation of the various knights of the early stories, the conflict and fall are not merely the tragedy of Arthur, an individual, but they are rather the tragedy of the whole Round Table, a society.

Endowed thus with such significance, Arthur's knights were no longer mere supernumeraries, but integral parts of the whole. If that whole does not manifest the special variety of unity of classical epic or tragedy, it has nevertheless the only kind of unity that really counts—the unity of theme and form. And that unity, it may be observed, is no less sophisticated than the classical unity. Indeed, if anything it is more sophisticated. Like the architecture whose growth paralleled the legend's development, Arthurian story's triumph was the unification of almost unbelievable diversity, the harmonization of the demands of matter with the aspiration of the spirit. If its unity is thus not geometrical, it is clearly organic; not imposed by canon, it rises out of the vital spirit of the feudal society whose aspirations it expressed.[102]

And also, just as French Gothic architecture, after passing through a series of great changes, quickly reached a perfected and comparatively unchanging type, the essential story structure of Arthur's reign also attained, though less rapidly, a formal and expressive completeness.[103] To summarize its essential narrative elements is, as it should be, to summarize its spiritual and moral dialectic: In a land racked by evil, a hero of mysterious though kingly birth makes his way to his throne, cleanses the land, and founds an ideal form of life, a society of glorious heroes. That society is tested in the material world by the fleshly passions of wife and friend, and in the world of spiritual absolutes by a mysterious quest. Found false to its ideal, the society is destroyed in a tragic denouement in which both its good and evil meet their end.

It is this exact correspondence of content and form, as well as the mythic evolution of the legend that explains the relatively fixed nature of the story, its obstinate rejection of significant alteration, and hence the failure of every later attempt at arbitrary addition or subtraction. There is "something impertinent," MacCallum observes, about the procedure of wholesale change adopted by many of the later authors who took up the story; "it rouses the same kind of recalcitrance that is felt when well-known historic characters are distorted in novel or drama."[104] And well it might, for such manipulations are in both cases tamperings with truth—with the truth of fact on the one hand and with the truth of imagination or poetry on the other hand. In the failure to appreciate the fixed nature of the essential Arthurian story, then, lies the explanation for the relative unsuccess of efforts to rouse Arthur from his long sleep in Avalon during most of the next three-and-a-half centuries.

2 ❦ A Slow Decline

ARTHURIAN STORY AND TRADITION
IN THE ENGLISH RENAISSANCE

ARTHUR IN TUDOR SOCIETY AND THOUGHT

Malory's great compilation of Arthurian story had been written during the last years of the English Middle Ages, prolonged or revived as they had been by the feudal anarchy of the Wars of the Roses. But the year in which *Le Morte Darthur* was finally published, 1485, was also the symbolic year of the battle of Bosworth, which conventionally signalizes the final decline of feudalism and the Middle Ages in England, and the beginning under Henry VII of the Tudor dynasty and of the English Renaissance proper. Scattered evidences of the spread of the New Learning are detectable in England before this date, of course, and a variety of medieval institutions and attitudes persisted with remarkable strength well into the Tudor period. Thus, chivalric notions, Arthurian romance, and Arthurian tradition maintained a considerable and apparently vigorous life even as late as the accession of James I. Nevertheless, it may be observed with some justice that, at the very moment when Arthurian legend had received its first great comprehensive treatment in English, the conditions for its proper understanding and artistic use were in fact fading away, to be replaced by attitudes and necessities fundamentally antipathetic to its essential shape and spirit.

To some extent, perhaps, the Arthurian legend suffered in a reaction of the English Renaissance against the Middle Ages in general. Tudor society, still recovering from the long bloody conflict of the Yorkist and Lancastrian factions, often thought of the whole Middle Ages as the bad old days.[1] Yet on the surface there was no direct rejection of such typically medieval institutions as chivalry. On the contrary, English humanists like Sir Thomas Elyot "tried to effect a conciliation between the ideals of chivalry and of classical antiquity, and the result of this fusion was the figure of the 'governor,' the new type of 'gentleman.' "[2] The medieval code of knightly conduct remained in many aspects of its verbal formula-

tion the code of the ideal Renaissance gentleman, but since the requirements of society had shifted from military prowess and religious devotion
to political skill and philosophical interests, the final result was to some
extent a concealed, even unconscious, transvaluation of medieval chivalry.[3]
Thus, although the Tudor Englishman speaks of chivalry and its code in
a way that would suggest a full sympathy with the ideals that medieval
romance had embodied, his terms often have a content essentially at
variance with their medieval meanings. Inevitably this discrepancy would
affect men's attitudes towards the Arthurian romances, in which medieval
conceptions are unmistakable.

The attack on the romances began early among the scholars, who
were naturally inclined to look askance at the imaginative literature of the
"supposedly obscurantist period which [had] preceded the dawn of humanism."[4] Erasmus scorned the tales of Arthur and Lancelot, and Vives
in his *De Officio Mariti* (1528) spoke sourly of stories "written in the
vulgar tonge, as of Trystram, Lancelot, Ogier, Amasus and of Arthur the
whiche were written and made by suche as were ydle & knew nothinge.
These bokes do hurte both man & woman, for they make them wylye &
craftye, they kyndle and styr up covetousnes, inflame angre, & all beastly
and filthy desyre."[5] To some degree, of course, the denunciation of the
romances proceeded from literary objections to their unreality, their extravagance, and the crudity of their medieval form as viewed by men
whose tastes had been developed in the study of the classics. Nashe lifted
a sophisticated eyebrow at "the fantasticall dreames of those exiled Abbie-
lubbers, from whose idle pens proceeded those worne out impressions of
the feyned no where acts of Arthur of the rounde table."[6] Graver souls,
however, reacted to Arthurian romance with passionate objurgations in
which it is difficult to distinguish doctrinal objections from moralistic
denunciation. Doubtless a part of the obloquy heaped on *Le Morte
Darthur* among others sprang from a puritan dislike of fiction on principle, but far more important was the view that the book was full of
"Romish superstition" and that its publication lent aid and comfort to the
Catholics,[7] at the same time that it represented behavior sure to corrupt
the young and innocent. Thus in *The Scholemaster*, Roger Ascham, one-
time tutor to Elizabeth, denounced not only Malory, but the whole body
of romances:

> In our forefather's tyme, when Papistrie, as a standyng poole couered
> and ouerflowed all England, fewe bookes were read in our tong, sauyng
> certaine bookes [of] Cheualrie, as they sayd, for pastime and pleasure,
> which as some say, were made in Monasteries, by idle Monkes, or
> wanton Chanons: as one for example, *Morte Arthure*: the whole

pleasure of which booke standeth in two speciall poyntes, in open mans slaughter, and bold bawdrye: in which booke, those be counted the noblest Knightes that do kill most men without any quarrell, and commit fowlest aduoulter[i]es by sutlest shiftes: as Sir *Launcelot* with the wife of King *Arthure* his master: Syr *Tristram* with the wife of King Marke his vncle: Syr *Lamerocke* with the wife of King *Lote*, that was his own aunte. This is good stuffe, for wise men to laugh at, or honest men to take pleasure at. Yet I know, when Gods Bible was banished the Court, and *Morte Arthure* receiued into the Princes chamber. What toyes, the dayly reading of such a book may worke in the will of a yong ientleman or a yong mayde, that liueth welthily and idelie, wise men can iudge, and honest men do pitie. And yet ten *Morte Arthures* do not the tenth part so much harme, as one of these books, made in Italie and translated in England.[8]

Nevertheless, as is suggested by the heat of Ascham's attack and the perpetuation of such abuse even into the seventeenth century, the romances continued to enjoy a considerable though declining vogue throughout the Tudor period.[9] From the coming of printing to England in the late fifteenth century to about 1575, the list of romances available remained almost constant.[10] The relatively large number of chivalric narratives published in expensive folios—such as all the Tudor editions of Malory—indicates that the audience for these works was still extensive in aristocratic or moneyed circles during the first three-quarters of the sixteenth century; an equally large number of metrical romances were available in quarto for a less discriminating public.[11] After 1575, however, the market declined steadily, partially as a result of the introduction of new types of imaginative literature, and even more because of the popularity of translations of late Spanish romances such as the Palmerin cycle, which attracted an almost exclusively middle-class audience.[12] The older Arthurian romances, particularly Malory, continued to exercise a fascination over a few members of the nobility and aristocracy such as Mary, Queen of Scots, and Sir Philip Sidney, who patterned not only parts of his *Arcadia* but some aspects of his life and death on the chivalry of the *Morte Darthur*.[13] But on the whole among the educated and the cultured, the romances were increasingly the objects of scorn, and their major audience was progressively lower on the social scale.[14] "It became more and more the custom," Professor Crane says, "to denounce the romances for their immorality, their lack of verisimilitude, their crudeness of form, and to sneer at them because of their popularity with uncultured readers."[15] The influence of Arthurian romance on the serious literature and thought of the time declined correspondingly.

This long though slowly diminishing interest in the romances is only one manifestation of the extraordinary vitality of the Arthurian tradition in the lives of all sorts of Tudor Englishmen. Among the folk, Arthurian tales must still have been widely told, judging from the large number of topographical features traditionally associated with Arthur and his men.[16] Solid middle-class citizens of London proudly supported the Fellowship of Prince Arthur's Knights, an archery society whose members assumed the names of Arthur's various knights, and whose annual shoots apparently commemorated Arthur and the Round Table.[17] Learned Cambridge dons like Nicholas Cantelupe in the fifteenth century and John Caius, Master of Gonville and Caius College, in the sixteenth century, argued gravely that Arthur had founded their university.[18] For the upper classes there were numerous reflections of Arthurian chivalry in such organizations as the Gentlemen-Pensioners and the Order of the Garter. The latter, according to William Harrison, writing in 1577, had been established by Edward III in imitation of Arthur's Round Table.[19] Chivalric tournaments paralleling those described in the romances, though they had been held as early as 1259 in England,[20] attained an especially high degree of popularity under the Tudors, with over forty recorded during Elizabeth's reign alone.[21] It seems likely, of course, that the popularity of such passages at arms derived more from the Renaissance passion for spectacle and pageantry than from any widespread sympathy with the ideals of medieval chivalry,[22] and equally probable that for the most part the interest in the romances was more a matter of fascination with exotic places and fantastic adventures than an entering into the intensely spiritual quality of Arthur's tragic story. Nevertheless, despite the great change in the intellectual climate between the Middle Ages and the Renaissance, the collapse of feudalism, and the shattering effects of the Reformation, it is clear that the Arthurian tradition still permeated the whole of Tudor society.

"Is it not amazing, then," Professor Greenlaw asks, "that almost alone of the great repositories of story . . . available, so little use was made of what we usually think of as the Arthurian legend?"[23] The five editions of Malory during the Tudor period testify that puritan objections did not kill the story, and, for that matter, as Professor Greenlaw points out, the writers of the time were accustomed to converting "Popish" materials to their own uses. Nor does the disuse of the legend rest on any feeling that the material was too unreal. On the contrary, it was just because the legend was regarded as real, as more or less historically true, that it fell into artistic limbo; ironically enough, the very quasi-historicity that had

allowed the survival of the Celtic myth into Christian times now condemned it to comparative desuetude.

TUDOR POLITICS, KING ARTHUR, AND THE
BATTLE OF THE HISTORIANS

It was the "historical" Arthur that Henry of Richmond seized on to
bolster his none-too-secure throne in the uneasy period that followed the
end of the Wars of the Roses. Proclaiming his inheritance of the blood of
Arthur and Cadwallader, Henry thus substantiated his right to rule, and,
in an attempt to strengthen the claim, christened his eldest son Arthur.
His younger son, Henry VIII, was luckier: born at Mona, he could claim
that he was the "sparke of fire" that was, according to Arthurian prophecy,
to be kindled at Mona; on such a basis he could claim not only the throne,
but also the Continental empire that Arthur had conquered.[24] Henry's
trappings at the Field of the Cloth of Gold (1520) made prominent display of hangings showing Arthur as a world conqueror,[25] and fourteen
years later in the Act of Supremacy he used the "fact" that Britain had
been an empire under Arthur to justify his claim of independence from
Rome.[26] In domestic politics, the claim that the Tudors carried in their
veins Arthur's Celtic blood, the common blood of England, Wales, Scotland, and Ireland, was used to further hopes, finally accomplished under
James I, for a unified British nation.[27] Such political uses of Arthurian
legend declined once the Tudors were firmly established. There does not
appear to have been any use of Arthurian material in the coronation celebrations of Edward VI, Mary, or Elizabeth. But in the last decades of
Elizabeth's reign, the legends were revived to support various imperial
and colonial claims to all of the British Isles and even to certain foreign
territories.[28] Clearly, Tudor interest in Arthurian story was something
more than a mere historical primitivism stimulated by growing nationalism,[29] something more than an "antiquarian revival of a glorious *past* of
British empire. It was a revival, to be sure, but it was a revival enhanced
by the belief that in the Welsh blood of Henry of Richmond the very
blood of Arthur had returned to a glorious *present* of British empire."[30]

The consequences of this belief for poets and playwrights were of far-
reaching and long-lasting effect. Involving as it did not only the stability
of the throne, but also—through the prophetic passages in both Geoffrey
and Malory—the succession itself, the story of Arthur was doubly dangerous. Thus, as Josephine Bennett points out, though it

> was easily the best material for epic poetry available for an English
> poet ... [,] while the struggle was going on over how much of it was

> fact and how much of it was fiction, anyone who attempted to make
> use of the Arthurian theme would find himself in immediate difficulty.
> . . . If he made use of the fictional matter, he would offend the historians
> by seeming to discredit Arthur as a historical figure. . . . If, on the other
> hand, he tried to make a story out of the authenticated parts of Arthur's
> history, he would find his material not only impossibly circumscribed
> but also subject to constant change of status.[31]

The result was an almost exclusive concentration on the "historical"
Arthur. Those authors who did attempt to handle the story carefully
eschewed its romantic or supernatural elements. Arthur's mysterious birth
and passing, the achievements of his knights, his sad betrayal by wife and
friend, the high quest of the Grail, all were discarded as "superstition" and
"fantasticall" imaginings, and—more importantly—as additions likely to
throw doubt on the crucially important "facts" of Arthur's existence.[32] In
such an atmosphere, Malory's account was clearly useless, and Geoffrey's
chronicle, "one of the most eagerly studied books of the time,"[33] assumed
the status of chief source of Arthurian story.[34]

But even Geoffrey was suspect.[35] Denounced as an extravagant fabri-
cator as early as the twelfth century, he had held an uncertain position in
the eyes of scholars almost from the beginning. Ralph Higden, whose
fourteenth-century *Polychronicon* was printed in 1482, 1495, and 1527,
doubted the truth of almost the whole of Geoffrey's account of Arthur.[36]
And Robert Fabyan's *New Chronicles of England and France* (1516),
though it gave Geoffrey's account, rejected all the magic elements as unhistorical.[37] Yet despite all this native skepticism, a storm of outrage
greeted Polydore Vergil's *Anglicae Historiae* when it appeared in 1534.
Commissioned many years before by Henry VII to write a history of
England, Polydore, whose hatred of Geoffrey ("more a poet than a historian"), combined with an innate skepticism, caused him to relate the
Arthurian story only "with extreme distaste,"[38] had picked an unfortunate
time to cast doubts on Geoffrey's Arthur, and in any case he was, of all
men, the wrong one to do it. An Italian by birth and a Catholic by religious conviction, he gave his book to the world in the very year that
Henry VIII was using Arthur's empire to support his independence from
Rome.[39] Angered by Polydore's skepticism, the learned John Leland set
himself to collect all the evidence he could find to support faith in Geoffrey; with the appearance of his *Assertio Inclytissimi Arturii Regis Britanniae* in 1544, the tide began to turn.[40] Even before Richard Robinson had
translated Leland's book in 1582 as *A Learned and True Assertion of the
Original Life, Actes, and Death of the Most Noble, Valiant, and Re-*

noumed Prince Arthure, Kinge of Greate Brittaine,[41] Holinshed's *Chronicle* had shown signs of renewed belief.[42]

It would be poor justice to the new scholarship of the English Renaissance to suppose that belief in Geoffrey's Arthur was universal. In general, the humanists seem to have sided with Polydore, and their view of the whole matter is probably summed up in the entry under "Arthurus" in Elyot's *Dictionary*:

> Arthurus, a kyng of England, whã it was called Britannia, a man of excellẽt prowesse in .xv. great battayles agaynst the Saxons, vanquished theim, and fynally drave the most parte of theim out of this roialme. he subdued Scotlande and Irelande, at that tyme beyng well inhabited, and in culture. And after kept an honourable house of valyant and noble personages, wherein was suche magnifycence, that it gave occasion to Frenchemen and Spaniardes, to exercise their wittes in avãsyng of Arthurs maiestee with incredible fables. whiche is no more to be mervayled at, than the semblable invencions and fantasies of the Grekes. All be it this Arthure was a veraie noble and famouse prince, yet of them, whyche wrote histories aboute his tyme, he was unremembred.[43]

If most of England's scholars trained in the humanistic discipline doubted the fabrications of Arthurian tradition, it is reasonable to suppose that the Tudor monarchs themselves placed little credence in the antiquarian claims that Arthur had been a world conqueror,[44] though they would scarcely have been Tudors had they been unwilling to make use of anything that would strengthen their dynasty. Nevertheless, credulity and skepticism in regard to Arthur flourished side by side throughout the sixteenth century, and, as T. D. Kendrick has said, "the struggle to apply to the British History the critical machinery of a new scholarship did not speedily result in an easy and inevitable triumph of the Renaissance mind, but was one that had to be sustained for over a century against a formidable deadweight of contrary opinion jealously preserved and defended by reactionary scholars of great learning and repute."[45]

Meanwhile, although the popular belief in Arthur was far from characteristic of the best and most intelligent historians and scholars of the time, it continued to gather strength in those whose patriotism and emotional devotion to the Tudor monarchy clouded their judgment.[46] Stow, who had in the 1565 edition of his *Summarie of Englyshe Chronicles* taken Fabyan's skeptical attitude toward Geoffrey's version, had come by the 1580 edition of his book to reinstate most of Geoffrey and had accepted the belief that Arthur had subdued thirty kingdoms.[47] And the Arthurian material in Camden's *Britannia* in 1586 makes it clear that faith in a great deal of Arthur's story as told by Geoffrey had become widespread and even "correct" among patriotic, popular antiquarians.[48] But although a large share of his regal éclat had been restored to him, Arthur had at the same time lost all his romantic glory. William Warner's *Albion's England* (1586) outlined the conqueror's achievements, but dismissed the supernatural elements with a blunt "the reste I credite not."[49]

Unfortunately, it was just in that "reste" that the only poetically useful Arthurian story lay. Stripped of his mythic origins, his fellowship of knights, and his fatally attractive queen, Arthur emerged from the heated controversies of the historians and antiquarians as naked of poetic interest, appeal, and significance as a Norman chapel reduced to its "original structure" by Sir Gilbert Scott. Directed by motives of political expediency and national pride, they had saved belief in the historic Arthur at the expense of making poetic treatment of the king impossible. And in so doing, as later events were to prove, the Tudors had initiated an irreversible process—a process by which, ironically, belief in Arthur's historicity was bound to grow weaker and weaker. Once Arthur's being had been poised on historical fact, it was almost certain that the increasingly powerful solvents of historical inquiry developing after the Renaissance would steadily wash away "fact" after "fact." Arthur's connection with the fortunes of the throne would make the process of erosion inevitable. And only when that process was complete, only when men had ceased wholly to believe in the historical Arthur, could they believe once more in the real Arthur, the king of romance. Only then would Arthur return to his Britons. Such a time was still far in the future. Meanwhile, however, there had come a lull in the historians' controversy, and the poets, who had avoided the theme during the years when Arthur's position was subject to constant revision,[50] began to feel its attractions once more.

THE ARTHUR OF THE *FAERIE QUEENE*

Among the first to become aware of the restored popular and antiquarian faith in Arthur was a young man who was just then casting about for a suitable subject for a verse epic, which, though he did not live to finish it, was destined to be the greatest glory of Elizabethan nondramatic poetry. Renaissance courtier and ardent patriot, Edmund Spenser was doubtless particularly sensitive to the imperialist ambitions and nationalist historical primitivism that had fostered the Arthurian revival in the 1580's.[51] But Spenser's own views on Arthur and his knights appear to have been considerably more complex than the conceptions of either the proponents of the New Learning or the antiquarian patriots. As a product of humanist education, he must have smiled at the naïvetés of

Leland and Camden, but as a poet aware of the value of traditional and legendary materials, he probably reserved another smile for the earnest fulminations of his friend E. K. against "certain fine fablers and lewd lyers, such as were the Authors of King Arthure the great and such like, who tell many an vnlawfull leasing of the Ladyes of the Lake, that is, the Nymphes," a gloss on Spenser's own allusion in *The Shepheardes Calender*.[52] In line with the best scholarship of his time, Spenser probably rejected most of Geoffrey's British History, including the supposed founding of Britain by Brutus, although he seems clearly to have accepted the historical truth of at least a minimal part of the story of King Arthur.[53]

But although Spenser rejected most of the Arthurian tradition's pretenses to historical veracity, he was still mightily attracted to the use of Arthur as the hero of the *Faerie Queene*. He himself declared that he "chose the historye of king Arthure, as most fitte for the excellency of his person, being made famous by many mens former workes, and also furthest from the daunger of enuy, and suspition of present time."[54] It is not, however, immediately clear how Arthur could be "most fitte" as a hero in a poem whose avowed "generall end" was "to fashion a gentleman or noble person,"[55] but if we recall that the medieval ideal of chivalry had been translated by the Renaissance into the code of the gentleman, the selection of Arthur is not so mysterious.[56] The most eminent representative of medieval chivalry and at the same time a ruler, seemed an obvious choice for the model of a perfected Elizabethan gentleman and governor. And this was even more so in Spenser's time than it would have been half a century earlier. As Caspari has noted,

> Spenser's romantic revival of an Arthurian past reflects the age and place in which he was living. . . . The fighting in Ireland, buccaneering, high adventure in overseas exploration and in the struggle against Spain had placed a new value on a man's military qualities. There was a crusading spirit among the great soldiers, adventurers, and patriotic pirates of the Elizabethan era which lent itself to symbolization in terms of a glorious trail of knightly battles in pursuit of foul beasts or in the defense of fair ladies. . . . It was not accidental, then, that Spenser should have portrayed Elizabeth's courtiers and heroes in medieval armor. His knights were crusaders; his age was more heroically reckless than Elyot's had been.[57]

Glorified by tradition, "made famous by many mens former workes," and consecrated in the national imagination, Arthur thus already had much in his favor as the subject of a Renaissance epic. Beyond this, in Spenser's view, his career was far enough away in time to permit all the manipulations necessary to the fulfillment of the poet's pre-established ethical scheme. Moreover, the use of Arthur would be both a handsome compliment to the Virgin Queen, and an opportunity for the presentation of a heroic past as a foundation for "a policy and prophecy of a greater England yet to be."[58] And if the poet could simultaneously suggest the lineaments of his patron, the Earl of Leicester, in the figure of Arthur, so much the better.[59]

Yet in the event, the choice was not so happy. Almost from the beginning, the place and character of Spenser's Arthur have occasioned the severest critical objections to the *Faerie Queene*.[60] John Hughes, Spenser's first editor, noted that although Arthur appeared in every adventure, "his Part is not considerable enough in any one of them . . . and we lose sight of him too soon to consider him as the Hero of the Poem."[61] Warton objected that Arthur "is only a subordinate, or rather accessory character," whose "magnanimity . . . breaks forth but seldom, in dim and interrupted flashes."[62] And Bishop Hurd shrewdly suspected that "the adventure of Prince Arthur, whatever the author pretended, and his critic too easily believed, was but an after-thought" and a mere expedient.[63] Later critics have been no kinder: Renwick asserted that "the place of Prince Arthur in the epic-romance was never quite clearly worked out; his appearances are fitful and unrelated," and Davis has called him "an abstraction" substituted for a "personality."[64] Such a chorus of discontent is to be explained in various ways. The older critics, no doubt, were troubled by what they felt to be a failure of unity.[65] But the dissatisfaction of later critics partly springs also, as Merritt Hughes has observed, from "the widening gulf" that modern scholarship has revealed between Spenser's Arthurian material and that of the Middle Ages.[66]

Just how wide that gulf is becomes clear from a consideration not only of what Spenser offers in the way of Arthurian story, but also of what he omits. Piecing together Arthur's history from its scattered appearances in *The Faerie Queene*, we learn that Arthur, child of Igrayne and Uther, had been spirited away to be raised by one Timon and educated by Merlin.[67] He dreams one day of the Faerie Queene, and sets out in search of her, bearing arms of magical properties made for him by Merlin.[68] In the course of his search he vanquishes such enemies as Orgoglio, Malegar, Corflambo, and Disdain.[69] None of these adventures belongs to the Arthurian tradition, although some of the older motifs are to be seen in the adventures of the subordinate heroes. Florimell's girdle recalls the various chastity-testing devices common in Arthurian romance; Crudor's mantle trimmed with the beards of knights and ladies' hair suggests King Ryence's mantle in Malory; the Blattant Beast pursued and finally captured by Calidore is, of course, a variation on the Questing Beast followed

by Lamorack and Pelleas in *Le Morte Darthur*.[70] But the extent to which
Spenser strayed from the traditional story is made clearer by what he did
not include. Of all of Arthur's famous knights, Tristram alone is intro-
duced, and only as a very minor figure.[71] Of Lancelot, Gawain, Percival,
Galahad, Palomydes, Kay, Bedivere, Gareth, and Geraint we hear nothing.
Nor do Guinevere, Iseult, Morgan la Fay, or Mordred have any place in
Spenser's poem.[72] It is true, of course, that most of these figures could
have had little if any place in a poem dealing with Arthur's career before
he became king. In the Letter to Raleigh, Spenser declared that if *The
Faerie Queene*, in which he intended to illustrate in Arthur a combination
of the private virtues, was "well accepted," he might "be perhaps encouraged, to frame the other part of polliticke vertues in [Arthur's] person,
after that hee came to be king."[73] But from the way Spenser dealt with
Arthur's story in the part of the poem that was finished, and from what
we may guess of the intended conclusion in which, it appears, the love-
smitten Arthur would at last find his Gloriana and tender his love and
service to her, it does not seem likely that he would have paid much attention to the essential elements of the medieval story, or to its inherently
tragic spirit.

That a great poet should have elected to deal with the old story in
such a fashion must have puzzled many readers. Clearly his neglect of the
traditional story did not rest on ignorance of its earlier forms. If Warton's
view that *The Faerie Queene* is extensively indebted to Malory is no
longer tenable, there is still no doubt that Spenser was well acquainted
with a considerable body of romance materials.[74] Yet the fact that he was
so indifferent to the Arthurian story's central structure and nature is not
inexplicable if it is seen in the light of the historical situation, Spenser's
own profoundly moralistic bent, and, perhaps, the nature of the evolution
of his plan for the poem.

Spenser was, as has already been suggested, awake to the political and
dynastic implications of the Arthurian story. The wide range of sources
that he drew on for the chronicle of British history that Arthur reads at
Alma's castle[75] shows that he was "as close a student of the historical
aspects of the story of Arthur as any of those who took part in the controversy."[76] The fact that the historians had denuded Arthur of his romance characteristics was far from daunting Spenser. On the contrary,
only through taking Arthur's historicity seriously (within his poem, of
course) could he serve both his political purpose of complimenting the
Virgin Queen and his literary intention of creating an epic poem. In line
with common Renaissance critical theory, he doubtless thought of the epic
as idealized historical fact, and with Camden, he was convinced of the

value of historical study in fostering a national spirit. Thus, appropriately enough, in the chronicle passages he makes "a knowledge of the nation's history and destiny the final preparation" for his hero, just as Virgil had done in the *Aeneid*.[77]

But why, then, it may be asked, did not Spenser at least utilize the "facts" of the Tudor historians' Arthur as the narrative basis or core of his poem? The answer may be that there was simply no room for such a treatment in Spenser's plan. Mrs. Bennett has argued[78] that Spenser's earliest plan had been "to honor his patriot Queen by substituting her for Arthur [and] giving to her the court and order of knighthood which traditionally belonged to Arthur."[79] The very device by which the hero-lover of Gloriana was to be integrated into the plot, i.e., the knight's dream of a lady and subsequent devoted quest of her, is not Arthurian; indeed, it is drawn from Chaucer's anti-Arthurian *Tale of Sir Thopas*.[80] Thus when Spenser was stimulated by the revival of Arthur's reputation in the 1580's to include him in his plan, there was no place for Arthur as king or world-conqueror.[81] But here as elsewhere, Spenser seems to have been governed by a conviction that room could always be found for one more good thing, and so he adopted the expedient of presenting Arthur as Prince Arthur "before he was king."[82] The solution, unfortunately, left him with an Arthur who was nothing but a name, since all that remained was the birth and youth of Arthur. And the mysterious birth of Arthur was interdicted, perhaps partially because it might cast doubt on Arthur's historicity, and even more because it had no relevance to the fashioning of a gentleman.[83] What was thus left was exactly that part of the hero's life that almost universally in heroic myth is a mere blank, the period after birth and before the conquering of his kingdom.[84] To fill this space, Spenser invented a series of romantic adventures accomplished in the course of a quest that had no connection with the traditional myth of Arthur. Nor did the impoverishment of the traditional hero stop there. In terms of both his earlier and his later plans, Spenser was now obliged to appropriate Arthur's Round Table to Gloriana, at whose court it became the Order of Maidenhead and, not altogether incidentally, an elegant compliment to the Order of the Garter.[85]

The replacement of the Knights themselves—Lancelot, Gawain, and the rest—by such creations as the Redcrosse Knight and Guyon was, aside from questions of chronological consistency, necessitated by another factor in Spenser's plan. That factor—moral allegory—also militated against a satisfactory handling of Arthurian story. If "the twelue priuate morall vertues" were each to be personified in a single knight, it was obvious that considerable difficulty would be involved in attempting to employ the old knights with all their traditional associations to illustrate the struggle toward perfection in one or the other of the moral virtues.[86] Hence, they were ignored; a crueller fate was reserved for their king:

> I labour to pourtraict in Arthure, before he was king, the image of a braue knight, perfected in the twelue priuate morall vertues, as Aristotle hath deuised, the which is the purpose of these first twelue bookes . . . . So in the person of Prince Arthure I sette forth magnificence in particular, which vertue . . . (according to Aristotle and the rest) . . . is the perfection of all the rest, and conteineth in it them all.[87]

The result goes a long way toward justifying Swinburne's strictures on "the lack of tangible form and line, of human flesh and breath and blood on the limbs and at the lips and in the veins of Spenser's active or passive and militant or triumphant congregation of impersonated virtues and vices."[88] It was not just humanity that the allegory took away from Arthur—it was also his tragic significance. "If," MacCallum observes, "the allegory sets forth the universal war of good and evil and the inevitable triumph of the good, Arthur had to be presented as practically invincible."[89] In this conception of his hero, Spenser appears also to have been influenced by the Renaissance mythographers' conception of Hercules. For them, "Hercules had come to possess the same typical value as Spenser's Prince Arthur, representing the ideal of a gentleman, perfected in all the virtues by a life dedicated to 'long labors' in pursuit of fame."[90] Moreover, both Renaissance epic theory and his own desire to celebrate the success of the nation and of the lineage of its sovereign were opposed to any unhappy ending for his hero.[91]

The truth is that everything was inimical to Spenser's handling of the Arthurian story. Mrs. Bennett's hypothesis that Arthur was "a late and superficial addition and not a basic ingredient in the poet's plans,"[92] even if taken as fact, could be only part of the explanation. The political implications of the legend at the time, current literary theory, Spenser's own complicated intentions, and his fascination with the elaborated ingenuities of his allegory—all conspired against his giving meaningful expression to the essential Arthurian story. The question of whether *The Faerie Queene* is a great poem is not at issue here. That it is so is admitted even by those—perhaps especially by those—who "would rather praise than read it." Its marvels of color and texture, of rhythm and tone have fed the imaginations of poets and plain readers for over three centuries. Still, it may be asserted that *The Faerie Queene* is not a great Arthurian poem. The adventures of the Redcrosse Knight, of Una and Britomart, perhaps of Calidore, stick in our minds, but it must be a rare reader who recalls

Prince Arthur distinctly, or who, for that matter, even in the actual reading of the poem becomes absorbed in his quest of Gloriana. Indeed, we are surprised to be reminded that *The Faerie Queene* is an Arthurian poem. And there is a reason for our surprise. Of the spirit of the great king of myth and romance, of his beautiful and terrifying triumph and tragic destruction through his sad-eyed queen and his noblest knight, there is nothing in *The Faerie Queene*—which is to say that it is, in a very real way, not an Arthurian poem.[93] .

THOMAS HUGHES AND OTHERS

While wholesale invention characterizes Spenser's approach to the legend of Arthur, slavish imitation is the most salient feature of the Tudor period's only other significant attempt to grapple with the subject. Thomas Hughes, a Cambridge M.A. and lawyer at Gray's Inn, had doubtless been impressed, like Spenser, by the Arthurian revival of the 1580's, and, again like Spenser, had been moved to compliment his sovereign by a poetic representation of her great forebear. But there all resemblance ends. *The Misfortunes of Arthur* (1588, N.S.), presented before Elizabeth by the Gentlemen of Gray's Inn, complete with choruses and dumb-shows,[94] abandons all the magical trappings of romance so dear to Spenser. Instead, Hughes, impelled by the prevailing and politically important popular faith in Arthur's historicity, concentrates on what he probably regarded as a genuine chronicle of dynastic transgression and retribution.

From the Argument, we learn how Uther, smitten with lawless passion for Igerna, fathered Arthur on her through Merlin's cunning, and afterwards slew Gorlois, her husband. After Uther's death from Saxon poison years later, Arthur took the throne and "delighted in his sister *Anne*, who made him father of *Mordred*." Still later, challenged by Rome, Arthur left his queen, Gueneuora, and his realm in Mordred's care. During the nine years when Arthur was fighting on the Continent, Mordred usurped the throne and was accepted by Gueneuora as her lover.[95] The play itself opens with Gorlois's ghost, risen from Hades, cursing the line of Pendragon for Uther's crime, which "dispoylde [him] erst of wife, of lande, and life" (I, i, 7). Gueneuora, learning of Arthur's imminent return and enraged by both Arthur's nine years' neglect and her own passion for Mordred, contemplates killing her husband or herself, and finally, stung by conscience, retires to a nunnery. Mordred, putting aside advice to throw himself on his father's mercy, unsuccessfully resists Arthur's landing, rejects Arthur's offer of peace, delivered by Gawin, and gathers a force of Irish, Saxon, and Pictish warriors. Arthur, out of love for his son and an unwillingness to submit his realm to civil war, still seeks peace, but at last is obliged by Mordred to go to war. In the fatal battle (reported by a *nuntius*), the opposing armies are frightened by storms and lightning, but at last Gawin is killed along with thousands of others. Mordred, mortally wounded, thrusts himself forward on Arthur's spear and gives Arthur the fatal blow. Arthur dies, imploring his comrades to let his death "be ay vnknowen, so that in euery Coast / I still be feard, and lookt for euery houre" (V, i, 177–78). The play closes with Gorlois's ghost returning to gloat over the working out of his revenge.

Hughes's story, as this outline indicates, is taken over largely from Geoffrey's "history." The addition of the crucial motif of Mordred's incestuous begetting, possibly derived from Malory,[96] tactless though it may have been in a play designed for Elizabeth's entertainment,[97] doubtless owes something to Hughes's awareness of the need for augmenting the pathos of the catastrophe as it had been presented by Geoffrey. But it owes a great deal more to the classical predilections of Hughes. The combination of Geoffrey's "historical" ruler with the incestuous monarch of romance must have appeared perfect to a writer intent on dramatizing British history in terms of Senecan tragedy. For a writer with the bloodstained horror of the *Thyestes* as his ideal, it was irresistible.[98]

Unfortunately, the story of Arthur, essentially Christian as it was and had long been, was not so easily adaptable to the classical mold. The incest motif posed an insoluble problem. If Arthur's incest was made an unwitting transgression (as it is in Malory), it could not serve as the motivation of a Christian tragedy, where choice is all. But if it was a willed sin, the sin was so hideous as to seriously weaken Arthur's typical character as the flawless king. In the event, Hughes seems almost to try to have it both ways. Arthur's incest with Anne appears to have been committed knowingly, yet at the same time the whole of Arthur's expressed awareness of the sin and his remorse for it is condensed into two brief speeches.[99] Even Mordred himself takes no particular interest in his origins. Arthur's real concern is with "the loue, which nature doth inforce / From kin to kin, but most from sire to sonne" (III, i, 41–42) and with his unwillingness to shed his people's blood in civil strife. Nor does the assignment of the precipitating sin to Uther mend matters.[100] However successful such a motivation might have been in classical tragedy, it left an irreparable hiatus in the ethical fabric of the story.

Hughes's devotion to his Senecan models accounts for more than structural faults. So extensive are his borrowings from the classical authors, particularly Seneca, that the play often seems more an exercise in learned ingenuity than a dramatic presentation of human passions. Whole scenes are mere pastiches of translations from Seneca and Lucan.[101] "Arthur, Mordred, and Guenevora," Cunliffe observes, "have apothegms assigned to them taken from so many and so different Senecan characters that all impression of individuality is in danger of being lost."[102] To Seneca's influence is also due Hughes's frequent use of *stichomythia*, the construction of scenes in terms of aphoristic debate, the rapid oscillation of emotion in his characters. In *The Misfortunes of Arthur* these devices frequently make the play wooden and rhetorical in the bad sense of the word, and the rapid conversion of the characters from one decision to another suggests not the tides of passion, but the jerkings of marionettes. But for all his faults as a dramatist, Hughes was one of a very few writers who attempted the Arthurian subject between the time of Malory and that of Tennyson who had a glimpse into the heart of its greatness. How well he might have handled it, had he been free of his adulation of the classics and the notions of his age about Arthur's historicity is suggested in Arthur's anguished response to the urgings of Cador and Howell to revenge himself on Mordred:

> . . . my Country cryes for due remorse
> And some reliefe for long sustained toyles [.]
> By Seas and Lands I dayly wrought her wrecke,
> And sparelesse spent her life on euery foe.
> Eche where my Souldiers perisht, whilest I wonne:
> Throughout the world my Conquest was their spoile.
>   A faire reward for all their deaths, for all
> Their warres abroad, to giue them ciuell warres.
>   . . . .
> Must they still ende their liues amongest the blades?
> Rests there no other *Fate* whiles Arthur raignes?
>   What deeme you me? a furie fedde with blood,
> Or some *Ciclopian* borne and bred for braules?
> Thinke on the minde, that *Arthur* beares to peace:
> Can *Arthur* please you no where but in warres?
>   Be witnesse Heauens how farre t'is from my minde,
> Therewith to spoile or sacke my natiue soile:
> I cannot yeelde, it brookes not in my breast,
> To seeke her ruine, whom I erst haue rulde.[103]

But to have sustained this note of moral grief, of tragic awareness, would have required genius beyond Thomas Hughes's modest talents. Indeed, it would have taxed the greatest of the Elizabethan dramatists. Yet in fact only the most minor playwrights seized on the legend, and their works are known to us only through noncommittal entries in the diary of that remarkable businessman of the Elizabethan theater, Philip Henslowe. Among these vanished plays, "Vterpendragon" seems to have enjoyed a fair degree of success in 1597. A year later we find Henslowe paying a certain R. Hathwaye £4 for "the playe of the lyfe of arthure"; then as now production costs dwarfed the author's income if we can judge from Henslowe's expenditure of £3 for a robe for the same play. The last Arthurian entry in the Diary concerns a loan to Thomas Downton in 1599 for "the Booke of Trystram de Lyons."[104]

The major Elizabethan dramatists, however, universally neglected the Arthurian legend. Some, doubtless, were discouraged by the restrictions entailed by the political commitment of the story of Arthur. Others, perhaps, were disqualified by contempt for the meaningless marvels of the medieval romances or by a lack of sympathy with its inherent moral and spiritual idealism.[105] Nor should simple ignorance of the artistically significant versions of the story be overlooked. Shakespeare, whose *Lear* and *Cymbeline* testify to his interest in the material of British history, seems especially to trouble such writers as MacCallum by his failure to treat the story of the noblest of the British kings. While his plays contain a number of Arthurian allusions, their association with Falstaff and other figures of fun suggests, as MacCallum points out, that Shakespeare did not take the legend seriously.[106] But the fact that his imagination was not touched by the tragic story of Arthur may rest on nothing more complicated than simple lack of acquaintance with its serious literary versions. All the allusions to Arthur in the plays suggest derivation from popular tradition, and nothing in his work indicates that he knew Geoffrey, Malory, or any other worthwhile form of the story.[107] Small wonder, then, that Shakespeare did not feel its attractions, though there is matter for regret that great Arthur, so truly "more sinned against than sinning," did not find a place beside Othello, Lear, and Macbeth.

Nor was any other important talent inspired during the Tudor period by the story, though a variety of insignificant works indicate that the Arthurian tradition maintained a certain literary vitality. *A Lytel Tretys of the Byrth and Prophecyes of Merlin*, published by Wynken de Worde in 1510,[108] probably was designed to cater to vulgar interest in prophetic works of all sorts. The early part of the century also saw the publication of several episodic romances on Sir Gawain, a figure of considerable popularity during the period if we are to judge from his frequent appearances.[109] During the long and heated controversy over Arthur's historicity, the knights of the Round Table are not heard of, but as the Tudor dynasty drew to a close, Arthur and his men once more appear in several minor works. Christopher Middleton's *History of Chinon of England* (1597) mentions the king briefly and also employs Lancelot, Triamore, and Tristram as foils for its chief character, though with customary Renaissance indifference to the essential story, Lancelot is made to fall in love with a certain Laura, and Guenevere and Iseult are omitted.[110] Another of these late Tudor romances had considerable success: Richard Johnson's *The Most Pleasant History of Tom a Lincolne, That Renowned Soldier, The Red Rose Knight, Who for His Valour and Chivalry was Sirnamed The Boast of England* (1599–1607) had reached its seventh edition by 1635.[111] A tedious performance in the euphuistic style, its connection with Arthur is essentially tangential, and even so it merely trades on the names of the heroes of romance, altering the traditional story freely. Its hero, Tom of Lincoln, is the offspring of an illicit love affair between Arthur and Angellica, daughter of the Earl of London. In his youth Tom organizes a band of outlaws, and later on he occasionally has the assistance of Launcelot, Tristram, and Triamore in the course of a series of absurdly improbable adventures that include a love affair with an Amazon and the successful wooing of Anglitora, the daughter of Prester John. The second part, which offers an account of Arthur's twelve battles and his peaceful retirement during the last seven years of his life, shows the same disposition to alter the traditional version of Arthur's career when it suited Johnson's convenience to do so. As for Tom himself, he is deserted by Anglitora and subsequently murdered by her paramour, a Soldan. Returning as a ghost, he incites his son, the Black Knight, to revenge him, and Anglitora also dies at her son's hand. The process of free alteration and extravagant expansion of Arthurian story could scarcely have been carried further. A somewhat more traditional view of the story is taken in the versified account of Arthur's reign included in Robert Chester's *Loves Martyr: or, Rosalins Complaint . . . with the True Legend of famous King Arthur, the Last of the Nine Worthies* (1601), obviously based on the less interesting chronicle versions.[112] How far the impoverishment of the tradition had gone by the end of Elizabeth's reign is made clear by the jejune doggerel of Thomas Deloney's "The Noble Acts of Arthur of the Round Table" (1603).[113] Yet even worse things lay ahead for Arthurian story under the Stuarts.

3 ❦ The Death of a Legend

ARTHURIAN STORY IN THE SEVENTEENTH AND EARLY EIGHTEENTH CENTURIES

The association of Arthur's fortunes with the stability of the throne, as we have seen, had placed serious limitations on the artistic use of the legend. But while the effects on the legend of this strange alliance had been debilitating under the generally popular monarchy of the Tudors, they were all but fatal under the increasingly unpopular rule of the Stuart family. Whereas many of the Tudor historians had, in response to the royal claims to kindred with Arthur, leaped to the authenticating of the legendary king and at least some of his conquests, the general movement of seventeenth-century historiography is in the direction of a skeptical discounting of even the fragments preserved by the preceding historians.

While this movement was to a large extent due, as we shall later see, to the Parliament party's steadily harder line against the claims of the Stuarts, it was also firmly rooted in the new mental attitudes toward science and imagination, historical fact and poetic fancy, developing through the period. And these attitudes were as destructive of the poetic Arthur as they were of the "historical" Arthur. Thus it was that although three of the greatest poets of the age were stirred to epic plans by the subject, one after another they abandoned it.

ARTHUR IN SEVENTEENTH-CENTURY POLITICS AND THOUGHT

Like the Tudors before him, James I was quick to see the usefulness of Arthur in bolstering his throne. Through both the Tudor and the Stuart lines, he was able to trace himself to Arthur's blood,[1] and by his relinquishment of separate titles to the two realms of Scotland and England and his taking instead the title of King of Great Britain, James made possible the assertion by his supporters that his accession fulfilled Merlin's prophecy that under the name of Brutus England and Scotland would be united once more as they had been under Arthur.[2] James sought in other ways to make use of Arthur's éclat in popularizing his rule. He imitated Arthur in a plan for the creation of a thousand new knights during his first years on the throne.[3] And for some of his subjects, "James was not only *like* Arthur; he was also considered to *be* Arthur returned to life again through his descendant, or at least to be the successor of Arthur."[4] This notion makes its appearance in Campion's *Masque at Lord Hays Marriage* (1606–1607), Camden's *Remaines,* Warner's *Continuance of Albion's England* (1606), and Ben Jonson's *Speeches at Prince Henry's Barriers* (1609).[5]

However auspicious such poetic gallantries may have appeared, the basing of the Stuart claims to the throne on Arthur's historicity was unlucky—both for the Stuarts and, in the event, for the Arthurian story. For as James began to press his theory of the divine right of kings, an automatic reaction against all his claims set in among the offended Commons and their supporters. Since the King's party traced its rights at least partially to the early British kings, the Parliament party turned also to history to vindicate the rights of the people.[6] In the ensuing search, it was discovered that the nation's oldest laws were Saxon in origin and contained no British words, only Germanic.[7] Such discoveries were accompanied by the discrediting of the notion of the settling of the island by Brutus and by a corresponding elevation of the Saxons, Arthur's traditional enemies, to the status of founders of the country's liberties.[8] With this view went a corresponding disparagement of the British kings, especially Arthur.[9] Indeed, the identification of Arthurian story with the fortunes of the legendary king's putative descendants during the century was so close that interest and belief in Arthur closely parallels the decline, fall, and restoration of royal ascendancy in England.[10]

Among the historians and historical poets, this parallel is particularly clear. Robert Nicols' *Winter Nights Vision,* an addition to the 1610 issue of *A Mirour for Magistrates,* presents an Arthur who professes to tell only the truth of his reign; nevertheless, Nicols mostly follows Geoffrey's account though he eliminates the motif of Arthur's bastardy.[11] In the following year, Speed, while accepting Arthur's historicity, doubted the romantic conquests and noted that they were probably responsible for disbelief in Arthur.[12] Even Samuel Daniel, one of the few men of his time to see the greatness of medieval civilization, was forced in his *History of England* (1612) to reject most of the legendary material.[13] Thus Arthur became "a man in force and courage aboue man and worthie to haue beene a subiect of truth to posterity and not of fiction."[14] But it was just this distinction that John Selden, writing in the same year, doubted could be made at all: "The *Bards* songs have, with . . . unlimited attribut so loaden him, that you can hardly guesse what is true of him."[15] Ten years later, Francis Bacon was still able to accept Arthur's existence, but suggested that much of the story was fanciful.[16] The only notable exception to this general current of skepticism before the Civil War was William Slayter's *Palae-Albion* (1619), a verse chronicle dedicated to James and therefore not surprisingly marked by a full faith in the British legends and a condemnation of those who doubted Arthur's historicity.[17]

As the Stuart sun waned, so did interest in Arthur, and during the Commonwealth he was all but forgotten. Dugdale's *Monasticon Anglicanum*, published first in 1655, mentions Arthur only in passing, and then in a purely antiquarian reference to Arthur's connection with Glastonbury.[18] After the Restoration, Arthur is heard of once more, but the view among historians seems commonly to have been that though Arthur had indeed existed, his accomplishments had been vastly magnified in the early chronicles. Churchill in 1675, Sammes in 1676, Stillingfleet in 1685, and Nicolson in 1696, all subscribed to this estimate.[19] But so deeply had the acid of skepticism eaten into the story by the end of the century that Sir William Temple, a conservative by nature, doubted Arthur's very existence.[20] Thus was reached the logical end of the process of historical questioning that Polydore Vergil had begun over 160 years before. But whereas the earlier doubters had been obliged to defend their position by pointing to improbabilities, the new historians had the support of vastly improved methods of historical study. During the controversy that had raged around Arthur and the nation's origins, historians developed such techniques as the test of chronology and critical examination of sources.[21] Exposed to their harsh light, the historical Arthur withered and dwindled into insignificance.

But what of the king of romance then? Once Arthur had been released from shoring up the Stuart cause,[22] he should have been free for artistic service. The fact is, however, that from the death of James I on, allusions to Arthurian story often reveal a note of contemptuous ridicule.[23] Hostility to an increasingly unpopular royal family no doubt entered into this revulsion of feeling. At the same time, the pangs of disillusionment are not to be underestimated: the fate of fallen idols, whether actual or ideal, is rarely kind. But beyond these shocks to Arthur's reputation, and perhaps even partially the source of them, were the far more serious and long-lasting effects of the profound shift in sensibility that characterizes the seventeenth century.

This shift, developing slowly at the beginning of the period and accelerated greatly after Descartes, took many forms: antischolasticism and the rejection of authority, empiricism and a devotion to mathematical or mechanistic explanation, rationalism and a preference for abstraction to particularization—for the sign to the symbol. But in all its forms the new philosophy stood firm for fact, for the "true nature of things," and ever more strongly opposed to "fancy" and imagination, "fiction" and myth.[24] The effects of such a world view on the use of Arthur are obvious. His historical "truth" reduced to nothing or at the most a mere shadow by the first roughly "scientific" historians, both he and his knights as figures of romance were victims of the century's general depreciation or rejection of "poetic truth." Poetry might be, as Locke was to put it, agreeable, but it was neither true nor reasonable.[25] And the basically unhistorical quality of the new rationalism made even more unlikely a sympathetic entering into the spirit of a medieval story.[26]

How far interest in the romances declined during the century may be gathered from the fact that although five editions of Malory had appeared in the course of the Tudor period, only one—and that the badly mutilated edition of 1634, carefully purged of oaths and popish superstitions—appeared between the Stuart accession and the nineteenth century.[27] In this respect Arthurian romance only participated in the general eclipse of the older literature during the period. In the 125 years before 1602, eleven issues of *The Canterbury Tales* had been published; between 1602 and 1778 there were just three editions.[28] Those occasional eccentrics who for one reason or another continued to read the old romances, or at least to collect them, apparently found the supply in England limited, and few new ones were written.[29] To some extent, of course, the creative triumphs of the Elizabethan age had replaced earlier literature in men's affections. Again, the ascendancy of classical tendencies in criticism, with a corresponding reaction to the barbarism of the medieval and early Tudor writers doubtless contributed to the neglect.[30] Beyond all else, however, it was the triumph of the faith in fact over faith in poetic truth that made impossible any really satisfactory treatment of the Arthurian legend during the seventeenth and eighteenth centuries.

DRAYTON AND JONSON

Despite the fact that everything was against its successful execution, the Arthurian subject continued to evoke high ambitions in the breasts of patriotic poets throughout the century. As lovers of their country, they all felt the proud enthusiasm that prompted Michael Drayton's exclamation: "For some aboundant braine, ô there had beene a storie / Beyond the Blind-mans might to have inhanc't our glorie."[31] Drayton himself was fired by even higher, or, certainly, more extensive aims. Of the work in which he celebrates Arthur at length—if in passing, perhaps no better description can be given than that afforded by its title page: *Poly-Olbion, or A Chorographicall Description of Tracts, Riuers, Mountaines, Forests, and Other Parts of This Renowned Isle of Great Britaine, with Intermixture of the Most Remarquable Stories, Antiquities, Wonders, Rarityes, Pleasures, and Commodities of the Same: Digested in a Poem.*[32] Like its author, *Poly-Olbion* was in many ways a holdover from the more spacious days of Elizabeth. Begun as early as 1598 and added to fitfully until the publication of the first eighteen Songs in 1612, it came to market too late.[33] Drayton had conceived his poem when antiquarian faith in Arthur was at its full; by the time it appeared, as the poet angrily declares, "Ignorance had brought the world to such a pass / As now, which scarce beleeves that *Arthur* ever was."[34]

For a man possessed of a "naturall inclination to love Antiquitie," it was indeed a "lunatique Age." But with undisguised contempt for those who "had rather read the fantasies of forraine inventions, then [*sic*] . . . see the Rarities and Historie of their owne Country delivered by a true native Muse,"[35] Drayton proceeded to recount various Arthurian incidents and legends whenever in the course of his survey he reached some topographical feature associated with the king. In Song IV, he gives a relatively full summary of Arthur's career, conquests, and death at "false *Mordreds* hand."[36] In this account neither Lancelot nor any of the other romance knights or adventures plays any part. Drayton's Arthur is, as we would expect, the king of the patriotic historians, particularly Geoffrey.[37] This and the aggrieved bitterness of his condemnation of "those fooles that all Antiquitie defame" because they discover some "fictive ornament" mixed with the "truth,"[38] show clearly that Drayton, no matter how much inspired by the subject, championed like the other poets of the preceding age what was coming to be an increasingly impossible approach. Even in his own book the new sense of historical fact had jostled uncomfortably against Drayton's conception of the story. The learned John Selden, speaking of the scholarly "Illustrations" that Drayton had asked him to prepare to accompany the poem, had, he said, "insert[ed] oft, out of the *British* story, what I importune you [i.e., the reader] not to credit."[39] But although the faith in Arthur's historicity that marks Drayton's approach was moribund, the patriotic possibilities of the material appear to have remained very much alive.

It was the desire to honor his country that prompted Ben Jonson to project "ane Epick Poeme jntitled Heroölogia of the Worthies of his Country rowsed by fame," and this poem, Drummond goes on to say, he "was to dedicate . . . to his Country." That Arthur would have been the hero or at least one of the heroes of this work seems likely from Jonson's assertion that "for a Heroik poeme . . . there was no such Ground as King Arthurs fiction."[40] The last word suggests that Jonson, having freed the story from the shackles of pseudohistory, might have been in the way to have achieved a successful treatment of Arthur. But there is more than enough evidence to indicate that had Jonson gone on with the plan, he would have failed to enter into the legend's spirit. In *The Speeches at Prince Henry's Barriers* (1609) and later in *Under-Woods* XLIII, "An Execration upon Vulcan," he condemns the institutions of chivalry and "the whole summe / Of errant Knight-hood, with the Dames and Dwarfes." In *The New Inn*, Lovel attacks the romances with a pungency worthy (not to say reminiscent) of Ascham: "Abortiues of the fabulous, dark cloyster, / Sent out to poison courts, and infest manners."[41] Since on the other hand he also disliked Spenser's freely inventive handling of Arthurian story,[42] it is rather difficult to guess just what he would have done with the material. Whatever it would have been, Jonson probably realized, as Miss Brinkley says, that the nation's sympathies were turning Saxon and "the time for the popularity of an Arthurian epic had passed."[43] At any rate he abandoned his plan. That he did so is most likely no occasion for regret. Classicist, rationalist, and satirist, he could scarcely have been more ill-suited to handle the dark medieval story of a king whose tragic fall hinged on the betrayal of high ideals.

MILTON AND THE ARTHURIAN SUBJECT

Much better adapted to the requirements of the Arthurian legend was the next poet who felt its appeal. Like Jonson, young John Milton was attracted by the story's patriotic potentiality, but unlike the older writer he seems to have had a sympathetic understanding of its spirit from childhood. In his youth, he tells us,

> I betook me among those lofty Fables and Romances, which recount in solemne canto's the deeds of Knighthood founded by our victorious kings; & from hence had in renowne all over Christendome. There I read it in the oath of every Knight, that he should defend to the expense of his best blood, or of his life, if it so befell him, the honour and chastity of Virgin or Matron. . . . Only this my minde gave me that every free and gentle spirit without that oath ought to be borne a Knight, nor needed to expect the guilt [*sic*] spurre, or the laying of a sword upon his shoulder to stirre him up both by his counsell, and his arme to secure and protect the weakenesse of any attempted chastity.[44]

The reminiscence bespeaks something more than youthful sympathy; it reveals a comprehension of the moral or ethical content of the romances and, beyond that, an understanding of that content in symbolic terms applicable to later times. As an all but official spokesman of the Puritan cause, he was bound to make a nod in the direction of the conventional abhorrence of the romances, "books which to many others have bin the fuell of wantonesse and loose living," but for him they had been "so many incitements . . . to the love and stedfast observations of that vertue which abhorres the society of Bordello's."[45] No wonder that in young manhood, chivalric romance remained among his favorite reading, the adventures that "great bards,"

> In sage and solemn tunes have sung,
> Of Turneys and of Trophies hung;
> Of Forests and inchantments drear,
> Where more is meant than meets the ear.[46]

And in later years his memory would still be haunted by

> . . . what resounds
> In Fable or *Romance* of *Uthers* Son
> Begirt with *British* and *Armoric* Knights[47]

and by

> . . . Fairy Damsels met in Forest wide
> By Knights of *Logres*, or of *Lyones*,
> *Lancelot* or *Pelleas*, or *Pellynore*.[48]

By 1639–1640, Milton's interest in the romances appears to have aroused in him hopes that he might some day write a poem on Arthur. In *Mansus*, he prays that Fate will give him such a friend as Manso, "If ever I shall recall in song the kings of my native land, and Arthur, who set wars in train even 'neath the earth [i.e., in Fairyland], or shall tell of the high-hearted heroes bound together as comrades at that peerless table, and O, may the spirit come to my aid—I shall break to pieces Saxon phalanxes under the might of Briton's warring."[49] In the *Epitaphium Damonis* (1640), it seems clear that an Arthurian epic has become a settled plan: "I shall sing of Igraine, mother-to-be, through fateful trickery, of Arthur, I shall sing of lying features, of the taking of the arms of Gorlois, guile, all, of Merlin."[50] The rest is silence, or something very like it. In 1641 in one of the controversial pamphlets that now began to absorb his energies, Milton hints vaguely that when the great work of reformation has been completed, "some one may perhaps" sing of God's benefactions "throughout all Ages" in "this great and Warlike Nation," but of the Arthurian epic no more is heard.[51] Instead, he appears by 1642 to be generally unsettled as to a possible subject, and in the nearly one hundred subjects, many of them drawn from British history, listed in the *Trinity College Manuscript*, Arthur finds no place.[52]

Explanations of this abrupt relinquishment of the subject so long and so lovingly considered have proliferated like mushrooms after a spring rain. As early as 1762, Bishop Hurd, noting that Milton manifests "thro' all his poetry, where his enthusiasm flames out most, a certain predilection for the legends of chivalry," suggested that "what led him to change his mind was, partly, . . . his growing fanaticism; partly, his ambition to take a different rout from Spenser; but chiefly perhaps, the discredit into which the stories of chivalry had now fallen by the immortal satire of Cervantes."[53] But some forty pages later, it was the triumph of Reason over "the portentous spectres of the imagination" which, "no doubt, was the main reason of his relinquishing his long-projected design of Prince Arthur, at last, for that of the Paradise Lost; where, instead of Giants and Magicians, he had Angels and Devils to supply him with the *marvellous*, with greater probability."[54] The same sort of impromptu plausibility and ill-considered speculation marks a great many later endeavors to explain Milton's abandonment of the Arthurian plan. Among the reasons advanced with varying degrees of conviction have been Milton's declining interest in the allegorical method;[55] his "increasing republicanism," which would have made a monarch-hero unsuitable;[56] his growing anti-Catholicism and concern with his own times;[57] and his disillusionment with his country's leaders.[58] Again, it has been suggested that "the historical material [which he was reading in the early 1640's] probably surprised him by its richness" and it is thus "not strange that we hear no more of the Arthurian epic after the time when Milton had become deeply interested in the non-legendary part of English story."[59] But the widest assent seems to have been given to the view that Milton "with his growing Puritanism looked askance . . . at fictions . . . , and with austerer veracity demanded the truth and nothing but the truth."[60] Such a crude dichotomy as this between "fiction" and "truth" may make Milton more of a Puritan—it certainly makes him less of a poet, and, for that matter, it would make *Paradise Lost* impossible also.

But perhaps Milton's abandonment of the Arthurian subject can be explained in a much easier way—and without the necessity of reducing the imagination of a great poet to such naïve fundamentalism. The very years in which Milton rejected the Arthurian legend mark the beginning of his active involvement in the religious and political controversies of the time. As a poet and teacher he had been able to see the story of Arthur as a glorious national legend; as a controversialist increasingly aligned with the Parliament party he would have found it difficult to overlook its political implications. "The legend which had supported Tudor absolutism," as Miss Brinkley says, and which was now associated with the more onerous absolutism of Charles I, was thus, it seems likely, irremediably defiled in Milton's mind.[61]

It is probably this fortuitous identification of the beloved legend and the loathed tyranny of the Monarchists that accounts for the about face that now characterizes his attitude toward Arthurian story in *The History of Britain*, which he began in 1645.[62] In the conventional view of this shift in attitude, Milton's

> youthful enthusiasm for a subject from British legendary history . . . rapidly cooled after he had begun a serious study of historical sources for the proposed poem; . . . this cooling was caused by his dissatisfaction with the sources; . . . his dissatisfaction arose from the confusion and consequent uncertainty of the sources, from the alleged incompetency of the monkish historians, and from a distrust by the poet himself of "Antiquarianism."[63]

This explanation overlooks two significant sets of facts. First, it suggests that Milton was disillusioned in the authenticity or historicity of Arthur, but as all his earlier references to the story make clear, Milton was not only well aware of its fabulous elements, but intended to include them in his plan: his Arthur fought in Fairyland and was conceived through Merlin's magic guile. Second, the explanation, in its elevation of the historian at the expense of the poet, ignores Milton's attitude in the *History* toward legend in general:

> He recognizes [Miss Brinkley tells us] that all early history is "obscur'd and blemisht with Fables," and that there are several reasons for not discarding all fabulous stories: some authors of judgment and learning accept as fact that which others hold to be fabulous; things held to be fabulous are sometimes found "to contain in them many footsteps of something true"; and finally, these stories are of value for the poets. . . . his history is a rich storehouse of fable.[64]

Of all these fables, the story of Arthur is the only one which Milton is concerned to refute,[65] and it he pursues with a vindictive rancor that reveals not so much a change of mind as a change of heart. In alluding to the battles of the Britons against the Saxons, he says "*Arthur*, as beeing then Cheif [*sic*] General for the *British* Kings, made great War; but more renown'd in Songs and Romances, then [*sic*] in true stories."[66] He is dubious that Arthur's father, Uther Pendragon, ever existed,[67] but his greatest skepticism is reserved for Arthur himself. "Such Authors as we have to follow," he says slightingly, assign the Badon Hill victory to Arthur.

> But who *Arthur* was, and whether ever any such reign'd in *Britain*, hath bin doubted heertofore, and may again with good reason. For the Monk of *Malmsbury*, and others whose credit hath sway'd most with the learneder sort, we may well perceave to have known no more of this *Arthur* 500 years past, nor of his doeings, then [*sic*] we now living; And what they had to say, transcrib'd out of *Nennius*, a very trivial writer yet extant. Or out of [Geoffrey of Monmouth's] *British* Book. . . . Others of later time have sought to assert him by old Legends and Cathedral regests. But he who can accept of Legends for good story, may quickly swell a volume with trash, and had need be furnished with two only necessaries, leasure, and beleif, whether it be the writer, or he that shall read. . . . And as we doubted of his parentage, so may we also of his puissance.[68]

And how, Milton asks sarcastically, are we to reconcile Arthur's power with the tale that "*Melvas*, King of that Country which is now *Summerset*, kept from him Gueniver his wife a whole year"? Moreover, there was not time in his reign for all his fabled acts, and, seeing that the Saxons constantly gained strength, there is not much likelihood of such deeds. Both chronology and probability are against his reputed foreign conquests.[69] Nor is the attack on Arthur the only presumptive evidence of Milton's political motivation. His bias against the British, associated, it may be supposed, in his mind with the Royalist faction, is manifest in his curtailment of the period of their eminence, his emphasis on their barbarism and cruelty, and his condemnation of their moral corruption. In sharp contrast, the Saxon element (beloved of the Parliament party) is portrayed in all of its orderliness, respect for learning, and virtuous strength.[70] Geoffrey and his *Historia*, the major sources of the Royalist historical claims, are special objects of Milton's contempt. He uses Geoffrey only "when others are all silent" and then denigrates him with such phrases as "the simple fraud of this Fable."[71] Everywhere we look, then, in the *History*, the conclusion seems the more likely that it was the political uses of Arthurian story that led to Milton's abandonment of his long-cherished plan.

In the last analysis, it was perhaps just as well that Milton was early turned aside from his first plan. It does not seem likely that he would have been long content with it in any event. For all the air of defiant self-justification in the older Milton's comparison of his "higher Argument" with that which had aroused his youthful enthusiasm, it seems clear that the choice was right for him, a poet

> Not sedulous by Nature to indite
> Warrs, hitherto the onely Argument
> Heroic deem'd, chief maistrie to dissect
> With long and tedious havoc fabl'd Knights
> In Battels feign'd; the better fortitude
> Of Patience and Heroic Martyrdom
> Unsung; or to describe Races and Games,
> Or tilting Furniture, emblazon'd Shields,
> Impreses quaint, Caparisons and Steeds;
> Bases and tinsel Trappings, gorgious Knights
> At Joust and Tourneament; then marshal'd Feast
> Serv'd up in Hall with Sewers, and Seneshals;
> The skill of Artifice or Office mean,
> Not that which justly gives Heroic name
> To Person or to Poem. Mee, of these
> Not skilled nor studious, higher Argument
> Remains.[72]

Nor would he, it may be suspected, have been capable of entering into the spirit of the lawless love on which the tragedy of Arthur's reign turns; for Milton, love "lights / His constant Lamp, and waves his purple wings" only in wedded love, not in "Court Amours" with their "Serenate, which the starv'd Lover sings / To his proud fair, best quitted with disdain."[73] The Grail quest would doubtless have received even less sympathy from Milton's thoroughly Protestant and Puritan mind.[74]

Again, while a simplistic confusion of "fact" with poetic truth need not be cited in explanation of Milton's relinquishment of the Arthurian epic, it is still possible to agree that more subtle notions of "truth" entered into his final choice. As Willey observes, "intolerance of all except what seemed to him *most real* was . . . a characteristic of Milton which linked him with his age, and vitally affected his choice of poetic subject."[75] Clearly the Biblical story, which still enjoyed the shared belief of nearly all Englishmen and which contained explicitly or implicitly the whole of man's moral and spiritual knowledge, was the "most real" and had the highest "truth value." And beyond these considerations, Milton was, Willey has finely observed, "probably guided by the irresistible bent of his own nature towards the kind of subject with which his genius was best fitted to deal. As Dr. Johnson truly remarked, Milton's characteristic port is 'Gigantick loftiness,' and it is permissible to doubt whether he could have employed his great powers to such effect upon any subject of a more 'human' or 'dramatic' kind."[76] At the same time, it is still possible to lament with Scott, if not in the same terms, what was lost in the abandonment of the Arthurian subject. It is not only the "sublime glow of his imagination," the "dignity of his language," and "his powers of describing alike the beautiful and terrible," which "would have sent him forth to encounter such a subject with gigantic might" and for which the old romances contained a thousand suitably "striking Gothic incidents."[77] Beyond these lay other and far more important qualities—qualities which would have made Milton of all those who touched on the subject between Malory and Tennyson the writer most capable of giving it significant expression. He alone possessed the tragic sense to its uttermost degree.[78] He more than any other might have read in the old story the high sorrow of a great ideal lost through the subjection of man's spiritual faculties to his passions, of a nation's subjection through the betrayal of its loftiest aspirations.[79] He above all others, in short, had the special and profound moral seriousness that was required to penetrate beyond the "tinsel trappings" and quasi-history to the essential mythic story.

DRYDEN'S ARTHUR

Neither the tragic sense nor moral seriousness are conspicuous qualities of the decades in which the third great poet of the seventeenth century came to consider—as Jonson and Milton before him had—the epic possibilities of the Arthurian story. Like his predecessors, Dryden shared the century's veneration for epic poetry as the highest and noblest kind of literary expression.[80] And in fact it appears that it was the theory and machinery of the form that most concerned Dryden when, sometime before 1684, he had "been long laboring in [his] imagination" a plan for providing proper "machines" for a Christian epic. It was this plan, he tells us, that, "I had intended to have put in practice, (tho' far unable for the attempt of such a poem,) and to have left the stage (to which my genius never much inclin'd me) for a work which would have taken up my life in the performance of it. This too I had intended chiefly for the honor of my native country, to which a poet is particularly oblig'd." The question of a suitable subject was decidedly secondary:

> I was doubtful whether I should choose that of King Arthur conquering the Saxons, which, being farther distant in time, gives the greater scope to my invention; or that of Edward, the Black Prince, in subduing Spain, and restoring it to the lawful prince, tho' a great tyrant, Don Pedro the Cruel; which, for the compass of time, including only the expedition of one year; for the greatness of the action, and its answerable event; for the magnanimity of the English hero, oppos'd to the ingratitude of the person whom he restor'd; and for the many beautiful episodes, which I had interwoven with the principal design, together with the characters of the chiefest English persons; wherein, after Virgil and

Spenser, I would have taken occasion to represent my living friends and patrons of the noblest families, and also shadow'd the events of future ages, in the succession of our imperial line.[81]

It seems likely from the particularity with which Dryden lists the advantages of the second subject and his manner of dealing with it, that it interested him far more than King Arthur.[82] In any event, there are ominous hints enough to still any regrets that he abandoned the project. Doubtless, as MacCallum observes, he would have followed nationalist pseudohistory rather than the romance story, and his alternative subject suggests Royalist and legitimist sympathies that would have made for a thoroughly topical treatment of the story.[83] His conception of epic theory would have militated even more against a satisfactory treatment. Since he was convinced that the epic required a "prosperous" conclusion,[84] he would have been obliged to omit the tragedy, which is at the heart of the Arthurian story. And since he believed that "machines" had been an essential element in the grandeur of classical epic, he had laid plans for supplying the place of the heathen deities with the "tutelar genii, who presided over the several people and regions committed to their charge." These spirits, drawn from "the perusing of one chapter in the prophecy of Daniel," and harmonized "with the principles of Platonic philosophy, as it is now Christianis'd, would have made the ministry of angels as strong an engine for the working up heroic poetry" as anything possessed by the ancients.[85] But for Dryden, poets might propose, but kings disposed, and so, "being encourag'd only with fair words by King Charles II, my little salary ill paid, and no prospect of a future subsistence, I was then discourag'd in the beginning of my attempt."[86]

With Arthur as a subject of the noblest poetic form abandoned, Dryden next, in a remarkable reversal, decided to make one more bid for the King's favor in 1684 by casting Arthur as the hero of a "Dramatick Opera," a form which in his own words was "principally designed for the Ear and Eye." But Charles disappointed him once more—this time he died before the play could be performed. Thus what Dryden described as "the last Piece of Service which I had the Honour to do, for my Gracious Master," a piece which doubtless had flattered Charles's policies through the same kind of political allegory he had used in his earlier "entertainments," had to be shelved.[87]

By 1691, when *King Arthur: or, The British Worthy* was finally performed, William and Mary were on the throne, and in order "not to offend the present Times," Dryden tells us, "nor a Government which has hitherto protected me, I have been oblig'd so much to alter the first Design, and take away so many Beauties from the Writing, that it is now no more what it was formerly."[88] The final version, despite Dryden's laments, was fitted out with "Beauties" enough to gain it immediate popularity; music by Purcell, dances by Priest, and such stage effects as a tree that gushes blood when struck by a sword, a fight between Arthur and Oswald "with Spunges in their Hands dipt in Blood,"[89] "Syrens" who "shew themselves to the Waste" (p. 276), and a forest scene which at the touch of a wand "changes to a Prospect of Winter in Frozen Countries" (p. 272) were doubtless then as now the ingredients of a hit. Nor was its story any less calculated to grieve the judicious. Its subject is the conflict between the Saxon leader Oswald, "revengeful, rugged, violently brave," and Arthur, who is

> all that's Excellent in *Oswald*
> And void of all his Faults: In Battle brave;
> But still Serene in all the Stormy War,
> Like Heaven above the Clouds; and after Fight,
> As Merciful and Kind, to vanquisht Foes,
> As a Forgiving God; . . . .
> . . . Praise is Dumb before him. (Page 248)

Ostensibly, the struggle between them is for the possession of Great Britain; the real object of their conflict, in true "musical" fashion, is the possession of "Fair, Blind, Emmeline" (p. 248), daughter of the Duke of Cornwall. It would be as tedious as it is unnecessary to relate in detail the complicated action in which Oswald, assisted by the heathen magician and priest, Osmund, and the "trusty Fiend," Grimbald, "a fierce earthy Spirit" (p. 251), abducts Emmeline, attempts to rape her, and withholds her from Arthur in an enchanted forest. Despite Merlin's best efforts,[90] which include a potion that restores Emmeline's sight, and the assistance of Philidel, another sprite, Arthur undergoes many trials, the most notable of which are magic temptations of the flesh by bathing nymphs and by a false spirit who emerges from a tree in the likeness of Emmeline. At the end, Arthur defeats Oswald in single combat, is rejoined to Emmeline, and is entertained by Merlin's Virgilian glimpse of the future in which

> Britons and Saxons shall be once one People;
> One Common Tongue, one Common Faith shall bind
> Our Jarring Bands, in a perpetual Peace. (Page 283)

How far this absurd story diverges from either history or romance is indicated by Dryden's sources. Though he claims to have "employ'd some reading about it, to inform my self out of *Beda, Bochartus,* and other Authors, concerning the Rites and Customs of the Heathen Saxons," he does not appear to have consulted any properly Arthurian work.[91] On the contrary, he preferred to assemble a mélange of motifs from such sources as Tasso (the enchanted wood), Spenser (Arthur's temptation by the "syrens"), and Shakespeare (the various sprites).[92] In the resulting hodgepodge nothing genuinely Arthurian remains beyond the name of his hero and his off-stage battles with the Saxons. Not only has the tragic love story of Guinevere and Lancelot been scrapped to make way for the dubious sentimentalities of the blind Emmeline; Arthur's Round Table of heroes has been replaced by a troop of "Guards," who, after one victory, their "Captain" tells us, are quite "debauch'd: / All Drunk or Whoring" (p. 260). The chivalric code has also suffered a change: "Whether by Force, or Stratagem, we gain; / Still Gaining is our End, in War or Love" (p. 261), a view which quite naturally leads Arthur to reply to Oswald's protestations of honorable intentions by calling him—in terms that suggest reproach rather than approbation—"so Cold a Lover" (p. 261). The fact is, of course, that both Oswald and Arthur are nothing but a pair of Restoration beaux. Hence, there is nothing surprising in the fact that Arthur on a desperate quest to rescue his beloved from momentary danger is obliged to debate with himself whether he should join the nymphs put in his way by magic:

> A Lazie Pleasure trickles through my Veins;
> Here could I stay, and well be Couzen'd here.
> But Honour calls; Is Honour in such haste?
> Can he not Bait at such a pleasing Inn? (Page 276)

And there is even less wonder that when he is tempted by the likeness of Emmeline, "panting with desire," he should declare

> By thy leave, Reason, here I throw thee off,
> Thou load of Life: If thou wert made for Souls,
> Then Souls shou'd have been made without their Bodies. (Page 278)

All of this accords well enough with the Charles II who "could not think God would make a man miserable only for taking a little pleasure out of the way." But with the great king of romance, who held his honor above his life, it has no remotest connection.

The final effect of the whole—to use the word loosely—with its compounding of sentimentalized blindness and exposed innocence, rhetorical passions, and febrile eroticism,[93] resembles a slightly sticky marshmallow sundae laced with absinthe and sprinkled with cantharides. Dryden's talents did not indeed lie in the direction of drama, and with his keen intelligence, probably even less in the direction of "Dramatick Opera." Yet he needed money, and to get it he pandered with cynical calculation

to the debased tastes of the Restoration audience. The result was a commercial product whose direct modern heir is the Broadway musical, a
form which then as now assembles insignificant drama, music, dance, and
spectacle into a highly salable and meretricious fantasy—or, as Dryden
himself put it, a "Trifle, which if it succeed upon the stage, is like to be
the chiefest Entertainment of our Ladies and Gentlemen this Summer"
(p. 241).

BLACKMORE'S ARTHURIAN EPICS

Whatever else might be said against him—and a great deal was—
trifling is the one literary offense with which the seventeenth century's last
aspirant to Arthurian epic cannot be charged. Richard Blackmore, who
boasted an M.D. from Padua and a certain prominence in Whig politics,[94]
was convinced that all poetry's "true and genuine End is by universal
Confession, the Instruction of our Minds, and Regulation of our Manners," and "*Epick Poetry*, as it is first in Dignity, . . . mostly conduces to
this End."[95] Nevertheless, "to write an Epick Poem is a work of that
Difficulty, that no one for near seventeen hundred years past has succeeded
in it; and only those two great wits *Homer* and *Virgil* before. That the
modern poets have been so unsuccessful, has not," Blackmore graciously
conceded, "proceeded so much from want of *Genius*, as from their Ignorance of the Rules of writing such a Poem; or at least, from their want of
attending to them." But clearly there could be little difficulty for a man
who had perused Aristotle, Horace, Rapin, Dacier, Bossu, and Rymer.
Thus, despite the fact, as he himself asserted, that "poetry had been so far
from being my *Business* and *Profession*, that it has imploy'd but a small
part of my Time; and then, but as my *Recreation*, and the Entertainment
of my idle hours,"[96] Blackmore did not hesitate to seize upon the subject
that Jonson, Milton, and Dryden before him had meditated as an epic
theme.

The product of this grotesque egotism was given to the world in 1695
as *Prince Arthur: An Heroick Poem in Ten Books*.[97] After an epic announcement of the subject, the poem opens *in medias res*. Lucifer, a supporter of the Saxon ruler, Octa, observing Arthur's ships on their way to
England from Neustria (Normandy), calls on Thor to provide a storm
which scatters Arthur's ships. The angel Uriel calms the winds, and
Raphael appears to Arthur, who has been driven on the Armorican coast,
to assure him of ultimate success. Hoel of Brittany, incited by a Fury,
Persecution, sets out to destroy Arthur, but in a mystic encounter with the
voice of God, learns that he must seek out Arthur to be converted by him

to Christianity. This, Arthur accomplishes by spending one day in recounting the Biblical story from the Creation to the Resurrection, and a second, to Hoel's unspeakable delight, in describing the final damnation of the guilty and the elevation of the innocent on the Last Day of Judgment. The evening (and the whole of Book IV) is passed at Hoel's castle where the bard Mopas sings a song of the "secret Maze of Nature,"[98] and Arthur's friend Lucius gives a review of British history. From this account we learn that the Britons under Uter had been betrayed by the Saxons, and Arthur, despite the prowess he had demonstrated in battle, had been ordered by Raphael after Uter's death to retire to Neustria where he was to wait ten years before returning. That time having elapsed, ten "orators" had come from Britain beseeching his return. It was on this journey to reclaim his throne that he was shipwrecked on the coast of Hoel's dominions.

With Hoel's assistance, Arthur reassembles his fleet, and after riding out another storm invoked by Lucifer, defeats Octa's navy and lands on the Danmonian shore (Devonshire). In a dream Arthur is allowed to see the line of the future kings of Britain. Meanwhile, Octa, disturbed by Arthur's growing power, sues for peace and offers to Arthur his daughter, Ethelina. Lucifer causes the Angels who guard Arthur's camp to withdraw their protection in indignation at the vices that Lucifer has sown among the men. Many are lost to various plagues before God's anger is assuaged by Arthur's prayers. Octa, encouraged by the weakness of Arthur's forces, attacks once more in force, but suffers another defeat.[99] Tollo, the Albanian (Scottish) king, together with Mackbeth and Mordred, king of the Picts, now joins Octa, but the Saxon forces are once more worsted and saved from annihilation only by a storm brought on by Lucifer. Finally, Tollo offers and Arthur accepts a challenge to single combat to settle the issue. Arthur is, of course, victorious, and the poem concludes abruptly with his triumphant acquisition of his throne.

Blackmore's second epic on the Arthurian subject, *King Arthur* (1697),[100] opens after Arthur as king has lost his wife, Ethelina, and has returned to Britain from a victorious campaign in Cimbria (Denmark). Besought by seven lords to deliver the Christians of Gallia (France) and Neustria (Normandy) from the oppression of Clotar, Arthur assembles his men, embarks, and is joyously greeted in Neustria. When they have advanced to the plain of Lutetia (Paris), Satan becomes alarmed, and in a great consultation in Hell, it is decided to stir up dissension in Britain. Appearing in disguise to Morogan and various prelates such as Miraldo, "a mitred Christian with a Pagan Mind,"[101] Discord stirs up a conspiracy against Arthur. Informed of the troubles at home, Arthur fights one battle with Clotar and succeeds despite heavy losses in crossing the Esia (Oyse) before returning to Britain, where he restores peace by granting a general amnesty to all involved in the conspiracy, although he reaffirms his policy of religious tolerance to sectarians.

Meanwhile, Satan, disappointed of his hopes to harm Arthur in Britain, receives God's permission to try Arthur for fourteen days. During the storm that Satan raises to drive Arthur's ship to the Orcades, a heavenly spirit appears to Arthur, warns him against the trials to come, but assures him all will be well as long as his faith is strong. On the island of Pamona, Satan carries Arthur to a mountain top where he vanquishes a fearful dragon, to a valley where he resists the Demon of Despair, and to a pleasure garden where he is briefly tempted by the lovely wanton, Fascinia. Warned by Gabriel, he falls back on the better part of valor and flees. In Gallia, meanwhile, Arthur's men have barely managed to fight off an attack by Clotar, and Clovis, captured in the fight, is sorely tempted by his wife, Merula, to abjure God and worship pagan idols to save his life. When he refuses and instead reconverts her to Christianity, Uriel saves them both. Arthur returns to his men, listens to a lengthy sermon by Caledon, and fights victoriously against Clotar. At Lucifer's inspiration, Clotar and his priest, Palmida, set on foot a plot to murder Arthur when he is on his way to confirm a peace treaty. One of the conspirators reveals the plot to Arthur, another battle ensues and even though Clotar attempts to raise the dead Bellcoran to aid him, Lutetia is taken and Arthur kills Clotar.

Despite Blackmore's attempts to suggest that "Geofry" of Monmouth was the "Foundation" of these two lengthy epics, it is clear that his sources are in fact anything but Arthurian.[102] Outside of the name of Arthur's father and the bare fact that Arthur did make war against the Saxons in England and against Denmark and Gaul abroad, Blackmore took scarcely anything from the Arthurian tradition, and what else he did borrow is perversely misapplied. Mordred is made a "king of the Picts," and Merlin, everywhere else Arthur's staunchest support, becomes, astonishingly enough,

> The Pagan *Briton Merlin*, that of late
> For his dire Art, driv'n from the *British* State;
> Did with the Pagan *Saxons* safely dwell,
> And kept his Correspondence up with Hell.[103]

Arthur's mysterious engendering and secret rearing are ignored; not one of the knights known to the legend remains to accompany him; his fatal queen has been replaced by Ethelina, who makes no appearance in the first epic and is dead before the second begins; and of the tragic ending, there is no hint.

But while Blackmore ignored Arthurian tradition, he was not backward about drawing on other sources. Although he says he "had been long a stranger to the Muses" and claims that he "had read but little *Poetry* throughout [his] whole life,"[104] his two epics are in actuality little more than remarkably ingenious pastiches of borrowed motifs from Homer, Virgil, Spenser, Milton, Dryden, and the Bible.[105] *Prince Arthur*, as Blackmore acknowledged, is particularly indebted to the *Aeneid*, and it is no exaggeration to say that his Arthur bears a closer resemblance to Virgil's *pius* hero than to Geoffrey's:

> Much to his Conduct he, much to his Arms,
> But more he trusted to *Devotion's* Charms.
> Of Triumph and Success he rarely fail'd,
> For those on Earth, and these in Heav'n prevail'd.[106]

Blackmore also confessed to "a few allusions to some *Inventions* of *Milton*" and "some thoughts" taken from Scripture; these words are a long way from suggesting how ruthlessly he plundered these sources.[107] Among the authors whom he fails to mention as originals, Tasso and Spenser (whom he was at pains to criticize for "*wild, unnatural,* and *extravagant*" allegory) seem to have played some part in his treatment of Arthur's career.[108] But as for the poet to whom he owed the most—his very subject itself—Blackmore had, in Dryden's offended words, "the baseness not to acknowledge his benefactor, but, instead of it, to traduce [him] in a libel." With all due allowance for wounded vanity, it seems clear that Dryden, whom Blackmore had indirectly attacked for licentiousness in the Preface to *Prince Arthur* and directly in the poem itself as Laurus, "an old, revolted, unbelieving Bard" (Book VI, p. 167), was correct in his assertion that the "City Bard" took his subject from "the plan of an epic poem on King Arthur, in my preface to the translation of Juvenal."[109]

Although Blackmore drew recklessly and not always candidly on literature for a variety of incidental motifs, it was to life—specifically William of Orange's life—that he turned for the main outlines of his story. In keeping with the theories of his age, he held that "the Action [of an epic] must be related in an *Allegorical* manner; and this Rule is best observ'd, when as *Divines* speak; there is both a *Literal* Sense obvious to every Reader, and that gives him satisfaction enough if he sees no farther; and besides another *Mystical* or *Typical* Sense, not hard to be discover'd by those Readers that penetrate the matter deeper."[110] What more natural, then, for the Whig physician, who claimed to have contributed "more to the Succession of the illustrious House of *Hanover* . . . than I ever boasted of,"[111] than to pitch on the career of William III, the events of the Glorious Revolution, and "the great Deliverer's" triumph abroad to be shadowed forth as the "*Mystical* or *Typical* Sense" of Arthur's adventures? It was to reinforce this parallel that Blackmore devised the expedient of having Arthur sent abroad to Neustria for ten years before he returned at the behest of ten "orators" to Britain to claim his throne, and it was for this purpose that he included the storm that prevented Arthur's first landing, just as a storm had frustrated William's first attempt in October of 1688 to cross the Channel.

Nevertheless, the identification of William with Arthur involved difficulties. For some eighty years the legendary king had largely found his upholders in the ranks of those of royalist, legitimist sympathies; he had, indeed, been identified with the Stuart line, a fact which, as we have seen, probably contributed to Milton's abandonment of the subject. No more impressed by this traditional alignment than he had been by the traditional story of Arthur, Blackmore brushed aside all difficulties. In one neat stroke he simply reversed the political bearings of the legend. The last of the Stuarts, James II, became Octa, king of the Saxons; the Protestants became the Christian Britons; the Catholics became the pagan Saxons; James's Protestant daughter and William's wife, Mary, became the Saxon princess, the "fair *Ethelina*, whose perverted Mind," in the opinion of her father's advisers, "to *Christian* Worship is too much inclin'd."[112] The first epic thus traces William's victorious campaign against the Stuart forces during the Revolution of 1688, and the second deals (rather too hopefully, as events were to prove) with William's French War against Louis XIV (Clotar) and the conspiracy of 1695 to assassinate William.[113] One of the more amusing results of the identification of William with Arthur is that when Arthur in a Virgilian dream sees the line of future British kings, he is allowed to see his symbolic referent as the last of the line, "the brave Nassovian . . . the great Deliverer to come," accompanied by his queen, Maria.[114] Such awkward moments are rare, however, and generally the allegory flows along with easy transparency.[115]

The attractions of such an epic variant of the roman à clef must have been great for the age in which topical allegory and satire were becoming increasingly dominant literary forms. Doubtless the not inconveniently difficult challenge that it offered to the ingenuity of the Whig audience for which it was intended accounts partially for the remarkable degree of popularity that *Prince Arthur* attained.[116] The poem ran through two editions in the year of its publication, and a third was issued in the following year.[117] Nor were there readers lacking to compare Blackmore favorably with Homer, Virgil, and Milton.[118] Whether William III shared such views is not known; it may have been only a regard for political loyalty that led him to make Blackmore one of His Majesty's Physicians in Ordinary and soon after to knight him.[119] Beyond the appeal of his allegory, Blackmore's staunch support of morality and his announced purpose in writing his *Arthurs*—"that the young Gentlemen and Ladys who are delighted with Poetry might have a useful, or at least a harmless Entertainment"[120]—probably also contributed to his popularity at a time when reaction had set in strongly against the laxity of Restoration manners in both life and literature.

The King's rewards, the mushrooming popularity, and the fulsome praise in some quarters, which Blackmore's epic had won him, were enough in themselves, as Dr. Johnson shrewdly observed, to enrage the critics.[121] John Dennis' *Remarks on Prince Arthur*, issued a few months after the third edition of Blackmore's poem had appeared, seems alone to have been motivated by a sincere and impartial concern for literary values. Although Dennis found some things to commend in *Prince Arthur*, he also found much wanting. Succeeding critics were scarcely so disinterested. Dryden as a Catholic and one who had little occasion for rejoicing at the coming in of the Prince of Orange would doubtless in any case have had little sympathy with Blackmore's stoutly Protestant apotheosis of William. When to these considerations were added Blackmore's unacknowledged appropriation of Dryden's plan for an Arthurian epic, his attack in the "*Provoking Preface*"[122] of *Prince Arthur* on the immorality of the stage, and his slurring portrait of Dryden in the poem itself as Laurus, it seems remarkable that Dryden waited so long to reply. When he did in 1700, he struck with all the malicious wit he was capable of: "I will deal the more civilly with his two poems, because nothing ill is to be spoken of the dead; and therefore peace be to the *manes* of his *Arthurs*."[123] And shortly afterwards he returned to the attack in a Prologue written for a performance of Fletcher's *The Pilgrim* in 1700:

> . . . if he would be worth a poet's pen,
> He must be more a fool, and write again;
> For all the former fustian stuff he wrote
> Was dead-born dogg'rel, or is quite forgot;
>
> . . . .
>
> At leisure hours, in epic song he deals,
> Writes to the rumbling of his coaches wheels,
> Prescribes in haste, and seldom kills by rule,
> But rides triumphant between stool and stool.

. . . .

We know not by what name we should araign him,
For no one category can contain him;
A pedant, canting preacher, and a quack,
Are load enough to break one ass's back.[124]

Pope, who shared Dryden's religious views, first moved against Blackmore
in defense of Dryden. Later, Blackmore unwisely attacked him per-
sonally, and Pope retaliated by making Blackmore, "the father of the
Bathos, and indeed the *Homer* of it," the main target of his *Peri Bathous:
Or the Art of Sinking in Poetry* (1728).[125] In *The Dunciad*,[126] the "ever-
lasting Blackmore," (II, 290), "who sings so loudly, and who sings so
long," (II, 256), triumphs by putting the entire audience of critics asleep
in a contest to discover

> . . . what author's heaviness prevails,
> Which most conduce to sooth the soul in slumbers,
> . . . *Hen*ley's periods, or . . . Blackmore's numbers. (II, 336–38)

Pope, however, was only adding a few acidulous drops to the torrent of
witty abuse which by the end of the century had already reached flood
tide. As Blackmore's most recent biographer tells us, "The Cheapside-
Knight was an obvious target and the Wits found the impulse to lampoon
him irresistible. His interminable epics, composed in coach and coffee-
house; his dullness and pomposity; his connexions with the City; and his
alternating between the practice of physic and poetry provided the Wits
with ammunition for many satiric allusions."[127] The high (or low, as one
chooses to regard it) point in the remorseless campaign against Blackmore
was reached in 1700 with the appearance of a collection of some forty
scurrilous lampoons by various hands and published under the ironic
general title, *Commendatory Verses, on the Author of the Two Arthurs,
and the Satyr against Wit*, written by "some of his particular Friends."[128]

Doubtless, there is some justice in Dr. Johnson's view that Blackmore
was "exposed to worse treatment than he deserved; his name was so long
used to point every epigram upon dull writers, that it became at last a by-
word of contempt."[129] Nevertheless, it is to this contempt alone that the
seventeenth-century Bavius owes what small measure of fame he still
has.[130] As a poet—in general terms—

> he studied no niceties of versification; he waited .for no felicities of
> fancy; but caught his first thoughts in his first words in which they
> were presented . . . . In the first suggestions of his imagination he
> acquiesced; he thought them good, and did not seek for better. His

works may be read a long time without the occurrence of a single line that stands prominent from the rest.[131]

As an Arthurian poet he was hopelessly on the wrong track, though here he but followed the lead of his age. An era obsessed with epic form called for heroic poetry. Even Blackmore would have realized that an attempt to force the romance materials with their Gothic unity into the narrower limits of classical epic would have been doomed from the start. At the same time, in the chilly light of the Age of Reason, even though one might still accept Arthur's historicity, one could scarcely accept the obviously fabulous elements recorded by the earlier historians. The result was that on the one hand the essential Arthurian story was interdicted by formal considerations. On the other hand anything imaginatively interesting in the "historical" Arthur was prohibited by rationalist notions of "truth." Tossed on the horns of this dilemma and deprived of the mythic Arthur and thus of Arthur's universal significance, Blackmore landed quite naturally on topical allegory. On the poems that resulted, the best verdict —from the viewpoint of the present—is provided by words that Blackmore leveled against Spenser's allegory: "This way of writing mightily offends in this Age; and 'tis a wonder how it came to please in any."[132]

MINOR SEVENTEENTH-CENTURY VERSIONS

Most of the seventeenth century's writers who had felt the challenge of the Arthurian story had been attracted by what they regarded as its epic possibilities. But the legendary king and various figures associated with him had also appeared in other less ambitious literary forms. Although the demand for romance declined steadily in the century, there were two editions in the first year of publication of *The Most Famous History of That Most Renowned Christian Worthy Arthur King of the Britaines, and His Famous Knights of the Round Table* (1660). By Martin Parker, a ballad writer commended by no less a critic than John Dryden, it is based generally on Geoffrey of Monmouth, though it omits Arthur's bastardy and the whole of the love interest.[133] In his account, Parker lists 150 of the Round Table knights who helped Arthur in such feats as the slaying of 46,000 Saxons in one battle. Possibly it was death that prevented Parker's carrying the story through to its end; at any rate, for whatever reason, it was left incomplete.

Parker's concern in the Preface to his work to vindicate Arthur's historicity suggests that faith in the legendary king was rapidly dying out even in popular circles. And it is clear that Arthur's counselor and supernaturally gifted assistant, Merlin, had a much wider repute among the lower classes of society. During the seventeenth century, over a dozen publications appeared to which Merlin's name and thereby his fame were attached. Some of these prophetical works were used to support Stuart claims to the throne; later examples are variously more or less specific predictions, astrological forecasts, and general almanacs.[134] Doubtless it was Merlin's fame among the vulgar that led William Rowley to write *The Birth of Merlin: Or, The Childe Hath Found His Father.*[135] The play, which gives a burlesque account of Merlin's mystic origin, centers on Uther's defeat of Vortigern, and is truly Arthurian only in the vision of a future triumphant Arthur with which it closes.

As for the great king himself, in the popular imagination he sank low enough during the century to be easily linked with such folk figures as Jack the Giant Killer and Tom Thumb. With the latter his connection had first been made early in the century in a popular ballad that grew to considerable length by various additions during the period.[136] A prose *History of Tom Thumb, the Little* based on the ballads appeared in 1621.[137] Another version of the popular ballads, *Tom Thumbe, His Life and Death: Wherein is Declared Many Maruailous Acts of Manhood, Full of Wonder, and Strange Merriment: Which Little Knight Liued in King Arthurs Time, and [was] Famous in the Court of Great Brittaine* (1630),[138] presents Tom as Arthur's dwarf. Having been granted any boon, he asks for all that he can carry away, but in the event can make off with no more than threepence.[139] From such folk elements and such puerile humor, it is clear that in such tales Arthur was being relegated to the nursery. And perhaps, as MacCallum observed, that was the best place for him "till he should be healed of the grievous wound that the rationalism of the period had dealt him, and return once more to gladden the hearts of his Britons."[140]

THE AUGUSTAN VIEW OF ARTHUR'S WORLD

The closing decades of the century that had seen Dryden's degradation of Arthur to a satyromanic soldier and Blackmore's equally ruinous elevation of him to a Whig paragon were also the opening years of an era in which Arthurian story was to vanish almost wholly from the literary scene. To be sure, some of the factors that had militated against the literary use of Arthur—his political involvement and, for that matter, any significant degree of faith in his historicity—had evaporated during the seventeenth century. But the rationalism that had begun to develop in the early part of that period—and which had even more essentially prevented proper handling of the legend—continued to gather force, and after the

Restoration it burst upon the world in a flood of shadowless and some-times cheerless light. In the *saeculum rationalisticum* that thus opened, everything was against the serious literary use of Arthurian legend. It is, of course, no longer possible to accept the crudely pejorative explanations of nineteenth-century critics, e.g., "It was the absence of . . . ideality in the eighteenth century, which sounded the death-knell of Arthurian Romance. . . . a century bereft of those high qualities of heroism, poetry, and faith which we discern in the mind of previous periods."[141] Nevertheless, it is clear that in many ways the Age of Reason was radically unsuited for sympathy with Arthurian legend. Infatuated with verifiable "truth," with classical notions of artistic decorum and unity, with "rational" religion, and with the limitless applicability of common sense, cheerful benevolence, and polished manners, the new age was necessarily opposed to the legend-ary and the mythical, to thematically or psychologically unified art, to "popery" and "superstition," and to the tragic sense of life's dark, savage, and passionate side. Ever ready to congratulate itself on the triumph of "civility" over "barbarism," it held in equal disdain the history, manners, art, and literature of the Middle Ages. In a word, Arthur and his world were doomed to contempt and ridicule during the dominance of ration-alist, Neo-Classic thought.

The scorn with which the Middle Ages were regarded manifests itself everywhere during the earlier eighteenth century. Among skeptics and Deists, whose hatred for organized religion had been generated by the general collapse of dogmatic belief in the wake of seventeenth-century science, a loathing for the greatest Age of Faith was natural. But even Roman Catholics like Pope could assert that

> . . . the same age saw learning fall, and Rome.
> With tyranny, then superstition joined,
> As that the body, this enslaved the mind;
> Much was believed, but little understood,
> And to be dull was construed to be good;
> A second deluge learning thus o'errun,
> And the monks finished what the Goths begun.[142]

In these words, Pope voiced what would be the settled view of the professional historians, if the phrase is applicable to the discussion of a period when history was, as Professor Black reminds us, "a species of literature, a humane study, an art rather than a science."[143] In Italy Vico saw the "barbaric times come back again" of the Middle Ages as a parallel to the Homeric period and a confirmation of his cyclical theory of history; Iselin in Switzerland was even harsher in his condemnation of a time

when "corrupt Christianity augmented ignorance, anarchy and grossness."[144] Voltaire described the Middle Ages as "a heap of crimes, follies,
and misfortunes, sometimes in one country, sometimes in another, for five
hundred years," and went on to declare that scholasticism had done "more
harm to reason and good scholarship than the Huns and Vandals."[145]
Convinced that the early Middle Ages "deserved as little study as the
doings of wolves and bears," he made use of them only as a means of
showing how man through science and reason had emancipated himself
from the dark errors of fanaticism.[146] Altering the metaphor and the time
span, Hume, who said he had chronicled the Middle Ages "chiefly as a
resource against idleness," scorned the Anglo-Saxon period as a "battle of
kites and crows," and regarded "the interval between Augustus and the
Renaissance as a great trough or depression, in which humanity wallowed
for more than a thousand years a prey to ignorance, barbarism, and superstition."[147] The dominance of this attitude as late as the last quarter of the
eighteenth century may be gathered from Gibbon's famous observation:
"I have described the triumph of barbarism and religion."[148]

This almost universal contempt among the historians (and, for that
matter, among their eager readers) for the Middle Ages is scarcely to be
wondered at. Neither the eighteenth century's conditions in scholarly
research nor its climate of opinion was conducive to an enlightened—let
the word stand—historiography. The century lacked adequate scientific
techniques for evaluating sources, and at the same time access to the
sources in archives was strictly controlled. The study of history was virtually absent from the curricula of the schools and universities. Beyond
these difficulties, there was an almost total absence of the historical
sense.[149] What J. B. Black says of Voltaire applies equally to all the historians of the time:

> It seems never to have crossed his mind that the medieval man, for
> instance, differs from the modern by the whole heaven. . . . Voltaire
> was content . . . to measure all ages against his own. If men acted
> differently or incomprehensibly in the past, they were either misguided,
> or imbeciles, or the story is a lie. The test of their significance is their
> intelligibility to an enlightened Frenchman of the eighteenth century.[150]

To some extent, such an attitude was a product of the ethical and philosophical purposes of the historians. History was a pragmatic study devoted to drawing moral and political lessons from the past through the
application of the undeviating standards of rational behavior to the events
of the past. The distant and "barbaric" Middle Ages were useful to such
a practice only as the source of horrid examples. But even more important

in the formation of this attitude was the smug satisfaction of the Age of
Reason with its own civilization. As Willey has observed, "In the early
and middle years of the eighteenth century the wealthy and educated of
Europe must have enjoyed the nearest approach to earthly felicity ever
known to man."[151] It is not difficult, then, to understand the conviction
that this age was the very pinnacle of human achievement, and that the
past, at least since the fall of Rome, was a dark nightmare from which
man had escaped only through a reliance on Reason.

With the civilization in which Arthur had legendarily moved and
reigned consigned to the rationalist's chamber of horrors, the arts and
literature of that civilization also fell under a cloud of contempt and
mockery. Among the writers and men of fashion who influenced and
formed contemporary taste, classical architecture, particularly Palladian
architecture, was from the time of Inigo Jones early in the seventeenth
century right through the earlier part of the eighteenth century the *beau
ideal*. For men of taste, whatever occasional lapses into nostalgia they
might have, the principles of symmetrical balance and chaste severity of
ornament, the disposition of the orders, and the geometrical adjustment of
proportions enunciated by Vitruvius and Palladio were the fixed stars.
For them, Gothic architecture with its "dim, religious light," its asym-
metry, its strange buttresses, its insistence on the dynamic opposition of
forces, and its luxuriance of ornament, was barbaric, irrational—the
product of papistry, bigotry, and dark superstition.[152]

As for the literature of the Middle Ages—the chivalric romances in
which Arthur had shone so gloriously—the Augustans felt obliged to
entertain an equal scorn. Already in 1694 the youthful Addison had displayed the fashionable reaction against the elements of knightly romance
in the work of "old Spenser," who,

> warm'd with poetic rage,
> In ancient tales amus'd a barb'rous age;
> An age that yet uncultivate and rude,
> Where'er the poet's fancy led, pursu'd
> Thro' pathless fields, and unfrequented floods,
> To dens of dragons, and enchanted woods.
> But now the mystic tale, that pleas'd of yore,
> Can charm an understanding age no more;
> The long-spun allegories fulsome grow,
> While the dull moral lies too plain below.
> We view well pleas'd at distance all the sights
> Of arms and palfries, battles, fields and fights,
> And damsels in distress, and courteous knights.

> But when we look too near, the shades decay,
> And all the pleasing landscape fades away.[153]

If this was true of the pseudomedievalism of *The Faerie Queene*, how much truer was it of genuine medieval works, of which even scholarly publication was condemned: "Every monkish tale & lye & miracle & ballad are rescued from their dust & worms, to proclaim the poverty of our forefathers, whose nakedness, it seems, their pious posterity take great pleasure to pry into; for of all those writings . . . , there is not one that is not a disgrace to letters, most of them are so to common sense, & some even to human nature."[154] And Addison reserved his choicest ridicule for

> books of chivalry, where the whole point of honor is strained to madness [and] the whole story runs on chastity and courage. The damsel is mounted on a white palfrey, as an emblem of her innocence; and to avoid scandal, must have a dwarf for her page. She is not to think of a man, till some misfortune has brought a knight-errant to her relief. The knight falls in love, and did not gratitude restrain her from murdering her deliverer, would die at her feet by her disdain. However, he must waste many years in the desert, before her virgin heart can think of a surrender. The knight goes off, attacks everything he meets that is bigger and stronger than himself; seeks all opportunities of being knocked on the head; and after seven years' rambling returns to his mistress, whose chastity has been attacked in the meantime by giants and tyrants, and undergone as many trials as her lover's valor.[155]

Dr. Johnson, possibly for reasons best known at the time to few, was content with a more magisterial comment:

> Nations, like individuals, have their infancy . . . . Whatever is remote from common appearance is always welcome to vulgar, as to childish credulity; and of a country unenlightened by learning, the whole people is the vulgar. The study of those who then aspired to plebian learning was laid out upon adventures, giants, dragons, and enchantments. *The Death of Arthur* was the favourite volume.[156]

Few of the "enlightened" readers to whom Johnson addressed these words could have had any firsthand acquaintance with "The Death of Arthur"; over a century had passed since the last publication of *Le Morte Darthur* in 1634. And the intellectual climate of the period was, as has been seen, not such as to make a new edition an attractive publishing venture.

HENRY FIELDING'S ARTHURIAN BURLESQUE

For an age that often spurned its medieval heritage with a polite smile of superiority (and something, perhaps, of the nervous vehemence of the *arriviste*), the most reasonable response to the great king of romance was ridicule—the most reasonable use, burlesque and farce. Of such applications of Arthurian material, the prime example is Fielding's *The Tragedy of Tragedies; or the Life and Death of Tom Thumb the Great* (1730, 1731).[157] This parodistic burlesque opens in Arthur's court soon after a great victory over the giants has been won by Tom Thumb, a minute though "mighty hero, / By Merlin's art begot."[158] King Arthur, "a passionate sort of king" and a somewhat timid husband, falls in love with Glumdalca, queen of the giants, whom Tom has brought captive to court. But she, unfortunately, is in love with Tom, and he in turn is in love with Arthur's daughter, Huncamunca. Arthur's queen, Dollallolla, "a woman entirely faultless, saving that she is a little given to drink, a little too much a virago towards her husband, and in love with Tom Thumb," conspires unsuccessfully with Lord Grizzle to prevent Tom's marriage to Huncamunca. The princess, a maiden "of a very sweet, gentle, and amorous disposition," is "equally in love with Lord Grizzle and Tom Thumb, and desirous to be married to them both." Enraged by Tom's marriage to Huncamunca, Grizzle rouses a rebellion, which Tom, alerted by the ghost of his father, puts down. But alas, as Merlin has prophesied, on his way back he is devoured by a red cow. When the dreadful news is brought to court, Dollallolla kills the messenger and is killed in turn by Cleora. Huncamunca thereupon kills Cleora, and Doodle, who kills her, is killed by Mustacha. King Arthur slays Mustacha and concludes the play with his own suicide.

This "charming and bloody catastrophe," which requires less than a dozen lines, and which the "editor," H. Scriblerus Secundus, proudly compares to the paltry five deaths that end Dryden's *Cleomanes*,[159] makes clear that the real target of Fielding's burlesque was not Arthurian story, but rather the ranting tragedies of the Restoration stage, with their strained situations and hackneyed motivations, their bombast, bathos, and shabby rhetoric. For *Tom Thumb* is quite literally a *Tragedy of Tragedies*; that is, it is a patchwork of travestied motifs, maliciously selected quotations, and parodied lines from the tragedies of Addison, Lee, Thomson, Banks, Dryden, and others.[160] To assist the reader in identifying his models, Fielding provided elaborate annotations by H. Scriblerus Secundus in which he draws "parallel passages out of the best of our English writers."[161] The jest is heightened by the brilliant twist of dating the composition of the play in "the reign of Queen Elizabeth," thus opening the question as to whether the tragic dramatists cited had borrowed from *Tom Thumb* itself.

The presence of Arthur in this bravura display of critical wit is, of course, largely fortuitous—the result of his association in the seventeenth century with the nursery tales of Tom Thumb.[162] What attracted Fielding were the great burlesque possibilities inherent in a tragic hero of minute proportions:

> Though small his body be, so very small
> A chairman's leg is more than twice as large,
> Yet is his soul like any mountain big.[163]

No doubt, however, it played well into his hand to have the glorious King Arthur to reduce to the vulgar, uxorious monarch who thus plans grandly the celebration of Tom's victory over the giants:

> Let other hours be set apart for business.
> To-day it is our pleasure to be drunk.
> And this our queen shall be as drunk as we.
>
> . . . .
>
> Though 'rack, in punch, eight shillings be a quart,
> And rum and brandy be no more than six,
> Rather than quarrel you shall have your will.[164]

And if his Arthur bears little resemblance to the king of romance, why that was only a part of the cream of the jest: "Are there not instances of plays," Scriblerus asks, "wherein the history is so perverted, that we can know the heroes whom they celebrate by no other marks than their names?"[165] The fact is that nothing at all of the essential Arthurian story is involved in Fielding's burlesque, and thus the story can sustain no damage at his hands. No harm is intended to serious things of value— only the puncturing of ludicrous posturing. And that is why even the most passionate admirer of the Arthur of romance can take no offense at the fine hilarities of *The Tragedy of Tragedies*.[166]

MERLIN IN THE NEO-CLASSICAL AGE

Although Arthur himself virtually disappeared from the literary scene during the first half of the century, his mage, Merlin, was still a figure of some interest. The larger part of this interest was, no doubt, confined to vulgar readers, and in any case was due to the wizard's vaticinative powers rather than to his association with Arthur and the world of romance. Among the various prophetical works of the time, John Partridge's *Merlinus Liberatus*, which had commenced annual publication in 1689 and continued to appear each year through 1707, has a fortuitous significance from its author's position as butt of the Bickerstaff hoax.[167] Not content with predicting and then announcing the death of the cobbler turned astrologer, Swift went on in 1709 to employ Merlin's name in a parting shot in the campaign, *A Famous Prediction of Merlin, the British Wizard, Written Above a Thousand Years Ago, and Relating to the Present Year 1709.*[168] Subsequent publications trading on both Partridge's name and title indicate that Swift failed to destroy the astrologer's reputation among the commonalty.[169] Nevertheless, the rapid decline in the number of such publications during the century suggests that, even among the readers of such ephemerae, the skepticism of the age of Reason had begun to do its work.[170]

Such vogue as Merlin did have still later in the century seems to have been due largely to an architectural whim—"childish silly stuff," King George called it—of Queen Caroline.[171] Merlin's Cave, a queer combination of "Gothic" windows and thatched roofs, including among its interior furnishings wax figures of Merlin and his scribe, was built in 1735 under the Queen's patronage in the royal garden at Richmond, and placed in the care of Stephen Duck, the thresher poet, and his wife. Merlin's Cave and another building at Richmond, the Hermitage, both built by Kent, soon became the centers of a storm of controversy, though it seems clear that Caroline's sympathy for Walpole rather than any inherent folly in the structures was responsible for the satire directed against them by Swift and Bolingbroke in the *Craftsman*. At any rate, the conflict appears to have stimulated revivals between 1736 and 1741 of *The Birth of Merlin* and Dryden's *King Arthur*, neatly adapted to the occasion by a change of title: *Merlin, or, the British Inchanter.*[172] Even more directly inspired by the new adornments of Richmond were Edward Phillips' *The Royal Chace, or Merlin's Hermitage and Cave*, a verse drama performed in 1735/6 (O. S.) and revived in 1740–1741.[173] Other efforts to capitalize on the public interest were Edmund Curll's *The Rarities of Richmond: Being Exact Descriptions of the Royal Hermitage and Merlin's Cave, With His Life and Prophesies* (1736), a mere bookseller's hackwork speculation, and *Merlin: a Poem . . . To Which is Added, the Royal Hermitage: A Poem* (1735).[174]

The most charming of the works to emerge in the wake of the controversy was Aaron Hill's unperformed *Merlin in Love: or, Youth Against Magic.*[175] For the plot of his pastoral, a "pantomime opera," Hill turned back to Arthurian tradition and the motif of Merlin's enchantment by Vivien or Nimue, and to this he added elements of the popular Italian comedy. The aged wizard, Merlin, in his wooing of young Columbine, is persuaded to lend her his magic wand, which she uses to change him by enchantment into an ass, thus leaving her free to continue her amours with young Harlequin. To this peculiar concoction, Hill added song, dance, and a variety of stage effects calculated to astonish the audience and bewilder the ingenuity of the producer. It is difficult to imagine why such carefully designed entertainment did not find an audience. Perhaps the market was saturated by the first comers, but curiously enough, public interest in the controversy over Merlin's Cave was not extinct as late as twenty years after its construction, if we may judge by the appearance in 1755 of *Merlin's Life and Prophecies . . . His Predictions Relating to the Late Contest About . . . Richmond Park, With Some Other Events Relating Thereto, Not Yet Come to Pass.*[176]

Such were the contributions of the first half of the eighteenth century to Arthurian literature: a literary burlesque involving Arthur only secondarily and modeled on a nontraditional juvenile tale, and a flurry of largely nontraditional treatments of Merlin inspired by a contemporary political squabble.[177] Doubtless, little more could be expected, opposed as the period officially was to the supernatural, to mythology and legend, and to the "Popish" superstition of the Middle Ages with all their rude emotionalism, their richly instinctual life, and their "barbarism." Such attitudes combined with the essentially anti-historical, critical, and satirical spirit of the times, and with what Willey has described as the "steady decline of what has been called the tragic sense of life,"[178] to make the absence of an adequate response to Arthurian story a foregone conclusion. To a casual observer of the English literary scene at the middle of the century, it would have seemed that the legend of Arthur had finally dwindled into extinction. Closer inspection, or, more properly speaking, hindsight, would have shown him that already—tentatively, inconsistently, even blindly, to be sure—the forces that would one day restore Arthur to his throne among British heroes were quietly gathering strength.

PART II

*Poetic Antiquarians
and Antiquarian Poets*

4 ❧ Arthur Stirs in Avalon

ARTHURIAN STORY AMONG THE PRE-ROMANTICS

The Age of Reason had all but finished the work begun at the Battle of Camlann. In the palmy days of the early eighteenth century, it seemed certain that Arthur would never return to comfort his Britons. But in the event, the hegemony of Dryden and Pope proved to be extremely precarious. Even as Pope was growing to manhood, there were signs about of the coming shift of sensibility and sympathy, of aesthetic and philosophical theory, that we now call Romanticism. As time passed, the oddly assorted and variously motivated interests that indicate a romantic revival —orientalism, gothicism, ethical optimism, primitivism, and religious enthusiasm—would coalesce into a set of wholly new attitudes toward earlier literature and the times that had produced it, particularly the Middle Ages.[1]

At first the change in attitude would have but slight effect on Arthurian story, but as fascination with the past grew stronger and more serious, publication of its literature more extensive, and successful poetic use of its materials more frequent, Arthur would assume an increasingly important position in literature. By the end of the century, an Oxford don would be able to assert confidently that "no Englishman, certainly no poetical Englishman, can hear with indifference of '—what resounds / In fable or romance of Uther's son.' "[2]

THE AUGUSTAN SETTLEMENT UNDERMINED

The events that led to this reversal of the rationalist contempt for the Arthur of romance had begun over a century before. In a sense, Rationalism was its own worst enemy in what had then transpired. "Stripping the truth bare was what that age and generation felt itself to be mainly engaged upon: stripping it bare of mythology and all the accretions of paganism and popery," says Professor Willey in summing up the intellectual atmosphere at the close of the seventeenth century and the opening

83

of the eighteenth.[3] But the process, as it turned out, was not exactly comparable to removing the rags and tatters of the past in order to arrive at "Beauty bare." It was, instead, more like unwinding a ball of yarn—when it was all over, there was nothing left. Locke's empiricism and his destruction of Cartesianism ended in "discrediting . . . the validity of the intellect as a means of arriving at the truth."[4] To this undermining of the faith in reason—carried even further by Hume—was joined a growing restiveness at the extensive editing of experience and feeling involved in the Neo-Classical compromise.[5] In literature, as Dryden had already understood, the rationalist exclusion of mythology had produced insuperable difficulties for the exercise of some of the most important varieties of poetic creativity.[6] Thus in the very years when Pope was laying the last capstone on the Augustan sea wall, ominous cracks were developing at its base. The sea of emotion, of romantic impulse and aspiration, pounded relentlessly, and the fissures in the wall slowly and inevitably widened.

Many of the early indications of the coming romanticism are of no direct importance to the later fortunes of Arthurian story, but the various new appeals to the desire for novelty, for irregularity in form and extravagance in emotion, show how imperfect the dominance of the Neo-Classical settlement was from the beginning. But the old legend was very much the beneficiary of the growing interest in the remains of post-classical civilization, especially the Middle Ages, when Arthur had reigned in romance if not in fact. Among the earliest signs of this interest is the development of enthusiasm for Gothic architecture.[7] While the Gothic revival seems to have had its inception among antiquarians, it was popularized by literary men, who soon substituted for the scholarly interests of Hearne and Stukeley, a "sentimental delight in decay."[8] This adulation of nature's malign effects on the works of man—another sign of the imperfect dominance of Neo-Classical attitudes—led as early as 1733 to the construction of elaborate sham ruins (neatly combined with such useful functions as stable space).[9] But the appeal of Gothic architecture went deeper. As Sir Kenneth Clark has noted, it lent itself splendidly to the summoning up of dreams of a savage and violent age, beloved fantasy material of an age bored with too much tranquillity, too little action.[10] The hashish of gothicism thus led to more than sham ruins and architectural pastiches like Walpole's Strawberry Hill: it led ultimately to one of the major manifestations of Romanticism, the Medieval Revival.

But ruins, whether real or artificial, were the possession of few. For the many, the appetite for escape into the past from the civility and the rationalism of the time could be more conveniently satisfied by recourse to books.[11] Hence, at least in part, the vogue, relatively slight at first, but

rising to something very like a mania later in the century, of collections of
what the age called "ballads." Such materials had already appeared frequently during the seventeenth century in various "garlands," "miscellanies," and in "courtesy," "compliment," "wit," and "drollery" books.[12]
In the eighteenth century, interest in ballads was at first largely an expression of interest in the "popular"; the association of ballads with "Gothic"
times was not to develop fully until after Percy's *Reliques*, and although
this earlier interest in the poetry of the folk has been seen as "romantic,"
it is more likely, as Friedman has argued, that the ballad revival during
the first half of the eighteenth century was in large part a product of the
Neo-Classical admiration for "simplicity."[13]

Certainly this is true of Addison's unintentional contribution to the
restoration of earlier literature through his two *Spectator* papers devoted
to praise of the "Ballad of Chevy-Chase." His conscious intention throughout the essays is to vindicate the Neo-Classical tenet of simplicity and to
oppose the "Gothic manner in writing," by which he means the "false
wit" and elaboration of Donne and other seventeenth-century writers, and
he chooses "Chevy-Chase" just because it demonstrates through its long
popularity the high value of simplicity. Thus he roundly declares that
"an ordinary song or ballad that is the delight of the common people,
cannot fail to please all such readers as are not unqualified for the entertainment by their affectation or ignorance."[14] But at the same time he
remains the orthodox Neo-Classicist in his method of demonstrating the
poem's excellence by extensive comparison with classical epic, a method he
vindicated by saying, "I feared my own judgment would have looked too
singular on such a subject, had not I supported it by the practice and
authority of Virgil."[15] Nevertheless, those who admired earlier poetry for
other reasons, perhaps, must have taken great comfort from the prestige
that Addison had thus conferred upon the ballads.[16]

Even before Addison had acclaimed "Chevy-Chase," one anthology
that contained such material had already appeared in the eighteenth century. Like most of the collections that came later, *A Choise Collection of
Comic and Serious Scots Poems Both Ancient and Modern* (1706–1711)
seems to have contained an assortment of love songs, satires, didactic
verse, and some genuine or at least traditional early ballads.[17] Several
new collections followed before the first quarter of the century was out.
Of these the most extensive was *A Collection of Old Ballads* (1723–1725),
supposedly edited by Ambrose Philips.[18] Allan Ramsay's *Scots Songs*
(1718, 1720) was succeeded in 1724 by his *Tea-Table Miscellany* and *The
Ever Green*.[19] While the latter was largely edited from the Bannatyne
MS, it also contained Lady Elizabeth Wardlaw's spurious *Hardyknute*,

an example of the imitation ballads being turned out, both avowedly and covertly, by Ramsay himself, and such writers as William Hamilton, David Mallet, and Thomas Parnell.[20]

Yet despite the flurry of publications of earlier literature in the first quarter of the century, only one Arthurian piece was printed, the insignificant "Sir Lancelot du Lake."[21] To some extent this near absence of Arthurian works from the early ballad collections is due to the fact that, even in the rather loose meaning of the term in the eighteenth century, there are relatively few Arthurian "ballads." The subject had not generally lent itself to brief treatment, and its elaborate courtly conventions had made it from the beginning the subject of an aristocratic literature, rather than of the popular literature to which authentic ballads belong. Perhaps more important is the consideration that the motivations behind the early eighteenth-century ballad revival would scarcely have encouraged an Arthurian revival. What these motivations were may be gathered to some extent from Allan Ramsay's Preface to *The Ever Green*:

> I have observed that *Readers* of the best and most exquisite Discernment frequently complain of our *modern Writings* as filled with affected Delicacies and studied Refinements, which they would gladly exchange for that natural Strength of Thought and Simplicity of Stile our Forefathers practised: To such, I hope, the following *Collection of Poems* will not be displeasing.

> I hope also the *Reader*, when he dips into these *Poems*, will not be displeased with this Reflection, That he is stepping back into Times that are past, and that exist no more. Thus the *Manners* and *Customs* then in Vogue, as he will find them here described, will have all the Air and Charm of *Novelty*; and that seldom fails of exciting Attention and pleasing the Mind.[22]

The craving for novelty could be most easily satisfied by ballads sufficiently recent in form to require a minimum of editorial labors for presentation to a nonscholarly audience.[23] At the same time, the anxiety to justify enthusiasm for such literature in terms of its historical value (a species of vindication not altogether unknown in critical circles today) was best served by ballads dealing with events and manners that were clearly historical, or at least believed to be so. But beneath these motives, there lay, unexpressed and doubtless unrecognized, the same force that moved men to enthusiasm for Gothic architecture—the desire for relief from the tranquillity of a too refined society.[24] What was wanted was the fantasy stuff of a society removed as far as possible from polish, restraints, complicated manners, and elaborate social codes. The chivalric heroisms and stately manners of the main Arthurian tradition would have been radically unsuitable. Far more satisfying were ballads of the blood and violence of border warfare, the pathos of jilted sweethearts, the weird thrills of ghostly lovers, the untrammeled passions of Scottish chieftains. The ruder and rougher the society reflected in the ballads, the better.[25] It was work for a later time, less satiated with order and decorum, to look to the earlier literature and the societies that it reflected for other—indeed, quite opposite—values.

Meanwhile, it appears that even this first wave of enthusiasm for earlier poetry had been premature. At any rate, after the first quarter of the century, it subsided quickly, and the next thirty-five years saw no significant new publication of such literature. During these years the rapidly growing reputation of Pope and the doctrines that he embodied raised Neo-Classicism to steadily greater heights of domination. Nevertheless, beneath the surface calm, the forces of change were slowly gathering strength. Here and there, faith in the ideals of the *saeculum rationalisticum* was sapped by its own skepticism, and as it weakened, men increasingly gave the advantage in comparisons to the nonrational, the powers of feeling and instinct, and to sentimental, primitivistic, and even sheerly anti-intellectual conceptions of man and nature.[26] The brilliance of Pope's genius and the personal vigor of his lineal successor, Dr. Johnson, tended to obscure the extent and strength of the new attitudes. Yet, in fact, the new forces, many perceptible since the beginning of the century, were converging into a current that would in the decade of the sixties throw up a great swell of enthusiasm for earlier literature and earlier societies, one surge of the tidal wave that would ultimately inundate the Neo-Classical settlement forever.

The harbingers of this new revival of earlier literature in the sixties were many. Among the earlier preparations for the revival were the development of Shaftesbury's doctrine of man's "natural" goodness, and the parallel development of the doctrines of Sensibility.[27] Views that elevated the "natural" at the expense of the "artificial" quite easily tended in the direction of sympathy with literatures that were thought to have sprung from the uninstructed hearts of the poet and the people. Akenside, in his *Pleasures of Imagination* (1744), asserted the necessity of an instinctive appreciation of beauty in the poet, an appreciation not to be gained by schooling or obedience to rules. Such a theory of literary primitivism soon led to direct attacks on Neo-Classicism. Joseph Warton's *Essay on the Genius and Writings of Pope* (1753) went so far as to suggest that although Pope was a supreme poet of his kind, the kind was of the second order; it lacked the sublimity and the artless spontaneity of Shakespeare and Spenser. And Young's *Conjectures on Original Composition* (1759) declared the inferiority of imitation of the classics to the inspiration of life and nature. The inspiration of nature—that was what the earlier poets had possessed; their instincts and emotions had not been "withered by skepticism: they dared and strove and believed and let themselves go."[28]

And there were other developments that prepared men to look sympathetically at earlier times and earlier poetry. The Evangelical movement founded by Wesley and Whitefield in 1739 was, with its emphasis on feeling, on emotional conversion, on enthusiasm, inimical to rationalist and Neo-Classicist ideals. At the same time, it must have encouraged those who were touched by it to feel a kinship with the vanished Middle Ages, when religion had been as personal, as emotional, and as non-rational as the Evangelicals were seeking to make it once more. Again, interest in Gothic architecture, growing slowly during the first part of the century, became an important vogue in the forties, with Walpole's Strawberry Hill begun sometime after 1747.[29] It seems likely that the enthusiasm for Gothic architecture is related to a revival of sympathy—at least imaginative sympathy—with medieval Catholicism as well as with medieval society and literature generally. At any rate, it is clear that by the middle of the century the time was at hand for a revival of the Middle Ages and medieval literature, of the times when Arthur had had his fabled existence and of the literature in which he had reigned.

THE REVIVAL OF MEDIEVAL LITERATURE

When that revival came it was both quantitatively and qualitatively different from the earlier wave of interest felt during the first quarter of the century. Dozens of volumes of earlier poetry appeared at fairly close intervals, and many of these were reissued in later editions. At the same time, a variety of works praising the nation's earlier literature and aimed at popularizing it or vindicating it against the sneers of Neo-Classicists found publishers and readers. While it is true that much of the older literature that was now published was not strictly medieval, nearly all of the collections contained at least some material either genuinely medieval, or at least old enough to be thought of as "Gothic" by eighteenth-century readers. "The word *Gothic*," Earl Wasserman observes, "as descriptive of a historical period was applied to almost any time before the middle of the seventeenth century."[30] Of genuine medieval literature—with the exception of Chaucer—the early eighteenth century knew little, and the revival of interest in early literature focused at first on the English Renaissance, a period in which linguistic changes presented no insurmountable problems and from which printed texts were still available. Outside of Shakespeare and the drama, Spenser was the main object of this new interest, and *The Faerie Queene* thus became "the starting point for any literary discussion of chivalry and 'romantic composition.' "[31] During the century there were nine printings of *The Faerie Queene*, and well over a hundred poems more or less directly imitative of it appeared.[32] But gradually other earlier literature was being revived and more and more readers were interesting themselves in it.

Beyond this growing awareness of the earlier poets, there was also an increase in understanding of the past. The work of the earlier antiquarians and scholars made the new admirers of medieval architecture and "Gothic" poetry more knowledgeable. Progressive disillusionment with rationalism, and changing conceptions of artistic creation made them more responsive to the spirit of medieval literature. Even the word *Gothic*, as Sir Kenneth Clark notes, shifted in meaning around the middle of the century: it "ceased to be a synonym for 'barbarous' or 'violent' and became associated with the poetry and chivalry of the middle age."[33]

The fusion of antiquarian interests and poetic sensibility that characterizes the new revival is particularly evident in two books that appeared around mid-century and probably contributed much to the impetus of the revival of earlier literature by giving it a certain cachet of scholarly approval.[34] The first of these, Thomas Warton's *Observations on the Faerie Queene of Spenser* (1754), was partially a response to the Spenserian revival. But whereas earlier admirers such as John Hughes[35] had been only diffidently commendatory, Warton was bold in asserting the virtues of Spenser's work—virtues that grew out of an appeal to the feelings and the imagination rather than the intellect.[36] Even more important was Warton's assertion of the necessity of historical imagination in criticism, the necessity of an awareness of other standards than those of Neo-Classicism:

> In reading the works of an author who lived in a remote age, it is necessary, that we should look back upon the customs and manners which prevailed in his age; that we should place ourselves in his situation, and circumstances; that so we may be the better enabled to judge and discern how his turn of thinking, and manner of composing were biass'd, influenc'd, and, as it were, tinctur'd, by very familiar and reigning appearances, which are utterly different from those with which we are at present surrounded.[37]

One of the most important of these "circumstances," Warton quite properly recognized, was the popularity of chivalric romance; and drawing on a knowledge of medieval and Renaissance romance remarkably wide for his day, Warton proceeded to demonstrate that the *Faerie Queene* was not the product of barbarous perversity, but rather the fine flower of original genius and historical situation. Even Dr. Johnson was struck by his method. "You have shown to all, who shall hereafter attempt the study of our ancient authors, the way to success, by directing them to the perusal of the books, which these authors had read," he wrote to Warton.[38] Warton's study of the *Faerie Queene* doubtless contributed much to the rehabilitation of Spenser. At the same time, his analysis of the sources of the poem, however faulty in detail, must have drawn many to a more sympathetic consideration of the vast wealth of medieval romances such as *Le Morte Darthur*, which the Age of Reason had allowed to fall into neglect. And if Warton had his reservations about what he called "the depths of Gothic ignorance and barbarity" of the Middle Ages and the "bad taste" that had preferred Ariosto to Tasso, it may well be that in such reservations lay his strength as a propagandist of the earlier literature.[39] His judicious assignment of praise and blame did not rouse the suspicions that would have been awakened by a more radical break with the intellectual tradition of his time.

A similarly complex though not inconsistent attitude toward the Middle Ages and their romances marks Richard Hurd's *Letters on Chivalry and Romance* (1762).[40] While Hurd's language seems to perpetuate Warton's depreciation of the past, his defense of romance carries Warton's plea for historical understanding a step further:

> The greatest geniuses of our own and foreign countries, such as Ariosto and Tasso in Italy, and Spenser and Milton in England, were seduced by these barbarities of their forefathers; were even charmed by the Gothic Romances. Was this caprice and absurdity in them? Or may there not be something in the Gothic Romance peculiarly suited to the views of a genius, and to the ends of poetry? And may not the philosophic moderns have gone too far, in their perpetual ridicule and contempt of it?[41]

As the names Hurd mentions may suggest, he is concerned not to praise the actual medieval romances, but rather to vindicate the Renaissance "epics," which had drawn on the chivalric romances. Genuine medieval romance he scorned without having read (p. 94), but the "manners" portrayed in the work of Tasso and Spenser had to be defended against the ridicule of the philosophic moderns, since such ridicule was the result not of wisdom, but rather of ignorance. Gothic or chivalric manners were a product of feudalism, and when feudalism had passed, so had its manners. Knowing little of those times, later men had refused to believe in the chivalric manners that the romances reflect (pp. 148–49). Moreover, the essentially fallacious application of the wrong Neo-Classical standards to the romances had misled the critics sadly.

> When an architect examines a Gothic structure by Grecian rules, he finds nothing but deformity. But the Gothic architecture has it's [*sic*] own rules, by which when it comes to be examined, it is seen to have it's merit, as well as the Grecian. The question is not, which of the two is conducted in the simplest or truest taste: but, whether there be not sense and design in both, when scrutinized by the laws on which each is projected. The same observation holds of the two sorts of poetry.[42] (Page 118)

Unlike Warton, Hurd did not base his defense on historical relativism. Instead, he presents something very like the doctrine of organic form:

> The general plan of a work, or what might be called the order of *distribution* . . . must be governed by the subject matter itself. It was as requisite for the Faery Queen to consist of the adventures of twelve knights, as for the Odyssey to be confined to the adventures of one Hero: Justice had not otherwise been done to [the] subject. . . . classic ideas of Unity . . . have no place here; if the poet has found means to give his work, tho' consisting of many parts, the advantage of . . . unity of design, and not of action. (Pages 121–22)

How, then, had such poetry come to be neglected? It had had the misfortune to be written just when Reason was "about to gain the ascendant over the portentous spectres of the imagination" and Reason's "growing splendour, in the end, put them all to flight, and allowed them no quarter even amongst the poets" (p. 153).

As the phrase "growing splendour" applied to Reason suggests, it would be a mistake to see Hurd as having given unreserved approval to medieval romance. In fact, to him, and to most of his contemporaries who felt the appeal of the past, genuine and unadulterated medieval romance was generally inferior to the Renaissance romances. As Ker says, "Not medieval poetry, but medieval customs and sentiments, were interesting; and so Hurd and many others who were tired of the poetry of good sense looked on Ariosto, Tasso and Spenser as the true poets of the medieval heroic age."[43] But Hurd was resolute in asserting the superiority of the "manners" of the Middle Ages and its institutions—medieval Christianity with the "superior solemnity of [its] superstitions" and chivalry with its "improved gallantry"—to those of both classical and modern times as subjects of "epic" poetry (p. 108). "What we have gotten" by the victory of reason, he says, "is a great deal of good sense. What we have lost, is a world of fine fabling" (p. 154).

With such attitudes assuming greater currency, it is not surprising that the decade of the sixties saw a movement to restore the "world of fine fabling" that had been lost. That movement was to grow in strength continuously; the great modern scholarly editions of medieval literature are but its latest products. But at first, scholarly accuracy—not to speak of simple honesty—was not much in evidence. It was the enterprising Scotsman James Macpherson who first detected and rushed to satisfy the new market. His Ossianic poems, which began to appear in 1760, are a notable if early example of the values of fitting the product to the consumer.[44] The enormous success of these purported "translations" from "the Gaelic or Erse language" doubtless owes something to Macpherson's genuine if modest poetic ability, but it owes a great deal more to the fact that these poems of life among third-century tribesmen signally vindicated current theories of the cult of Sensibility.[45] A primitive people, living in a natural state, it was supposed, would produce not only a morally good society, but also beautiful poetry. And this, it appeared, was just what had happened: in rhythms that bore an altogether proper resemblance to those of the Hebrew Bible, and in language and images that suggested the simplicity of a heroic age, "Ossian" celebrated the lives and deeds of the early warriors, "knowing nothing of money or luxuries, awed by the wild grandeur of nature, sentimental and melancholy in mood, and, although brave in battle, merciful to their enemies."[46] The fifteenth century was the ground of the other notable impostor of the decade, Thomas Chatterton. His *Rowley Poems*, paraded as the work of a certain Thomas Rowley, a monk, catered like Macpherson's work to the theories of the time, and like Macpherson's third-century Caledonia, his late medieval England was imbued with a love of nature and an artless benevolence.[47]

The success of such forgeries and especially the fact that Macpherson's imposture, despite Dr. Johnson's skepticism, was not clearly revealed until much later depended on more than the theories of the Sensibility school.[48] Macpherson also catered to rising nationalist feelings, which were finding outlet in tracing national greatness to the origins of the nation in the distant past. The desire to show the superiority of the Northern peoples was handily fed by the "discovery" of an epic poet as great as Homer if not greater.[49] Besides these emotional and intellectual commitments that favored belief in the genuineness of the Ossian poems, the simple unsophistication of the day in respect to the study of medieval literature played its part. As Ker notes, "an admiration of the Middle Ages need not lead to a study of medieval philology . . . . In literature, a taste for the

Middle Ages generally meant, first of all, a taste for Spenser, for Elizabethans—old poetry, but not too old."[50] To some extent this was a linguistic matter—knowledge of the medieval forms of the languages was the imperfectly mastered acquirement of a few scholars. It was not, after all, until Tyrwhitt's edition of Chaucer in 1775–1778 that Chaucer's metrical regularity was recognized, and a great many of the most important medieval texts were not to achieve publication until the next century. And anyhow, it was not the past itself that the readers of Ossian and the ballad collections wanted. It was the image of the past for which they hungered—"the light that never was, on sea or land"—the excitement and impossible glamor of the imagined past, and, above all, release from the staleness of the present.

BISHOP PERCY AND "ANCIENT POETRY"

Nevertheless, Gresham's law for once failed to operate. More and more often, genuine medieval literature began to show up in the stream of collections of older poetry issuing from the presses, and here and there a thin trickle of Arthurian pieces made its appearance. In 1764 Evan Evans published in a slender quarto *Some Specimens of the Poetry of the Antient Welsh Bards* containing less than a dozen early Welsh poems accompanied by English prose translations.[51] Evans' notes to several Arthurian allusions in the poems show a fair acquaintance with the traditional versions of the story. The following year, 1765, saw the publication of Thomas Percy's *Reliques of Ancient English Poetry, Consisting of Old Heroic Ballads, Songs, and Other Pieces of Our Earlier Poets, Together with Some Few of Later Date*, a book that "summarizes and climaxes the neoclassic interest in the ballads; and . . . is the most influential book in the romantic phase of the [ballad] revival as well."[52] Half a century later Wordsworth would describe it as having "absolutely redeemed" English poetry, and for Scott it summoned up a fantasy world of high romance in which at thirteen he would miss his dinner and at fifty-five, lose his fortune.[53]

By modern standards, the *Reliques* is an extraordinary hodgepodge About a quarter of its 180 pieces were taken from the famous "Folio MS" collection of ballads and other poetry assembled late in the first half of the seventeenth century. The rest were drawn from a variety of manuscript and printed sources and include a great deal of late material—inferior modern imitation ballads, Elizabethan and Cavalier lyrics. Percy's methods of dealing with his texts involved wholesale alteration, substitution, conflation, addition, rearrangement—in short, everything but scholarly accuracy. The fact is that, in keeping with the attitude of his time toward the editing of most vernacular texts, neither Percy's motives nor his methods were scholarly.[54] Indefatigable in his attempts to hit the shifting taste of the period, he had worked hard for a number of years to make his collection a success.[55] He might assert publicly of his collection that "such specimens of ancient poetry have been selected, as either show the gradation of our language, exhibit the progress of popular opinions, display the peculiar manners and customs of former ages, or throw light on our earlier classical poets" (I, 8),[56] but privately he was well aware that neither philological interest nor historical curiosity was the important concern. "The public," he had written to Warton in 1762, "seem to loath all common forms of Poetry; & requires some new species to quicken its pall'd appetite."[57] Again, he might claim that his object had been "to please both the judicious antiquary and the reader of taste," but his endeavor "to gratify both without offending either" (I, 11) was, as Ritson soon made evident, impossible. And the fact is, as his editorial methods— even his curious tripartite organization—show, Percy was after the broad suffrage of readers "of taste."

Yet whatever the defects of Percy's collection, or, more probably, because of them, the book seems to have done more than any other publication of the century to stimulate and feed interest in medieval story.[58] In the history of Arthurian literature, the *Reliques* occupies a special place as having made possible through its six crude Arthurian pieces a wide familiarity with some elements of the traditional story. Four of these brief Arthurian poems were taken from the "Folio MS." "The Boy and the Mantle" details a variety of chastity tests by which Guenever is proved to be a "whore" and Arthur a "cuckold." "The Marriage of Sir Gawaine" is a variant of the tale told by Chaucer's Wife of Bath. "The Legend of King Arthur" and "King Arthur's Death" provide in very scant outline the story of Arthur's birth, military triumphs, betrayal, and passing, after Mordred's fatal wound.[59] In addition to these ballads, Percy transcribed as "King Ryence's Challenge" a small song from the entertainments presented to Elizabeth at Kenilworth in 1575, and reprinted for the second time in the century Deloney's "The Noble Acts of Arthur of the Round Table," this time more clearly entitled "Sir Lancelot du Lake."[60] In these few poems, comprising altogether less than a thousand lines of verse, and marked by the coarseness of touch characteristic of the ballad composers' attempts to deal with chivalric material, little if any of the grandeur of Arthurian story shows through. But at least they gave Percy's readers in a very rough fashion a glimpse of the essential elements of the legend. The ballads were enough, perhaps even the best thing, to whet the readers' curiosity, and this curiosity Percy responded to in his notes and his essay "On the Ancient Metrical Romances, &c."[61] In both, Percy shows himself well read if not scrupulously attentive to detail. He knows and quotes extensively from Malory, and appears to have read a variety of other metrical and prose romances, both English and French.[62] Significantly, he breaks from the old editorial tradition in basing his discussions of Arthurian matters not on the historians and pseudohistorians, but rather on the purely literary and avowedly fictional sources.[63] Thus through Percy's work, the story of Arthur—and now, not as a problematical king of dubious history, but as a monarch of romance—began once more to be familiar knowledge among the literate and the cultured.

Percy had spoken of these "rude songs of ancient minstrels" with a freedom from vulgar enthusiasm altogether fitting for a man who would one day be elevated to the bishopric of Dromore. Of these "barbarous productions of unpolished ages," these artless "effusions of nature" (I, 1), he professed to have been "long in doubt, whether, in the present state of improved literature they could be deemed worthy the attention of the public." "In a polished age, like the present," he was "sensible that many of these reliques of antiquity will require allowances to be made for them" (I, 7–8). The public as it turned out—and doubtless as Percy expected—was not only ready, it was even eager to make allowances; a second edition was called for before two years were out.[64]

THOMAS WARTON AND OTHER GOTHIC ENTHUSIASTS

The success of the *Reliques* and the renown it won its editor encouraged other men of antiquarian sympathies to try their luck. The audience to which Percy had appealed continued to grow, and, in what remained of the century, it provided a ready market for over a dozen different collections of earlier literature of one sort or another.[65] All of these various collections of "old ballads" and "old songs" edited by Herd, T. Evans, Pinkerton, Ritson, and Ellis doubtless contributed to the impetus of the Medieval Revival to which, at the same time, they owed their success. Under the exacerbated lash of Ritson's accurate scholarship, there slowly emerged a new attitude toward the editing of vernacular texts, a new tradition of intelligent authentication, precise transcription, editorial honesty, and bibliographical responsibility. But the eighteenth-century collections after Percy's *Reliques* did little to assist directly the revival of Arthurian story. Ritson, whose keen interest in the legend took a largely historical turn, contributed no more than a careful reprinting of "Sir Lancelot du Lake" in his *Select Collection of English Songs* (1783).[66]

The year 1786 saw the first appearance in modern English of several brief Arthurian *lais* or romances translated from LeGrand d'Aussy's modern French *Fabliaux, ou contes du XIIe et du XIIIe siècles* (1779–1781).[67] Six years later, John Pinkerton, who like Bishop Percy had been exposed to Ritson's stinging sarcasm,[68] included two long alliterative metrical romances dealing with Gawain in his *Scotish Poems* (1792).[69] Both of these —"Gawan and Gologras," reprinted from an early sixteenth-century Scottish edition, and "Sir Gawan and Sir Galaron of Galloway," transcribed from manuscript and conjecturally dated before 1440 by Pinkerton[70]—are tedious examples of the late Scottish tradition of popular narrative. But if neither of these third-rate poems had any influence on the Arthurian revival of the next century, they are nevertheless significant as indicating a turning of editorial attention from lyrics and ballads (in which Arthurian story neither had been nor could be well employed) to the longer narratives of the past, especially the medieval romances, in which Arthur and his knights had shone most resplendently.[71]

One of the more powerful stimulants to this shift in interest came from Thomas Warton. Warton, whose antiquarian sympathies had been roused in childhood by his father's admiration for Gothic architecture, and to whom medieval themes were "falsely stil'd" as "unclassic," spent his life declaring: "Nor rough, nor barren are the winding ways / Of hoar Antiquity, but strown with flowers."[72] Indeed, as his biographer observed, "Every subject, connected with the ages of Chivalry and Romance, with Gothic manners and Gothic arts, was contemplated with peculiar fondness by Warton."[73] What he had earlier done for Spenser, Warton now set out to do for all early English poetry in his ambitious and influential *History of English Poetry* (1774–1781).[74] In this wide-ranging ("scaturient" is Scott's unexpectedly harsh word for it) and detailed survey, Warton not only discusses the origins of the Arthurian story, but at the same time sympathetically examines a number of individual romances.[75] And in a burst of enthusiasm, he exclaims,

> I cannot help observing, that English literature and English poetry suffer, while so many pieces of this kind [i.e., metrical romances] still remain concealed and forgotten in our manuscript libraries. They contain in common with the prose-romances ... amusing images of antient customs and institutions, not elsewhere to be found, or at least not so strikingly delineated: and they preserve pure and unmixed, those fables of chivalry which formed the taste and awakened the imagination of our elder English classics. The antiquaries of former times overlooked or rejected these valuable remains, which they despised as false and frivolous; and employed their industry in reviving obscure frag-

ments of uninstructive morality or uninteresting history. But in the present age we are beginning to make ample amends: in which the curiosity of the antiquarian is connected with taste and genius, and his researches tend to display the progress of human manners, and to illustrate the history of society.[76] (I, 208–9)

In this preference for romance to pseudohistory, and in his recognition of the story of Arthur's being carried away to Avalon by an "Elfin princess" as a "beautiful romantic fiction" (I, sig. h3ᵛ), Warton follows Percy's lead. At the same time, he foreshadows the developments of the next century when the "historical Arthur" who had so long stood in the way of adequate artistic treatment of the legend would be discarded and replaced by the Arthur of romance.[77] Yet he himself, it will be seen, fell back on pseudohistory in his one significant Arthurian poem, "The Grave of King Arthur."

The History of English Poetry doubtless conferred an important new prestige on earlier literature and thus stimulated interest in the publication and study of medieval romance, but its author, as witness his laureateship, was no hot-eyed revolutionary. As B. Ifor Evans has observed, Warton "is like an eighteenth-century gentleman who has no desire to give up his Palladian residence because there are 'gothic' ruins in the garden; above all he does not wish to live in the ruins."[78] The motives behind the revival of interest in medieval literature were, Warton supposed, those of curiosity and self-gratulation.

> In an age advanced to the highest degree of refinement, that species of curiosity commences, which is busied in contemplating the progress of social life, in displaying the gradations of science, and in tracing the transitions from barbarism to civility.
>
> That these speculations should become the favourite pursuits, and the fashionable topics, of such a period, is extremely natural. We look back on the savage condition of our ancestors with the triumph of superiority; we are pleased to mark the steps by which we have been raised from rudeness to elegance: and our reflections on this subject are accompanied with a conscious pride, arising in great measure from a tacit comparison of the infinite disproportion between the feeble efforts of remote ages, and our present improvements in knowledge. (I, i)

The knowledge of early manners to be derived from the study of earlier literature, Warton says, "teaches us a just estimation of our own acquisitions; and encourages us to cherish that cultivation, which is so closely connected with the existence and the exercise of every social virtue" (I, ii). Like most of his fellow editors and scholars in the century (and even Scott in the next), he feels constrained to justify the study of early literature in terms of its educative value, its "genuine delineations of life in its simplest stages" (I, iii).[79] If such arguments derive mainly from a genuine ambiguity of attitude in the late eighteenth century toward the older poetry, they also owe something to the fact that the medieval revival did not proceed unopposed. As late as the nineties, Ritson glumly predicted of his *Pieces of Ancient Popular Poetry* that it would "have few charms in the critical eye of a cultivated age,"[80] and excluded from his *English Anthology* poetry before 1500 on the grounds that "the nicety of the present age [would be] ill disposed to make the necessary allowances for the uncouth diction and homely sentiments of former times."[81] Clearly, Neo-Classical ideals, no matter how moribund, were not yet dead.

Nevertheless, the view was making headway that earlier literature was not merely a matter of historical interest—that it was, in fact, actually superior to the poetry of the Age of Reason. In 1783 in one of the dissertations prefixed to his *Select Scotish Ballads*, Pinkerton, with a certain partisan vigor, perhaps, could assert that "the music of the most barbarous countries has had effects that not all the sublime pathos of Corelli, or animated strains of Handel, could produce. Have not the Welsh, Irish, and Scotish tunes, greater influence over the most informed mind at this day than the best Italian concerto?"[82] And when he drew the architectural parallel so dear to the critics of the time, the advantage was all with the earlier poets: "The laboured productions of the informed composer [of tragic poetry] resemble a Greek or Roman temple; when we enter it, we admire the art of the builder. The rude effusions of the Gothic Muse are like the monuments of their architecture. We are filled with a religious reverence, and, forgetting our praise of the contriver, adore the present deity" (I, xxxv).

Behind such assertions lay theories of poetic creation and subject matter widely at variance with Neo-Classical emphasis on reason, taste, the "rules," and the probable and universal. The humbling consideration that "an age advanced to the highest degree in refinement" had been unable to approach Homer in what the age agreed in describing as the highest poetic type—the epic—had long been obvious. As early as 1735 James Blackwell had pointed out that Homer's greatness lay in the often unrecognized fact that Homer was a primitive poet celebrating a primitive society in a primitive language.[83] The parallel between Homeric times and manners and the Middle Ages and "Gothic manners" had been drawn at length by Bishop Hurd.[84] Following his lead, Warton had been constrained to admit that the Middle Ages had been "favorable to poetry"; indeed, "ignorance and superstition, so opposite to the real interests of human society, are the parents of imagination" (II, 462). And the revolution wrought by reason had seriously depleted the poet's resources:

> Setting aside the consideration of the more solid advantages, which are obvious, and are not the distinct object of our contemplation at present, the lover of true poetry will ask, what have we gained by this revolution? It may be answered, much good sense, good taste, and good criticism. But in the mean time, we have lost a set of manners, and a system of machinery, more suitable to the purposes of poetry, than those which have been adopted in their place. We have parted with extravagancies that are above propriety, with incredibilities that are more acceptable than truth, and with fictions that are more valuable than reality.[85] (II, 463)

Nor was it only in point of subject matter and beliefs that the earlier poets were the superiors of the Neo-Classicists. The fact was, Pinkerton declared, that poetry is "the original language of men in an infant state of society in all countries. It is the effusion of fancy actuated by the passions: and that these are always strongest when uncontrolled by custom, and the manners which in an advanced community are termed polite, is evident" (I, xvi). The ancient bards, just because "their mode of expression was simple and genuine," had "touched the passions truly and effectively" (I, xxiii). The stuff of poetry is nothing as transitory and liable to displacement as the constructs of the Reason or appeals to the Reason. The real matter of poetry is the human heart—its real appeal is to the passions: "We may laugh at Sir Isaac Newton, as we have at Descartes; but we shall always admire a Homer, an Ossian, or a Shakspere" (I, xxiv).

Doubtless, it is easier for the modern reader to laugh at Ossian than at Newton. Still, Pinkerton's statement indicates the vigor with which a critically supported enthusiasm for medieval literature and civilization flourished in the 1780's. A century before, Newton had brought light to "nature's laws . . . hid in night." Now a new generation was beginning to roll back the darkness of the Dark Ages. Patrons of the circulating libraries would go on seeking the delicious *frisson* of its shades in the shabby cousin of the Medieval Revival, the Gothic novel. But soberer readers—and, for that matter, some readers of Gothic fiction in their soberer moods—were seeking out and developing a more informed comprehension of the Middle Ages. As this search continued, it would lead inevitably to the revival of sympathy for Arthurian story.

THE HISTORIANS AND THE MIDDLE AGES

Meanwhile, what was needed for the development of a clearer and

thus ultimately more accurately sympathetic image of the Middle Ages
was the assistance of serious historians. Unfortunately, history had waited
on the literary studies for its cue.[86] And the cue had been confused by the
fact that literary men who were capable of great respect for medieval
literature were very frequently dominated by the rationalist historians in
their attitudes toward the civilization that had produced the literature
they so much admired. Thus Evan Evans, speaking of the thirteenth-
century Welsh bards whose poetry he had translated, was led to say, "It is
true, they lived in times when all Europe was enveloped with the black
cloud of bigotry and ignorance; yet, even under these disadvantageous
circumstances . . . poetry shone forth with a light, that seems astonishing
to many readers."[87] It is not surprising, then, that in general the historians
during the second half of the eighteenth century carried on the habit of
ignorant depreciation of the Middle Ages that they had inherited from
Voltaire and Hume. But the doctrine of the evolution of humanity,
enunciated by Leibniz, was beginning to encourage at least a more
thorough if not more sympathetic study of the period out of which modern times had evolved.[88] Thus Robertson, though he manifests the usual
contempt for the institutions of the Middle Ages, did devote a large work,
his *View of the State of Society in the Middle Ages* (1769), to what Peardon has called "a remarkable attempt to elucidate the main forces at work
during a thousand years of European history."[89]

But it is mostly the influence of literary historians, theoreticians, and
critics, combined toward the end of the century with Burke's historical
relativism and reverence for the past and its traditions, which served to
transform the historians' treatment of the Middle Ages in the latter part
of the century. The influence of Hurd, Percy, and Ossianism is obvious
in the works of such historians as Lord Lyttelton, Robert Henry, and
William Russell.[90] While these writers show a steady rationalist contempt
for the "rubbish of Monkish Annals"[91] and many other aspects of medieval Christianity and society, they also manifest a common admiration for
what was noble in feudalism and chivalry, and a common enthusiasm for
medieval poetry and its "beautiful extravagances of romantic feeling."[92]
In another group of historians—Gilbert Stuart, John Whitaker, and John
Smith—the primitivist notions of the times and the rising popularity of
nationalist history provoked attempts to trace the sources of English
virtues and English liberties to early medieval times.[93] In contrast to such
highly speculative writers, Joseph Strutt in *A Complete View of the
Manners, Customs, Arms, Habits, etc. of the Inhabitants of Britain*, combined historical zeal with a sympathetic love of the past to produce the
first significant social history of the Middle Ages.[94] The progress toward

a re-evaluation of the Middle Ages in the works of these various historians was of considerable importance; nevertheless, as Peardon has shown, the period between Hume and Hallam was essentially transitional. Although it laid the groundwork for a great school of medieval historians to come, it produced no lastingly great work of its own.

In this, historical writing but shared in the nature of the age. Poised between a dying Rationalism and Neo-Classicism on the one hand and a not yet fully formed Romanticism on the other, it performed the thankless task of preparing the soil for new growth. The rationale of sensibilitarian primitivism by which it had thrown off the domination of Neo-Classicist ideals, at the same time seriously obscured its view of the Middle Ages and medieval literature. On the positive side, the age did manage partially to rehabilitate the past, and through its love of the past it was led, as Fairchild observes, to "most of the changes in theme, form, and technique which sounded the knell of pseudoclassicism."[95] But the age was unable to exploit its own revolution. It created no great literature based on medieval themes. What it did create was an attitude of mind—a readiness to sympathize with what it considered (often incorrectly) the literature and life of the Middle Ages. How far that attitude had spread by the last decade of the century may be gathered from the reliance on its appeal that Burke (a man not likely to misestimate his audience) manifests in his great lament for the passing of chivalry:

> The age of chivalry is gone. That of sophisters, economists, and calculators, has succeeded; and the glory of Europe is extinguished for ever. Never, never more shall we behold that generous loyalty to rank and sex, that proud submission, that dignified obedience, that subordination of the heart, which kept alive, even in servitude itself, the spirit of an exalted freedom. The unbought grace of life, the cheap defence of nations, the nurse of manly sentiment and heroic enterprise, is gone! It is gone, that sensibility of principle, that chastity of honour, which felt a stain like a wound, which inspired courage whilst it mitigated ferocity, which ennobled whatever it touched, and under which vice itself lost half its evil, by losing all its grossness.[96]

Yet despite the currency of the attitudes at which Burke's eloquence was aimed, poets of the latter part of the eighteenth century were little touched by the tradition of the greatest exemplars of the chivalry Burke praised—Arthur and his knights. A number of poetically inclined antiquarians like Percy and Warton displayed familiarity with Arthurian story, and a few inferior Arthurian ballads and romances had been made widely available.[97] But for various reasons most of the significant poets of the period largely ignored the legend. Neither Cowper nor Burns, as might be expected, makes any mention at all of the story, and even Thomas Gray, despite his interest in Celtic antiquities, alludes but once to Arthur, and then only very briefly to the Arthur of Welsh folk tradition, rather than to the king of romance.[98]

The fact is, as Gray's solitary reference to Arthur and the whole of the poem in which it occurs, *The Bard*, indicate, the Pre-Romantics were not so much interested in the poetic themes of the past as they were fascinated by its customs and manners—not its spirit but its hardware and furniture. Their minds were not impressed by the human similarity of the Middle Ages to their own age, but rather by the differences. It was precisely the pastness of the past that made that past dear to them. Hence it was in the spirit of a sort of mental antique collecting that they approached the long ago. And what they brought back was not something for present service, but a number of grotesquely carved chairs, each with a tasseled velvet cord across its arms, to set between the Chippendale sideboards and the Adam mantelpieces.

THOMAS WARTON AS ARTHURIAN POET

The specialist of the age in this sort of interior decorating was Thomas Warton. A life spent in antiquarian studies had admirably stored his mind with medieval knickknacks. Hence in his own poetry, as his biographer observed, "In one department he is not only unequalled, but original and unprecedented: I mean in applying to modern poetry the embellishment of Gothic manners and Gothic arts; the tournaments and festivals, the poetry, music, painting, and architecture of 'elder days.' "[99] Warton's "Ode at Valeroyal Abbey," along with its "reflections on the benefits derived to modern times from monastic institutions," thus also contains "some fine touches of Gothic painting" (I, cxlv). Two of Warton's sonnets include specifically Arthurian materials. "Written at Stonehenge" alludes to the tradition that the structure was reared by Merlin's magic aid. "On King Arthur's Round Table, at Winchester" takes as its subject the ruins where "Venta's Norman castle still uprears / Its rafter'd hall" and what there "High-hung remains, the pride of warlike years, / Old Arthur's Board," on which the names of Arthur's champions were inscribed in "marks obscure" by "some British pen" (II, 158–59). What chiefly interests Warton in both of these poems, however, is not the themes of medieval romance, but the physical vestiges of medieval times, marked by Time's "slow vengeance."[100]

The same disposition to delight in the quality of "pastness," or what might be called the "historicalness" of medieval material, manifests itself in Warton's one extensive treatment of an Arthurian theme. "The Grave of King Arthur" (1777), an "ode" in octosyllabic couplets, is based not on a romance episode, but instead takes as its framework an incident in the passage of Henry II through Wales on his way to put down a rebellion in Ireland.[101] To Henry, sitting in state, comes a Welsh bard who in "fabling rime" tells the consequence of the last battle between Mordred and Arthur, who is, surprisingly,

> By Mordred's faithless guile decreed
> Beneath a Saxon spear to bleed!
> Yet in vain a paynim foe
> Arm'd with fate the mighty blow;
> For when he fell, an elfin queen,
> All in secret, and unseen,
> O'er the fainting hero threw
> Her mantle of ambrosial blue
> And bade her spirits bear him far,
> In Merlin's agate-axled car,
> To her green isle's enamell'd steep,
> Far in the navel of the deep. (II, 57 and 59–60)

But this account of Arthur's passing and of the promise that he will some day return is quickly countered by a second bard "of aspect sage," who declaims:

> Not from fairy realms I lead
> Bright-rob'd Tradition, to relate
> In forged colours Arthur's fate;
> Though much of old romantic lore
> On the high theme I keep in store:
> But boastful Fiction should be dumb,
> Where Truth the strain might best become. (II, 63–66)

The fact, it appears, is that "when Arthur bow'd his haughty crest," his men carried him to "Joseph's towered fane, / In the fair vale of Avalon," and there he was buried in an unmarked grave (II, 67–69). Told by the bard that it is his task to renew "the faded tomb, with honour due," Henry, in a burst of royal piety (or antiquarian fervor?) "scorns awile [sic] his bold emprise" of putting down the Irish rebellion and begins to plan a new tomb at Glastonbury (II, 71, 74).[102]

Of this curious poem it is easy enough to say with MacCallum that it is one of the best that Warton ever wrote,[103] without thinking it a very good poem in itself. Warton's poetic endowment was slender at best, and his work shows one of the commonest marks of the minor poet—an unquestioning contentment with the poetic forms, techniques, and conventions of his time. There is no hint that he was anything but perfectly satisfied with the personified abstractions, the "purified" diction, and the steady rhymes of the Augustans as a medium for expressing a new subject matter and an altered sensibility. Doubtless this inconsonance of form and matter accounts partially for the oddly flatted effect of "The Grave of King Arthur." But even more destructive is the simple inadequacy of Warton's response to his favorite material. How imperfectly he had grasped the spirit of the Middle Ages may be easily deduced from his bland bestowal on a twelfth-century Welsh bard of a fine Rationalist discrimination between "boastful Fiction" and "Truth," with a clear preference for the latter. How far he was from appreciating the poetic possibilities of Arthurian story is clear from the simple fact that he obviously shared the bard's partiality. The result, not surprisingly, is scarcely a significant addition to Arthurian literature, although it does seem permissible to suppose that the serious use of the theme by the poet laureate may have added something to its attractiveness in the eyes of other poets.

WILLIAM HILTON'S ARTHURIAN TRAGEDY

Of the other attempts during the second half of the century to give poetic expression to the Arthurian story, it is not too harsh to say that the obscurity in which they languished from the beginning was not undeserved. The author of one of these curious efforts, William Hilton, is so little known to fame that not even his birth or death dates can be ascertained.[104] And his *Arthur, Monarch of the Britons, A Tragedy* seems to have achieved no circulation beyond a group of North of England subscribers to the publication of his *Poetical Works* in 1775–1776.[105] In most respects, Hilton's play follows the pseudohistorical tradition fairly closely. "I collected my materials," he says, "from such histories of [Arthur] as fell in my way," and despite the fact that most of these are "very dark," Hilton asserts, "that [Arthur] did exist, and so magnanimously excel, seems indubitably certain" (I, xiii–xiv). Whatever the particular "histories" were, Hilton's plot, with the exception of minor variations, derives ultimately from the account of Arthur in Geoffrey's *Historia*. Arthur is called back from a campaign in Britanny by news that Mordred has usurped the throne and married Guinever. Assisted by Cador, Galvan (Gawain), and Hoel, and counseled by Druis, a "priest and philosopher" whom he sometimes visits "to converse of *Nature* and of *God*" (II, 181), Arthur prepares war against Mordred, who is assisted by Saxons, Picts, and traitorous Britons. Guinever, racked by conscience, seeks reconciliation with Arthur, but is denied even converse with him or his friends by Arthur. Lacking her, Mordred loses heart, and Arthur, who has rejected the suggestion that the attack begin at night on the ground that "*my* soldiers chuse the open day; / Their hearts are honest, and they scorn what's mean" (II, 192), now begins a series of battles in which the foe is finally routed and Mordred killed. Arthur himself is mortally wounded, and after magnanimously pardoning Guinever, dies, bequeathing his throne to Constantine with the injunction, "Remember, prince, that *Britons* must be free!" (II, 247).

Arthur's dying words summarize the dominant theme of Hilton's play; they also reflect the temper of the time when it was written. According to Hilton's note (II, 169), *Arthur, Monarch of the Britons* was finished in November of 1759,[106] a date which fits in well with the author's observation that in the writing of the play he had been "not a little actuated by that innate love of national liberty, which with *Britons*, kindles at our birth, grows with our years, and with our strength refines!" (I, xiv). In 1759 the triumph of British arms and policies abroad as a result of Pitt's brilliant conduct of the Seven Years' War had unified England in an excited sense of patriotism and national pride.[107] At such a time the celebration of a national hero, "godlike" Arthur, as one who had "set the oppressed free" abroad and "often prov'd religion's friend," must have seemed marvellously appropriate, and no less so would have appeared the sage advice of Arthur's counselor, Druis:

> Union! and virtue! these alone must save
> From threaten'd ruin. These alone prevent
> The complicated schemes of foreign foes.[108]

Indeed, in Hilton's view, it seemed altogether likely that British virtues would recommend themselves even to Arthur's foes. Withgar, the Saxon general, and Pictutius, the Pict general, looking ahead to the time when the Britons will have been finally conquered, rejoice in the prospect that they themselves and their descendants will then ". . . mount to fame, / And, warm'd with freedom, into Britons grow" (II, 239).

Apart from its unintentional humor, the naïve historicism of this prophecy does little but call attention to Hilton's anxiety to plaster over a basic defect in his design. For the attempt to use Arthur, essentially a mythic or moral hero, as a patriotic hero runs head on into two inherent contradictions. To begin with, no matter how much the histories and pseudohistories varied in detail, they were in agreement on one hard fact: that some of Arthur's greatest triumphs had been over the Germanic invaders, the very people who had most contributed to the ethnic structure, political ideals, and even the language and name of modern England. And the ultimate destruction of the work of his reign had also come at the hands of the future English. More importantly, his story, even in the accounts of the historians, was further disqualified for use as patriotic material by the fact that the issue of Arthur's life and work was unsuccessful in practical terms. Unlike that of the ordinary patriot hero, his was no story of high sacrifice for the ultimate good of his country; it was rather a story of noble achievement lost forever through the treachery of those for whom he had labored.[109] Dryden, whose *King Arthur* may have been in Hilton's mind, had evaded the issue by a freely invented happy ending. Hilton, more historically conscientious, tried to meet the difficulty by providing the foes of his Arthur with an odd prevision of ethnic destiny, a sort of drive toward cultural *Lebensraum*. The result, if it is less meretricious than Dryden's play, can hardly be said to be more successful.

The comparison is not inapt. For despite the fact that Hilton shows a certain Pre-Romantic tendency in his choice of the Arthurian theme for serious use and in his general reliance on his medieval sources, his work belongs essentially to the Augustan age. What additions he did venture upon—the ever-impending but still avoided rape of Guinever, the braggadocio of the cowardly traitor Molus, and the web of suspicions that he constructs to alienate Arthur and his friends—reflect the worst elements of mid-eighteenth-century drama. All the routine improbabilities of disguise, recognition, and motivation are there. Nor is he any more original in his prosy, end-stopped blank verse or in his sensibility. For emotion he offers at best only shabby rhetoric; for thought, Popian commonplace.[110]

Nevertheless, *Arthur, Monarch of the Britons* has a significance as the first completed attempt in nearly two centuries to make serious and meaningful use of the Arthurian story with full fidelity to medieval sources. Not since Thomas Hughes's *Misfortunes of Arthur* had a writer been content to leave the major outlines of the medieval tradition unchanged. That the tradition Hilton drew on was that of pseudohistory instead of romance doubtless owes as much to his rationalist tendencies and the age's general ignorance of the romances as it does to his patriotic purposes. But in his effort to apply the old story without drastic alterations to new needs, he shows a new attitude, and he distantly foreshadows far better treatments to come.

RICHARD HOLE'S PRE-ROMANTIC ARTHURIAD

The thirty years that separate the completion of Hilton's *Arthur* and the publication of *Arthur: or, The Northern Enchantment* (1789) cover most of the important events in the incipience of Romantic sensibility.[111] The book's author, Richard Hole, rural clergyman, antiquarian, versifier of Ossian, student of Scandinavian antiquities and the origins of Oriental fiction, and minor poet, was himself a figure to delight literary historians —a textbook instance of the Pre-Romantic.[112] Even the Augustan couplets and the "refined" diction in which he wrote his "Poetical Romance in Seven Books" reflect the characteristic Pre-Romantic failure to reconcile form and subject.[113] No less typical is the fact that what interested him most were the stage trappings, the "extravagant" incidents, the "grotesque beauties," of "Gothic" times, rather than the spirit, the narrative integrity of genuine medieval romance. In the style of his day, Hole admired the "boldness" of conception of the "old metrical romances" (in whose num-bers he clearly included Renaissance romances[114]); they were, he believed, "taken from life" and they had thus "afforded the author greater pleasure than many correct, but uninteresting productions of more modern times. Trusting that others might possess the same feelings, he has adopted such of their peculiarities as would afford the greatest scope for poetical imagry and description" (p. viii).[115]

The "imitation of the old metrical Romance . . . with some of its harsher features softened and modified" that resulted goes far to justify— at least in respect to the traditional Arthurian story—Hole's declaration that "though he dare[d] not . . . claim originality, he [had] not infre-quently attempted it" (pp. iv, viii). The main action begins after the death of Uther when, in the absence of Arthur, Hengist the Saxon seizes power in Britain with an army of Saxons and Scandinavians and spreads "death and havock o'er [the] hapless land" (p. 46).[116] Merlin flees with his daughter Inogen, the beloved of Arthur, to a forest retreat, where the Genius of the Isle appears to him and endows him with heavenly powers to assist and advise Arthur in his struggles with the Heathen. But Arthur, misled by illusions created by the Fatal Sisters, who are assisting Hengist, allows himself, in violation of the heavenly command delivered by Merlin, to become separated from his men. The Fatal Sisters, in an attempt to "impede / What heaven's eternal wisdom has decreed" (p. 52), have sought to destroy Arthur in a storm at sea and only Merlin's powers have saved him. As punishment for breaking the heavenly command, Arthur is condemned to undergo alone a series of trials and adventures before he is restored to his friends, Gawaine, Cador, Lancelot, Lionel, Cradoc, Hoel, and such Celtic heroes as Maronan, Conal, and Fiacha. At the last mo-ment he arrives and stems the tide of battle against the united Saxon and Scandinavian armies. Meanwhile, Hengist, who has hitherto avoided

Arthur's vengeance by the magical aid of the Fatal Sisters, is magically disguised as Arthur and thus manages to lure Inogen from her refuge and almost rapes her before she escapes and he himself is killed by one of his own followers who naturally mistakes him for Arthur. Arthur himself, grieved at first by what he takes to be her treachery, has his confidence restored by Merlin's explanation, and so takes Inogen as his Queen. Thus by Arthur's brave obedience to heaven's commands, his realm is restored, and through their own mistaken efforts, the Fatal Sisters' champion, Hengist, is killed, and they themselves are bound fast for evermore in Hell. Thus is fulfilled the prophecy made at Inogen's birth:

> Doom'd in severest woe thro' life to pine,
> Unless thou fliest from him thy soul approves,
> And he rejects thee who most dearly loves:
> Yet whosoe'er in wedlock takes thy hand,
> Reigns from that hour supreme in Britain's land. (Page 29)

This was "originality" all right, if only by a process of indiscriminate combination. True, there are some elements of romance, such routine motifs as magical castles and hideous creatures that disappear before the hero's resolute bravery.[117] There is even something of the complicated romance method of interweaving separate narrative strands. But much more important to the structure of the poem were the conventions of Virgilian epic: the beginning *in medias res*, the hero's shipwreck on a friendly strand as the result of a storm roused by supernatural enemies, the narration of antecedent events to his hosts, the "machinery" by which both hero and anti-hero receive supernatural assistance, even a descent into the underworld[118]—all these hail from a tradition far different from medieval romance. And there was still more to come in this cultural potpourri: "some of the characteristic manners of the Northern nations." Such figures as the Fatal Sisters were, of course, not meant to be strictly Scandinavian; they, like the romance elements, had been adapted to the "genius of [the] Poem." This "mixture of Scandinavian manners with the ideal ones . . . of chivalry" is justifiable on the ground that "they were really and originally the same" (p. xi).[119] And what more proper for ornament to these antiquities than an admittedly "free use" of "some descriptions and allusions in the poems attributed to Ossian" (p. viii)?[120]

Much more obvious, though unacknowledged, is the omnipresent influence of Milton's epic. Even the incident that serves to illustrate the central theme—Arthur's fall from grace through disobedience to heaven's single, arbitrary command and his subsequent condemnation to wander alone through Britain—derives from *Paradise Lost*. And Hole's conception of the "eternal will" and man's freedom is clearly Miltonic, as in Merlin's rebuke to Arthur's murmur against the "unjust fate" under which he labors: "High heaven permits these evils men create; / Whilst they, what folly caus'd, impute to fate" (p. 16). Heaven, Merlin has been told, intends Arthur's good,

> But since 'tis man's with liberty of will
> Heaven's kind intents to frustrate or fulfill;
> With dauntless valour he must prudence join. (Page 54)

Nor is Hole less indebted to Milton's imagery. Hengist's lance, "vast as the pine on Norway's storm-beat shore" (p. 85), is doubtless a pale enough reflection of Satan's spear, but Milton's "darkness visible" debased to Hole's "horror visible" becomes strangely ludicrous (p. 173).[121]

Amid all these levies on romance and classical, pseudosavage, and Christian epics, Hole seems to have neglected the Arthurian story alone. Apart from a few proper names, evidently drawn from the Arthurian pieces in Percy's *Reliques* (see Hole's footnotes, pp. 92–93), and the basic situation of Arthur's youthful struggle with the Saxons, little remains of the traditional story. It was not that Hole doubted Arthur's authenticity; behind the fabulous tales, he was sure there was a nucleus of fact. The truth is simply that Hole was not interested in either the king of history or the monarch of tradition. Following the common Pre-Romantic theory of poetic sensibility, Hole put great emphasis on the "Fancy," that is, inventiveness uncurbed by Reason or Rules. Indeed, the thing that united the poet and the (by now) canonized rustic swain was Fancy. The fairies who entertained Inogen, Hole declares, were still to be seen by poets and such noble primitives:

> Thus potent fancy can the sense enchain,
> Form, and embody forth her airy train
> In simplest minds, and give to vacant eyes,
> What sterner Wisdom to her sons denies,
> Impressions sweet and strange! alike her sway
> Th' inventive bard and humble swain obey.
> Yet we in one, their lot so different, find
> The daring efforts of the glowing mind,
> That "scales invention's heaven." While censure vain
> And keen derision mock th' unletter'd swain,
> Tho' to his view ideal forms arise:
> And Fancy gilds them with her brightest dyes![122] (Page 185)

With the imagination turned into a supplier of supernatural baubles and "daring" invention given free rein, it is no wonder that Hole's Arthur became "merely an ideal personage; his atchievements groundless and imaginary; not to be examined at the bar of historic truth, but of poetic credibility" (p. iii).

The distinction, for all its neatness, is misleading. What Hole failed to grasp, as many failed in an age awkwardly attempting to re-introduce mythic or traditionary materials into literature, was that imaginative or poetic materials have their "facts," their fixed relationships, as much as history does. Arthur was, like Oedipus or Hamlet, not merely a name or a character about whom the poet might weave whatever fancies he might card and spin in his mind. He was, instead, a character identified and made significant by certain "facts" in his career. Quite precisely he *was* the events of his life, as is any character in fiction. It was not enough for Hole to present Arthur as "the darling theme, the wonder of our days," a leader whose men were "with ardent souls inspir'd, / Taught by his rules, by his example fir'd." To show him as possessing a "fearless soul" that "amid opposing dangers greater swells," as one whom "force could ne'er o'erthrow," though fraud might, and as one divinely appointed, "Far to diffuse religion's sacred light; / And whelm the Pagan gods in endless night," approached the traditional conception of Arthur's character (pp. 13–14, 52, 56, 67). But to eliminate the essential story in which this character had its significance, the story in which this character both partially created and suffered its tragic fate, was to fling a challenge to the imagination which Hole (and probably any other poet) was incapable of supporting. With such an approach, even had Richard Hole not been "the meanest of the tuneful train," as he describes himself, it seems unlikely that he would have produced anything very far beyond the "feebler lay" that resulted (p. 4).

Hole's announced intention was to write a "poetical romance," and he had, as he modestly thought,

> Presume[d] t'unfold a tale of other days[,]
> Such, as of old to Fancy's ear addrest,
> Perchance had struck the sympathizing breast;
> When lovely were our maids, and brave our youth,
> When virtue valour crown'd, and beauty truth. (Page 4)

Putting aside the question of whether this is an accurate picture of any past, it seems quite permissible to doubt that any medieval reader would have been struck. The fact is, as Hole's sentimental affection for "mould'ring walls" "clasp'd by rude ivy" (p. 4) suggests, he, like his fellow Pre-Romantics was moved not by the undying humanness of the past, but precisely by its material pastness, and his view of the spirit of that

past was characteristically unhistorical. It may be wondered just what a
medieval reader—no matter how "sympathizing" his breast—would have
made of Merlin's account of his forest retreat:

> By Deva's stream, mid vales and mountains rude,
> Sweet to the pensive mind is solitude.
> Most sweet to study nature's secret laws,
> And trace her wonders to the primal cause.
> What deep instruction the reflecting mind,
> Benignant nature, in thy works can find!
> The leaf that quivers in th' autumnal gale,
> The flower of spring that in the lonely vale
> Blooms unregarded, equally proclaim,
> With yonder orbs that deck th' ethereal frame,
> Their great Creator's wisdom. (Pages 30–31)

And how far would a feudal knight have concurred in the view that "nor
pomp, pride, conquest, sooth the troubled breast / Like acts humane" (p.
136)?[123] Even Merlin's final injunction to Arthur with its references to
"laws" and "arts" seems more applicable to the third George than it does
to the legendary Arthur:

> Crush stern oppression, and the wrong'd redress;
> Fight to protect, and conquer but to bless.
> Let laws maintain, let arts adorn thy sway;
> And blend the olive with the victor bay!
> By acts like these, the first of names acquire;
> The friend of human-kind, thy country's sire. (Page 253)

The objection to such anachronisms does not rest on any view that
the proper aim of the poet is the construction of minutely "accurate" historical dioramas. Indeed, one of the glories of the Arthurian legend, or
any other great legend for that matter, has been its adaptability to the
expressive needs of widely varying cultures. The real objection is that in
the intellectual and imaginative gropings of the transitional period during
the second half of the eighteenth century no large or significant expressive need seems to have emerged. The time seems only to have generated
a proliferation of modish ideas. At any rate, it is certain from the number
of such ephemerae tangled in the gum of his poem that Hole was little
able to escape from the fashionable notions of his own day into the time-
less world of romance. This is perhaps no more than to say in a round-
about way that Hole was a minor poet, and his *Arthur: or, The Northern
Enchantment*, a minor poem.

Even so, Hole has a place of some importance in the history of the

Arthurian story. In his arbitrary revision of the central story, he harks back to the old approach of free invention. But in his explicit declaration of independence from pseudohistory, in his halting recognition of romance as the proper land for Arthur's exploits, and in his attempts to adapt Arthur's story to a great and serious theme, Hole suggests the future course of the legend's history and combines several important requisites of a successful treatment of the story. That he did not achieve success is to be blamed partly on his own disabilities, partly on the age's.

The period in literary history that was now drawing to an end had done much to prepare the way for the coming of the fully developed romanticism of the nineteenth century, and thus, ultimately, for the second great flowering of the Arthurian legend. The last half of the eighteenth century had seen a steadily quickening interest in medieval literature and the publication of a growing body of that work, although very little of the longer narrative poetry of the Middle Ages had been restored to common day from the archives and libraries. Following the lead of amateurs and literary scholars, historians had also begun a slow process of revision of the rationalist disdain for the culture and institutions of Medieval Europe. If much of the growing enthusiasm seems today wide of the mark—sentimental thrill-seeking—it still represents a genuine progress toward sympathetic understanding of the Middle Ages. Nevertheless, no great expression of either the Middle Ages or the Arthurian legend grew out of the Pre-Romantic period. To some degree this might be explained as the result of simple ignorance of the great medieval romances. But far more effectively it is a result of the fact that the age was imaginatively and intellectually divided against itself. The pull of the old common-sense certainties rarely failed to clog the flights of the most "enthusiastic" imagination. Extravagance of feeling went unequally yoked with Rationalist notions of reality. It was not, however, an age of productive tension, but rather one of pathetically split sensibility, of emotional flux and imaginative indecision. And thus, as Evans has pointedly observed, "the eighteenth century in its striving toward a world of romantic imagination is led to antiquarianism, to literary forgery, to the tale of horror, but never the great poetic achievement."[124]

5 🦋 The Past Restored

ROMANTIC MEDIEVALISM
AS PREPARATION
FOR ARTHUR'S RETURN

The fortunes of Arthurian story have been from the beginning closely linked with romanticism in the broad sense of that term. Indeed, the high Middle Ages, in which the legend first achieved great artistic expression, have been quite properly called the "Golden Age" of romanticism.[1] Only with the introduction of classical and pseudoclassical notions in the Renaissance had the story begun to lose vitality, and during the domination of Neo-Classicism it had died back completely, not to quicken again until the coming of the Romantic Revival. In the fully developed Romanticism of the first third of the nineteenth century, Arthurian story would once again excite wide interest among readers and poets, and serious new efforts would be made to adapt the old subject to the expressive needs of a new age.

There are a number of profound changes in the intellectual climate of the age that are obviously conducive to such an Arthurian revival. The discontent with the present, which had turned men's eyes to the past in the late eighteenth century, becomes increasingly strong in the new century. The half-hearted Gothicism of Walpole and Warton gives place to a full-fledged and passionately espoused Medievalism. The study and publication of medieval literature rises steadily toward flood tide. Out of such studies, particularly as they were absorbed and given new expression by Walter Scott and other antiquarian poets, and out of the Romantic validation of sympathy as a way of knowing, grows a new and vastly altered conception of the past. Both poets and historians begin to revive the Middle Ages not as a quaint and fortunately outgrown stage of man's progress, but rather as a living reality to which the present might well put itself to school. Seen in this light, the chivalry that had ideally governed Arthur's court could be regarded as a code for modern gentlemen; the Christian church of Arthur's time, as the model for modern piety; and the feudal organization of his land, as the pattern for a modern society.

Beyond such attitudes, there were deeper elements in the Romantic sensibility that were not merely congenial but even essential to an adequate treatment of the story of Arthur. The conviction that the ideal world was more real than the world of mere appearances, the rejection of the excogitated in favor of the imaginatively perceived, the preference for the products of the unconscious mind to those of rational calculation—all these bear a clear relationship to the problem of treating a story that is mythic in origin and suffused with spiritual idealism.

The conditions, then, for successful use of Arthurian story seem obviously to be present in the Romantic period. And a number of poets, both major and minor, did feel the attractions of the theme. Their attempts to grapple with it often show seriousness of purpose and a dawning comprehension of the problems posed by the legend. But in the end none of these new versions can be described as entirely successful. Even so, several of them are significant as pointing the direction that poets who would master the Arthurian story would have to take. That direction would involve first a fine respect for the basic outlines and the tragic spirit of the myth of Arthur and his reign. The new approach would also include a sensitive understanding of the essential setting of the story—a setting that was not medieval but rather quasi-medieval, for the story had taken place not in an archaeological past, but in an imagined past, the past of romance. This comprehension of the inviolability of the essential Arthurian story in its spirit and setting as well as in its events is, to a very large degree, the product of characteristically Romantic attitudes toward the past.

ROMANTIC MEDIEVALISM

An interest of some sort in the past is doubtless all but universal in imaginative men, but in the Romantic temperament the interest often amounts to something like obsession. The reasons are not far to seek. The process of stripping the "truth" bare, of de-mythologizing the world, which had begun in the seventeenth century, had continued unabated; but what Pope had welcomed as "light," for later poets was turning into "cold philosophy." As they watched, more and more of the "awful rainbow" of experience was being reduced to the "dull catalogue of common things." Instinctively, the Romantic poets and their readers sought to find a world safe for angels' wings. For some, of course, the search led to a world of inner experience safe from rational analysis, or to the world of children and simple primitives uncrippled by the reasonable and the proper.[2] But for many others, the way lay in the direction of the past—not so much the actual past as the fabled and fabling past. In this rejection of the present, the Romantics closely resembled the practice of the authors of medieval romance (from which, of course, the word Romantic had its origin). The past on which the romancers had drawn was a nebulous long ago; the past that attracted the nineteenth-century Romantics was quite particularly the Middle Ages.[3] Indeed, so marked is Romantic interest in the medieval past that Heine even identified Romanticism specifically as "the reawakening of the Middle Ages . . . a passion-flower blooming from the blood of Christ," and for Sismondi the defining themes of Romanticism were congruent with the three great motifs of medieval romance: love, religion, and chivalry.[4] If, as the obvious examples of Byron and Shelley remind us, such equations require considerable qualification, it is still possible to say that the Middle Ages largely replaced classical antiquity as the focus of Romantic historical interests.[5]

Nor is there much occasion for wonder in this selection of medieval times as a *beau ideal*. For the Romantic poets who turned to the past, the Middle Ages—above all other times—were the "obvious spiritual home," as F. L. Lucas puts it. They were "mystical, mysterious, and remote" and all the more attractive for having been "finally killed at the Renaissance by this hated Classicism."[6] Whether we define Romanticism as the pursuit of violent feelings, as a re-vindication of emotion and imagination, or as an affirmation of the superiority of the intuitive or spiritual over sense experience and scientific fact, it is clear that the Middle Ages, with their violence, their willingness to feel and believe, and their lack of interest in empirical observation, were ideally adapted to the needs of the Romantic temper.[7]

And there are other, perhaps deeper reasons for the sympathy that the Romantics felt for the Middle Ages. The relationship between nineteenth-century Romanticism and medieval romance is after all more than a matter of mere etymology. Each grows out of parallel though not identical impulses. In its longing to put aside the world of rationality and rigid social codes, and to liberate the unconscious or intuitive powers from the domination of the conscious mind,[8] Romanticism seeks to unleash the mythopoeic energies that in the Middle Ages had created the great romances of Arthur and his knights. Again, both romance and Romanticism are founded on revolt—the one against the purely theological ideals of medieval society, the other against the rationalist, mechanistic notions of later days.[9] Both are based on the idealization of human love beyond anything known to either classical or Neo-Classical conceptions.[10] Both are uninterested in the simple, factual, phenomenal world, and both are strongly attracted to the supernatural and the superrational. It is true that medieval poets and readers appear to have had quite naturally the

"suspension of disbelief" that for the Romantics would have to be qualified as "willing" or, sometimes, even, as "willed." And it is also true that
the revolt of the romancer aimed at uneasy compromise with the dominant theological values of medieval society rather than at open conflict.
But with all these discounts, the spiritual kinship of medieval romanticism
and nineteenth-century romanticism is clear. And it is this similarity of
informing spirit that properly distinguishes fully developed Romantic use
of the Middle Ages from the antiquarianism of the Pre-Romantics—the
time-eroded stones of Warton's Gothic battlements from the "argent
revelry" that fills Keats's medieval castle on the Eve of St. Agnes.

The earlier Romantic Medievalism that imaginatively warmed the
long ago to such glittering life did not in general aim at a historically
accurate reconstruction of the past. "Romanticism," Lascelles Abercrombie has said, "does not recollect the past; it fashions the past anew—as it
ought to have been."[11] The past that many of the Romantic poets thus
both half-created and half-perceived was not the Middle Ages of the historians, nor even the Middle Ages of authentic medieval literature. On
the contrary, it was frequently a vaguely medieval-ish past derived from
sources and filtered through imaginations that were anything but genuinely medieval. For Coleridge, struggling to escape from a world of
Godwinian rationalism, the "medieval" past afforded a world in which the
supernatural was natural, a refuge from the domination of "fact." Although Wordsworth looked but rarely at such early times, when he did so
he sought and found the unsophisticated goodness and simple endurance
he had discovered in the shepherds of his childhood.[12] For Keats, the
imagined past was filled with a sensuous opulence and gorgeous color that
could blot from the mind the smoke-blackened streets of London. In all
of these medievalisms—the plural is justifiable—it is clear that although
the earlier Romantics breathed a new life into the past, they made no
break with the sources of eighteenth-century medievalism. Their Middle
Ages were still the peculiar eighteenth-century conflation of historical
scraps and mangled ballads, the spurious medievalism of Chatterton and
Ossian, and the Renaissance survivals of medieval romance in Spenser
and other Elizabethans. From such soil, watered by the Romantic imagination, might grow *The Eve of St. Agnes* and *La Belle Dame sans Merci*,
Christabel and *The Ballad of the Dark Ladie*—poems which are not really
re-flowerings of medieval materials, but rather completely new species.
What did not, indeed could not, spring from that soil was a new flowering
of the Arthurian story. For that to happen a different medievalism was
needed—a medievalism in which the Romantic spirit would blend with a
loving study of the physical and spiritual texture of medieval life and of

the genuine medieval literature in which Arthurian story had first flourished.

SCOTT AS MEDIEVALIST

Paradoxically enough, the man who did most to bring about this new knowledge and understanding of the medieval past was the one writer among the great Romantics who most clearly harked back to the eighteenth century. Whether as antiquarian and editor of medieval texts, as popularizer of the Middle Ages through his verse and prose romances, or even as adapter of the Arthurian legend, Walter Scott was, as B. Ifor Evans pungently observes, "the eighteenth-century romantic, with genius added."[13] Unlike Coleridge and Keats, who combined physical elements or atmospheric qualities of a vague long ago into completely new wholes, Scott tirelessly sought to know the past as it actually had been and to reconstruct it with the minutest fidelity—at least insofar as such a reconstruction was consistent with his keen sense of what the public would welcome.

Scott's fascination with the past, begun in youth, nourished at the outset on eighteenth-century antiquarianism and later on German pseudo-medievalism, bore its first notable fruit in the ballad collection that he called the *Minstrelsy of the Scottish Border* (1802, 1803).[14] Like Bishop Percy's collection—the only one that exceeded Scott's in popularity and influence—the *Minstrelsy* is marked by extensive concessions to the official literary taste of the day and by a thorough sophistication of its texts in the direction of appealing to a popular audience rather than to scholars. Following the success of the *Minstrelsy*, Scott next contributed to the revival of medieval literature his edition of the thirteenth-century metrical romance *Sir Tristrem* (1804).[15] Since his MS was defective, he composed a pastiche conclusion based on the motif of the black or white sails, and thus restored to modern English readers for the first time one of the great stories connected with the Arthurian cycle.[16] In both this remarkable conclusion and in what Swinburne called the "mixture or alternation of lazy negligence with strenuous energy," which marked Scott's editorial work on occasion, Scott betrays his eighteenth-century origins.[17] Nevertheless, his antiquarian pursuits are marked everywhere by an infectious excitement, laborious industry, and wide if indiscriminate knowledge. And if his enthusiasm seems oddly naïve to modern scholars, and his freedom in handling early texts reprehensible, it must be remembered that his age would probably have ignored a colder and more accurate scholarship.

From popularizing the past through the revival of its own literature, Scott turned next to his own reconstructions of the past, first in a series of verse romances and later in a pageant of prose blendings of romance and the novel. The enormous popularity of these works, the extent to which they produced an emotional sympathy for the Middle Ages in a vast body of the most various readers, and their deep and wide-ranging influence on subsequent generations are almost impossible to exaggerate. Years later Newman would name Scott's romances as one of the great fostering elements of the Oxford Movement, and Young England owed even more to them.[18] Swinburne's praise of "the sovereign masterpieces . . . of the royal and imperial master, Sir Walter Scott," is no more than an echo of the feelings of all the Victorian poets and artists who turned to the Middle Ages for inspiration and materials.[19] Beyond youthful reformers and poets in search of new themes, Scott's influence made itself felt with equal strength among practical men of affairs and historians as various as Thierry, Macaulay, Ranke, and Barante.[20]

In any explanation of this popularity, something, doubtless, is due to Scott's own literary merits. But a great deal more is due to his remarkable tact—continued from his editorial labors—in adapting his materials to the tastes and expectations of his age. Thus Scott's verse romances such as *Marmion* and *The Lady of the Lake* are a subtle blending of medieval romance with the rugged spirit of the early ballads—a spirit that Scott's contemporaries had come to expect from "medieval" literature. "This crossbreeding," Fairchild observes, "did much to preserve the reputation of the medieval romance at a time when imitations of the genuine courtly article could have found favor with but few readers." And Scott was equally sensitive as to the materials that would interest his time. In both romances and historical novels, to quote Fairchild again, "he exploited chiefly those elements of the past which any normal reader of his own day would have found picturesque and exciting."[21] At the same time, Scott made no disturbing departure from the eighteenth-century program of adding to such pleasures the salutary medicine of historical instruction. The avowed intention of *The Lay of the Last Minstrel* was "to illustrate the customs and manners which anciently prevailed on the Borders of England and Scotland. . . . As the description of scenery and manners was more the object of the author than a combined and regular narrative, the plan of the Ancient Metrical Romances was adopted, which allows greater latitude in this respect than would be consistent with the dignity of a regular Poem."[22] This was not merely comforting—it went a long way toward guaranteeing success in an age which could thus satisfy its demand for edification while it freely indulged its appetite for romantic thrills.

And if the thrills often owed more to Gothic horror fiction, German and English, than to medieval sources, so much the better—they were just the thrills his audience expected of the Middle Ages.[23] Beneath such obvious reasons for Scott's popularity, there were other, perhaps deeper, appeals. "In showing feudalism and chivalry in gradual decay," Professor Neff notes, "Scott appealed to the loyal fears of a vast body of readers who, like himself, had seen the French Revolution menace their extinction."[24] And although the passing of time allayed the pangs of that traumatic event, time also brought with it new evils that endowed Scott's novels and poems with even stronger appeal. As more and more of English life was touched by the bleak monotony of industrialism and materialism, readers would increasingly turn to Scott's imaginary Middle Ages for color, vitality, and high idealism.[25] But whether it was out of historical curiosity, or in pursuit of the mysterious, or in flight from an ugly present that they read Scott, one thing is safe to say: no writer who came to maturity from the 1830's on—indeed, no Victorian of any intellectual pretensions at all—remained untouched by Sir Walter's glamour.

There remains to be considered what was, at least for his own age, perhaps the most important reason for Scott's popularity and influence, and at the same time the greatest fulfillment of the eighteenth-century antiquarianism from which he had sprung. "These Historical Novels," wrote Carlyle in 1838, "have taught all men this truth, which looks like a truism, and yet was as good as unknown to writers of history and others, till so taught: that the bygone ages of the world were actually filled by living men, not by protocols, state-papers, controversies and abstractions of men."[26] It seems an uncritical claim to the modern reader who summons to mind such sterling nonentities as Quentin Durward or even the engaging but still externally realized Louis XI. Yet if there are really no "living men" among the major figures in Scott's historical poems and novels, there is something that made Carlyle and the age think there was. There is a kind of life, or an illusion of life, produced not by the characters, but instead by the infinitely detailed stage settings, the lovingly reconstructed minutiae of daily life in the past. It was Scott's sheer informedness about the past that made possible such thickness of texture, but in his hands, the dead, impersonal facts that Warton and Strutt had collected and recorded so zealously were galvanized into a semblance of vitality.[27] To the twentieth-century reader, trained to look for psychological analysis or moral agony, it all may seem as tedious as the "protocols" and "controversies" Carlyle scoffed at. But to men of the nineteenth century, it was the opening of a new vision of the past, and the transition from the Gothicism of a few antiquarians to the fully developed Medievalism of the nineteenth century.

So ubiquitous, indeed, is the name of Scott in all the manifestations of nineteenth-century medievalism that it is not easy to escape the impression that he was the sole begetter of the Medieval Revival. Yet in fact, Scott was but the most popular exponent of a new attitude toward the Middle Ages that was working in the minds of men everywhere, and everywhere the gimcrack Gothicism and the sentimental, amateurish antiquarianism of the eighteenth century were yielding place to a progressively more educated, more informed, and more truly sympathetic medievalism. Something of this development in the plastic arts had already been visible in the shift from the Rococo Gothic, as Sir Kenneth Clark calls it, of Strawberry Hill, built at the opening of the Pre-Romantic period, to the much more impressive Romantic Gothic of Beckford's Fonthill Abbey, built at the end of the period.[28] Now, in the new century, both the popularity of Gothic architecture and the knowledgeableness of its admirers began to grow rapidly. After 1805, engravings of Gothic buildings made up almost all of the illustrations in the influential *Gentleman's Magazine*. In the same year Britton began to publish as a purely commercial venture a series of *Architectural Antiquities of Great Britain*, which were aimed at a wide audience and which brought to their readers for the first time archaeologically reliable notions of Gothic form. When they could afford it, the lovers of medieval architecture went further— they built their own Gothic buildings. At first the style was confined to residential architecture, but after the Church Building Act (1818) 174 of 214 new churches erected between 1818 and 1833 were more or less Gothic. Windsor Castle, completed in 1830, was also derived from the new and knowledgeable enthusiasm for Gothic architecture. Thus by the close of the Romantic period the place of Gothic was fully established once more, and a correspondingly thriving market had been created for ready-made Gothic ornaments in stone and wood as well as cast iron, cast stone, and even papier-mâché. Clearly, medievalism was becoming the dominant note in the architectural thought of a vast number of Englishmen.

The Medieval Revival was, of course, built of more than the detail-crowded pages of Scott's romances and the accurate reproductions of Gothic ornaments on country villas and Commissioners' churches. These are but the most dramatic evidences of the triumph of Medievalism that was to become ever more deeply and truly consolidated throughout the century. Scott may well have contributed more than any other to that victory, but he was still only one of a host of scholars, editors, and historians, at home and abroad, who both strengthened his lead and at the same time drew inspiration from his example.

THE NEW HISTORY

In Europe, the great intellectual movement toward the rehabilitation of the Middle Ages found some of its most effective proponents among historians, over whom the impulses of both poetic and nationalist romanticism exercised full sway. As early as 1774 Herder had demanded that reason be supplemented by feeling in the study of the past. Man's development, he urged, had been no mechanical process, but rather an organic growth comprehensible only by sympathy, a willingness to apply other standards of judgment to other times. Observed thus, the Middle Ages, despite some dark passages, revealed great accomplishments in learning, the arts, and in social institutions such as chivalry and the church.[29] Herder's views were soon to be confirmed by an even more forceful argument against Rationalist historiographical attitudes—the French Revolution, an event that "drew together firmly the converging lines of Romantic literature and historical works of similar inspiration," as Professor Neff says. "By writing large the fact that no society is exempt from change, it forced men to contemplate the past, whether with regret of something lost whose charm was only fully perceived in the losing, or for aid and example in building toward a better future."[30] Herder's notions thus fell on fertile ground. In Germany they resulted in a school of historians of Teutonic origins, such as Jacob Grimm, in such sympathetic chroniclers of the medieval church as Neander, and most importantly in the romantic nationalist historians like Böhmer, Wilken, Voigt, Raumer, and Luden. Inspired and sensitized by romanticism, these men turned to the Middle Ages for exotic excitement. Saddened and frustrated by the divisions and defeats of German nationalist impulses, they drew from the Middle Ages stories of German greatness. As Luden put it for them all, "The need of self-respect sent us back to our fathers."[31] The picture which they painted contributed largely to the formation of a widespread sympathetic attitude toward the Middle Ages, and in the case of Raumer's *Hohenstaufen* (1823–1825), provided material for a host of subsequent artistic treatments of the Middle Ages.

Among French historians, also, the Romantic movement inspired a new appraisal of the Middle Ages, though here the seminal work was that of the romantic devotee Chateaubriand, whose *Génie du Christianisme* (1802), a strange melange of narrative, emotional religiosity, and Catholic apologetics, roused the Middle Ages to glowing life. Under his influence,

Michaud's *Histoire des croisades* (1811) reversed the eighteenth century's contemptuous view of that great quest. Chateaubriand's emotion also had its part in Thierry's *Conquête d'Angleterre* (1825), but the real inspiration of Thierry's combination of erudition with imaginative color and warmth was Walter Scott. Barante's scholarly yet moving *Histoire des ducs de Bourgogne* (1824) shows the same influence.[32] As in Germany, these new historians did much to gain a sympathetic hearing for the Middle Ages among the general public.

In England, however, the influence of Romantic notions on professional historians was comparatively slight, and the contribution of such historians to the Medieval Revival was correspondingly smaller. In a sense, Scott, a poet and novelist, was, as Herford pointed out long ago, "the true Romantic historian of [the] period."[33] Abroad, he had taught historians how to bring the Middle Ages alive with color and warmth, but his romantic approach to historiography touched his soberer countrymen far less.[34] Nevertheless, study and reappraisal of the Middle Ages occupied the attention of a number of important English historians. Sharon Turner (whose work Scott had studied with profit) initiated professional study of the English Middle Ages in his *History of the Anglo-Saxons* (1799–1805) and his *History of England from the Norman Conquest to 1509* (1814–1823). The first of these works he saw as illustrating "the conversion of ferocious pirates, into a highly civilized, informed, and generous people," and in the second he argued that the Middle Ages, despite the neglect of them by previous historians, were the period "within which our political relation, our religion, literature, language, manners, laws, and constitution, have been chiefly formed."[35] But for all his enthusiasm, Turner had lost more than the eighteenth century's contempt for the Middle Ages; he had also lost its ability to make history popular. His style is heavy, his attitude moralizing, and his narrative lacking in clarity, vigor, and color. Lingard's *Antiquities of the Anglo-Saxon Church* (1806) and his *History of England* (1819–1830) not only shared the defects of Turner's work, but also substituted a chilly objectivity for Turner's enthusiasm. While his work contributed to the state of knowledge of the English Middle Ages, Lingard himself had little sympathy with one of the central institutions of his period, chivalry, and still less for the Medieval revival in his own time.[36] An even more stubbornly "enlightened" attitude marks what has been called "the first great history after Gibbon," Hallam's *View of the State of Europe During the Middle Ages* (1818).[37] Suspicious of Romantic illusions about the past, convinced that miracles were but the impostures of a church whose history was "one long contention of fraud against robbery" recorded in the "annals of barbarism," Hallam lacked the most elementary imaginative sympathy with his subject.[38] His instinct for analysis rather than dramatization and his contempt for the picturesque fully justified Mignet's judgment that he had "rather the intelligence than the sentiment of the past."[39] Still, he did devote a long history to a serious, carefully prepared, and often finely reasoned survey of the period. He and his predecessors, Turner and Lingard, along with a number of lesser historians of similar bent, clearly contributed much to English knowledge of the Middle Ages. But at the same time, it is equally clear that among professional historians in England there was no parallel to the fervently passionate approach of re-creation seen in the Continental Romantic historians. The works of the British historians lacked color, warmth, poetic attractiveness, and it is thus only to be expected that their direct effect on the artistic and popular Medieval Revival was little more than negligible.

MEDIEVALIST PROPAGANDISTS

While dispassionateness marked the approach of the academic historians to medieval times, the same can scarcely be said of a group of publicists and men of letters who began in the 1820's to turn from Scott's romantic interest in the past for its own sake to a full validation of the Middle Ages as a repository of vital lessons for the present. All of these men would have agreed with Carlyle's later announcement of purpose: "We will . . . strive to penetrate a little . . . into a somewhat remote Century; and to look face to face on it, in hope of perhaps illustrating our own poor Century thereby."[40] Charged with serious purpose and high enthusiasm, Cobbett, Southey, and Kenelm Henry Digby portrayed a Middle Ages not below the present in physical and spiritual well-being, but instead well above it. Drawing on Lingard for his information and on his own violent dislike of Protestant prejudice for his vigor, Cobbett in his *History of the Protestant Reformation* (1824) presented contrast after contrast between a happy, secure Middle Ages under a unified Church and a nineteenth century plagued with industrial misery and spiritual unrest.[41] Even more influential were Southey's *Colloquies* (1829), two volumes of imaginary conversations with Sir Thomas More. While Southey, whose sympathies were scarcely Romanist, attempts to give a somewhat more balanced view of the past than Cobbett, he still provides a number of contrasts highly partial to the Middle Ages; "bad as the feudal times were," he observes, "they were less injurious than these commercial ones to the kindly and generous feelings of human nature, and far, far more favourable to the principles of honour and integrity."[42] For an age in which the premium placed on "kindly and generous feelings" indicates a nagging fear of emotional and spiritual dryness, the appeal of such a picture of the Middle Ages was immediate, and the influence of both Cobbett and Southey in popularizing the Medieval Revival was understandably enormous. So direct was the influence of Southey on the earliest political action group with medievalist aims that George Smythe did not hesitate to call him the true founder of the Young England movement.[43]

Another crucial formative influence on the movement and the oddest of the romantic medievalists was Kenelm Henry Digby (1800–1880), a man who has been virtually forgotten today.[44] Yet in his own day Digby touched some of the finer minds of the age, and few medievalists had more influence than he. His youthful conversion to Roman Catholicism bore strange fruit in an equally youthful book, *The Broad Stone of Honour, or Rules for the Gentlemen of England* (1822), an extraordinary fusion or confusion of Scottian medievalism, romantic Catholicism, English and German Gothicism, and enthusiasm for chivalric romance and Wordsworthian nature.[45] Digby's three great subjects are the Middle Ages, Christianity, and Chivalry, and his approach to them is by means of a "history of heroic times, arranged chiefly with a view to convey lessons of surviving and perpetual interest to the generous part of mankind," or as he elsewhere puts it, a "history of the middle ages, as far as it concerns the origin, spirit, and institutions of Christian Chivalry."[46] Some idea of the scope as well as of the desultory arrangement of this "history" may be suggested by an abridgement of the Argument of one volume:

> Religion in all ages essential to Chivalry . . . How the Crusades may be justified . . . To defend the Catholic faith a perpetual obligation . . . Laws of Chivalry were directed to make men religious . . . Examples of devout Knights . . . Of Hermits and Monastic Orders . . . The charity and benevolence of ancient manners . . . The profound and solemn spirit of Knights . . . The doctrine of the holy Angels . . . On the love which men had for the ceremonies and offices of the Church . . . How everything bore a devotional aspect . . . That the Middle Ages were ages of great virtue.[47]

But it is impossible to convey by practicably brief quotation the curious texture of the work: its endless seriatim marshaling of quotation, allusion, and anecdote from every conceivable source; its naïve jumbling of fact and fiction, of quotations from the speeches of Malory's characters cheek by jowl with others from Wordsworth and grave doctors of the church; its narrative elements from German horror fiction and its language from Wardour Street.[48] Yet for all its hortatory rhetoric, its slightly crack-brained pietism, its vulgarly argued *noblesse oblige*, and its grossly sentimentalized version of medieval life, it is not difficult to understand the book's appeal to two generations of young men. What youthful idealist (or snob) could have remained untouched by Digby's challenge:

> You are born a Gentleman. This is a high privilege, but are you aware of its obligations? It has pleased God to place you in a post of honour; but are you conscious that it is one which demands high and peculiar qualities? Such, however, is the fact. The rank which you have to support requires not so much an inheritance, or the acquisition of wealth and property, as of elevated virtue and spotless fame.[49]

True, to a more skeptical age, Digby's medieval chivalry is the chivalry of Scott in his most benevolent vision of the Middle Ages, and his medieval atmosphere in reality is the atmosphere of the Gothic novels, but of such were made the Middle Ages that his readers stood ready to receive. With the addition of what amounts to a society of initiates and an admirable combination of ethical idealism, aesthetic ritualism, and youthful piety, the mixture was irresistible. Young England was swept off its feet, and the vision of Lord John Manners, Ambrose de Lisle Philips, even of John Ruskin, was colored forever by the young man who had once kept his knightly vigil in King's College Chapel, his ears echoing with the clashing swords and solemn speeches of Arthur and his knights.[50]

The Medievalist apologists—Digby, Cobbett, and Southey—did little, of course, to create an objective image of the Middle Ages. Quite the contrary—they made an impossible Golden Age of feudal times. Nevertheless, they did contribute to something ultimately much more important for the Medieval Revival—the development of a wide audience for whom the Middle Ages became a daily imaginative reality, a standard point of reference, a familiar and beloved home of the spirit. Their view was an illusioned one, doubtless, but in that fact lay the very source of its strength.

MEDIEVAL ROMANCE RESTORED

Nevertheless, the illusion was increasingly built during the Romantic period on a more and more thorough and accurate knowledge of medieval literature. There is, of course, no real paradox in this—the poetry of the Middle Ages is itself the stuff of dreams, just as Arthur was the monarch of an imagined Golden Age. The appetite for earlier literature, stimulated at first by the conflated ballads and occasional scraps of longer medieval narrative published in the preceding century, was now ready for more and stronger meat, and a procession of editors, scholars, and critics rushed to satisfy its demands.

With the death of Joseph Ritson in 1803, most of the great eighteenth-century editors were gone from the scene. Their places were taken by a new generation of scholars with materially different attitudes, interests, and methods. Whether it was Ritson's shrill ghost still ranging for revenge, or only an inevitable intellectual development that brought the change, the nineteenth-century editors show a considerable advance in accuracy, exactness, and respect for their texts. By modern standards, it is true, their work seems occasionally marred by mistaken theorizing, desultory research, fanciful linguistic manipulation, and an enviably easy assumption of competence to undertake any inquiry. But at the same time there is a fine excitement, an admirable industry, and an impressive knowledgeableness in the new publications.[51]

The shift in expressed attitudes toward the publication of early texts is less marked. The eighteenth-century justification of such publications as ancillary to historical studies persisted in a half-hearted fashion throughout the Romantic period. Earlier literature, David Laing observed in 1822, was "valuable, no less in enabling us to trace the history and progress of our language, than in assisting us to illustrate ancient manners and amusements, of which [it] often contain[s] the liveliest representations," but he also asserted proudly that "little apology . . . will be looked for, on submitting to the Publick a collection . . . of our Ancient Popular Poetry[, which is] allowed to possess a value, sanctioned by Time, of which neither prejudice nor fashion can deprive [it]."[52] A few years earlier, Utterson, with a glance in the direction of Walter Scott, had chosen a new line of defense for the new editions of earlier literature: they afforded poets "interesting images of ancient manners, which, chosen by taste, and remodelled by genius, tend to enliven the narrative, and increase its interest."[53] But, as the lameness of such arguments suggests, medieval literature was increasingly being edited, published, and read for its own sake. Utterson himself admitted that the publication of earlier literature no longer threw important new light on the past; at best it only afforded "corroboration of former conjecture, which is thus strengthened into conviction."[54] The fact is that "fashion" and "prejudice" were all in favor of medieval literature. A public composed exclusively of historians, philologists, and poets could scarcely account for the volume of publication of early texts in the first third of the century, nor does it seem likely that such a public alone could have supported the foundation of the great book clubs and publishing societies through which so many medieval texts were now beginning to find their way to the light of day again.[55]

But it is the preference of the early nineteenth-century editors and their public for medieval romance as opposed to balladry that marks the greatest departure from the traditions of the preceding century. Scott himself had followed the new direction when he turned from the *Minstrelsy* to the editing of *Sir Tristrem*. Besides such editions of separate romances, the period between 1800 and 1829 was to see the publication of no less than eight collections including or made up entirely of early romances. The first to appear, Ritson's *Ancient Engleish Metrical Romanceës* (1802) included several Arthurian pieces (*Ywain and Gawain, Launfal, Libeaus Desconus*, and *The Marriage of Sir Gawain*) and a preface and extensive annotations revealing the extraordinary breadth of Ritson's knowledge of Arthurian literature.[56] The next two collections, Henry Weber's *Metrical Romances* (1810)[57] and Utterson's *Select Pieces of Early Popular Poetry* (1817), although they included no Arthurian material, made large additions to the stock of romances available to modern readers. In 1822 David Laing included *The Awntyrs off Arthure* in his *Select Remains of the Ancient Popular Poetry of Scotland*, a collection which he followed up in 1826 with his *Early Metrical Tales*.[58] Hartshorne's *Ancient Metrical Tales* (1829) also played a part in popularizing medieval metrical romance.[59] The market for English prose romances appears to have been more limited. At any rate, when Thoms in his *Collection of Early Prose Romances* (1827–1828) set out to do for the prose romances what Ritson and others had done for the metrical romances, the response to his work, which included the Arthurian *Tom a Lincolne*, was disappointingly small.[60]

The extent to which these collections restored medieval English romance to nineteenth-century England was considerable, but their direct effect on the Arthurian revival was slight. The Arthurian romances included in the collections were few and for the most part inferior English renderings of Continental versions. It was rather through collections of "specimens" or abstracts that the central Arthurian story as it had appeared in the great French forms and in the better English versions was made available in the first years of the century, and this process of popularization was largely the work of one scholar—George Ellis (1753–1815), whose eighteenth-century rearing is apparent in the ironic detachment that qualified his enthusiasm for medieval literature. His first contribution to the Arthurian revival was made in 1801 when he added to the second edition of his *Specimens of the Early English Poets* a series of parallel passages dealing with the festivities at Arthur's coronation and drawn from Geoffrey, Wace, Laȝamon, and Robert of Gloucester.[61] Four years later Ellis published his *Specimens of Early English Metrical Ro-*

mances (1805), a heterogeneous collection of abstracts, prose résumés, and generally brief quotations from the originals.[62] In the book's lengthy, erudite, and closely reasoned "Historical Introduction Intended to Illustrate the Rise and Progress of Romantic Composition in France and England" and in the text itself, Ellis supplied a detailed account of the central Arthurian story and its development. After a brief consideration of Gildas and Nennius, he gives a full summary of Geoffrey, which is followed by an examination of the Welsh Arthurian materials, some of which were already being published in *The Myvyrian Archaiology of Wales* (1801–1807).[63] After this study of the origins of the Arthurian legend, Ellis goes on in a section devoted to "Romances Relating to King Arthur" to give detailed résumés (interspersed with quotations) of *Arthour and Merlin* and the stanzaic *Le Morte Arthur*.[64] Where his romances left the legend incomplete, Ellis supplied from other sources an account of the birth and rearing of Lancelot and illustrated that hero's relations with Guinevere by including a summary of Chrétien's *Conte de la Charette*. Ellis' method of linked prose summaries was also adopted by John Dunlop in his *History of Fiction* (1814), in which a comprehensive view of the Arthurian cycle is provided by means of carefully joined résumés of such French prose romances as *Merlin*, the *St. Graal*, *Perceval*, *Lancelot du Lac*, *Tristan*, and *Artus*.[65]

The fact that a second edition of Dunlop's book was called for in two years suggests its popularity; its influence on the Arthurian revival, however, appears to have been slight.[66] But the influence of Ellis' work is manifest. Fairchild's assertion that it "did for medieval romance almost what Percy's *Reliques* had done for the medieval ballad,"[67] may involve some exaggeration, but it is exaggeration of the truth. The contribution of Ellis' *Specimens of Early English Metrical Romances* to the revival of Arthurian romance is understandably large. For the first time in the modern period, Ellis presented a rounded, coherent, and faithful view of the central Arthurian story; his lucid prose eliminated the discouraging linguistic difficulties of the original texts; and his elegant summaries eliminated the more obvious *longueurs* of his sources. In short, the essence of the legend in a comprehensible and easily readable form was restored to modern readers. Little wonder then that for the generation that was young in 1805, "George-Ellis-specimens" could be used almost as a synonym for chivalric romance, and less wonder that incidents from his account would become part of the imaginative staple of the minds of poets and other ordinary, nonscholarly readers.[68]

What is surprising in all this publication of medieval romance and the accompanying revival of interest in the Arthurian cycle is the fact that

Malory's *Le Morte Darthur*, the one great compilation in English of the whole body of Arthurian romance, should have remained so long out of print. Among scholars and antiquarians, of course, knowledge of Malory's work had never lapsed completely, and as early as the middle of the eighteenth century Warton had focused considerable attention on the book. Percy and Ritson were well acquainted with Malory, and Scott in 1803 spoke of the book as being "in the hands of most antiquaries and collectors."[69] Nevertheless, *Le Morte Darthur* had not been reprinted since Stansby's corrupt version of 1634; and in the nearly two centuries since that edition, it and the previous editions must surely have become scarce.[70] At the same time an extensive market for a new edition was being created. Ellis had borrowed from Malory Sir Ector's noble lamentation over Launcelot's body for the conclusion to his "Romances Relating to King Arthur."[71] Scott in 1803 had described *Le Morte Darthur* as "a work of great interest, . . . curiously written in excellent old English, and breathing a high tone of chivalry."[72] Later, addressing himself to a wider, more popular audience in *Marmion* (1808), he praised the book more enthusiastically:

> The romance of the Morte Arthur contains a sort of abridgement of the most celebrated adventures of the Round Table; and being written in comparatively modern language, gives the general reader an excellent idea of what romances of chivalry actually were. It has also the merit of being written in pure old English; and many of the wild adventures which it contains are told with a simplicity bordering upon the sublime.[73]

These "wild adventures," Scott somewhat disingenuously told his readers, he "would have illustrated . . . by more full extracts," except that "this curious work is about to be republished."[74] It was, in fact, about to be "edited" by Scott himself, who had told the publisher Millar in October of 1807: "I have referred to this curious work so frequently in Marmion that I am sure if that poem sell[,] a small edition of the romance [i.e., *Le Morte Darthur*] will go off."[75]

Yet for all the build-up, the projected edition did not appear. Learning that Southey was preparing an edition of Malory for Longmans, Scott, with characteristic generosity, resigned the project to him. Southey, who had declared that if there "were . . . an Academy of the Round Table, I believe myself worthy of a seat there in point of knowledge," had taken up the task as "work after my own heart."[76] But for some reason Longmans appears to have delayed the printing of the work, and two years later (1809) it became Southey's turn to relinquish the editing of *Le*

Morte Darthur in favor of Scott, in whose hands, now busied with more profitable activities, the project finally languished altogether.[77] The net result of this perverse comedy of errors was that the first nineteenth-century appearance of Malory was delayed for almost a decade after the time had obviously been ripe for its republication.

When Malory's *Le Morte Darthur* was finally reprinted, three separate editions appeared in the space of two years. The first of these, published in 1816 by Walker and Edwards as *The History of the Renowned Prince Arthur, King of Britain*, is no more than an ill-edited and inaccurate reprint of Stansby's expurgated 1634 edition.[78] The other edition to appear in 1816 was published by R. Wilks under the title of *La Mort d'Arthur* and is said to have been edited by one Joseph Haslewood. It too is based on the 1634 text, but despite its shrill claims of superiority to the Walker and Edwards edition, it is if anything inferior. Not content with retaining most of the errors of the 1634 edition or even with adding yet others through the compositors' misreading of the black letter of the original, Haslewood felt obliged to further expurgate his already expurgated source:

> . . . some sentences highly needed pruning, to render the text fit for the eye of youth; and that it might be no longer secreted from the fair sex. This has led to a very careful revisal of the whole Work; every indecent allusion has been carefully expunged; and the work may now, with confidence, be placed in the hands of the most scrupulous. But the objectionable and, indeed, obscene passages are certainly preserved in the rival edition of two volumes. . . . The name of our great Redeemer, which too often occurs in the original . . . has . . . been varied to a simple appeal to Heaven, or the attribute of mercy.[79]

Haslewood's tender concern for "youth" and "the fair sex," and the miniature format of the volumes, which required excruciatingly small type in both of the 1816 editions, indicate clearly that both publishers had a wide, popular body of readers in mind. By contrast, the sumptuous quarto volumes of *The Byrth, Lyf, and Actes of King Arthur*, which Southey finally "edited" for Longmans in 1817, testify that this, the third nineteenth-century edition of Malory, was aimed at a narrower, not to say more affluent, audience.[80] The lengthy Preface, for which Southey had read "much black letter, at some cost of eyesight and no little expense of time"[81] displays, as Wright acidulously observed, "the extensive and indiscriminate reading for which the poet was celebrated, but [does] little towards explaining or illustrating his text."[82] Nevertheless, the book had its value in making available once more through a generally accurate reprinting the text of Caxton's 1485 edition.[83] Thus by the end of 1817, after nearly two centuries of neglect, Malory's "noble and Ioyous hystorye of the grete conquerour and excellent kyng[,] Kyng Arthur" had been suddenly restored in three editions to a body of readers no longer composed only of "noble prynces[,] lordes and ladyes[,] gentylmen or gentylwymmen," but including scholars and poets and plain readers of all conditions of life.[84]

Whatever else publishers may be accused of, insensitivity to what the public wants can scarcely be numbered among their faults. It seems reasonable to suppose that the almost simultaneous appearance of three editions of Malory was the result of the expectation of a large and ready market for Arthurian literature.[85] Something of that expectation probably also operated in the belated publication in 1825 of Joseph Ritson's *Life of King Arthur*, a book which Ritson's publishers had summarily refused a generation earlier.[86] Ritson's intention in this remarkable work was, as his biographer has summarized it, "to provide an authentic source-book of the trustworthy passages in medieval history and literature dealing with the beginnings of the Arthurian legend."[87] "No character, eminent in ancient history," Ritson declared with customary vehemence, "has ever been treated with more extravagance, mendacity and injustice than the renowned Arthur," particularly in the "romantic fables" of Geoffrey of Monmouth and the shameless lies and forgeries of the monks of Glastonbury.[88] As to just what might be accepted as historical fact after the fabulous elements had been dissolved away, Ritson was a great deal less positive. Indeed, he nowhere declares directly for a belief in Arthur's historicity. But while the total effect of the book is somewhat inconclusive, the skeptical objectivity, the careful reasoning, and the extraordinary erudition that he brought to his task fully justify Annette Hopkins' estimate of Ritson as the "first modern Arthurian scholar." Though his work has been undeservedly ignored, Ritson clearly "introduced or revived, and in some instances solved, a surprising number of problems which are commonly supposed to have originated with Arthurian scholars from the mid-nineteenth century, on, or at least not to have been critically dealt with before."[89] Ritson's *Life of King Arthur* appears to have been equally neglected in its own time. That its relegation of practically every poetically useful element of Arthur's career to the status of fiction should have had so little consequence on the very eve of the great Victorian revival of the matter of Arthur is eloquent testimony of how completely insignificant the question of Arthur's historicity had become to the artistic use of the legend.[90]

THE ARTHURIAN THEME AND THE MAJOR ROMANTICS

Thus by the last years of the Romantic period proper a climate of opinion richly sympathetic to Arthurian story had come into being. This responsiveness had not, of course, developed overnight, and, indeed, the fact is that most of the major Romantic poets remained relatively untouched by the great theme.[91] To some extent this is to be explained by the slowness with which mythic materials in general—so long banished during the Enlightenment—were reinstated in the ranks of viable, serious poetic subjects. Again, various idiosyncrasies of the poets themselves doubtless militated against the use of Arthurian materials. But probably most important was the matter of chronological accident. Extensive republication of authentic Arthurian romance had not begun until well after the end of the impressionable, formative years of these poets. Blake was born in 1757, Wordsworth in 1770, Coleridge in 1772, and thus, excepting always those writers with a specifically antiquarian bent, the legend could have had but little place in the most central imaginative fiber of the minds of the earlier Romantic poets.

In the poetry of William Blake, the earliest born of these poets, despite Northrop Frye's assertion that Arthurian myth was "integral to Blake's symbolism," there appears to be no clear reference to Arthur, and certainly no recounting of the Arthurian legend.[92] Yet Blake wac acquainted in a rather confusing way with some elements of the story—probably through Geoffrey of Monmouth, Milton's *History of Britain*, certain Welsh materials, and a variety of antiquarian sources.[93] These sources, together with his own mystical elaborations of what he found in them, seem to have been the foundation of one of the "portable frescoes" exhibited in 1809—a work, now lost, advertised as "The Ancient Britons—Three Ancient Britons overthrowing the Army of armed Romans; the Figures full as large as Life—from the Welch Triades."[94] This picture, described by Blake with characteristic innocence as "not inferior to the grandest Antiques," portrayed the "last Battle of King Arthur" from which "only Three Britons escaped; these were the Strongest Man, the Beautifullest Man, and the Ugliest Man; these three marched through the field unsubdued, as Gods, and the Sun of Britain set, but shall arise again with tenfold splendour when Arthur shall awake from sleep, and resume his dominion over earth and ocean."[95] Along with these three Britons, who signified respectively "the human sublime," "the human pathetic," and "the human reason," the picture included a battlefield strewn with armored Romans and naked Britons, dead and dying, a bard playing on his harp as he succumbs, Druid temples "similar to Stone Henge," and a sun sinking behind the mountains, "bloody with the day of battle."

However strange this conflation may sound to modern ears, the mixture of history, romance, and Ossianism, in which Arthur is outfitted with a band of naked Britons and made to fight his last great battle not against the Saxons, but against the Romans, seemed perfectly proper to Blake:

> This picture . . . supposes that in the reign of that British Prince, who lived in the fifth century, there were remains of those naked Heroes in the Welch Mountains; they are there now, Gray saw them in the person of his bard on Snowdon; there they dwell in naked simplicity; happy is he who can see and converse with them above the shadows of generation and death. The Giant Albion, was Patriarch of the Atlantic; he is the Atlas of the Greeks, one of those the Greeks called Titans. The stories of Arthur are the acts of Albion, applied to a Prince of the fifth century, who conquered Europe, and held the Empire of the world in the dark age, which the Romans never again recovered. In this Picture, believing with Milton the ancient British History, Mr. B. has done as all the ancients did, and as all the moderns who are worthy of fame, given the historical fact in its poetical vigour.

In Blake's time, all this was scarcely as mad as it may seem today. As Professor Hungerford has shown, Blake is here following very closely in the footsteps of various speculative mythographers who, during the last quarter of the eighteenth century, came close to dominating the study of mythology and cultural origins.[96] Among these earnest researchers, a conception that might be called a monomyth theory became a standard way of dealing with the myths of the past. Thus Blake was on what seemed to him solid ground in his explanation of the equation of Albion, Atlas, and Arthur: "The antiquities of every Nation under Heaven, is [sic] no less sacred than that of the Jews. They are the same thing, as Jacob Bryant and all antiquaries have proved."[97] Blake's willingness to alter the received "facts" of Arthur's career only reflects another notion current among the mythographers: that all myths had been corrupted in later times. Hence it was necessary to reduce the myths to their "original" form. By this process the identity of the various myths became wonderfully clear. And, since the original myths were, it was assumed, divine communications to men, these "restored" myths could be used by a poet like Blake both to make his own visions clear, and to authenticate them. The attractiveness of such theories to the visionary Blake is obvious, and his description of his picture "The Ancient Britons" is testimony to how far he followed them.

The effect on a later audience with rather different notions about myth and tradition is another thing. Those of us unhappily confined to the "shadows of generation and death" may well wonder at Arthur's last battle being waged against the Romans, who, as a matter of clear historical fact, had abandoned Britain over a century before the reputed date of the battle of Camlann. We may even wonder whether past events so thoroughly subordinated to "poetical vigour" have any claim to be called "historical fact" at all. But one thing we can have no doubt about: the fact that even the highly independent and original Blake was as late as the first decade of the nineteenth century still dominated in his treatment of Arthurian story by something of the same naïve historicism and antiquarianism which had molded and marred the various Pre-Romantic treatments of the legend.

Of the other important Romantic poets whose careers opened before the turn of the century, only one, Walter Scott, was largely affected by Arthurian story. Doubtless both Wordsworth and Coleridge in their youth knew something of the adventures of the legendary king through the scraps of Arthurian material printed in the ballad collections and through Percy's notes in the *Reliques*, a book to which, said Wordsworth in 1815, every "able writer in verse of the present day" was indebted.[98] But such slight acquaintance was not sufficient to move either of them to take up the old legend. Wordsworth's admiration for the *Reliques* was an admiration for what he regarded as the simplicity and freedom from affectation of England's earlier literature rather than for its subject matter. In his sixties—after he had read Malory—he would, it is true, attempt an Arthurian poem, but by that time the central fires of his poetic imagination had long been banked.[99] Coleridge, who responded more creatively to the eighteenth-century medievalism of his youth, did write a number of vaguely medievalistic poems, but to the Arthurian story he made no allusion except for one passing reference to Merlin.[100] By the time the whole story of Arthur was once more available, the poet Coleridge had disappeared into clouds of metaphysical speculation at Highgate, and in any event he had customarily turned to the past for atmosphere, not for story. The other Lake poet, Southey, might much more reasonably have been expected to write an Arthurian poem. Antiquarian by inclination, medievalist and conservative, practiced editor and translator of romances, and writer of lengthy verse epics based on romantic and more or less traditionary themes, Southey had begun his acquaintance with Arthurian story in early youth. "When I was a schoolboy," he tells us, "I possessed a wretchedly imperfect copy [of Malory], and there was no book, except the Faery Queen, which I perused so often, or with such deep contentment."[101] But when he grew older, as MacCallum has pointed out, the irregularities, both ethical and aesthetic, of genuine medieval romance shocked Southey, upset his judgment, and led him to prefer the prim and tedious *Amadis of Gaul* to *Le Morte Darthur*.[102] All that was left to memorialize the schoolboy's enthusiasm—and superior taste—was a valueless introduction to an unedited edition of Malory and a stray allusion in *Madoc* (1805) to the "crystal Ark" in which "sailed Merlin with his band of Bards."[103] Southey's fellow antiquarian Scott suffered no such change of heart; the full responsiveness of his boyhood to the world of old romance underwent no diminution in "the light of common day." And thus he alone of the major figures of the first generation of Romantic poets was destined to make an influential contribution to Arthurian literature.[104]

By the springtime years of the second generation of Romantics—Byron (b. 1788), Shelley (b. 1792), Keats (b. 1795)—the Arthurian story, albeit in fragmentary, curtailed form, had become much more accessible through the publications of Ellis, Scott, Weber, and other antiquarians. Yet none of the three produced an Arthurian work. Byron, whose Rationalist skepticism and admiration for the Neo-Classicists must go a long way toward qualifying the conventional image of him as the arch-Romantic, appears to have had a general contempt for medievalism, a contempt only the stronger for his political liberalism. The one Arthurian poem that he seems to have valued was Hookham Frere's burlesque of the theme, and here it was not the story but the form and manner that he admired and soon emulated.[105] As for Shelley, it is clear that neither his Godwinian rationalism nor his revolutionary political attitudes would have been very consistent with a sympathy for medieval romance or medieval chivalry, even had he been conversant with them, which, in fact, he was not.[106] At any rate, the whole of Shelley's poetic work contains nothing Arthurian beyond a single trivial reference to "Merlin's prophecy."[107]

Of the great triumvirate of later Romantics, Keats alone was equipped with the sensibility and sympathy to have taken up the Arthurian story. He "of all the romantic poets," as Professor Fairchild observes, "derive[d] the most nourishment from the beauty of olden things as preserved by the genius of the past." His various poems with medieval themes show a steady progress from Spenserian medievalism and "excessive reliance on inferior contemporaries and on eighteenth-century medievalists to direct personal contact with the works of the great writers of the past," Dante, Chaucer, Boccaccio.[108] Although his knowledge of the Arthurian story may have been limited at first to what he could glean from the résumés in Dunlop's *History of Fiction*, he also had one of the 1816 editions of Malory among his books.[109] By 1818 his familiarity with the material was sufficient to permit him to relish fully and report in detail Charles Brown's amusingly indecent banter turning on such Arthurian characters as the Lady of the Lake and the Lord of the Isles.[110] But the trip on which he had laughed at Brown's Arthurian puns was cut short by Keats's developing an ominously sore throat. The seed that had been planted in Keats's fertile imagination never grew beyond a sprout, the allusion to Merlin in *The Eve of St. Agnes* (1819): "Never on such a night have lovers met, / Since Merlin paid his Demon all the monstrous debt."[111] No "high-piléd books" were to "hold like rich garners the full-ripened grain" of the Arthurian poetry that Keats might have written. With his delight in the texture of the past, his instinctive sympathy for the "huge cloudy symbols of . . . high romance," his perfect tact in handling antique materials, and his rapidly increasing intellectual and moral seriousness in the last work, it is hard not to believe that Arthurian literature may well have lost one of its most splendid chapters through Keats's death at twenty-five.

6 ❦ Arthur Wakes in Avalon

ARTHURIAN LITERATURE OF THE ROMANTIC PERIOD

Although the major Romantics largely ignored the mythic king, the attractiveness of his story to the poetically inclined was very much on the rise. Thus the first third of the nineteenth century saw the appearance of almost twice as many treatments of the Arthurian legend as had been produced during the entire century preceding. None of these new attempts is wholly successful, to be sure, but the range of approaches they exhibit is of considerable interest and significance. Some of the least satisfactory, the poems of Thelwall and Frere and the prose fictions of Peacock, look back quite obviously to the arbitrarily inventive approach of Dryden and Richard Hole or to the genial irreverence of Fielding. Others, like Scott's *Bridal of Triermain* and Wordsworth's *The Egyptian Maid*, while they show the authors working outside the channels of their central inspiration, manifest clearly the growing reverence for the form and spirit of the old romances that was the unique contribution of the Romantic era to the development of Arthurian story. And, finally, one unfinished redaction by a minor poet, Reginald Heber, looks ahead unmistakably to the full restoration of the king of romance in the age to come.

JOHN THELWALL'S ARTHUR

The first man to enter the lists with Arthurian story in the nineteenth century was the radical reformer, elocutionist, and poetaster John Thelwall (1764–1834).[1] Although his political opinions were sufficiently advanced to land him temporarily in the Tower under indictment for sedition, his poetic ideals were retrograde enough to imprison him for life in the murky twilight of the pre-Romantic sensibility. Nowhere is this clearer than in his handling of the legend of Arthur. *The Fairy of the Lake* (1801), described in Thelwall's subtitle as a "Dramatic Romance," is as tasteless a concoction of freely manipulated romance elements, scrambled pseudohistory, "Cambrian" tradition, Northern mythology, and plain nonsense as can easily be imagined.[2] At the opening of this closet drama, Rowenna, child of Hengist and Queen of Britain, rejoices at the news that her husband Vortigern, the King, has carried off Guenever, his daughter and the unwilling object of his incestuous desires. Encouraged by this development and the ambiguous prophecy of a "Chorus of Invisible Spirits," Rowenna pursues her wicked plans to gain Arthur for herself. That worthy, meanwhile, wanders about disconsolately with a beer-swilling Tristram whose celebrations of the wonders of drink are obviously intended for comic relief. Arthur's men have already been spirited away from him; Tristram soon follows, another victim to Rowenna's magic spells, and finally Arthur himself is laid asleep by her wand, but upon awaking stoutly resists her more natural charms. At this point the Lady of the Lake appears, restores Arthur's men to him, and all march off to battle to save Guenever, whose ruin is imminent, according to some wax tablets that Arthur happens to have turned up. In the concluding act the evil Rowenna poisons Vortigern, attempts to burn Tristram and Guenever in a tower, and perishes herself in flames. The Lady of the Lake rescues Tristram and Guenever, and Arthur is crowned in Caer-Leon. Such a brief summary necessarily omits the large part played in the spectacle by assorted supernatural beings: "Hela, Queen of the Infernal Regions," "Urd, Verandi, and Schulda, The Fatal Sisters," "Incubus, a frozen demon," "The Giants of Frost; Demons of the Frozen Regions; Demons of the Noon, &c. &c."[3] Nor can summary suggest the variety of songs, dances, elaborate scenic effects, and other *divertissements* that serve to obscure the basic poverty of the action.

What is immediately clear, however, is that the traditional romance versions of the Arthurian story have had no part in Thelwall's play. His ultimate sources were, instead, the accounts of the romantic historians, especially that of Nennius, from whom Thelwall seems to have had, directly or indirectly, the motif of Vortigern's marriage to Hengist's daughter and his incestuous relation with his own daughter.[4] As for the telescopings of time by which Guenever becomes that daughter and Arthur becomes a contemporary of Hengist and Vortigern, figures dead before Arthur's birth in the traditional accounts of the British kings, these were, as Thelwall put it, only "liberties for which, as a poet, I hope to be pardoned."[5] Something of the same argument is used to support his heavy drafts on Northern mythology: "The Cambrian superstitions harmonize so readily with those of the Northern nations; and the mixed and illegitimate christianity of those times borders so closely upon paganism, that, I trust, the combination will not destroy the *poetic probability*

of either."[6] A generation or two earlier, the public's pardon for such historical and cultural conflations might easily have been relied upon; by
the beginning of the nineteenth century the development of the historical
spirit must have made them seem strangely out of date to many readers.

The fact is that Thelwall's real models were equally out of date. For
the mixture of Scandinavian and Celtic antiquities, he possibly found sanc-
tion in Richard Hole's "poetical romance." For such plot elements as
Arthur's sexual temptation and his magic-frustrated attempts to rescue
Guenever from impending rape, as well as for the elaborate operatic form
of the play, he clearly drew on Dryden's *King Arthur*. Even the texture
of Thelwall's play is derivative in a peculiarly old-fashioned way: shreds
and patches of Elizabethan blank verse and scraps of Miltonic diction
and syntax embedded in an overall glaze of late Augustan rhetoric.

In poetry, moreover, wholes are frequently something less than the
sum of their parts, and Thelwall's *Fairy of the Lake* ends up an even
sadder mistake than Dryden's *King Arthur*. If Dryden's Arthur is a
decline from the glorious hero of romance, he is still a man of action.
Thelwall's Arthur does not have even that much to commend him. Indeed, as Thelwall's title suggests, it is the Lady of the Lake who is the
heroic principal in this play. She it is who rescues Arthur from enchantment and she unaided rescues Guenever from Vortigern's flaming tower.
Thelwall's Arthur could scarcely be more the *roi fainéant*. This submer-
sion of Arthur under the weight of "romantic" Northern and "Cambrian
superstitions" thus marks the *Fairy of the Lake* as a belated survival of
the pre-Romantic approach to the legend.

FRERE'S ARTHURIAN BURLESQUE

In contrast to Thelwall's pale manipulation of an Arthur far more
Drydenesque than traditional, deliberate burlesque in the mood of the
high good humor of Fielding's *Tragedy of Tragedies* is the aim of John
Hookham Frere's quasi-Arthurian "epic."[7] Originally published as a
*Prospectus and Specimen of an Intended National Work, by William and
Robert Whistlecraft, of Stow-Market, in Suffolk, Harness and Collar-
makers, Intended to Comprise the Most Interesting Particulars Relating
to King Arthur and His Round Table* (1817–1818), *The Monks and the
Giants*, to give the poem its more traditionally accepted title, was left
unfinished after having reached a length of considerably over two hundred *ottava rima* stanzas.[8] As Frere's original title suggests, his chief aim
in the poem was comic. "There are," he explained later, "two kinds
of burlesque, of both of which you have admirable examples in Don
Quixote":

There is the burlesque of imagination, such as you have in all the Don's fancies. . . . Then there is the burlesque of ordinary rude uninstructed common sense, of which Sancho constantly affords examples. . . . My first intention in the "Monks and the Giants" was merely to give a specimen of the burlesque treatment of lofty and serious subjects by a thoroughly common, but not necessarily low-minded man—a Suffolk harness-maker.[9]

It is, of course, part of the jest that the story of Arthur and his knights, "reckon'd the best King, and bravest Lords, / Of all that flourish'd since the Tower of Babel,"[10] that this English Sancho Panza sets out to sing is in the event neither essentially Arthurian nor, for that matter, much of a story at all. Thus the entire first Canto is given over to a static description of Arthur's court in which the knights, though they have "refin'd and perfect manners" (I, 10), are nevertheless

> . . . prepar'd, on proper provocation,
>   To give the lie, pull noses, stab and kick;
> And for that very reason, it is said,
> They were so very courteous and well-bred. (I, 11)

Among the ladies, "majestical, reserv'd, and somewhat sullen" (I, 12), move Arthur's chief knights: Launcelot, the best of all the knights Great Britain ever had, "except, perhaps, Lord Wellington in Spain" (I, 13); Tristram, "somewhat more learned than became a Knight, / It was reported he could read and write" (I, 22); and Gawain, fearless in battle and flawless in courtesy. Into this court at Christmas time there comes in the second canto a "crook'd damsel" with news that a party of Giants have carried off a number of ladies on their way to court. Gawain and Tristram, who set off in hot pursuit, "blockade" the "fort" of the Giants, attempt a surprise attack at night, are discovered in a manifestly disadvantageous position, and yet inexplicably conquer:

> The Giants ran away—they knew not why—
> Sir Tristram gained the point—he knew not how—
>   He could account for it no more than I.
> Such strange effects we witness often now;
>   Such strange experiments true Britons try
> In sieges, and in skirmishes afloat,
> In storming heights, and boarding from a boat. (II, 40)

The remaining two cantos are concerned with the earlier depredations of the Giants against a community of Monks whose bell had enraged the Giants, and thus these earlier events doubtless represent "Whistlecraft's" conception of a suitable return to the beginning of the story after a properly "epic" opening *in medias res*.[11]

But was that all there was to the "Intended National Work"—a harmless jest at the expense of an imaginary Suffolk harness-maker? Frere's contemporaries thought not, and in the face of his repeated disavowals of any such intention, they remained stubbornly convinced that the poem concealed the political satire they expected from an erstwhile contributor to the *Anti-Jacobin*. Frere even claimed that attempts to unravel an allegory that, according to him, was nonexistent led to his discontinuance of the poem.[12] There is, however, at least some reason to suspect that Frere was not altogether candid in his protestations. He himself admitted that he had not always been able to submerge himself into Whistlecraft: "I have no doubt I did occasionally diverge into something which was more akin to one's own real feeling on the subjects which turned up, and thus misled my readers."[13] The "subjects which turned up" strikingly suggest at times something very close to Frere's "own real feeling"—the conduct of the Peninsular campaigns (1808–1813), from the early stages of which Frere himself had returned with a marred reputation. At any rate, although it would require a minute examination of the war in Spain and Portugal to demonstrate the matter beyond doubt, it seems difficult to explain on any other grounds such carefully specified but dramatically and narratively unnecessary elements as Tristram's inexplicable victory over the Giants, or his earlier retirement for three days from the "blockade" of the Giants' "fort" in order to snare a bird "much like a Pheasant, only crimson red, / With a fine tuft of feathers on his head" (II, 21). Indeed, the whole adventure is characterized by exactly the lack of discipline and responsiveness to central command that Wellington inveighed against so bitterly in Spain.[14]

Whatever the truth of these guesses may be, it is certain that the target of Frere's satire was not Arthurian romance; in fact, not even the central inspiration of the poem is to be found in the story of Arthur. For the form and the manner of the work with its apparently capricious transitions from grave to gay and back again, Frere drew on the Italian models of burlesque medley poetry that he found in Pulci, Berni, and Casti, especially the *Morgante Maggiore* of the first.[15] And the primary object of his satire, as he had said, was the "ordinary rude uninstructed common sense" of his author, Whistlecraft, just as the object of Cervantes' supremely intelligent fooling in his portrayal of Sancho is neither the Don nor chivalric romances, but rather the ultimately inadequate crudity of Sancho's all too earthy vision of reality. From the Arthurian tradition Frere drew little indeed: a few of the more renowned heroes, the characteristic motif of a quest begun by an injured damsel's arrival at Arthur's court, and a passing allusion to King Ryence's challenge. In the event, neither Arthur nor Launcelot participates in the action, and the story itself is completely nontraditional. But it is significant that in what little Frere did take from the legend, he reveals a disposition to treat the essentials of the old story tenderly. In the generally comic context of the poem, the portrait of Launcelot's secret grief of conscience, for example, is disconcertingly serious:

> Yet oftentimes his courteous cheer forsook
>   His countenance, and then return'd again,
> As if some secret recollection shook
>   His inward heart with unacknowledged pain;
> And something haggard in his eyes and look
>   (More than his years or hardships could explain)
> Made him appear, in person and in mind,
> Less perfect than what nature had design'd. (I, 15)

And the portrayal of Gawain is equally untouched by "Whistlecraft's" pedestrian imagination:

> The coarsest natures that approach'd him near
>   Grew courteous for the moment and refin'd;
> Beneath his eye the poorest, weakest wight
> Felt full of point of honour like a knight. (I, 27)

The precise sources of Frere's Arthurian material are difficult to define. The characterization of Gawain reveals a familiarity with the earlier traditions of the story before Gawain, the flower of courtesy, had been degraded by the growing ascendancy of Launcelot to the ambiguous role which he plays in the later romances. The sketch of Launcelot, on the other hand, suggests that Frere had also been imaginatively impressed by the later versions, probably Malory's. Frere's acquaintance with Arthurian literature had doubtless begun early, and probably was one fruit of his association with George Ellis, who may very well have communicated a portion of his knowledge of earlier literature to Frere, and doubtless some of his enthusiasm.[16] At any rate it is clear that Frere was at home with both the matter and the spirit of Arthurian romance, and it is indicative of the imaginative sympathies of the new romantic age in which he wrote that although his basic intention was a burlesque poem, he avoided any wholesale recasting of either the structure of the traditional story or its essence.

  The Monks and the Giants has a small but secure niche in literary history as the reviver of *ottava rima* in English and as the direct inspiration of Byron's *Beppo* and thus indirectly of *Don Juan*.[17] Frere's poem has, perhaps in only a lesser way, some of the more attractive qualities of its greater progeny; it also has some of the faults. It is amusing (for a time); its surface sparkles with ingenious rhymes and acute aphorisms; it tickles the mind with its abrupt shifts from the comic to the serious (also for a time); and ultimately it may jade the palate and weary the mind with its lack of significant structure and its inconsequence. In spite of Frere's disarming admission that the poem is modeled on the "wand'ring Bards of Yore" who "never laid a plan" (II, 1), the shapeless cannot be made shapely by elevating shapelessness to an aesthetic principle. And for all of Frere's obvious affectionate respect for the old legend, the use of Arthur and his knights as elements in witty burlesque was opposed not only to the bias of the tradition, but also to the sensibility of the age, and thus after a certain *succès d'estime, The Monks and the Giants* faded from what little public attention it had had and became one with rare vintage ports and minor classical satirists.

PEACOCK AND ARTHURIAN STORY

Similarly special tastes seem to characterize the "fit audience though few" of the other author of the period who sought to bend Arthurian matter to the purposes of satire. That the subject appealed strongly to Thomas Love Peacock may be gathered from his four attempts to embody parts of it in his work, but that his sensibility was adapted to the task of giving significant form to the old legend may be doubted from the outset. His first forays into Arthuriana were two commercial products for the juvenile book market. *Sir Hornbook: or, Childe Launcelot's Expedition, A Grammatico-Allegorical Ballad* (1813), a versified outline of grammar, has little connection with the old romances beyond the name of its hero, Childe Launcelot, who, with the aid of Sir Hornbook, sets out to scale the steep hill of grammatical knowledge, meeting and subduing on the way such opponents as "Sir Substantive . . . / With Adjective, his lady bright," and Sir Verb.[18] Equally pedagogical in intent and somewhat more Arthurian in substance was *The Round Table: or, King Arthur's Feast* (1817) in which Arthur, after his passing from the Battle of Camlan, is, according to the Introduction,

> represented as inhabiting a solitary island, under the influence of the prophet Merlin; by whose magic power he is shown all the kings and queens who have sat on the throne since his death, and giving to them a grand feast, at his old established round table, attended by their principal secretaries, dukes, lords, admirals, generals, and a long train of

courtiers. The kings are of course mentioned in the order of succession. The allegory is illustrated as concisely as possible in the notes. So many histories of England being published for the use of young persons, we have only attached the names of the kings, and to such instances as might not be considered sufficiently explanatory.[19]

What the feelings of the Regency moppets were for these gifts from doting maiden aunts is not recorded, but it is indicative of the increasing reinstatement of the Arthurian story in the popular mind that Peacock and his publishers sought to trade upon the éclat of Arthurian names and situations in these two ventures. As a prelude to his later attempts to deal with the story, there is something suspicious in the fact that he could use the material at all for such purposes. The truth is that for all of Peacock's romantic interests in wild scenery and a somewhat ambivalent approval of the Middle Ages, his roots were firmly planted in the eighteenth-century past, and there is more than a little of the old Rationalist mockery in his attitude toward the medieval hero:

> King Arthur sat down by the lonely sea-coast,
> As thin as a lath, and as pale as a ghost:
> He looked on the east, and the west, and the south,
> With a tear in his eye, and a pipe in his mouth.[20]

Something of the same attitude is revealed in Peacock's first effort to handle the legend for an adult audience. *Calidore*, an abandoned fragment of a satirical prose fantasy, turns on the adventures in nineteenth-century England of a young man who has come thither from the island of Terra Incognita on which the unaging Arthur, Merlin, Guenever, Launcelot, Gawaine, Kay, and Bedevere have been living since Arthur was carried away after the Battle of Camlan by the "Ladies or Nymphs of the waters."[21] Aside from the whimsical violation of the tradition involved in peopling this new Avalon with Arthur's false queen and false friend, his magician and his nephew, both lost before the last battle, Peacock blithely proceeds to reject the whole Christian bias of the legend. Basically classicist, atheist, and epicurean in sympathies, he must have derived huge merriment from his decision to deposit Arthur and his court on an island already taken over by Pan, Bacchus, Jupiter, and other antique deities. These gods of the elder world, Arthur learns, had been driven thither by the goddess Necessity when men had destroyed the pagan images and temples and had "built ugly structures on their ruins, where, instead of dancing and rejoicing as they had been used to do, and delighting [the gods] with spectacles of human happiness, they were eternally sighing and groaning, and beating their breasts, and dropping their lower jaws, and turning up the whites of their eyes, and cursing each other and all mankind, and chanting . . . dismal staves."[22] Arthur's ready agreement to a life of merriment, both gustatory and sexual, which Pan and Bacchus require of him and his knights, whatever affinities it may have with the whimsical amorality and inconsequence of early Welsh poetry, sorts but ill with the grave Christian King of romance. But as with Frere, the real object before Peacock was satire, and Arthur and his knights are little more than an arbitrarily chosen point of departure for a series of rollicking attacks on religious fanaticism, paper money, hard-drinking Welsh parsons, and Coleridgean metaphysics.

Satire is also one motive of Peacock's last romp in the fields of Arthurian story, *The Misfortunes of Elphin* (1829). But by this time, his interest in early Welsh literature, already apparent in *Calidore*, had been considerably augmented by his marriage to a Welsh woman, and his lengthy if not altogether serious study of Welsh under her tutelage. Indeed, if we are to believe the testimony of Edith Nicolls, his grand-daughter, *The Misfortunes of Elphin* was largely written as an outlet for Peacock's translations—perhaps verse adaptations would be more accurate—of the various triads and other Welsh poems that he intercalated so lavishly in his prose text.[23] Be that as it may, the main plot elements and the characters in the book no longer rest on a vague mental image of Arthurian story, but instead are based firmly on the traditional materials of Wales.

The central story—if it may be so designated in a book that seems determined to have no center—is combined from a variety of Cambrian legends and motifs, which he found in such publications as *The Myvyrian Archaiology of Wales* (1801–1807), Edward Davies' *Mythology and Rites of the Druids* (1809), and *The Cambro-Briton* (1819–1822).[24] The first of Prince Elphin's misfortunes is the loss of the best part of his land through the failure of the drunken Seithenyn ap Seithyn Saidi to care for the embankment that had kept out the sea. Later, after he has married and when his people are hard pressed for food, he suffers another apparent misfortune in finding in his fishing weir one night nothing but a coracle containing the infant Taliesin, the bard to be. When Taliesin has grown to manhood, Elphin is abducted by Maelgon Gwyneth, a king of North Wales, and held captive while Maelgon's son Rhûn attempts to disprove Elphin's assertion that his wife is the chastest and the most beautiful woman in Britain. Although Rhûn's attempts are thwarted by a variety of ruses, Elphin's daughter Melanghel refuses to marry the devoted Taliesin until he manages to free Elphin. This feat he finally accom-plishes through King Arthur's aid, having earned that monarch's grati-

tude by convincing the bibulous King Melvas, who has long held Gueny-
var captive, that he should restore the abducted queen to her husband.

The connection of Arthur with this loosely knit story is clearly of the
most tangential order. Even so, Peacock devotes a considerable amount
of space to a circumstantial description—significantly derived in large part
from Hoare's *Giraldus Cambrensis* (1806) rather than from the romance
sources[25]—of Arthur's court and such retainers as Sir Cradock and his
chaste wife, Gawain, Tristram, Kay, Bedwyr, and such bards as Llywarch
the Aged, Aneurin, and Merddin Gwyllt or Merlin the Wild. As for the
relation of the great and tragic medieval King Arthur, the flower of
chivalry, to Peacock's primitive Celtic warrior-kinglet, a man whom Maelgon bluntly describes as a "man of great prowess" but also a "cuckold,"[26]
there is scarcely any. Even the story of Gwenyvar's abduction by Melvas,
a motif apparently taken from a Life of St. Gildas,[27] is but the pale
original of the high chivalric adventure that it developed into in the
succeeding romances.

While *The Misfortunes of Elphin* thus lacks the beauty of the late
medieval versions, it fails at the same time to capture the archaic charm of
Peacock's Welsh originals. The fantastic and supernatural elements of
the early poetry were either not congenial to Peacock's classical and highly
rational sensibility or perhaps they were inconsonant with his satirical
purposes. At any rate, they were regularly ignored, and in their place was
supplied a wealth of minutely detailed historical reconstruction of sixth-
century Welsh life. The antiquarian zeal with which this out-of-the-way
knowledge was woven together was, of course, in keeping not only with
Peacock's own interests, but also with the temper of his age. Nevertheless, although the *mise en scène* is constructed with elaborate fidelity to
the place and period that Peacock had chosen, the spirit in which the
whole is approached could hardly be more deliberately modern.[28]

For, as in *Calidore*, the real targets of Peacock's wit were the men and
the notions of his own day, and indeed it is only when his shafts strike
there that his humor comes fully alive. Seithenyn's great—and greatly
drunken—defense of the embankment against charges that it is in a
dangerous state of decay, must surely be almost as hilarious today as it
was in the days before the First Reform Bill put the arguments of
Canning and Wellington aside forever:

> "Decay," said Seithenyn, "is one thing, and danger is another.
> Everything that is old must decay. That the embankment is old, I am
> free to confess; that it is somewhat rotten in parts, I will not altogether
> deny; that it is any the worse for that, I do most sturdily gainsay. It
> does its business well: it works well: it keeps out the water from the

land, and it lets in the wine upon the High Commission of Embankment. Cupbearer, fill. Our ancestors were wiser than we: they built it in their wisdom; and, if we should be so rash as to try to mend it, we should only mar it."

The beauty of the embankment, Seithenyn goes on to say, lies precisely in the fact that "some parts of it are rotten, and some parts of it are sound." Those who would seek to interfere in the workings of such a system are, quite clearly,

> perverse people, blind to venerable antiquity: that very unamiable sort of people, who are in the habit of indulging their reason. . . . I would not be so presumptuous as to say, I could build anything that would stand against [the sea] half an hour; and here this immortal old work, which God forbid the finger of modern mason should bring into jeopardy, this immortal work has stood for centuries, and will stand for centuries more, if we let it alone. It is well: it works well: let well alone. Cupbearer, fill. It was half-rotten when I was born, and that is a conclusive reason why it should be three parts rotten when I die.[29]

His oration completed, Seithenyn collapses in a drunken stupor, the embankment crumbles, and the flood of humor breaks in a crowning foam of wit.

But in the end, such moments are too rare, even for a book of moderate length, and the final impression is one of confused and sometimes irreconcilable intentions. By falling back on the Welsh sources, Peacock had accepted distinctly inferior materials, and had cut himself off from the far greater and more vigorous later flowerings of the legend. The attempt to combine accuracy of milieu with characters and events that had never had any real being outside of myth and folklore seems equally ill considered. And finally, the addition of a topically satirical purpose, no matter what its momentary triumphs might be, serves ultimately only to call attention to the lack of genuine imaginative vitality in the whole.[30] The playful charm of Peacock's fancy was occasionally capable of galvanizing these disparate elements into something that looked like life, and his wit along with his political opinions earned the work a number of favorable reviews. But the time for enlisting Arthur in the service of burlesque and satire was past. A new audience had developed, and that audience ignored Peacock's book.[31] *The Misfortunes of Elphin* accordingly left no mark on the subsequent development of Arthurian story, and instead fell into its destined place among the not inconsiderable number of minor satires whose admirers characteristically tend to think them rather funnier than they are.

The failure of both Frere and Peacock to create Arthurian treatments capable of appealing widely to the audience of the Romantic period is, to be sure, largely a function of their own characters. Neither lacked the requisite acquaintance with older literature, and neither was deficient in antiquarian knowledge of the texture of the medieval past. But what was essential to any successful new version of the great central Arthurian story was the additional quality of reverence, and reverence is precisely what is conspicuously absent in both writers. They simply would not (perhaps "could not" is closer to the facts) take the Arthurian story seriously, nor was it in their natures to aspire to a noble and dignified re-creation of that story for their own time.

JOHN LEYDEN

Such aspirations had already stirred in the heart of one young Scotsman at the very beginning of the century. John Leyden (1775–1811), philologist, linguist, ballad collector, and minor poet by choice, preacher and physician by profession, had rendered Scott great assistance in the collecting and compilation of the *Minstrelsy of the Scottish Border*. Among other antiquarian friends he numbered the great bibliophile Richard Heber, Joseph Ritson, and the ubiquitous George Ellis.[32] Through their books, their correspondence, and his own indefatigable researches, Leyden appears to have gained an extraordinary antiquarian competence and a fairly detailed mastery of the available medieval versions of Arthur's story. That it touched him deeply may be gathered from the tone of the Arthurian passages in his *Scenes of Infancy* (1803), a sort of Poly-Teviot-dale recalling Drayton's fine inclusiveness and his elegiac celebration of older manners and beliefs, but, fortunately, not his verbosity.[33] In the most striking of Leyden's Arthurian allusions, he offers a sample of the

> . . . strains the harp of haunted Merlin threw,
> When from his dreams the mountain sprites withdrew;
> While, trembling to the wires, that warbled shrill,
> His apple blossoms waved along the hill.
> Hark! how the mountain-echoes still retain
> The memory of the prophet's boding strain!
>   "Once more, begirt with many a martial peer,
> Victorious Arthur shall his standard rear,
> In ancient pomp his mailed bands display;
> While nations, wondering, mark their strange array,
> Their proud commanding port, their giant form,
> The spirit's stride, that treads the northern storm:
> Where fate invites them to the dread repast,

> Dark Cheviot's eagles swarm on every blast;
> On Camlan bursts the sword's impatient roar;
> The war-horse wades, with champing hoofs, in gore;
> The scythed car on grating axle rings;
> Broad o'er the field the ravens join their wings;
> Above the champions, in the fateful hour,
> Floats the black standard of the evil power."[34]

The accents of this song are unmistakably sincere, and the poet's approach is manifestly governed by an awareness of the dignity of the ancient hero. But from the Celticist primitivism implicit in his allusion to the Caledonian Merlin,[35] and from the Ossianic grimness and fatalism of the atmosphere, it is clear that Leyden was largely conditioned by the pre-Romantic period in his view of Arthurian story. Moreover, as his highly conventional couplets and his colorless, consciously "lofty" diction suggest, Leyden's talent was slender and unoriginal at best. A greater imaginative vitality than his would be required to breathe life into the subject, and Leyden himself thought he recognized that strength in his friend Walter Scott,

> ... with whom, in youth's serenest prime,
> I wove, with careless hand, the fairy rhyme,
> Bade chivalry's barbaric pomp return,
> And heroes wake from every mouldering urn![36]

Maturity, however, had brought its doubts and its financial difficulties. Leyden was forced to take up foreign service to mend his fortunes. Meanwhile, before he left, he donned the robes of the oracle and glanced into the future:

> Say, who is he, with summons strong and high,
> That bids the charmed sleep of ages fly,
> Rolls the long sound through Eildon's caverns vast,
> While each dark warrior rouses at the blast,
> His horn, his faulchion grasps with mighty hand,
> And peals proud Arthur's march from Fairyland?
> Where every coal-black courser paws the green,
> His printed step shall evermore be seen:
> The silver shields in moony splendour shine—
> Beware, fond youth! a mightier hand than thine,
> With deathless lustre, in romantic lay,
> Shall Rymour's fate, and Arthur's fame display.[37]

SCOTT AS ARTHURIAN POET

The "mightier hand" was, of course, Walter Scott's, and, as such things go, Leyden's prophecy must have seemed a safe one in 1803. Scott had already shown a promising talent for verse romance. His antiquarian interests were bringing him an unsurpassed mastery of the history, the physical circumstances, and, to a lesser degree, the spirit of medieval life. His acquaintance with chivalric romance was wide; his affection for it, a dominant motif in his imaginative life. And for the man who edited *Sir Tristrem* and for long contemplated doing the same for Malory, romance meant above all else the undying thrills of Arthurian romance:

> . . . on the ancient minstrel strain
> Time lays his palsied hand in vain;
> And . . . our hearts at doughty deeds,
> By warriors wrought in steely weeds,
> Still throb for fear and pity's sake;
> As when the Champion of the Lake
> Enters Morgana's fated house,
> Or in the Chapel Perilous
> Despising spells and demons' force,
> Holds converse with the unburied corse;
> Or when, Dame Ganore's grace to move,
> (Alas, that lawless was their love!)
> He sought proud Tarquin in his den,
> And freed full sixty knights; or when,
> A sinful man, and unconfess'd,
> He took the Sangreal's holy quest,
> And, slumbering, saw the vision high,
> He might not view with waking eye.

That Scott himself as late as 1807–1808 when these lines were written still intended to fulfill Leyden's prediction seems clear:

> The mightiest chiefs of British song
> Scorn'd not such legends to prolong:
> . . . .
> Warm'd by such names, well may we then,
> Though dwindled sons of little men,
> Essay to break a feeble lance
> In the fair fields of old romance.[38]

Yet despite all his enthusiasm and all his knowledge, the quest was not for Scott. The subject lay outside his own creative range, and in the end, the lance that he did finally break in the lists of Arthurian romance was among his feeblest.

Of Scott's one attempt to deal at length with Arthurian materials, *The Bridal of Triermain* (1813), few of his admirers would be inclined to say that it is either very characteristic or very impressive as a poem. Even its genesis and the peculiar circumstances surrounding its publication suggest that Scott's own attitude toward the poem was one of uncertainty or uneasily mixed purposes. Begun originally with no intention beyond furnishing a fragmentary "imitation" of his own style printed under the name "Caleb Quotem," the poem seems to have strangely seized Scott's fancy. But even when he completed it as a serious work, he held on to the deception of publishing it as a professed imitation by an unnamed author who was suspected, as Scott intended, to be his friend William Erskine.[39] Just what the ultimate motives were for this "systematic mystification" is not altogether certain; Scott's later explanation that it was a trap for the reviewers is probably honest as far as he knew his own mind, but certain elements in the deception suggest a more complex motive.[40]

Even more obscure are the reasons for the peculiarly elaborated structure of the work as a whole. The poem begins with a lengthy Introduction in which a modern minstrel named Arthur woos his purse- and class-proud mistress Lucy by singing a romance "Of errant knight and damozelle; / Of the dread knot a wizard tied, / In punishment of maiden's pride."[41] Within the romance of the medieval Sir Roland de Vaux's quest which the lovesick minstrel sings, there is yet another romance, "a mystic tale, by bard and sage, / . . . handed down from Merlin's age" (I, ix), told by one Lyulph, which traces the antecedent history of Gyneth, the sleeping beauty whom Sir Roland finally rouses from the five hundred years' sleep to which her fatal pride had brought her.

The poem thus involves three lines of action. Of these the first, the framing device in which the narrator Arthur woos and ultimately wins the proud Lucy in spite of social and economic obstacles, seems on the surface to be a quite arbitrary addition to the romance of Roland and Gyneth. The various introductory and concluding passages in which the Arthur-Lucy story is developed are, it is true, in keeping with the general motif of the marriage quest, but it is equally true that they serve no necessary function of development or clarification of either that motif or of the poem as a whole. Even the pious Lockhart was constrained to describe them as "unfortunate."[42] Nevertheless, if they have no function in the public poem, they may have had an important place in the poet's private fantasy world, and their presence hints at an explanation for Scott's curious impulses toward concealment manifested in both the publication of the poem and in the poem itself.

What the secret was is suggested by the fact that the scenery and the style of life portrayed in the framing story are clearly those of Gilsland, the small watering place where Scott himself had wooed and won Charlotte Charpentier in 1797. Following this clue, Dame Una Pope-Hennessy has noted that "we may read a lyrical rendering" of Scott's courtship in the Introductions.[43] Such a reading, however, scarcely accounts for the description of the young minstrel's love as "Lucy of the lofty eye, / Noble in birth, in fortunes high, / She for whom lords and barons sigh" (Introduction to Canto I, iii). There is nothing to suggest that Charlotte was haughty, and whatever other valuable qualities she may have had, she was if anything somewhat below her young husband in both rank and fortune.[44] To find the real original of Lucy, we must look to Scott's earlier love, Williamina Belsches, a young lady whom Grierson describes as "certainly his most passionate . . . love."[45] Williamina, unfortunately, had belonged "by birth and expectations . . . to a higher level of society" than her suitor, and she ended by rejecting a bitterly disappointed Scott in whose breast the pain of injured merit still rankled years afterwards.[46] In real life there was nothing to be done about the "social wants that sin against the strength of youth," but in the world of fantasy the spirit could have its victory. Thus in the Introductions, Scott, reversing the unpleasant facts, handily combined the longed-for Williamina with the successful and lyric courtship at Gilsland of the obtained Charlotte. The actual winning of the proud fair, passed over in silence in the Introductions, was expressed in symbolic terms at yet another remove from the hateful jars of reality; it is in the story of Sir Roland that the hero manages by over-coming dozens of supernatural obstacles to make clear his real worth and thus to liberate the lady from her spell of pride to live happily ever after with the poor but noble baron.

The process of redressing the disappointments of life by romantic fantasy was abiding in Scott. Usually it takes the relatively innocent form that we find in the story of Sir Roland, a form in which the frail, bookish, game-legged Edinburgh advocate was able to see himself as a noble and martial young man who wins fame, wealth, and love in a series of freely invented adventures. But that was not enough this time—the psychic damage of Williamina's rejection required stronger medicine, and thus the Introductions, wholly redundant and diffusive from an artistic stand-point, were added to satisfy the subconscious longing. But with this, the guilty wish came too near the surface. Hence the elaborate and prolonged efforts at concealment, at transferring—quite ambiguously to be sure—the authorship by means of an almost obsessively labored hoax to Erskine. And hence, perhaps, even the confusing structure and the strangely split moral burden of the poem. The overt moral of Roland's quest is unexcep-tionable: success attends valiant self-control; but there is another darker moral buried in the third layer of the poem, Lyulph's Tale: pride brings on a living death. It is as if the dangerous latent content had found a structural means to conceal itself—even from the poem's author. Such an interpretation is not labored for the cheap purpose of laying bare the pathetic self-deception of one of the most great-hearted gentlemen our literature has known. Were that all to be derived from the inquiry, the mystery of the unsatisfactory structure of *The Bridal of Triermain* might well have been left unexplained. But the role of personal fantasy in the explanation of Scott's failure to write a great Arthurian poem is too large to be ignored.

What remains of the poem after the otiose Introductions are cleared away is a more or less typically Scottian romance into which an Arthurian episode of almost equal length has been inserted. Sir Roland de Vaux, Baron of Triermain, dreams in his sleep of a maiden so lovely that he decides she must be his bride; in order to find out if she is real, he sends to Lyulph, a "sage of power / . . . sprung from druid sires" (I, vi), who informs him that the damsel is indeed real and still to be won "though there have glided since her birth, / Five hundred years and one" (I, ix), a marvel which he explains in the lengthy intercalated "Lyulph's Tale." Learning that Gyneth, the maiden of his dreams, lies in spellbound sleep in a mysterious disappearing castle in the Vale of St. John,[47] Roland goes there and after difficulties finally manages to enter the castle where he bravely strides unharmed through a hall of tigers, resists the riches offered by four maidens, and afterwards the advances of four oriental "slaves to love" (III, xxxi). Leaving them in order to go "where the feelings of the heart / With the warm pulse in concord move; / . . . where Virtue sanctions love" (III, xxxii), he next endures a dark, poisonous passageway, and finally the offer of royal power proferred by French, German, and Spanish maids. At his assertion that he prefers to be "A free-born Knight of England free, / Than sit on Despot's throne" (III, xxxvi), a fourth maiden—of England—declares that the spell has been broken by Roland, who has thus surmounted Fear and the "snares . . . / Spread by Pleasure, Wealth, and Pride" (III, xxxvi). Roland rushes on, finds and wakens the lovely Gyneth as lightning flashes, thunder rolls, and the castle falls asunder.

While there is nothing specifically Arthurian in this freely invented story, the range of Scott's vocabulary of stock medieval story motifs is a signal illustration of how long and how deeply he had drunk at the well of old romance. The central formula of the quest for the dreamed-of maiden is derived from Chaucer's *Tale of Sir Thopas*, as the motto on the title page of the poem as well as its irregularly rhymed octosyllabics and trimeters suggest. For such other standard motifs as the spellbound maiden and the disappearing castle that falls to the ground when a spell is broken, it is pointless to search for specific inspiration, although for the allegorized temptations that Roland overcomes, Spenser may be confidently offered as the source.

How Gyneth came to be in the situation from which Roland rescues her is the subject of "Lyulph's Tale," the only properly Arthurian part of *The Bridal of Triermain*. Long, long ago, King Arthur, having left Guenever at home and ridden out in search of adventure, entered a castle of maidens and there easily fell into dalliance with Guendolen, a child of a human mother and a pagan Genie. When the time finally came for Arthur's departure, Guendolen shed a tear and "pressed / The foldings of her silken vest! / At her reproachful sign and look, / The hint the monarch's conscience took" (II, vi–vii), and so he swore that if Guendolen's child should be a son, it would be his heir, and if a girl, then

> To chuse that maid a fitting spouse,
> A summer day in lists shall strive
> My knights,—the bravest knights alive,—
> And he, the best and bravest tried,
> Shall Arthur's daughter claim for bride. (II, vii)

In the fifteen years that followed, Arthur overcame the Saxons in twelve battles, killed the giant Rython, and defeated Lucius of Rome. Then one Pentecost day as Arthur sits feasting with his knights there comes a maid on a white palfrey. It is Gyneth, his daughter by Guendolen, and she claims the performance of his vow. In the competition that ensues, all the knights join save Tristrem, Lancelot, and Caradoc,

> And still these lovers' fame survives
>   For faith so constant shown,—
> There were two who loved their neighbours' wives,
>   And one who loved his own. (II, xviii)

Observing the heat of the conflict that follows, Arthur begs Gyneth to stop the fight before any of his knights are killed, but she proudly refuses, and he, bound by his oath, allows the fight to continue until "seemed in this dismal hour, that Fate / Would Camlan's ruin antedate, / And spare dark Mordred's crime" (II, xxv). Just at this moment, however, a young kinsman of Merlin's is mortally wounded, and the magician, arriving in a storm, stops the fight and lays on Gyneth for her pride a chilling curse: she shall sleep in lone penance in the Vale of St. John until a knight "for feat of arms as far renowned / As Warrior of the Table Round" (II, xxvi) shall wake her. Who that knight will be some five hundred years later has already been seen.

In this episode, as in that of Roland de Vaux, Scott has again freely combined stock elements from medieval romance. The castle full of maidens with a princess who is got with child by a visiting knight he might have had from the story of either Lancelot or Percival; the coming to court of the child of such a liaison may easily have been derived from the story of Galahad. But it is not sources that are of real interest here. What is of the last moment is the approach that Scott has taken toward his material. Abandoning the method of arbitrary recasting of the central story that Spenser and Dryden had followed, Scott was content to sketch in the major outlines of the old legend unchanged, and to attach loosely to that story a new and original episode. It was, of course, the approach that many of the medieval romancers had followed, and by which the central legend of Arthur had been swelled to an immense body of stories. But more importantly, it was an approach born out of the new Romantic temper, a temper that fully and reverently accepted Arthurian romance as true—true poetically—and therefore not subject to arbitrary alteration and rearrangement. In this respect *The Bridal of Triermain* may be justly described as the first example of the distinctly modern reflowering of the legend.

This is not, of course, to say that it is fully satisfactory either as a treatment of the Arthurian story or even as a poem of any sort. Its structure, whatever subconscious satisfaction it may have afforded Scott, is defective, and its hero is an insipid projection of Scott's daydreams. Indeed, it is not too much to say that the whole poem is stultified by a pervasive immaturity, best suggested, perhaps, by the jejune "moral truth in fiction's veil" (Conclusion, ii) with which Roland de Vaux's adventure ends:

> . . . this was what remain'd of all
> The wealth of each enchanted hall,
>   The Garland and the Dame:—
> But where should warrior seek the meed,
> Due to high worth for daring deed,
>   Except from LOVE and FAME! (III, xxxix)[48]

If such sentiments are innocuous, they are also vapid. Things are not quite that simple in either life or literature, and in fact such a view is likely to blunt the sense for finer distinctions in both ranges of experience.

Something of this coarsened perception seems to be involved, at any rate, in Scott's view of the central Arthurian story as it appears in *The Bridal of Triermain*. The standard fixtures of the legend, as we have seen, he leaves unaltered: the Arthur-Guenever-Lancelot triangle, Arthur's triumphs over Saxons, giants, and Rome, and the foreshadowed fatal battle at Camlan with Mordred. Similarly, the tradition of Arthur's court as a center of chivalry, a bulwark against anarchy and paganism, is carefully preserved:

> ... all who suffered causeless wrong,
> From tyrant proud or faitor strong,
> Sought Arthur's presence to complain,
> Nor there for aid implored in vain. (II, xi)

But Scott's reading of Arthur's character departs so widely from tradition that the final product is a great deal closer to an indiscreet Regency clubman than to the *flos regum* of romance. From the "wily monarch" who calculatingly "guess'd" that Guendolen's initial reserve showed "more ardent passions in the breast" (I, xxi) to the shamefaced lover who promises the injured maid to provide for his by-blow, Scott's Arthur cuts a poor figure, and the situation is little improved by the author's pedestrian reflection: "Where lives the man that has not tried, / How mirth can into folly glide, / And folly into sin!" (I, xxi). It is true, of course, that the younger Arthur of the old romances twice fell into amorous dalliance, but that was *before* his marriage with Guenevere. And there is nothing in the romances that could have justified an Arthur who "lies loitering in a lady's bower" while

> The Saxon stern, the pagan Dane
> Maraud on Britain's shores again.
>
> . . . .
>
> Heroic plans in pleasure drown'd,
> He thinks not of the Table Round;
> In lawless love dissolved his life,
> He thinks not of his beauteous wife. (II, i-ii)

Nor does the discovery of this liaison disturb Guenever when she sees Gyneth's reception by Arthur; on the contrary, in what amounts to an ethic of sexual reciprocity, she gazes "unruffled at the scene, / Of human frailty construed mild, / Looked upon Lancelot, and smiled" (II, xv). Frere's Whistlecraft could scarcely have debased the conscience-searing tragedy of the lovers of the legend more ruinously.

This reduction of the "huge cloudy symbols" of romance to beings of such all-too-human stature suggests that it is perhaps just as well that Scott never attempted an independent retelling of the central story of Arthur's birth, triumphs, betrayal, and defeat. For although at first glance Scott, with all his antiquarian interests and his love for old romance, seems the ideal man to have presented that story anew to the world, the fact is that the legend was as far outside his creative range as its tragic spirit was beyond his sensibility. What did stir his creative impulses may be seen in one after another of Scott's chivalric romances: a poor but noble young man—a sort of Horatio Alger hero in plate armor—through a profusion of exciting deeds of derring-do manifests to all the world the ambition, valiance, strength, and honor that ultimately win for him fame, wealth, and love. It was, of course, Scott's beloved personal fantasy, but it was also a fantasy he shared with thousands upon thousands of readers. When to this formula Scott added his magical and lovingly detailed reconstruction of a glamorous past, he achieved the zenith of his own aims, and the delight of his audience—in whom the spirit of historical curiosity was steadily quickening under the influence of the Romantic revival— knew no bounds.

But the essential Arthurian story was radically unsuitable for such development. In its somber world of strained and divided loyalties, of honor shattered on the paradoxes of existence, of high and noble aims grievously defeated, there was no place for facile wish-fulfillment to operate. Here ideals and bravery earned no automatic dividends, and here human love was not happy reward but melancholy pain. From such a story Scott's fantasying impulse doubtless drew back with a shivering awareness of its inability to survive in such dark waters. Nor was Arthurian romance congenial to Scott's other basic impulse—that of a sedulous reconstruction of the past. For the story of Arthur, as Scott must have realized, can be assigned to no actual past. Its King and his knights belong neither to the sixth century in which the annalists would put them, nor to the twelfth century from which they took their chivalric traits. They belong instead to a vaguely medieval world in which the physical facts that Scott loved to marshal matter little, and in which the emotional facts, which were beyond Scott's ability to deal with, count for everything.[49]

Thus although long beguiled by the story, which he seems to have loved deeply and sincerely, Scott in the end produced only *The Bridal of Triermain* in which a hasty outline of the Arthurian legend is used as background for a newly invented and mythically irrelevant tale of adventure. It is significant of the coming attitude that Scott refrained from any wholesale recasting of the central story, and doubtless his example moved others to the same respect for the legend. But in terms of direct effect, outside of two hackwork dramatizations of the poem, *The Bridal of Triermain* seems to have had little influence on the subsequent development of the story in the nineteenth century.[50] To that development Scott's contribution was made in other ways. He created not Arthurian poems, but rather an audience eager for them. He, more than any other man, made the world of medieval romance an integral part of the mental fabric of the nineteenth century, and, he, beyond all other exemplars, sent a generation of poets to

> . . . seek the moated castle's cell,
> Where long through talisman and spell,
> While tyrants rul'd, and damsels wept,
> Thy Genius, Chivalry, hath slept.[51]

WORDSWORTH AND ARTHURIAN LEGEND

The medievalism that marked so many of Scott's vast historical canvases, his romantic vignettes, and his genre scenes entered but rarely into the quiet landscapes of Wordsworth, the one other major Romantic to concern himself with the Arthurian legend. In his younger days, medievalism did have some effect on his poetic theories, though it had none on his poetry, and in any event it was a medievalism thoroughly eighteenth-century in character. He admired and praised earlier literature for its simplicity and its sincerity, but, it must be remembered, for him "older poetry" largely meant, as it did for most of his generation, a haphazard conflation of Spenser, Percy's ballads, Chatterton's pastiches, and scraps of Ossianic verse. The "naïve" simplicity of the old ballads may have suggested the form and quality of some of the poems in *Lyrical Ballads*, but Wordsworth's subject matter was "incidents and situations from common life."[52] To some degree Wordsworth's rejection of the past in favor of everyday scenes and events may have been determined by his reaction against the "gross and violent stimulants" of the "frantic novels . . . and deluges of idle and extravagant stories in verse" in which the "Gothick" impulse was largely making itself felt in the decade before the end of the century.[53] Much more instrumental, however, was what Willey has identified as Wordsworth's "instinctive repudiation of any concrete mythology" as a result of the rationalist, scientific tradition in which he had been formed:

> Any translation of his experience into myth, personification or fable [would have been] inevitably a lapse toward a lower level of truth, a fall, in fact, from imagination to fancy. Poetry exists to transform, to make this much-loved earth more lovely; . . . in former times men could express their sense of fact, without misgiving, in mythologies. But since the coming of the enlightened age this was becoming almost impossible.[54]

Yet for all his avoidance of the romantic past during the first years of his poetic career, Wordsworth, like the younger Milton, seems to have been deeply moved at an early stage of his life by medieval romance. Among the subjects that he early considered for poetic treatment, according to *The Prelude*, the elder stories ranked high:

> Sometimes the ambitious Power of choice, mistaking
> Proud spring-tide swellings for a regular sea,
> Will settle on some British theme, some old
> Romantic tale by Milton left unsung;
> More often turning to some gentle place
> Within the groves of Chivalry, I pipe
> To shepard swains, or seated harp in hand,
> Amid reposing knights by a river side
> Or fountain, listen to the grave reports
> Of dire enchantments faced and overcome
> By the strong mind, and tales of warlike feats,
> Where spear encountered spear, and sword with sword
> Fought, as if conscious of the blazonry
> That the shield bore, so glorious was the strife;
> Whence inspiration for a song that winds
> Through ever-changing scenes of votive quest
> Wrongs to redress, harmonious tribute paid
> To patient courage and unblemished truth,
> To firm devotion, zeal unquenchable,
> And Christian meekness hallowing faithful loves.[55]

But Wordsworth's central creative impulse was not to be put off long by such attractions. For him, again as it had been with Milton, the "last and favourite aspiration" mounted "with yearning toward some philosophic song."[56] It was not for him to find some

> little band of yet remembered names
> Whom I, in perfect confidence, might hope
> To summon back from lonesome banishment
> And make them dwellers in the hearts of men
> Now living, or to live in future years.[57]

His special mission was, as B. Ifor Evans has suggested with great discrimination, "to present experience without the intrusion of a mythology," to use description and exposition rather than narrative as the means of communicating his unique experience of life.[58]

Nevertheless, the specialization of the creative impulse that produced "Tintern Abbey" and the "Immortality Ode," however much that specialization may have been an indirect result of eighteenth-century rationalism, is not to be thought of as an antagonism or hostility to early myth and legend. On the contrary, Wordsworth seems to have had from his earliest days a fondness for the distant past and its poetry. And as the years passed, as his youthful revolutionary ardors were cooled by Napoleon's career through Europe, as nature came to be less "all in all" for him and the visionary gleam was replaced by the still, sad music of humanity, as, in short, the romantic naturalism of his youth gave way to the romantic conservatism of his later years, Wordsworth turned more and more often to the storied past. In such poems as the "Song at the Feast of Brougham Castle" and "The White Doe of Rylstone" (1807–1808), he celebrated quasi-historical traditions of early modern times. Later in a number of the *Ecclesiastical Sonnets* (1822) and in such minor narrative works as *Artegal and Elidure* (1820), he turned to the remoter "British" past, drawing heavily on Geoffrey of Monmouth and on Milton's *History of Britain*.

To the more frankly fabulous romances of the past, Wordsworth was temperamentally less well suited, perhaps. Yet his youthful reading of what Arthurian materials were available to him had struck chords in his mind that continued to vibrate long afterwards in various loving allusions to the legend. In reading Geoffrey, for instance, he seems to be especially touched by what he finds there of

> Spenser's fairy themes,
> And those that Milton loved in youthful years;
> The sage enchanter Merlin's subtle schemes;
> The feats of Arthur and his knightly peers;
> Of Arthur,—who to upper light restored,
> With that terrific sword
> Which yet he brandishes for future war,
> Shall lift his country's fame above the polar star![59]

And Arthur's might in battle is again celebrated in one of the *Ecclesiastical Sonnets*: "Amazement runs before the towering casque / Of Arthur, bearing through the stormy field / The virgin sculptured on his Christian shield."[60] Among the lesser figures of Arthurian story, the "Lady of the Mere, / Sole-sitting by the shores of old romance," Joseph of Arimathea, and Merlin also make their brief appearances in his verse.[61] But it was not until after he had read Malory in one of the 1816 editions that Wordsworth was finally to write an independent Arthurian poem, and even when he did, the inspiration was not really either the legendary king or any of his knights.

"The Egyptian Maid; or, The Romance of the Water Lily" (1835) follows Scott's method of attempting to integrate a more or less freely invented episode into a relatively unaltered traditional Arthurian framework.[62] As the poem opens, Merlin at first admires an approaching ship, "The Water Lily," and then in a fit of peevish envy raises a storm that destroys the ship. The "meek and guileless Maiden" whom the ship carried is cast up lifeless on a rock.[63] Nina, the Lady of the Lake, rebukes Merlin and then brings him the Maiden, "of breath and bloom forsaken" (l. 138), with instructions to carry her through the air in his swan-drawn car to Arthur's court. There Arthur explains that the Maiden was the daughter of an Egyptian ruler whose land Arthur had freed and who had sworn to "turn to Christ our Lord, / And his dear Daughter on a Knight bestow / Whom I [i.e., Arthur] should choose for love and matchless labours" (ll. 226–28). Upon Merlin's declaration that the intended groom must be made known by some miracle that shall occur when the right man touches her hand, each knight vainly attempts the feat. But when Galahad, who had earlier seen the Maiden in a vision produced by Nina, touches her, she returns to life, and the two are quickly married to the strains of a moralizing anthem sung by angels.

The central story of "The Egyptian Maid," which thus concludes with the marriage of Galahad, is clearly nontraditional, but for the *mise en scène* that forms its background Wordsworth drew freely and at the same time reverently on Arthurian sources, especially Malory.[64] From Malory he took the many names of the knights who seek to revive the Maiden, and to Malory's story he is indebted for his conception of most of the traditional characters in the poem: Percival, who is "devoutest of all Champions" (l. 273); Gawain, who is filled with "princely cheer" (l. 287); Tristram, who does not grieve at his failure to rouse the Maid because "the fair Izonda he had wooed / With love too true, a love with pangs too sharp, / From hope too distant, not to dread another" (ll. 292–94); Launcelot, who hopes to wake the Maid because "from Heaven's grace / A sign he craved, tired slave of vain contrition" (ll. 295–96); and Guinever, "who looked passing glad / When his touch failed" (ll. 297–98). The Arthur who rules splendidly over this court and whose life is filled with warfare in the service of Christ is an equally respectful transcription from the legendary sources, and even Nina, the Lady of the Lake, "a gentle Sorceress, and benign, / Who ne'er embittered any good man's chalice" (ll. 94–96) can easily be derived from the ambiguous character in the romances who so carefully guarded the fortunes of Arthur and Pelleas. But in two characters the departure from the tradition is considerable. A Galahad who takes a maid to wife is a far cry from the maiden knight who alone finally achieves the Quest of the Grail in the old romances because of his perfect chastity. And of the "Grave Merlin" whose "freakish will" leads him in "envious spleen" to sink the ship he had first "hailed with joy" (ll. 21–27), the old story affords no counterpart.

This relatively elaborate characterization of Merlin, however irrelevant and even contradictory it may be to the figure of the enchanter of the traditional story, is of paramount importance to the poem's underlying meaning. For "The Egyptian Maid" is no mere adventure in fairyland. It is, instead, a complex allegory of the older Wordsworth's brooding perceptions and thoughts about the conflict of scientific rationalism with imagination, of aesthetic hedonism with Christian ethics.[65] In that allegory Merlin, "a Mechanist, whose skill / Shames the degenerate grasp of modern Science" (ll. 19–20), stands clearly for the rational or scientific intellect as Wordsworth conceived it, albeit with a poetically necessary increase of power over natural forces.[66] In his youth Wordsworth had been able to condemn with something like easy gaiety the intellect that murders to dissect; in his maturity the image of the mind that explains all nature by mechanical laws had become considerably darker. The immense powers of the scientific intellect over nature, he seems to have felt, were actively and malevolently opposed to the beauties of the imagination and its joyful, instinctual life. Thus Merlin, in whom no more than rudiments of natural imaginative sympathy still exist, at first "gazed with admiration" (l. 14) at the lovely ship, but then, "provoked to envious spleen"—to a destructive hatred of the beautiful thing that his way of knowing makes incomprehensible to him—"he cast / An altered look upon the advancing Stranger / Whom he had hailed with joy, and cried, / 'My Art shall help to tame her pride'" (ll. 25–28). In the resulting storm of the intellect, the Egyptian Maid is all but destroyed, and the lovely ship is lost. Such is the fate of both moral and aesthetic beauty in a world in which the intellect has cut itself off from imagination as a way of knowing, and thus from moral knowledge. That fate is not, however, wholly dependent on the murdering intellect. Merlin's power is after all subject to Heaven's will, and the storm was, as the angels' nuptial song declares, but a "Heaven-permitted vent / Of purblind mortal passion" (ll. 364–65).

Why the storm was permitted is to be understood only in terms of the symbolic significance of the ship itself. Unlike the figure of Merlin, which bears the marks of conscious manipulation, the ship seems to have been a spontaneous creation of Wordsworth's imagination, and it is correspondingly both more complex and more substantial. It was around the ship's name, "The Water Lily," casually mentioned in a trivial conversation, that the entire poem had first begun to crystallize in Wordsworth's mind.[67] And it was from its name that he was led by an obvious association to the salient feature of the ship, a figurehead of a goddess rising from a lily flower—an image that, as he carefully explained in his headnote to the poem, had been "suggested by the beautiful work of ancient art, once included among the Townley Marbles, and now in the British Museum."[68] The symbolic value of the ship on at least one level is suggested by this association with the antique sculpture. For the ship seems partly to stand for all the joyous, instinctual life of the imagination and for the artistic creations of that life. The figure on its prow is "the old Egyptian's emblematic mark / Of joy immortal and pure affection" (ll. 77–78); like the imagination, the ship seems not to be restricted by mere physical laws—the "bright Ship . . . seemed to hang in air" (l. 4); and as it approaches, it grows in size like the moon, that favorite Romantic symbol of the imagination. Even to Merlin it seems more beautiful than anything ever "built with patient [i.e., rational?] care" (l. 17).

How then are we to explain Wordsworth's willingness to allow this manifestation of the precious imagination to perish in a "Heaven-permitted" storm? The answer lies in what he thought was false in the ship itself. For the ship that Merlin wonders at is still but "work of mortal hands" (l. 5), and the image on its prow is "a sign of heathen power" (l. 75); it lacks the sanctifying element of Christian morality and Christian compassion—the moral sensibility that increasingly interested Wordsworth. Thus although "she was fair, / Luminous, blithe, and debonair (ll. 51–52), she is quickly sunk by the storm raised by Merlin's rational intellect. The echo from Milton's celebration of pure joy in *L'Allegro* is significant; her joy lacks the necessary admixture of compassion. We may grieve as the poet does at her fate, but, as Wordsworth tells us with careful italics, she had no heart or brain to "*feel* her own distress; / Nor aught that troubles us" (ll. 59–60). The ship is, then, the type of a beautiful, joyous, but at the same time pagan, heartless hedonism. As such its association in Wordsworth's mind with the "beautiful work of ancient art . . . in the British Museum" is entirely understandable. Doubtless he had experienced the characteristic Romantic nostalgia in gazing on the goddess's "antique smile," and like Keats he must have felt poignantly its freedom from moral struggle, its calm, "all breathing human passion far above," which for the Romantics distinguished the antique from the modern.[69] And for Wordsworth the distinction between the pagan hedonism of the world's youth and the soberer morality of its later days had a more personal significance: it directly paralleled his own development from the "glad animal movements" and "dizzy raptures" of youth to the "moral being" of maturity. If there is an ambivalence in his exclamation at the sinking of the ship—"Grieve for her, she deserves no less" (l. 55)—it is the same ambivalence that colors the "Immortality Ode." But in the storm of intellectual doubt, the antique hedonism was of no avail: "The Flower, the Form within it, / What served they in her need?" (ll. 367–68). The old instinctual joy was thus destroyed along with the voluptuous symbolic image at its prow of a goddess rising from a blossom of which the "leaves revealed / The bosom half, and half concealed" (ll. 129–30).

But "though nothing can bring back" this "glory in the flower," to borrow from the Ode, there remains some recompense. "A fairer than herself" (l. 63) was borne by the ship—"a meek and guileless Maiden" (l. 66), whose heathen origin and subsequent conversion to Christianity as well as her passage in the ship from a heathen to a Christian land symbolically delineate the evolution of a higher moral nature from the old pagan joy. Because "the Maid to Jesu hearkened, / And kept to Him her faith," she had reached "the destined strand" (ll. 375–82). And in contrast to the sunken goddess, the Maid is found by Nina "Unstripped of her attire" (l. 137)—the stubborn negative is not without its significance. How then shall we account for the fact that this personification of Christian moral consciousness is left "of breath and bloom forsaken" (l. 138) by the storm? In their nuptial song, the angels offer an explanation:

> Who shrinks not from alliance
> Of evil with Good Powers
> To God proclaims defiance
> And mocks who [sic] he adores.
>
> A Ship to Christ devoted
> From the Land of Nile did go;
> Alas! the bright Ship floated,
> An Idol at her prow.[70] (ll. 355–62)

In short, the new and higher life of moral imagination, of spirituality, cannot be joined to the old hedonism. If the moral imagination is to be put above the shipwreck of scientific, rationalist enquiry, it cannot rely on the mere instinctual joy of youth, whether Wordsworth's own, or civilization's. It must, on the contrary, put its faith in the Christian godhead.

But that is not the end of the matter. If the moral beauty or moral imagination for which the Maiden stands is to function effectively in the world, it must join itself to Christian moral action. It lies, as it were, in a passive trance until it is touched by moral conduct. Thus Galahad, who had already dreamed of ideal moral beauty in dreaming of the Maiden, and who is the emblem of perfect moral purity in action, is alone capable of waking the Maiden, and in their union is symbolized the perfect wedding of spirit and conduct. Such a union, it is to be noted, has also required the efforts of benignity on the part of Nina, who rescues the

Maiden from the rocks, and the contribution of intellect on the part of Merlin, who, when properly subordinated to benignity, brings the Maiden to court and there ordains the vague test for the Maiden's groom. And significantly in his search for the test, the limitations of intellectual knowledge are revealed to Merlin: "Much have my books disclosed, but the end is hidden" (l. 174).

Thus the poem represents a sort of allegorical version of the "Immortality Ode," a statement in terms of Arthurian romance of the farewell to youthful hedonism and the assumption of moral maturity that he had presented discursively in the earlier poem. Yet "The Egyptian Maid" is far from being poetically as successful as the Ode. For its failure, several explanations offer themselves. To begin with, it may be suspected that this excursion into romantic allegory involves a radical misapprehension by Wordsworth of his own peculiar talents. His imagination was, it is true, profoundly symbolic, but this symbolic bent in him lay in the direction of concrete idealism; for him objective phenomena shadowed forth the ideal, but they were nonetheless real and important in themselves. The very concreteness, the precise physical notation of his imagination, was opposed to the intellectual equation-making of the allegorist. He was on safe enough ground, perhaps, with the symbol of the ship—the imaginatively fused nucleus around which the poem had grown, or, as he put it, had risen out of his mind "like an exhalation."[71] Merlin, who as a wizard, it may be supposed, was the element that linked the initial image with Arthurian story, is rather more consciously formed, but he is still a fully imagined and precisely constructed symbol. But from this point on the symbols and their articulation become less and less satisfying in substance, more vague in significance. The Maiden is physically lifeless for most of the work; poetically she is dead from beginning to end. Like Nina and Galahad, she is all but bereft of concrete qualities. And the marriage, intended as the resolution of the poem, is just as much lacking in conviction and clear significance. Neither the Maiden nor Galahad has been enough distinguished one from the other as symbols to make the union of the two an effective symbolic statement. True, it can be read as the integration of Christian moral imagination with Christian moral conduct, but the actual impression is rather one of purity marrying purity or spiritual devotion wedding spiritual devotion.

If the trouble with the poem, then, springs initially from Wordsworth's having forced his imagination into an alien field of creation, it may be suspected that he also—and far more disastrously—forced his utterance beyond his deepest insights. The precision with which both Merlin and the ship are defined indicates that Wordsworth had very clear and intense convictions about the arrogance of the rational intellect and the ambivalent beauty of antique (or youthful) hedonism. The contrasting vagueness of Nina, the Maiden, and Galahad suggests that he was a good deal less convinced about the need of putting one's faith absolutely and specifically in Christ. This is not to say that Wordsworth was a hypocrite. There is no reason to suspect the candor of his High Church Anglicanism, and the conscious sincerity of "The Egyptian Maid," like that of the *Ecclesiastical Sonnets*, is equally beyond doubt.[72] But unfortunately they lack the overwhelming psychological and emotional conviction of the great early poems. In those, Wordsworth had been content to find "abundant recompense" for the loss of youthful joy in a doctrinally unspecified "faith that looks through death," in a "sense sublime / Of something far more deeply interfused," but in his later years the poet strove intellectually to equate these perceptions with the theological formulations of the Church of England. "The Egyptian Maid" is split by the inevitable discrepancies of the attempt: he *knew* that rationalism could destroy the glad life of imagination and intuition; he *thought* that moral sensibility required a founding basis in Christian doctrine.

As an Arthurian poem "The Egyptian Maid" is perhaps even less successful. Nevertheless, it is of considerable interest to the study of the later development of the legend. In his generally reverent borrowing from the major outlines and characters of the legend, Wordsworth like Scott illustrates the new Romantic respect for what may quite properly be called the poetic facts of the tradition—a sort of archaeological accuracy in imaginative terms. Much more than Scott, Wordsworth recognized in the legend its inherent bias toward symbolic significance and sought to use it as a carrier of moral and spiritual perceptions, to give it fresh meaning for a new age. But he also, again like Scott, failed to respond creatively to the old cycle itself. He respected it, but he failed to understand that its potential greatness lay not in a collection of characters to be used as a background, but rather in the stories themselves, of which the characters were but actors with fixed rôles. Moreover, even though Wordsworth spurned any wholesale reconstruction of the legend, he was still not able to avoid conflict with its facts in his attempt to add a new link to the mythic chain. Scott had already found it necessary to blacken Arthur's character out of recognition in order to tie his story of Gyneth into the cycle. Wordsworth now fell into a similar misreading of the function of Galahad, who in the legends is always the maiden knight upon whose perfect virginity the achievement of the Grail is based. If Galahad marries, what happens to the Grail quest? And if the Grail quest is eliminated, why any Galahad at all? To revert to the very process of gradual accretion of episodes by which the legend had developed in the Middle Ages must have seemed an eminently safe and admirably pious approach to the use of Arthurian story. But in practice, as the examples of Scott and Wordsworth make clear, it was a remarkably dangerous method. To a casual inspection the old legends with all their appearance of fortuitously jumbled disorder might seem to offer many a loose end to which a new story might be attached, many a vacancy in which a new episode might be lodged; but on closer examination the cycle reveals a mysterious organic integrity from which foreign grafts tend to be rejected as meaningless additions, and in which one apparently insignificant alteration will jangle throughout the whole structure as an alteration of the relations of all the other elements.

REGINALD HEBER

Of the conception that the true greatness of the Arthurian cycle lay precisely within the already established relationships of its characters and stories, only one man in the Romantic period seems to have caught a glimpse, hazy though it was. And Reginald Heber (1783–1826), now remembered best for the missionary hymn "From Greenland's Icy Mountains" and for his generous self-immolation during his service as Bishop of Calcutta, was scarcely fitted to deal with the story whose secret he had seen. His placid temperament and his gentle piety were as unequal to the violence and tragic passion of the old legend as his delicate constitution was to the savage heat and dark diseases of the foreign land that ultimately claimed his life.[73] But while Heber's inspiration was not robust, it was nevertheless of long standing. Beginning with a childhood fondness for Spenser, he had gone on to fill his mind with ballads, the old romances, and, still later, the earlier work of Scott. Years later one of his college friends was to recall a walk in which a discussion of "the old fabliaux and romances" was climaxed by Heber's declaration that "it was a very easy style, and [that] he could imitate it without an effort; and as he went along, he recited, composing as he recited, the happiest imitation of the George-Ellis-specimens which I ever saw."[74] The product of Heber's peripatetic composition, committed to paper the following day, was the "Boke of the Purple Faucon," a brief burlesque of chivalric romance turning on the adventures of one Sir Claudius Pantagruelle, who is sadly given to cannibalism.[75] Read as an undergraduate attempt at parody, it is a mildly amusing jest; as an exercise in literary pastiche it indicates a sensitive and detailed acquaintance with the more obvious features of the medieval romance materials that had come Heber's way.

And both the poem and the conversation that led to it are impressive evidence of how far the antiquarians' enthusiasm for the past had managed to reinstate medieval romance in the imaginations of educated Englishmen by the first decade of the nineteenth century.

Heber's next attempt to exploit the romance materials that thronged his imagination was a completely serious effort to write a modern version of the Arthurian cycle. Begun sometime between 1810 and 1812, this new *Morte D'Arthur*, as he entitled it, was soon to fall afoul of Heber's growing pastoral duties, and was finally to be put aside unfinished.[76] But before that he completed enough of the fragment to show clearly that he intended to integrate all the important Arthurian tales into a single long work centering on the tragic relations of Arthur, Ganora (i.e., Guinivere), Lancelot, and Modred. In short, the poem was generally to follow the format of Malory's work. Yet there were also significant differences, as a glance at Heber's story suggests.

The poem opens well after Arthur's glory has been established by his triumph over the Saxons and his conquest of Gallia and Ireland. At Pentecost he brings to his court and marries Ganora, to all appearances a lowly village damsel, but actually, unbeknownst to all, the daughter of Ladugan, who had concealed her as a babe in the wilds of Derwent. During her life there, Ganora had fallen in love with a "forestere" who called himself Cadwal and who had mysteriously disappeared some seven years before; now at Arthur's court she makes an inward resolve to forget this first love. At this point, the wedding feast, from which Lancelot is absent on a quest, is broken up by the entrance of a bleeding white hind pursued by a huntress who warns Ganora of future unhappiness unless she kills the hind, who has run to her for shelter. Ganora refuses, the damsel vanishes, and Arthur, suspecting his sister's magic arts, defies them with a

> portentous smile of hate and scorn,
> Which each strong furrow, stronger made to be,
> By toil, and care, and ruthless passion worn,
> And recollected guilt of youth's tempestuous morn! (I, liv)

Why Arthur suspected his sister's hand in this event and what his guilt was appears in the next canto. In youth Arthur, moved to a fit of anger upon discovering the "unpermitted love" of his sister Morgue and Paladore, had killed the latter, whereupon Morgue had leaped from a cliff only to be borne up by an enchantment and carried to the fays whom she thus came to rule as "goblin leader of a goblin crew" (II, xxvii). Just now she is at court disguised as the white hind; during the night she resumes her human form and plots the destruction of Arthur and the elevation of her son by Paladore, Modred, who hungers not only for the throne, but also for Ganora, who had been promised him by his mother. Time passes and one day Ganora wanders into a chapel that contains the Grail. In the wall paintings she recognizes the likeness of Cadwal, her early lover. The name inscribed above it is Lancelot. After raving at his desertion of her, she weakly begs that her "tempted heart" will break while her will is still "pure." With prayer she recovers her composure, and later, upon questioning her maids about Lancelot, learns that he disdains all women of the court, nursing a love for some unknown damsel said to live in Derwent. At this melodramatic discovery, the fragment comes to its end.

With the exception of the slight but important alterations that Heber thus introduces into the motivation of the legend, the broad outlines of his story could easily have been derived from a number of versions of the Arthurian tradition. Nevertheless, as both the title of the poem and several details indicate, Malory was probably his main source.[77] From the fifteenth-century *Le Morte Darthur* he had, for example, the suggestion for the white hind pursued by a huntress that interrupts the nuptial feast, and also the opening of the Balin story that concludes the second canto.[78] At the same time, Heber appears to have ranged freely through a number of other sources. Both Morgue's name and her youthful indiscretion with Paladore seem to have been suggested by one of George Ellis' notes to Way's translation of Le Grand's *Fabliaux*.[79] From Ellis' own *Specimens of Early English Metrical Romances*, he drew yet other materials lacking in Malory, among them the account of Lancelot's parentage and his rearing by the Lady of the Lake.[80]

This inclusion of the *enfance* of Lancelot, an element strikingly absent in Malory, who introduces that hero with a disconcerting abruptness into his narrative, suggests that Heber intended to go Malory one better in presenting a synoptic view of the whole body of Arthurian story. At the same time, the care with which he weaves in this and other subordinate tales such as the hopeless love of Tristan and Yseult (sung by a bard at the nuptial feast in Canto I) and the beginning of the Balin story indicates that he planned to unify the old episodes in a manner much more orderly than that of Malory's often haphazard and formally unmotivated *rifacimento*. He meant, in short, to reduce the old romances into what he called "a sort of epic poem."[81]

Unfortunately, the sensibility that was inclined to see the Arthurian legend in epic terms was not content to stop at a praiseworthy endeavor to regularize its narrative structure. It also sought to iron out other "irregularities" in the content of the legend, and to do this Heber was obliged to depart in important ways from his sources. To begin with, there was the question of the supernatural. In the old romances, the whole story from Arthur's mysterious birth to his equally mysterious passing is wrapped in magic. For Heber, a man reared during the unsettled struggle of rationalism and romanticism, it was apparently acceptable enough—even desirable—to make use of the supernatural for ornament, much as his age decorated the essentially rational plots of its Gothic novels with mysterious events, and its symmetrical architectural plans with Gothic crockets and finials. What was unpleasant and to be avoided was allowing the central story to rest on the supernatural. Thus the origins of Arthur are ignored and the whole motivation of the central action is made rationally explicable.[82] Even that most supernatural of all objects, the Grail, is treated with an odd indifference to its mysteriousness in the old stories: in Heber's poem it stands in full view as one of the furnishings of one of the chapels of Arthur's castle.[83] With the subtraction of the mythically important supernatural elements, all that was left were the harmless (and trivial) thrills of such fairy-tale magic as enchantments, spells, and transformations—the mere gimmickry—or "machinery"—of the supernatural.

Even more unpleasant to Heber than the mythic bearings of the story were its moral irregularities. In his efforts to deal with the tragically passionate infatuation of Arthur's queen and friend, the gentle Anglican clergyman fell back on serious modifications of the tradition. Ganora thus becomes "a village maid, who rank nor splendour knew" (I, vi); the source of the love between her and Lancelot is made to be a wholly innocent youthful troth plighted when both were unmarried. The result is predictable. The emotional interest in Heber's *Morte D'Arthur* is shifted almost exclusively to the soul-searchings of the unfortunate innocent harboring a sinful passion in her breast, and the fierce tragedy of the old myth is converted to a bittersweet tale of star-crossed lovers, a sentimental epic of bad conscience.[84] Such a theme had a sure and obvious appeal to Heber's well-developed homiletic tendencies, and he emphasized it unsparingly from beginning to end. When, for example, Ganora dreams of her early love and thus reveals it to the watchful Morgue, Heber is quick to draw the appropriate *significatio* about such guilty thoughts "e'en to wakeful conscience unconfest":

> And think'st thou, man, thy secret wish to shroud
>> In the close bosom's sealèd sepulchre?
> Or, wrapt in saintly mantle from the crowd,
>> To hug thy darling sin that none may see?
> A thousand, thousand eyes are bent on thee.[85] (II, lxi)

It is true, to be sure, that the Arthurian story has had from an early time a profoundly moral bent, and indeed every great treatment of the legend has drawn much of its strength from this moral significance. But there is a world of difference between the moral and the moralistic, and it is the latter that moved Heber.

There is another world of difference between the spirit of medieval romance and the upholsterer's Gothic that seems basically to have attracted Heber. "Like some gay child," to use the words he applies to his heroine, he drew "a simple bliss . . . / From every gaud of feudal pageantry, / And every broider'd garb that swept in order by" (III, viii). Like Scott, the chief master of the antiquarian school in which he worked, Heber was strong for archaeological accuracy,[86] and, at the same time by an odd paradox, like most of the members of that school, he was also inclined to conflate details of Arthurian story with historical fact or with other fabulous elements foreign to the cycle. Hence the curious lament for the "Celtic glories" destroyed by the Saxons (III, i), and hence the strange assertion that Balin's first victim was "Erin's Cucullin." That neither Irish story nor other Celtic antiquities have any place in the chivalric romance of a mythic king who rules an essentially feudal realm seems to have momentarily slipped Heber's mind.

The risk of injustice in the criticism of an unfinished poem is inescapable, yet on balance it does not seem likely that Heber's *Morte D'Arthur* would have been a successful work had it been completed. Not only was his conception of the legend inadequate—despite all that is commendable in his attempts to reduce the confusions of the old stories to order—but also, and perhaps more important ultimately, his tastes and talents as a poet were thin and derivative. Like other minor poets of his time he moved uneasily between the conventionalized diction of the Neo-Classicists and a sort of spurious Miltonic grandiloquence.[87] Even the selection of the difficult Spenserian stanza reflects the Spenserian revival of the preceding century; no matter how ideally suited it had been to Spenser's leisurely, allegorical, and richly ornamented poem, its use by Heber reveals an insensitivity to the relation of ends to means in a work that obviously required swift and vigorous narrative to cover its chosen ground. Indeed, it may not push hypothesis too far to suspect that the very difficulties of the stanza played their part in the abandonment of the poem. At any rate, as he was to say later, he "had no time to take [it] up as anything more than an occasional amusement, and merely as such [it] cost me too much trouble and time to answer my purpose."[88] And thus the first attempt since the fifteenth century to give a serious and comprehensive expression to the whole corpus of Arthurian legend was set aside unfinished.

Although the Arthurian epic had become too onerous for Heber, he had not lost interest in the subject, and in 1816 he turned to a much less ambitious use of the material in *The Masque of Gwendolen*.[89] This also was left unfinished, but unlike the earlier work, the poem appears to lack but a few lines for its completion. The story is a combination of elements of the Merlin legend with others from the *Marriage of Gawain*. Gwendolen, who has encouraged Merlin in order to learn his secrets, finally spurns his proposal because of his demonic connections, and is thereupon transformed into a loathly hag by the magician's art. Rescued by Titania and the fairies from suicidal despair, she is soon comforted to learn that Merlin has himself been locked away from the upper world by the power of one of his own spells applied by his "elfin paramour," the Lady of the Lake. Arthur, meanwhile, in a fit of anger at the contumacy of one of his knights, Llewellin, has vowed that the offender shall die unless Gawain can learn "Merlin's Secret" as to what women most desire. In the very nick of time, Gawain does learn the secret from Gwendolen—"Power is their passion"—and so releases Llewellin, but now he is called upon to fulfill his promise to marry the loathsome Gwendolen. After some revulsion he kisses her, makes the sign of the cross in his terror, and thus unwittingly releases her from the curse.

The inspiration for this poem appears to have come from a number of sources, illustrating once more Heber's broad command of the Arthurian materials available at his time. The association of the name Gwendolen with Merlin probably results from Merlin's having had a wife of that name in the *Vita Merlini*.[90] The immurement of the magician, Heber could have found easily in Malory. For the motif of the loathly lady and the question of what women most desire, Mrs. Heber suggested Chaucer's *Wife of Bath's Tale* as a source, but in fact the old ballad of "The Marriage of Sir Gawaine," printed in Percy's *Reliques*, shows much closer resemblances.[91] The addition of Titania and the fairies to these relatively standard Arthurian materials seems to have been Heber's own idea, and reflects once more, as indeed the tone of the whole masque does, the early romantic lack of discrimination between the realms of fairyland and the domain of the mythic Arthur. And it is to the airy, tricksy world of the former that *The Masque of Gwendolen* properly belongs.

In his retreat from the difficulties of the larger *Morte D'Arthur*, Heber had thus regressed to the old approach of free adaptation and combination if not of reckless invention. What he produced was doubtless a pleasant enough entertainment to relieve the ennui of a country house, but at the same time he had been obliged to substitute the tinsel of fairy glamor for the rich hangings of the old story. Yet his willingness to fall back on the lower subject, should not be allowed to obscure the fact that Heber first in modern times had perceived that the true greatness of the Arthurian legend was to be tapped by following more or less closely and reverently its own long-established relations. Nor should the moralistic bias of his sensibility conceal from us his awareness that the story could be the fully rounded image of moral truth. The way that Heber had thus pointed, no matter how dimly, probably had no direct effect on the later versions of the story. Nevertheless, it strangely prefigured the very course that Tennyson would take some two generations later.

AN ENGLAND READY FOR ARTHUR'S RETURN

By the end of the first third of the nineteenth century, it is clear, both from the number of attempts to turn Arthurian story to aesthetic account and from its attractiveness to men as various in stature and tastes as Peacock and Scott, Heber and Wordsworth, that the legend of the mythic king was well on its way to complete reinstatement among the great poetic matters. But at the same time, none of these Romantic treatments, it must be confessed, managed to exploit to the full the potentialities of the subject. To some extent this failure was probably a result of the very antiquarian and historical interests that had done so much to revive the old story. Nearly all of the Romantic writers who took up Arthurian story show an odd predilection for relating the legend to historical fact or to local topography. Peacock had cut his Arthur down to a rough warrior kinglet and Scott had laid his Gyneth asleep in a castle in the Vale of St. John.[92] But such attempts to historicize or localize the Arthurian stories are inherently contradictory, and far from lending credibility to the legend, they are but disturbing and irrelevant reminders of another order of reality. The truth of the material is poetic or imagined truth, and Arthur ruled not in history but rather in the "long, long ago" over a kingdom that had never existed save in the minds of men, a realm that had little to offer to the impulse for historical reconstruction that delighted the age. At any rate, whether the blame be laid to the irreconcilable conflict of antiquarian impulse and the nature of romance, or to the simple inadequacy of such writers as Thelwall and Heber, or to the unsuitableness of the material itself to the special genius of Scott and Wordsworth, the fact remains that all the Romantic versions of the Arthurian story are stillborn. Their interest as groping efforts to deal with the great mythic subject of the Middle Ages and as illustrations of the difficulties inherent in the material is considerable, but their actual contribution to the development of Arthurian legend is small.

The real contribution of the Romantic period was the development of a climate of opinion, a new sensibility, in which Arthurian story in the coming age could flourish again as it had not done since the end of the Middle Ages. Of this new sensibility, one of the most significant formative elements was the subtle sympathy for the past produced by the Romantic historical sense. The Middle Ages had interested the pre-Romantics considerably, but as a repository of the decorative, the quaint and picturesque. History as we know it today—as a sympathetic quest for the spirit of bygone times—might almost be called a nineteenth-century invention. "Nowhere before our time," Renan wrote, "do I find the immediate feeling for the life of the past. . . . Our century was the first to have that kind of finesse which grasps, within the apparently colorless uniformity of ancient accounts, traits of manners and characters which no longer have analogues in the present state of society."[93] Comprehended in this fashion, the historical and literary monuments of the Middle Ages received a new validation. No longer a sentimental waxworks for the curious, they became a real human time, a repository of values for the new age.

Among these values, none had a greater impact on the new sensibility than the institution of chivalry, the very system of which Arthur and his Round Table constituted an enduring symbolic expression. Bishop Hurd had long ago recognized its importance in medieval thought, but to him it was largely interesting as a source of superior poetic subjects. Even before the end of the eighteenth century, Burke had attached a deeper significance to the knightly code by equating the excesses of the French Revolution with the passing of chivalry. To Walter Scott, a generation later, chivalry had taken on even greater importance: "Excepting only the change which flowed from the introduction of the Christian religion, we know no cause which has produced such general and permanent difference betwixt the ancients and the moderns as that which has arisen out of the institution of Chivalry."[94] And Scott's essay was but one rivulet in a flood of books on chivalry that poured from the presses between 1815 and 1830.[95] In the most influential of these, *The Broad Stone of Honour*, Kenelm Digby had defined chivalry as "that general spirit and state of mind which disposes men to heroic and generous actions and keeps them conversant with all that is beautiful and sublime in the intellectual and moral world." For Digby, clearly, chivalry was not a mere historical phenomenon—it was a continuing guide to thought and conduct. The view was shared by G. P. R. James, whose *History of Chivalry* (1830) flatly declared that this "most glorious institution that man himself ever devised" had bequeathed to the modern world "a treasure of noble feelings and generous principles."[96] To be sure, men like the aging Canning, who had begun to see England's greatness in terms of her trade and industry, might welcome the substitution of the "age of oeconomists and calculators" for the age of chivalry whose passing Burke had lamented.[97] But among the young and idealistic—the Victorians to be—the noble code that had motivated Arthur and his knights had become more than an object of antiquarian interest: it was a gauge of the quality of modern life and, indeed, a way of living that life. As they grew older, they might recall their youthful loves a bit sheepishly; like Burne-Jones they might murmur that the works of Digby were "sillyish books," but they would probably add with him—a bit defiantly—"I can't help it, I like them."[98] And that was all there was to it—a new sensibility had been created, one which would welcome the return of Arthurian chivalry.

Beyond the new historical sense that thus revivified the knightly code, there were other more concrete elements in early nineteenth-century society that operated to make chivalry attractive. The feudal anarchy that had called forth chivalry as an organizing and civilizing principle in the Middle Ages was reappearing more and more in modern counterparts in prereform England. The lives of thousands upon thousands withered away in the lint-filled air of Manchester's mills, and other thousands were driven back to animal clawings for existence in the gloomy depths of the coal mines of the North. The old sense of social responsibility that had characterized the government when power had resided mainly in the hands of the landed gentry and aristocracy was being steadily replaced by the traditionless individualism of the new industrialists and plutocrats.[99] As early as 1802 Cobbett was complaining, perhaps exaggeratedly, that "the ancient nobility and gentry of the kingdom have, with a very few exceptions, been thrust out of all public employments. . . . A race of merchants and manufacturers and bankers and loan jobbers and contractors have usurped their place."[100] The productive capacity of the country was completely unorganized and uncontrolled, and even in government the bureaucracy operated with a feudalistic disregard for the Crown.[101] And at the same time that all these evidences of a divided, disorganized society were accumulating, the power of the monarch, the one abiding symbol of unity, was visibly declining into a "harmless fetish," as Halévy calls it.[102] Even the ranks of the aristocracy were not safe from the incursions of the new money men, as the extensive creation of new peers and knights by Pitt and others during the first fifteen years of the century made clear.[103] If birth was not the distinguishing characteristic of a gentleman, neither could money or party service be accepted as adequate qualifications by thoughtful men.[104] With social values in such a state of flux, all that was left to distinguish the gentleman was his behavior. Little wonder then that several generations of Englishmen—both those who were secure in their status and those who were reaching toward status— devoutly embraced the code of chivalry that lay so ready to hand and by which a gentleman's behavior might be governed and the new plutocratic feudalism civilized and subordinated to the community. The wide adoption of this idea thus did much to create in time yet to come a fully sympathetic audience for the legend of a king who had unified a strife-torn realm and created in it a glorious chivalry ruled by high selflessness.

But in the last analysis the greatest contribution of the Romantic period to the later Arthurian revival was something much less tangible than either historical sensitivity or an adulation of the chivalric code. The real gift of the period was the Romantic sensibility itself, with its full belief in the poetic imagination as a way of knowing, its full faith in its own imagined creations. For it is here that the *rapprochement* of Romanticism and romance is most vital. *The Rime of the Ancient Mariner* and medieval romance are at one in the impression that they give of absolute and unquestioning faith in the ultimate reality of their events and characters, no matter how supernatural or contrary to ordinary reality. With the end of the Middle Ages a new attitude had become apparent in adaptations of romance materials. There is an inescapable impression of ambivalence towards the mythological in nearly all of the attempts from the Renaissance to the nineteenth century to deal with the Arthurian subject. For both the intellectually self-conscious writers of the sixteenth century and the more empirically inclined rationalists of the next two centuries, the myth with its supernatural elements continued to be attractive. The mythic, the supernatural were "poetical," and they could be used consciously to add delight to poetry or they could be manipulated as a thoroughly serious symbolism of systematic moral truth. But such uses were distinct from any felt belief in the reality of the materials and there is a corresponding lack of conviction on a narrative level in the poems in which they occur. This was doubtless entirely proper—the mythic was not to be confused with reality. Reality lay either in the rarified reaches of pure intellectual systems or alternatively in the actual physical world where it was observed by the senses and measured by the rules of probability.

For the Romantic, however, reality was not to be found either in the world that was seen "through the eye" or in abstract systems of philosophical idealism. "The good, the true, and the beautiful," as Bernbaum observes in describing the Romantic temper, "were interwoven with [man's] human existence and earthly environment. It was the highest function of literature and art to portray man and his world in such a way that the presence of the infinite within the finite, of the ideal within the actual, would be revealed in all its beauty."[105] The merely factual world was not the limit of faith; its physical laws were not the boundaries of conviction. Seen thus, poetic myth might once more take on a validity similar to that which it had had for the Middle Ages. No longer either fanciful embellishment or bloodless moral paradigm, the poet's myth was truth itself, and its characters and events could call for full poetic faith. In short, by its reaction against both empiricism and rationalist realism, Romanticism had recreated in its willing surrender to the shaping powers of the imagination something of the climate of belief in which the Arthurian story had first flowered.

The fact that the legend of Arthur did not find its great re-expression within the conventional chronological limits of the Romantic period does not invalidate this view. Neither a clear understanding of the medieval spirit nor the best of the genuine medieval romance materials was widely available during the formative years of most of the Romantics. But in the age to come there would be a body of Englishmen to whom the Middle Ages were more than an antique shop full of quaint artifacts and to whom Arthurian legend would offer more than the faint fragrance of the past. For the young men who would write and read the poetry we call Victorian, the Middle Ages would be a heritage fully entered into, a treasury of moral and poetic inspiration, a home for the spirit, a realm in which high ideals and action believably flourished. And as the heirs of the Romantic sensibility, they would find in the myths of Arthur and his knights truth that goes beyond fact, and

> Sorrow that is not sorrow, but delight;
> And miserable love, that is not pain
> To hear of, for the glory that redounds
> Therefrom to human kind, and what we are.
>
> (*The Prelude*, XIII, 246–49)

NOTES

PREFACE

1. So vast is the field of medieval Arthurian studies and so riddled with controversy that until fairly recently only one survey, James Douglas Bruce's *The Evolution of Arthurian Romance from the Beginnings down to the Year 1300* (2 vols., *Hesperia*, "Ergänzungsreihe: Schriften zur englischen Philologie," Hefte VIII-IX; Göttingen and Baltimore, 1923), appears to have met with any degree of general approval. To a large extent Bruce's book has now been replaced by *Arthurian Literature in the Middle Ages: A Collaborative History*, ed. Roger Sherman Loomis (Oxford, 1959). For a brief scholarly survey for the general reader, see Roger Sherman Loomis, *The Development of Arthurian Romance* (London, 1963). There is no single, up-to-date bibliography. For the earlier material, the standard work is Bruce's *Evolution of Arthurian Romance*. Later publications are listed in *Bibliography of Critical Arthurian Literature*, Vol. I (1922–1929) compiled by John J. Parry for the MLA (1931), Vol. II (1930–1935) compiled by Parry and Margaret Schlauch for the MLA (1936), Vol. III (1936–1939) compiled by Parry and Schlauch for *MLQ* (1940), and continued annually in *MLQ* through 1963; Paul A. Brown assisted Parry for 1954 and after 1955 became the sole compiler. The standard serial bibliography in Arthurian studies today is the *Bulletin Bibliographique de la Société Internationale Arthurienne*, issued annually since 1949, Vols. 1–18 ed. Jean Frappier, thereafter by Lewis Thorpe; unfortunately the *Bulletin* excludes most studies dealing with the story of Arthur after the sixteenth century. For an extensive listing of versions of the Arthurian story published since 1800 together with critical works dealing with these versions, see Clark S. Northup and John J. Parry, "The Arthurian Legends: Modern Retellings of the Old Stories: An Annotated Bibliography," *JEGP*, 43 (1944), 173–221; and Parry's supplement in *JEGP*, 49 (1950), 213–16. The reader should be specifically cautioned against A. E. Curdy's frequently erroneous "Arthurian Literature," *RR*, 1 (1910), 125–39 and 265–78.

2. Since MacCallum's book and other works mentioned in this preface are

all cited elsewhere in my notes and listed in the bibliography, I have refrained from giving full citations here.

3. The same ground is covered in what appears to be an even more cursory manner in K. F. Plesner's *Engelsk Arthur-Digtning* (1925). Another very brief survey is E. M. R. Ditmas, "King Arthur in Literature," *Books*, No. 331 (1960), 159–64.

4. E[ugène] V[inaver], Review of Reid's *The Arthurian Legend*, in *RES*, 16 (1940), 331–32. The preface of Reid's book carries the date 1938; it was reprinted without alteration in 1960.

5. The limitations of Barber's work may be gathered from the reviews by Robert W. Ackerman (*CE*, 23 [1962], 512), R. T. Davies (*RES*, NS 13 [1962], 399–400), Helaine Newstead (*Speculum*, 37 [1962], 600–601), and Nathan Comfort Starr (*MLQ*, 23 [1962], 401–402).

6. Also useful for the sixteenth and seventeenth centuries are Charles Bowie Millican's *Spenser and the Table Round: A Study in the Contemporaneous Background for Spenser's Use of the Arthurian Legend* (1932), and William Edward Mead's "Arthurian Story in the Sixteenth Century," in his edition of Christopher Middleton's *Chinon of England* (EETS, Original Series No. 165; 1925), pp. xxv–xlvi.

7. W. Lewis Jones's *King Arthur in History and Legend* (1911, 1914) ignores most of the latter-day Arthurian works, but makes a few interesting comments on Tennyson's *Idylls*. David Jones's "The Myth of Arthur" (in *For Hilaire Belloc: Essays in Honor of His 72nd Birthday*, ed. Douglas Woodruff [1942]) has some challenging remarks on the problems of converting mythic materials to modern uses. Richard Paul Wülker's *Die Arthursage in der englischen Literatur* (1895) is too sketchy to be of value. The same applies to Robert Spindler's "Die Arthursage in der viktorianischen Dichtung" (*Britannica: Max Förster zum sechzigsten Geburtstage* [1929]). Mention must also be made of W. A. Nitze's *Arthurian Romance and Modern Poetry and Music* (1940), which, in fact, scarcely touches on modern poetry.

8. The earliest of these studies dealing with specific Arthurian themes appears to have been Wolfgang Golther's *Tristan und Isolde in den Dichtungen des Mittelalters und der neuen Zeit* (1907). See also T. Sturge Moore, "The Story of Tristram and Isolt in Modern Poetry," *The Criterion*, I (1922), 34–49 and 171–87; Maurice Halperin, *Le Roman de Tristan et Iseut dans la littérature anglo-américaine au XIXe et XXe siècles* (1931); Elisabeth Gutbier, *Psychologisch-ästhetische Studien zu Tristandichtungen der neueren englischen Literatur* (1932); Lucien Wolff, "Tristan et Iseult dans la poésie anglaise au XIXe siècle," *Annales de Bretagne*, 40 (1932), 113–52; Alfred Ehrentreich, "Tristan und Isolde in der neueren englischen Literatur," *Englische Studien*, 49 (1934), 220–36; Anna-Marie Wangelin, *Die Liebe in den Tristandichtungen der viktorianischen Zeit* (1937). Nineteenth-century treatments of the Grail theme are considered in J. S. Tunison's *The Graal Problem from Walter Map to Richard Wagner* (1904); Wolfgang Golther's *Parzival und der Gral in der*

Dichtung des Mittelalters und der Neuzeit (1925); and Louis Rigaud's "Le Graal au service de la morale victorienne," *Lumière du Graal*, ed. René Nelli (1951). Ella Vettermann analyzes sources of the Victorian versions of the Balen story in her *Die Balen-Dichtungen und ihre Quellen* ("Beiheft zur Zeitschrift für romanische Philologie," Vol. LX; 1918).

9. Studies of the literary fortunes of particular Arthurian characters are found in B. K. Ray's *The Character of Gawain* (Dacca University Bulletin, No. XI; 1926); August J. App's *Lancelot in English Literature: His Rôle and Character* (1929); Sister Mary Louise Morgan's *Galahad in English Literature* (1932); Elise Francisca Wilhelmina Maria Van Der Ven-Ten Bensel's *The Character of King Arthur in English Literature* (1925). In this group of character studies may also be included William Edward Mead's "Outlines of the History of the Legend of Merlin," *Merlin, or The Early History of King Arthur*, ed. Henry B. Wheatley, I (EETS, Vols. X, XXI, XXXVI, and CXII; 1865–1899), v–cclvi.

1. THE GROWTH OF A LEGEND: ARTHUR IN THE MIDDLE AGES

1. Roger Sherman Loomis, *Celtic Myth and Arthurian Legend* (New York, 1927), pp. 353–54; see also Loomis, *The Grail: From Celtic Myth to Christian Symbol* (Cardiff, 1963), pp. 20–27. The study of the origins of Arthurian story and, for that matter, of most of the developments in the legend before the Renaissance is extraordinarily fraught with uncertainty and disagreement. Professor Loomis' observation about the literature itself—that "consistency, harmony, fixity are not its outstanding qualities" (*Arthurian Literature in the Middle Ages: A Collaborative History*, ed. Roger Sherman Loomis [Oxford, 1959], p. xvi)—applies with equal force to the scholarship as a body. In the account that follows I have leaned heavily on James Douglas Bruce, *The Evolution of Arthurian Romance from the Beginnings Down to the Year 1300* (2 vols., Hesperia, "Ergänzungsreihe: Schriften zur englischen Philologie," Hefte VIII–IX; Göttingen and Baltimore, 1923); Loomis, *Celtic Myth*; *Arthurian Literature*, ed. Loomis; Robert Huntington Fletcher, *The Arthurian Material in the Chronicles* ([Harvard] Studies and Notes in Philology and Literature, Vol. X; Boston, 1906; new ed., New York, 1958); and E. K. Chambers, *Arthur of Britain* (London, 1927). Fortunately, it is as unnecessary to our purposes as it is beyond my competence to trace out in detail the development that I here attempt to summarize in only the broadest outline.

2. Loomis, *Celtic Myth*, p. 4.

3. Matthew Arnold, *The Study of Celtic Literature*, ed. Alfred Nutt ([London], 1910), p. 53. These lectures, delivered at Oxford in 1866, were first published in book form in 1867. M. W. MacCallum (*Tennyson's Idylls of the King and Arthurian Story from the XVIth Century* [Glasgow, 1894], pp. 3–4) also quotes Renan to something of the same effect from a review that

had appeared in *Revue des Deux Mondes* in 1854; it is of significance to the study of the later revival of Arthurian legend that such a view of the origins of the story was becoming common by the mid-nineteenth century.

4. For a convenient summary of the earlier attempts at identification, see MacCallum, *Idylls of the King and Arthurian Story*, pp. 4 ff. and Loomis, *Celtic Myth*, p. 350.

5. For Nennius, see Fletcher, *Arthurian Material*, pp. 8–30.

6. Rachel Bromwich in *Arthurian Literature*, ed. Loomis, p. 47. Clark S. Northup ("King Arthur, the Christ, and Some Others," *Studies in English Philology: A Miscellaney in Honor of Frederick Klaeber*, ed. Kemp Malone and Martin B. Ruud [Minneapolis, 1929], pp. 309–19) offers a number of interesting speculations as to the process by which "the warrior of Mount Badon" became "the magnificent emperor-god." Both the Christ story and that of Arthur, Northup suggests, may result from the "growth of national spirit and the passionate desire for a liberator" among a subjugated people. "Starting as men who captured the favor of the people, . . . both [Arthur and Christ] were elevated to the godhead. In both cases the process was probably gradual; it went on for decades, perhaps for generations." Interestingly enough, there is some evidence, from the twelfth century on, that medieval typology saw in Arthur a type of Christ; see Sister M. Amelia Klenke, "Some Mediaeval Concepts of King Arthur," *Kentucky Foreign Language Quarterly*, 5 (1958), 191–98.

7. Bromwich in *Arthurian Literature*, ed. Loomis, pp. 44–48. The MSS are of the thirteenth century and later, but, as Miss Bromwich points out, they show "marks of high antiquity."

8. Here again dating is a problem, but the poem, which occurs in the *Book of Taliesin*, is, according to Kenneth Hurlstone Jackson (in *Arthurian Literature*, ed. Loomis, p. 16), probably of pre-Norman date.

9. *Ibid.*, p. 15; cf. Idris Llewelyn Foster in *Arthurian Literature*, ed. Loomis, pp. 32–38. The version in the *Red Book of Hergest* is, according to Miss Foster, not older than the second half of the eleventh century.

10. The *Annales Cambriae* (*ca.* 950) mention "the Battle of Camlann, in which Arthur and Medraut fell" (Jackson, in *Arthurian Literature*, ed. Loomis, pp. 4–5).

11. Loomis, *Arthurian Literature*, pp. 64–71.

12. One of the latest scholars to survey Arthur's historicity, K. H. Jackson, is forced to say that to the question of whether Arthur ever existed, "the only honest answer is, 'We do not know, but he may well have existed' " (*Arthurian Literature*, ed. Loomis, p. 1). Jackson and Loomis (*Celtic Myth*, pp. 350–51) represent the commoner scholarly view that the probabilities are in favor of Arthur's historicity. See also John Jay Parry's posthumously published "The Historical Arthur," *JEGP*, 58 (1959), 365–79. For a convincingly argued rejection of that view, see Lord Raglan's *The Hero: A Study in Tradi-*

tion, Myth, and Drama (The Thinker's Library, No. 133; London, 1949), pp. 73–82.

13. John J. Parry and Robert A. Caldwell in *Arthurian Literature*, ed. Loomis, p. 85.

14. Geoffrey's sources and the extent of his originality are both uncertain, though the evidence is against his claim to having used "a very old book in the British language." See *ibid.*, pp. 81–85, and Fletcher, *Arthurian Material*, pp. 49–115, for discussions of the sources. See also W. Lewis Jones, "Geoffrey of Monmouth and the Legend of Arthur," *Quarterly Review*, 205 (July, 1906), 54–78, and J. S. P. Tatlock's monumental *The Legendary History of Britain* (Berkeley and Los Angeles, 1950).

15. Geoffrey's account is conveniently summarized by Fletcher, *Arthurian Material*, pp. 48–49. The full text in translation is easily available in *The History of the Kings of Britain*, trans. Lewis Thorpe (The Penguin Classics, No. L170; Baltimore, 1966). *Histories of the Kings of Britain*, trans. Sebastian Evans (Everyman's Library, No. 577; London and New York, 1912) is far less satisfactory.

16. Parry and Caldwell (*Arthurian Literature*, ed. Loomis, p. 84) say that Geoffrey "made of Arthur's court a glorification of the courts he knew."

17. *Ibid.*, p. 88. The most extensive list of the MSS is to be found in Acton Griscom's edition, *The Historia Regum Britanniae of Geoffrey of Monmouth* (London, 1929).

18. Geoffrey was the chief source of Wace's *Roman de Brut*, one of the most important of the romances in chronicle form, and, through Wace, of Laȝamon's *Brut* (*Arthurian Literature*, ed. Loomis, pp. 94–95 and 105). Wace added the motif of the Round Table (i.e., the physical object and its ceremonies) to the story. Layamon emphasizes Arthur's personal prowess in battle and his importance as a protector of law. He also suggests that Guinevere was willfully treacherous to Arthur.

19. Parry and Caldwell, *Arthurian Literature*, ed. Loomis, p. 75.

20. Loomis, *Arthurian Literature*, p. 53.

21. For our purposes, it is unnecessary to trace these pre-Malorian developments in detail; their direct influence on later English treatments of the story was negligible, and the contributions that they made to the story are largely reflected in Malory, whose work will be examined later. Even so, I must warn the reader that my summary represents a conflation of literary events over a period of nearly four centuries.

22. Elise Francisca Wilhelmina Maria Van Der Ven-Ten Bensel, *The Character of King Arthur in English Literature* (Amsterdam, 1925), p. 2.

23. MacCallum, *Idylls of the King and Arthurian Story*, p. 81.

24. Loomis, *Arthurian Literature*, p. 59.

25. Loomis, *Celtic Myth*, p. 3.

26. Loomis, *Arthurian Literature*, pp. 59–60.

27. It may be observed in passing that neither "verve" nor storytelling

ability is markedly characteristic of later instances of vogues in subject matter, e.g., the Gothic tale, Western stories, science fiction, etc.

28. Loomis, *Arthurian Literature*, p. 561.

29. MacCallum, *Idylls of the King and Arthurian Story*, pp. 38–39. While the *Zeitgeist* approach to literary problems is less fashionable today than it was in MacCallum's day, it still seems to me to have considerable value in dealing with questions of vogue in a subject matter. Of course it must not be forgotten that the Middle Ages include many times in many places among many kinds of men, and MacCallum's explanation must be qualified by saying that it applies to the social classes that produced and consumed the imaginative literature we call romances. For an interesting (and somewhat Marxist) examination of the conformation of Arthurian story to various stages in feudal history, see A. L. Morton, "The Matter of Britain: The Arthurian Cycle and the Development of Feudal Society," *Zeitschrift für Anglistik und Amerikanistik*, 8 (1960), 5–28.

30. For the persistence of barbarism and violence in the Middle Ages, see J. Huizinga, *The Waning of the Middle Ages: A Study of the Forms of Life, Thought and Arts in France and the Netherlands in the XIVth and XVth Centuries* (London, 1952; first published in English translation, 1924), esp. chap. I.

31. F. J. C. Hearnshaw, "Chivalry and Its Place in History," *Chivalry: A Series of Studies to Illustrate Its Historical Significance and Civilizing Influence*, ed. Edgar Prestage (London, 1928), pp. 4–9. On the development of chivalry, see also Charles Moorman, "The First Knights," *Southern Quarterly*, 1 (1962), 13–26; rpt. with minor changes in Moorman's *A Knyght There Was: The Evolution of the Knight in Literature* (Lexington, 1967), pp. 9–26.

32. See W. T. H. Jackson, *The Literature of the Middle Ages* (New York, 1960), p. 93; Maurice Valency, *In Praise of Love: An Introduction to the Love-Poetry of the Renaissance* (New York, 1958), pp. 38–42.

33. Huizinga, *Waning of the Middle Ages*, p. 38.

34. *Ibid.*, chap. V.

35. MacCallum, *Idylls of the King and Arthurian Story*, p. 41. Huizinga (*Waning of the Middle Ages*, pp. 30 and 163) says "In the Middle Ages the choice lay, in principle, only between God and the world, between contempt or eager acceptance, at the peril of one's soul, of all that makes up the beauty and charm of earthly life," and adds that in the Middle Ages an "absolute dualism" between the two "dominated all thinking and living."

36. Quoted by W. T. H. Jackson, *Literature of the Middle Ages*, p. 15.

37. Hearnshaw (*Chivalry*, ed. Prestage, pp. 24 and 32–33) lists a number of the more usual particulars of the chivalric code.

38. *Ibid.*, pp. 9–15.

39. For analyses of *amour courtois* and its origins, see C. S. Lewis, *The Allegory of Love: A Study in Medieval Tradition* (London, 1938), pp. 1–43, and John Jay Parry's introduction to his edition of Andreas Capellanus' *The*

Art of Courtly Love (New York, 1941), pp. 3–21. Recent scholars have gravely questioned Parry's conception of Andreas' *De Amore* as a serious exposition of the doctrines of courtly love. D. W. Robertson, Jr. ("The Subject of the *De Amore* of Andreas Capellanus," *MP*, 50 [February, 1953], 145–61), considers the book an ironic attack on concupiscence, and W. T. H. Jackson ("The *De Amore* of Andreas Capellanus and the Practice of Love at Court," *RR*, 49 [December, 1958], 243–51) takes it to be a tongue-in-cheek account of actual court practices. Cf. also John F. Benton, "The Court of Champagne as a Literary Center," *Speculum*, 36 (October, 1961), 578–82.

40. See Sir Herbert Grierson, *The Background of English Literature, Classical & Romantic, and Other Collected Essays and Addresses* (2nd ed.; London, 1950), pp. 278–79. Grierson goes so far as to identify chivalry with the secular spirit (pp. 282–83). Cf. Huizinga, *Waning of the Middle Ages*, chap. IV. Moorman argues convincingly that it was the addition of courtly love to chivalry that "supplie[d] the knight not only with a character, a set of values, and a potential conflict capable of literary treatment, but with an occupation—knight-errantry—out of which plot and action may be constructed" ("The First Knights," p. 22).

41. Huizinga, *Waning of the Middle Ages*, p. 47.

42. The Council of Clermont (1095), in whose injunctions we find one of the earliest expressions (if not the first) of the chivalric oath (Hearnshaw, *Chivalry*, ed. Prestage, pp. 8–9), precedes by only a year the date on which, as Loomis has argued, we have evidence for the telling of Arthurian tales as far as Bari in Italy, and by little more than a decade the terminal date for the Arthurian sculptures on an archivolt of the Modena cathedral (*Celtic Myth*, pp. 5–11).

43. C. W. Previté-Orton (*The Shorter Cambridge Medieval History* [2 vols.; Cambridge, Eng., 1952], I, 316) in a discussion of "the theocratic nature of Charlemagne's monarchy," expresses medieval attitudes toward the emperor thus: "He was the new David, the Lord's anointed, chosen to guide the Christian people in the City of God on earth. . . . He was the God-given autocrat of Western Christendom." Cf. W. T. H. Jackson (*Literature of the Middle Ages*, p. 71): "Charlemagne was a consciously Christian king, and it is not remarkable that, under the impact of the Crusades, he should have been viewed essentially as a monarch working in the service of Christianity."

44. MacCallum, *Idylls of the King and Arthurian Story*, p. 49. MacCallum's argument, which I am following here, suffers from the curtailment necessitated by my approach. Cf. W. T. H. Jackson's comment: "The indeterminate nature of its [i.e., Arthurian story's] historical background made it possible for writers to develop their own ideas of chivalry and to build upon them an ideal world which incorporated the best and highest of human aspirations of the day. The stories of Troy and Alexander . . . left too little freedom to the author. . . . Historical characters were hard to turn into a

medieval ideal, and none of the attempts is fully successful" (*Literature of the Middle Ages*, pp. 158–59).

45. Since 1947 the standard edition in Malory studies has been *The Works of Sir Thomas Malory*, ed. Eugène Vinaver (3 vols.; Oxford, 1947). A 2nd edition (Oxford, 1967) includes a number of corrections and some new material in the introduction. Nevertheless, because some twenty years of Malory scholarship are based on the 1st edition, my subsequent references to Vinaver's text are to the earlier edition unless otherwise specified. Vinaver's text is also available in a one-volume edition (London, 1954). The standard edition of Caxton's text is *Le Morte Darthur*, ed. H. Oskar Sommer (3 vols.; London, 1889–1891). In light of the fact that all editions of Malory known to the period covered in my book follow Caxton more or less closely, Sommer's edition, unless otherwise specified, is the source of all my future references to *Le Morte Darthur*. Caxton's text in modernized spelling is conveniently available in *Le Morte D'Arthur* (2 vols.; Everyman's Library, Nos. 45–46; London and New York, 1906).

46. Caxton's general title was apparently drawn from the last *explicit*, though Malory obviously intended it to apply to only the last romance in his series, i.e., the one which in point of fact deals with *le Morte Darthur*; Caxton's title was not repeated by any editor before the nineteenth century, but has in modern times become the "standard" title for the work (Malory, *Works*, ed. Vinaver, I, xxxiii). Caxton also deleted all but the last of Malory's colophons, divided the work into a sequence of "books" and "chapters," and made a number of stylistic alterations. See also Vinaver in *Arthurian Literature*, ed. Loomis, p. 543.

47. Andrew Lang in Malory, *Le Morte Darthur*, ed. Sommer, III, xv.

48. The first of these quotations is drawn from Sir Thomas Malory, *Morte D'Arthur*, ed. Sir Edward Strachey (The Globe Edition; London, 1868), p. viii; the second is from the revised edition of 1901, p. xiii.

49. George Saintsbury, *The English Novel* (London, 1913), p. 25, as quoted by Vinaver in Malory, *Works*, I, xxxiv.

50. Malory, *Works*, ed. Vinaver, I, vi and xxxii. Vinaver has continued to enunciate this view in roughly the same terms in his subsequent publications: "Le Manuscrit de Winchester," *BBSIA*, 3 (1951), 75–82; *The Works of Sir Thomas Malory* (1 vol.; London, 1954), p. vi; *The Tale of the Death of Arthur* (London, 1955), p. vii; *King Arthur and His Knights* (Boston, 1956), pp. xii-xiii; "Sir Thomas Malory," *Arthurian Literature*, ed. Loomis, pp. 541–52; "On Art and Nature: A letter to C. S. Lewis," in J. A. W. Bennett (ed.), *Essays on Malory* (Oxford, 1963), pp. 29–40; and Malory, *Works*, ed. Vinaver, 2nd ed., I, xxxv–li (of particular interest because it includes a new section on "The Problem of 'Unity'" in which Vinaver seeks to answer his critics). It is perhaps worth adding that although Vinaver once argued himself for some sort of unity in the *Morte Darthur*—a fact on which his opponents comment—even when he did he still declared that "on the whole [Malory] failed to weld

the rambling episodes of the French cycle into a harmonious whole, and retained a mass of stories unconnected with each other and often irrelevant to the main theme" (*Malory* [Oxford, 1929], p. 110).

51. The leading proponent of a closely unified *Morte Darthur* has been R. M. Lumiansky: "The Relationship of Lancelot and Guenevere in Malory's 'Tale of Lancelot,'" *MLN*, 68 (1953), 86–91; "The Question of Unity in Malory's *Morte Darthur*," *Tulane Studies in English*, 5 (1955), 29–39; "Two Notes on Malory's *Morte Darthur*: Sir Urry in England [and] Lancelot's Burial Vow," *Neuphilologische Mitteilungen*, 58 (1957), 148–53; "Gawain's Miraculous Strength: Malory's Use of *Le Morte Arthur* and *Mort Artu*," *Études Anglaises*, 10 (1957), 97–108; "Malory's 'Tale of Lancelot and Guenevere' as Suspense," *MedStud*, 19 (1957), 108–22; "Malory's Steadfast Bors," *Tulane Studies in English*, 8 (1958), 5–20. Lumiansky's most active seconder has been Charles Moorman: "Malory's Treatment of the Sankgreall," *PMLA*, 71 (1956), 496–509; "Courtly Love in Malory," *ELH*, 27 (1960), 163–76; "The Relation of Books I and III of Malory's 'Morte Darthur,'" *MedStud*, 22 (1960), 361–66; "Internal Chronology in Malory's *Morte Darthur*," *JEGP*, 60 (1961), 240–49; "Lot and Pellinore: The Failure of Loyalty in Malory's 'Morte Darthur,'" *MedStud*, 25 (1963), 83–92. All of these essays by Moorman reappear in his *The Book of Kyng Arthur: The Unity of Malory's Morte Darthur* ([Lexington], 1965). Several articles defending Malory's unity against Vinaver's view have been put forward by Thomas C. Rumble: "The First *Explicit* in Malory's *Morte Darthur*," *MLN*, 71 (1956), 564–66; "Malory's *Works* and Vinaver's Comments: Some Inconsistencies Resolved," *JEGP*, 59 (1960), 59–69; "Malory's *Balin* and the Question of Unity in the *Morte Darthur*," *Speculum*, 41 (1966), 68–85. See also Mary E. Dichmann, "Characterization in Malory's *Tale of Arthur and Lucius*," *PMLA*, 65 (1950), 877–95; and Gilbert R. Davis, "Malory's 'Tale of Sir Lancelot' and the Question of Unity in the *Morte Darthur*," *PMASAL*, 49 (1964), 523–30. Four of the articles cited above (Dichmann, *PMLA* [1950]; Lumiansky, *MLN* [1953] and *MedStud* [1957]; and Moorman, *PMLA* [1956]), together with other chapters by Thomas L. Wright, Thomas C. Rumble, and Wilfred L. Guerin, are printed in *Malory's Originality: A Critical Study of Le Morte Darthur*, ed. R. M. Lumiansky (Baltimore, 1964).

52. For the earlier acceptance or, at any rate, lack of disagreement with Vinaver's view, see reviews of the 1947 ed. of the *Works* by J. A. W. Bennett (*RES*, 25 [1949], 161–67) and Margaret Schlauch (*New York Times Book Review* [September 12, 1948], p. 28) and William A. Nitze's "Arthurian Problems," *BBSIA*, 5 (1953), 83–84. So little has been written in defense of Vinaver's thesis that D. S. Brewer was prompted to wonder "if any reputable scholar in English studies still accepts Professor Vinaver's view that Malory wrote eight separate works" (rev. of *The Book of Kyng Arthur*, by Moorman, *MLR*, 62 [1967], 109). It is of course possible, as Elizabeth T. Pochoda observes, that "there are partisans of Vinaver who have not defended him in

print because he has been able to do such an energetic job on his own behalf"
(*Arthurian Propaganda: Le Morte Darthur as an Historical Ideal of Life*
[Chapel Hill, 1971], p. 13).

53. William Matthews, reviewing *Malory's Originality*, ed. Lumiansky,
says "neither Vinaver's complete separateness or these essayists' fused and
welded unity fits all the facts of the book"; much in the case presented by the
proponents of such unity is "hardly more than say-so," "sky-scraping structures
[built] on very small sands" (*Speculum*, 41 [1966], 155–59). Reviewing the
same book, Alison White notes a "naive reiteration that Malory consciously
planned literary effects, as if he were the star performer in a Writers' Work-
shop" (*HAB*, 15, No. 2 [1964], 69). See also Helaine Newstead, rev. of
Essays on Malory, ed. Bennett, *Medium Ævum*, 33 (1964), p. 236; Robert H.
Wilson, rev. of *Essays on Malory*, *Criticism*, 6 (1964), 93; and R. T. Davies,
rev. of *The Book of Kyng Arthur*, by Moorman, *RES*, NS 17 (1966), 428–30.
The controversy is surveyed briefly by Edmund Reiss, *Sir Thomas Malory*,
Twayne's English Authors Series, No. 35 (New York, 1966), pp. 26–30; and
far more extensively by Stephen Knight, *The Structure of Sir Thomas Malory's
Arthuriad*, Australian Humanities Research Council Monographs, No. 14
(Sydney, 1969), pp. 5–34. Knight concludes that "there are elements of unity
and elements of disunity in the Arthuriad, and it seems impossible to explain
either element away" (p. 34).

54. C. S. Lewis, "The English Prose *Morte*," *Essays on Malory*, ed. Bennett, p. 22.

55. The tendency to regard *unity* and other terms dealing with relative
integration as absolutes may be seen clearly in R. M. Lumiansky's assertion:
"Obviously, a critic cannot logically champion both of these assumptions:
Malory's lack of conscious artistry, and Malory's employment of conscious
artistry" (rev. of *Essays on Malory*, ed. Bennett, *MP*, 62 [1964], 159). What
is obvious is that no writer has ever totally possessed or totally lacked conscious artistry; accordingly, the logical assumption to champion would be
that any given work will manifest evidence of some *degree* of conscious artistry.
A just estimate of that degree is part of the business of criticism.

56. This is not to be taken as the ritual shudder at the largely imaginary
horrors of the "intentional fallacy." On the contrary, questions of intention,
pace Wimsatt and Beardsley, are often real and inescapable, and there are
methods that may lead to their resolution (see E. D. Hirsch, Jr., *Validity in
Interpretation* [New Haven and London, 1967]). But questions of a writer's
structural intentions cannot be resolved by looking at his text alone or at his
handling of his sources when, as is the case with Malory, the exact text of his
sources is unknown to us.

57. One wonders if Vinaver's decision to give his text, as he puts it, the
"appearance of a modern novel" by using modern paragraphing has not,
ironically, contributed to the tendency to look for modern fictional unity
(Malory, *Works*, ed. Vinaver, 2nd ed., I, cxxv).

58. Rev. of *Essays on Malory*, ed. Bennett, *Medium Ævum*, 33 (1964), 236.

59. C. S. Lewis in *Essays on Malory*, ed. Bennett, p. 22.

60. D. S. Brewer, rev. of *The Tale of the Death of King Arthur*, ed. Vinaver, and "The Question of Unity in Malory's *Morte Darthur*," by Lumiansky, *Medium Ævum*, 25 (1956), 22; and "'the hoole book,'" *Essays on Malory*, ed. Bennett, p. 42.

61. Brewer in *Essays on Malory*, ed. Bennett, p. 41. The middle ground (between Vinaver and the school of Lumiansky) represented by the essays and reviews by Brewer, Matthews, Lewis, and Newstead already cited is also, if I interpret him correctly, occupied by R. H. Wilson in his rev. of Malory, *Works*, ed. Vinaver, *MP*, 46 (1948), 136–38; "How Many Books Did Malory Write?" *University of Texas Studies in English*, 30 (1951), 1–23; "The Prose Lancelot in Malory," *University of Texas Studies in English*, 32 (1953), 1–13. See also Brewer's "Form in the *Morte Darthur*," *Medium Ævum*, 21 (1952), 14–24; and Richard Leighton Greene, rev. of *Malory's Originality*, ed. Lumiansky, *JEGP*, 66 (1967), 120–24.

62. MacCallum, *Idylls of the King and Arthurian Story*, p. 85.

63. Malory, *Works*, ed. Vinaver, I, lii. The method, a combination of the *ordo artificialis* and the *digressio*, is discussed at length by Vinaver (I, xlix–lii).

64. [Thomas Malory], *The Byrth, Lyf, and Actes of King Arthur: of His Noble Knyghtes of the Round Table, Theyr Merveyllous Enquestes and Aduentures, Thachyeuyng of the Sanc Greal; and in the End Le Morte Darthur, with the Dolorous Deth and Departyng out of this Worlde of Them Al*, ed. Robert Southey (2 vols.; London, 1817), I, xxxi–xxxii.

65. Malory, *Works*, ed. Vinaver, I, lviii. Cf. pp. lii–lviii for an analysis of Malory's method.

66. John Erskine appears to have this contrast in mind when he observes that the "peculiarity of [Malory's] account is the dramatic vigor of the incidents, as over against the psychological interpretation which is the charm of most other versions" (*The Delight of Great Books* [Indianapolis, 1928], p. 71).

67. Cf. Malory, *Works*, ed. Vinaver, I, xxiii, and Vinaver in *Arthurian Literature*, ed. Loomis, pp. 546–47. But despite Malory's rationalizing tendencies, the sense of the marvellous, as Professor Vinaver points out, is not lost (*ibid.*, p. 547).

68. Lang, in *Le Morte Darthur*, ed. Sommer, III, xiii. Strachey, while conceding "that Morte Arthur exhibits a picture of a society far lower than our own in morals, and depicts it with far less repugnance to its evil elements, on the part either of the author or his personages, than any good man would feel now," still was convinced that Malory "does for the most part endeavour, though often but in an imperfect and confused manner, to distinguish between vice and virtue, and honestly to reprobate the former; and thus shows that his

object is to recognize and support the nobler elements of the social state in which he lived, and to carry them towards new triumphs over the evil" (Malory, *Morte D'Arthur*, ed. Strachey [1868], p. xiii). With this view, contrast Vinaver's assertion that such notions rest on a confusion between Malory's text and Caxton's preface (Malory, *Works*, ed. Vinaver, I, xxi).

69. William Matthews, rev. of *Malory's Originality*, ed. Lumiansky, pp. 156–57. A far more extensive inventory of inconsistencies could be compiled from Vinaver's commentary in the *Works*, though some of these would properly be subject to Rumble's contention that the commentary contains "a number of inaccuracies" ("Malory's *Works* and Vinaver's Comments: Some Inconsistencies Resolved," p. 59). The proponents of a highly unified *Morte Darthur* have labored to justify many of what they regard as only "apparent" inconsistencies, but even they are forced to concede that "cases remain which do not yield to . . . explanation" on the ground of Malory's "probable purposes" (*Malory's Originality*, p. 7). Rumble's use of "the bulk of Malory's work, the number and variety of its sources, and the conditions under which it was written" ("Malory's *Works* and Vinaver's Comments," p. 69) as explanation will, of course, satisfy readers only to the extent that they share the assumptions of the Lumiansky school. What is one scholar's "simply . . . need for minor revision" (*Malory's Originality*, p. 7) is another's "astonishing carelessness" (Newstead, rev. of *Essays on Malory*, ed. Bennett, p. 236).

70. Most of Malory's editors and critics prior to 1947 paid remarkably little attention to his defects, glaring as they often are. Indeed, their comments sometimes suggest that they are not even talking about the book itself, but rather—might one say?—about an emotion recollected in tranquillity; consider, for instance, this observation: "Every incident . . . is 'simple,' that is to say, complete in itself, while making a part of the whole story" (Malory, *Morte D'Arthur*, ed. Strachey [1901], pp. ix–x). A balanced analysis is to be found in E. K. Chambers' *English Literature at the Close of the Middle Ages* (Oxford History of English Literature; Oxford, 1945), pp. 191–95.

71. The same curiously offhand dismissal is given to the death of another important character, Sir Lamorak. Malory's use of the inferior version of the Tristram story together with his tendency to subordinate Tristram's importance as compared to Lancelot's had unfortunate consequences for later treatments of the story, according to Maurice Halperin (*Le Roman de Tristan et Iseut dans la littérature anglo-américaine au XIXe et XXe siècles* [Paris, 1931], pp. 14–15), since it was to Malory that many of the English poets turned. Whatever the general truth of this view, it does not apply to Tennyson's version.

72. In recognizing such faults (at least as I see them), I do not mean to overlook the importance of the Grail Quest to Malory's development of his overall story, an importance suggested by P. E. Tucker's "The Place of the 'Quest of the Holy Grail' in the 'Morte Darthur,'" *MLR*, 48 (1953), 391–97,

and even more forcefully by Charles Moorman in "Malory's Treatment of the Sankgreall" and *The Book of Kyng Arthur*, pp. 28–48.

73. Vinaver in *Arthurian Literature*, ed. Loomis, p. 541. How much Malory's account has become part of the mental furniture of the educated twentieth-century mind can be gauged by an allusion to the accidental precipitation of the battle of Camlan in Herman Kahn's *On Thermonuclear War* (Princeton, 1961), p. 525.

74. The early editions of Malory, all in black letter, are as follows: Caxton (1485), W. de Worde (1498), W. de Worde (1529), W. Copland (1557), Th. East (*ca.* 1578), and W. Stansby (1634). The account of these editions given by Sommer (Malory, *Le Morte Darthur*, ed. Sommer, II, 2–9) appears to be accurate in the main, with the exception of East's edition, for which he suggests the date 1585. But, as Josephine Waters Bennett has shown, the evidence suggests that 1578 is a much more likely date (*The Evolution of "The Faerie Queene"* [Chicago, 1942], p. 76, n. 46). Bennett also denies the existence of an additional quarto form of East's edition listed by Sommer. Of the black letter editions, those of 1498 and 1529 were apparently entitled *The Booke of Kynge Arthur and of His Noble Knyghtes of the Rounde Table*; those of 1557 and 1578(?) both have title pages beginning *The Story of the Most Noble and Worthy Kynge Arthur*; and that of 1634 has the significant alteration, *The Most Ancient and Famous History of the Renowned Prince Arthur, King of Britaine*. According to Strachey, "each succeeding edition departs more than the previous one from the original of Caxton; but if we compare this of 1634 with Caxton's, we find the variations almost infinite. Besides remodelling the preface, dividing the book into three parts, and modernizing the spelling and many of the words, there are a number of more or less considerable variations and additions" (Malory, *Morte D'Arthur*, ed. Strachey [1868], p. xv). The nature of these variations may be gathered from the preface to the edition: "In many places this volume is corrected (not in language but in phraseology) for here and there king Arthur or some of his knights were declared in their communication to swear prophane, and use superstitious speeches, all (or the most part) of which is either mended or quite left out by the paines and industry of the compositor and corrector of the presse; so that as it is now, it may pass for a famous piece of antiquity, revived almost from the gulph of oblivion, and rescued for the pleasure and benefit of the present and future times" (quoted in Malory, *Le Morte Darthur*, ed. Sommer, II, 13, n. 1). Of the editions before the seventeenth century, a total of nine copies appear to be known (this figure is a composite derived from Malory, *Le Morte Darthur*, ed. Sommer, II, 2–9, and Bennett, *Evolution of "The Fairie Queene,"* p. 76, n. 46). Louis Rigaud's curious claim that three editions of Malory appeared during the eighteenth century ("Le Graal au service de la morale victorienne," *Lumière du Graal*, ed. René Nelli [Paris, 1951], p. 283) is manifestly in error. The nineteenth-century editions will be discussed in their proper place in chap. 5.

75. "The Tale of Sir Gareth of Orkney" is a possible exception. Several critics committed to the hypothesis of a thoroughly unified *Morte Darthur* and proceeding from the fact that the French source of the tale is unknown have argued that Malory invented the story as a part of his presumed effort to unify the whole work (see Wilfred L. Guerin, "'The Tale of Gareth': Chivalric Flowering," in *Malory's Originality*, ed. Lumiansky, pp. 99–117; Moorman, *The Book of Kyng Arthur*, p. 100, n. 4). Yet everything we do know about Malory's methods elsewhere makes such an invention unlikely; as Vinaver says, "it is safe to assume . . . that such a source existed" (Malory, *Works*, ed. Vinaver, 2nd ed., III, 1427).

76. Cf. Malory, *Works*, ed. Vinaver, I, lxxviii–lxxxv. My view of what I here call the central story in the *Morte Darthur* was formed before I had encountered Charles Moorman's eloquent and impressively detailed *The Book of Kyng Arthur*. Although Moorman puts an emphasis on the Grail Quest and the Lot-Pellinore feud that I do not, and though I find myself finally unconvinced by much of his argument for an all but total unity in Malory, it is a distinct satisfaction to me that we are very much in agreement in seeing the major subject of the *Morte Darthur* as "the rise, flowering, and decay of an almost perfect civilization" (p. 50).

77. Thus the earlier references to the incest motif all occur in the early part of what is in the Winchester MS "The Tale of King Arthur"; the later references are confined to the latter part of "The Most Piteous Tale of the Morte Arthur saunz Gwerdon" (Malory, *Works*, ed. Vinaver). The corresponding references in Caxton's text are I, xix, xx, xxviii; II, x, xi; XX, xix; XXI, i, ii, iv, viii.

78. To a very large extent the tendency of the earlier critics to over-emphasize the importance of the incest motif probably grew out of a desperate desire to find an epic unity, a continuous chain of cause and effect running throughout the length of the *Morte Darthur*. Thus Strachey, after having declared that "the Epic is the story of the past, a cycle of events completed, [in which] may be traced a thread of destiny and providence, leading either to a happy triumph over circumstances, or to a tragic doom," finds the "cycle of events" in Uther's crime that leads to concealment of Arthur's parentage, which in turn leads to Arthur's incest, which produces Mordred, who finally brings doom upon his father (Malory, *Morte D'Arthur*, ed. Strachey [1901], p. xi). The story was, of course, dramatized from this point of view in Hughes's *Misfortunes of Arthur* (see my chap. 2).

79. Charles Moorman, the most recent critic to examine Arthurian story as myth, took the view that the Lancelot-Gwenyvere adultery is the unifying theme in Malory and declares that the central conflict is "between chivalric duty and romantic love" (*Arthurian Triptych: Mythic Materials in Charles Williams, C. S. Lewis, and T. S. Eliot* [Perspectives in Criticism, No. 5; Berkeley and Los Angeles, 1960], pp. 32 f.). Elsewhere, e.g., *The Book of Kyng Arthur*, Moorman regards the Lancelot-Gwenyvere intrigue as one of

three interconnected strands which "unify the narrative framework of the book" (p. 50). Nevertheless, he still sees that of these "three controlling motifs, the most immediately compelling is the story of the two lovers," who are, "in a manner of speaking, Malory's hero and heroine" and the object of "the reader's first concern" (p. 13).

80. Loomis, *Celtic Myth, passim*; Tom Peete Cross and William A. Nitze, *Lancelot and Guinivere: A Study on the Origins of Courtly Love* (Chicago, 1930). See also Bensel, *Character of King Arthur*, pp. 18 and 51.

81. Bensel, *Character of King Arthur*, p. 207.

82. Quoted by William Albert Nitze in *Arthurian Romance and Modern Poetry and Music* (Chicago, 1940), p. 43.

83. August J. App, *Lancelot in English Literature: His Rôle and Character* (Washington, 1929), p. 17.

84. Malory, *Works*, ed. Vinaver, I, xxvii.

85. *Ibid.*, I, xxiv–xxv.

86. Cf. Bensel, *Character of King Arthur*, pp. 146–47.

87. Vinaver in *Arthurian Literature*, ed. Loomis, p. 546. Lang seems to have recognized the importance of both the exaltation of Arthur and the fatal love of Lancelot and Guinevere in terms of the essential story: "The slight unity that we find in the earlier parts, before the Graal becomes an aim and end, before the love of Lancelot brings a doom on all, is in the character and position of Arthur" (*Le Morte Darthur*, ed. Sommer, III, xv).

88. Nevertheless, there have been a number of attempts in the present century to deal artistically with this dubiously historical figure. Nathan Comfort Starr's view is that "contemporary novelists have added fresh and original material to the legend in 'modernizing' Arthur by making him more ancient; in other words, by reviving the shadowy Celt who probably fought against the Germanic invaders of Britain in the sixth century" (*King Arthur Today, The Arthurian Legend in English and American Literature 1901–1953* [Gainesville, Fla., 1954], p. 84). My own view, derived from such examples as I have looked at, is that they have in fact added nothing of value to the legend and that what these writers have produced is nothing but the tepid oatmeal of amateur historical fiction.

89. Loomis, *Celtic Myth*, p. 3.

90. Professor Nitze says "A legend that is so persistent has in it elements which are of transcendent value; that is to say, elements rooted in the genius or the ethos of the nation itself. As long as there is a British nation, composed of Norman, Saxon, and Celtic strains, so long will there be an Arthurian legend!" (*Arthurian Romance*, p. 2). This seems to overlook the long vogue of the legend on the Continent, but it does correctly assign the survival of the story to "transcendent" elements. Their root is not in the nation, but in the human race.

91. Charles Moorman (*Arthurian Triptych*, pp. 20–26) argues that in its earlier forms in Geoffrey and the chronicles, the Arthurian story is close to

"legend" as defined by Bethe and Langer, but even closer to "folk-history." It is only in the later versions in the romances where it achieves thematic unity and becomes an examination of the larger issues of society and God that it is to be called myth, according to Moorman. Whatever the value of the distinction for anthropologists, I am inclined to doubt its usefulness to literary criticism. In the present study "myth" and "legend" have been used more or less interchangeably. For the difficulties of arriving at a precise definition of the term *myth*, see Harry Levin's "Some Meanings of Myth," *Myth and Mythmaking*, ed. Henry A. Murray (New York, 1960), pp. 103–114. *Myth* in this analysis of Arthurian literature is used to refer to stories whose origins appear to reside in the racial imagination or in the workings of the nondiscursive mind and which are capable of fascinating the minds of generation after generation of men—as stories, rather than as specific literary works. That any myth must somewhere have been actually uttered for the first time by some individual or by many individuals in different places is doubtless true, but not significant. What is important is that these first myth-utterers and their audiences almost certainly seized upon the myths as truth rather than invention. It is characteristic of myth as opposed to the *ad hoc*, consciously invented story that it has imaginative value apart from its treatment, it is capable of moving men simply as story, and it remains in the imagination as a viable formulation of felt truth long after the details of any specific literary incarnation have passed. Since the myth is an expression or paradigm of imaginative truth in the same way that an algebraic formula is an expression of certain logical truths, its general conformation cannot be altered without contradicting the intuited psychological, moral, or spiritual truth that it conveys. It should go without saying that there are, of course, other kinds of great and significant literature. For some reservations about the application of myth criticism to medieval literature, see Charles Moorman, "Myth and Mediaeval Literature: *Sir Gawain and the Green Knight*," *MedStud*, 17 (1956), 158–61.

92. For an extended treatment of this myth type, see Otto Rank, "The Myth of the Birth of the Hero: A Psychological Interpretation of Mythology," *The Myth of the Birth of the Hero and Other Writings* (New York, 1959), pp. 1–96. Despite all the indicators of the mythic status that Arthur achieved (whatever his genesis), Charles Moorman argues that "while the knights of the Arthurian story are largely mythical in origin, the king himself is the legendary magnification of a historical figure" ("King Arthur and the English National Character," *New York Folklore Quarterly*, 24 [1968], 107).

93. Lord Raglan (*The Hero*, pp. 177–89) draws up a pattern of twenty-two motifs or typical incidents derived from the careers of Oedipus, Theseus, Romulus, Heracles, Perseus, Jason, Bellerophon, Pelops, Asclepios, Dionysus, Apollo, Zeus, Joseph, Moses, Elijah, Watu Gunung, Nyikang, Sigurd, Llew Llawgyffes, Arthur, and Robin Hood. Of the twenty-two points, Arthur's story manifests nineteen. For a series of parallels between Arthur and Christ,

see Northup in *Studies in English Philology*, ed. Malone and Ruud, pp. 311–17.

94. Raglan, *The Hero, passim*, esp. pp. 144 ff.

95. Rank (*Birth of the Hero*, pp. 3–13), after a brief survey of the various schools of myth interpretation, suggests strongly that the advocates of the various "natural" or "astral" interpretations have shared with early myth-makers in this anxiety to avoid the less pleasant psychic content of the myths by projecting such motifs as incest and patricide into the heavens or the growth cycles of nature.

96. For a thoroughgoing application of Jung's notions of the "collective unconsciousness" and its "archetypal patterns" to literary criticism, see Maud Bodkin, *Archetypal Patterns in Poetry: Psychological Studies of Imagination* (New York, 1958). Rank (*Birth of the Hero*, pp. 65–96) deals specifically with psychological interpretation of the myth of the birth of the hero.

97. Charles Moorman sees Malory as giving particular and consistent emphasis to this inherently tragic spirit of the story ("Malory's Tragic Knights," *MedStud*, 27 [1965], 117–27; rptd. with minor changes in *A Knyght There Was*, pp. 97–112).

98. This is not to say, of course, that there are not successful, even great treatments of individual adventures of Arthur's knights that take place before the debacle of Arthurian society, although even in these a large part of the reader's sense of beauty and consequence is, I suspect, the result of the resonance that the tragic central story lends to episodes in which it has no explicit place. But the important point is that Arthur's career is poetically or mythically meaningless apart from its tragic conclusion.

99. Ernest Rhys, *Gwenevere: A Lyric Play, Written for Music: The Music by Vincent Thomas* (London, 1905), pp. v–vi.

100. Bensel, *Character of King Arthur*, p. 1.

101. It is true, of course, that in the classical myths the welfare of the society is involved with the welfare of the hero to some extent. But the emphasis is quite different: the fall of the hero does not mean the equivalent fall of the society as it does in Arthurian story.

102. The comparison between Arthurian legend and Gothic architecture is, quite naturally, a commonplace in the literature. Most of the critics, however, appear to be so dominated by classicist notions that the comparison usually accepts the charge of disunity. Thus Professor Nitze tells us in a curiously old-fashioned way that in Arthurian romance, as in a Gothic cathedral, "imaginative content again and again outstrips the sense of external form. . . . Such a structure . . . must often be judged as to its separate features, not as to its entity. What counts artistically is the parts of the edifice. . . . We are fascinated by the separate motifs, in their varying, diversified expression, not in the Arthurian cycle as a unity. The main reason for this deficiency, if so one regard it, is that the Middle Ages are essentially an era of aspiration" (*Arthurian Romance*, p. 95).

103. The development of the Gothic style and its relative stabilization as seen in the High Gothic of the Cathedral of Chartres and afterwards in the cathedrals of Rheims, Amiens, and Beauvais is lucidly surveyed in Nikolaus Pevsner's *An Outline of European Architecture* (5th edition; Pelican Books, No. A109; Harmondsworth, 1957), pp. 74–102, esp. 87–93. The same kind of design stabilization had, of course, taken place in Greek architecture with the Parthenon. It is significant, however, that the balance achieved in Gothic is, as Pevsner says, "not the happy, seemingly effortless and indestructible balance of the Greeks" (p. 87). It is, on the contrary, "a balance of two equally vehement drives towards two opposite directions" (p. 90). In short, it is the balance of paradox, for only in paradox could an essentially paradoxical social ideal find its formulation. Yet, to quote Pevsner again, "this balance of high tensions is the classic expression of the Western spirit—as final as the temple of the 5th century B.C. was of that of the Greek spirit" (p. 92).

104. MacCallum, *Idylls of the King and Arthurian Story*, p. 194.

2. A SLOW DECLINE: ARTHURIAN STORY AND TRADITION IN THE ENGLISH RENAISSANCE

1. In the absence of anything like historical imagination or exact notions of historical methodology, the tendency among Tudor historians to equate the entire Middle Ages with the disorders of the Wars of the Roses was all but universal; Samuel Daniel appears to have been one of the few historians who saw the greatness of medieval civilization. See May McKisack, "Samuel Daniel as Historian," *RES*, 23 (July, 1947), pp. 233–34.

2. Fritz Caspari, *Humanism and the Social Order in Tudor England* (Chicago, 1954), p. 14.

3. Ruth Kelso, *The Doctrine of the English Gentleman in the Sixteenth Century* (University of Illinois Studies in Language and Literature, Vol. XIV; Urbana, Ill., 1929), pp. 48, 70–71. Cf. Caspari, *Humanism*, pp. 5, 18–19. Considerable insight into the processes of this shift is afforded by Arthur B. Ferguson's *The Indian Summer of English Chivalry: Studies in the Decline and Transformation of Chivalric Idealism* (Durham, 1960).

4. McKisack, "Samuel Daniel," p. 234.

5. From a translation published sometime after 1546; quoted by Ronald S. Crane in *The Vogue of Medieval Chivalric Romance During the English Renaissance* (Menasha, Wis., 1919), p. 12. In the following discussion of the place of chivalric romance in the Tudor period, I am much indebted to Professor Crane's work.

6. Quoted from Nashe's *Anatomie of Absurditie* (1589) by William Edward Mead, "Arthurian Story in the Sixteenth Century," in his ed. of Christopher Middleton's *Chinon of England* (EETS, Original Series No. 165; London, 1925), p. xxxii. Cf. Crane, *Chivalric Romance*, pp. 18 and 20.

7. Josephine Waters Bennett, *The Evolution of "The Faerie Queene"* (Chicago, 1942), pp. 75–76.

8. Quoted from Arber's reprint (p. 80) by Mead, in his edition of *Chinon of England*, pp. xxx–xxxi. The same mixture of doctrinal and moral objection is observable in Nathanial Baxter's allusions to the "infamous legend of K. Arthur" with such "whoremasters" as Lancelot and Tristram, and the "vile and stincking story of the Sangreal" (quoted from Baxter's dedication to a translation of Calvin's *Sermons* [1578] by Bennett, *Evolution of "The Faerie Queene,"* p. 75).

9. Among others who condemned the romances on ethical grounds, Crane (*Chivalric Romance*, pp. 12, 18–20) lists Tyndale (1528), Meredith Hanmer (1577), Gosson (1582), Thomas Bowes (1594), Meres (1598), Henry Crosse (1603), Burton (1621), and William Vaughan (1626). For other interesting work on the later fortunes of the romances, see Mother Edith E. McShane's *Tudor Opinions of the Chivalrous Romance: An Essay in the History of Criticism* (Washington, 1950) and Mary Patchell's *The Palmerin Romances in Elizabethan Prose Fiction* (Columbia University Studies in English and Comparative Literature, No. 166; New York, 1947). For a parallel in France to the slow decline of the vogue of romances, see Nathan Edelman's *Attitudes of Seventeenth-Century France toward the Middle Ages* (New York, 1946), pp. 152–53.

10. Crane, *Chivalric Romance*, p. 1.

11. *Ibid.*, p. 9.

12. Patchell, *Palmerin Romances*, p. 22. Cf. Crane, *Chivalric Romance*, pp. 14–16. For a suggestion that the excitement of the "brave new world" of commercial expansion and the voyages of discovery played a part in diminishing interest in the marvels of long ago, see Elise Francisca Wilhelmina Maria Van der Ven-Ten Bensel, *The Character of King Arthur in English Literature* (Amsterdam, 1925), p. 154.

13. For Mary Stuart's romance reading, see Crane, *Chivalric Romance*, p. 23. For a study of the extensive indebtedness of the *Arcadia* to Malory, see Marcus Selden Goldman, *Sir Philip Sidney and the Arcadia* (Illinois Studies in Language and Literature, Vol. XVII, Nos. 1–2; Urbana, Ill., 1934–1935), pp. 192–205. According to Professor Goldman, Ben Jonson told Drummond that "S.P. Sidney had ane intention to have transformed all his Arcadia to the stories of King Arthure" (p. 192), and in the *Defense* Sidney asserted that "honest king *Arthure* . . . will never displease a souldier" (p. 193). The similarity of gesture to such fantastic points of honor in Arthurian romance is obvious in Sidney's removal of his leg-armour in order to make his protection equal that of his friend, Sir William Pelham; the action accounted for his fatal wound at Zutphen.

14. Louis B. Wright, *Middle-Class Culture in Elizabethan England* (Ithaca, N.Y., 1958), p. 376.

15. Crane, *Chivalric Romance*, p. 18; cf. p. 23.

16. Cf. Mead in his edition of *Chinon of England*, p. xxix.

17. Charles Bowie Millican, "Spenser and the Arthurian Legend," *RES*,

6 (April, 1930), 167–69. Spenser's schoolmaster, Richard Mulcaster, belonged to this group. The inspiration of the fellowship, patronized by Henry VIII and Elizabeth, appears to have been the proficiency at bowmanship of Prince Arthur of Wales, eldest son of Henry VII.

18. *Ibid.,* pp. 171–72.

19. Ivan L. Schulze, "Notes on Elizabethan Chivalry and *The Faerie Queene," SP*, 30 (April, 1933), 156.

20. Roger Sherman Loomis, "Chivalric and Dramatic Imitations of Arthurian Romance," *Medieval Studies in Memory of A. Kingsley Porter* (2 vols.; Cambridge, Mass., 1939), I, 81.

21. Schulze, "Elizabethan Chivalry," pp. 148–49. For a thorough study of the various manifestations of the Arthurian tradition in Tudor and early Stuart life, see Charles Bowie Millican's *Spenser and the Table Round: A Study in the Contemporaneous Background for Spenser's Use of the Arthurian Legend* (Harvard Studies in Comparative Literature, Vol. VIII; Cambridge, Mass., 1932).

22. M. W. MacCallum, *Tennyson's Idylls of the King and Arthurian Story from the XVIth Century* (Glasgow, 1894), pp. 115–16.

23. Edwin Greenlaw, *Studies in Spenser's Historical Allegory* (Johns Hopkins Monographs in Literary History, Vol. II; Baltimore and London, 1932), p. 52; cf. p. 53. Miss Bensel (*Character of King Arthur*, p. 154), however, asserts that "in view of the literary constellation of this time, it is no matter of surprise that the great minds of the age did not seek their inspiration in the romantic matter of Britain. [The new ideals of the Renaissance could] hardly be symbolized and advocated by the Arthurian champions of typically medieval virtues." This explanation overlooks the fact that a number of great minds were attracted to the subject, and the notion that the Arthurian champions could not have symbolized Renaissance ideals seems more theoretical than actual; after all, it is not medieval ideals that Tennyson celebrates in the *Idylls.*

24. Roberta Florence Brinkley, *Arthurian Legend in the Seventeenth Century* (Johns Hopkins Monographs in Literary History, Vol. III; Baltimore and London, 1932), pp. 1–3. Recently Sydney Anglo ("The *British History* in Early Tudor Propaganda," *Bulletin of the John Rylands Library*, 44 [September, 1961], 17–48) has argued that the "Tudor use of the descent from the primitive rulers of Britain was not an innovation; and . . . the Tudor use of the *British History* was not as extensive nor as important as has been supposed" (pp. 19–20).

25. Greenlaw, *Spenser's Historical Allegory*, p. 40. But cf. Anglo ("Early Tudor Propaganda," p. 34), who contradicts Greenlaw on the Arthurian symbolism at the field of the Cloth of Gold.

26. Lilian Winstanley, "The Arthurian Empire in the Elizabethan Poets," *Aberystwyth Studies*, 4 (1922), 60.

27. *Ibid.,* p. 59.

28. Bennett, *Evolution of "The Faerie Queene,"* pp. 68–69. Miss Brinkley (*Arthurian Legend*, p. 3) asserts that Arthurian material was used throughout Elizabeth's reign to reassure the people of her intention to bring them peace and prosperity. Mrs. Bennett (p. 69) takes special issue with Miss Brinkley's declaration that "the Arthurian ancestry of Elizabeth was given especial emphasis at the time of her coronation." The evidence seems to support Mrs. Bennett's contention that there was a certain falling off in the political uses of Arthurian material during a period stretching from Henry VIII's consolidation of his claims to the latter half of Elizabeth's reign.

29. Greenlaw, *Spenser's Historical Allegory,* p. 20.

30. Millican, *Spenser and the Table Round,* p. 9.

31. Bennett, *Evolution of "The Faerie Queene,"* pp. 73–74, see also p. 76.

32. Cf. Bennett, *ibid.,* p. 67; Greenlaw, *Spenser's Historical Allegory,* pp. 39–40, 47, and 54; Homer Nearing, Jr., *English Historical Poetry, 1599–1641* (Philadelphia, 1945), p. 110.

33. W. Lewis Jones, *King Arthur in History and Legend* (2nd ed., The Cambridge Manuals of Science and Literature; Cambridge, Eng., 1914), p. 118.

34. For a detailed study of Geoffrey's direct and indirect influence on a wide variety of Elizabethan plays and poems, see Ludwig Oehninger, *Die Verbreitung der Königssagen der Historia Regum Britanniae von Geoffrey of Monmouth in der poetischen Elisabethanischen Literatur* (Kitzingen a/M, 1905).

35. My account of the attempts of chroniclers and historians to handle the story of Arthur is based on Robert Huntington Fletcher, *The Arthurian Material in the Chronicles* ([Harvard] Studies and Notes in Philology and Literature, Vol. X; Boston, 1906; new ed., New York, 1958), *passim*; Mead in his edition of *Chinon of England,* pp. xxv–xxviii; and Bennett, *Evolution of "The Faerie Queene,"* pp. 64–72.

36. *Ibid.,* pp. 175, 181–82; Mead, ed., *Chinon of England,* p. xxv. On the other hand, John Hardyng's *Chronicle* (*ca.* 1436) seems to give full credence to Geoffrey and even includes the founding of the Round Table and the Grail Quest as sober history (Fletcher, *Arthurian Material,* pp. 251–52). Two editions of Hardyng were published in 1543 (Mead, ed., *Chinon of England,* p. xxvi).

37. Fletcher, *Arthurian Material,* pp. 255–59. Fabyan's book, written about 1493, had a wide effect through John Rastell's abridgement in *The Pastime of People, or The Chronicles of Divers Realms, and especially England* (1529). According to Mrs. Bennett (*Evolution of "The Faerie Queene,"* pp. 65–66), Fabyan was echoed in the historical writings of Cooper, Grafton, Thomas Elyot, John Twyne, and Stow, at least in the latter's earlier editions.

38. Quoted by Denys Hay, *Polydore Vergil: Renaissance Historian and Man of Letters* (Oxford, 1952), pp. 113 and 110.

39. Polydore appears to have begun his book about 1506, and though a

first draft was completed in 1513, publication was delayed until 1534. A second edition with many alterations appeared in 1546, a third in 1555. For discussion of these editions and Polydore's still-extant MS, see Hay, *Polydore Vergil*, esp. pp. 9, 79–82. Hay also prints an original MS criticism of the Arthurian legend, which Polydore appears to have felt was "too forthright to print" (pp. 122 and 199).

40. Mead, ed., *Chinon of England*, p. xxvii. Mrs. Bennett (*Evolution of "The Faerie Queene,"* p. 67) includes Bale among the early defenders of Geoffrey. For further information on this battle of the historians, see Nearing, *English Historical Poetry*, pp. 106 ff.

41. Mead, ed., *Chinon of England*, p. xxviii.

42. Bennett, *Evolution of "The Faerie Queene,"* p. 66.

43. [Sir Thomas Elyot], *Bibliotheca Eliotae: Eliotis Librarie* (n.p., 1548), s.v. "Arthurus." This work was originally published as *The Dictionary of Syr Thomas Elyot* (1538). The entry here quoted appeared first in the edition of 1545. It also appears in virtually the same form in Thomas Cooper's *Thesavrvs Linguae Romanae & Britannicae etc.* (1565).

44. T. D. Kendrick, *British Antiquity* (London, 1950), pp. 41–42.

45. *Ibid.*, p. 77; cf. p. 65.

46. *Ibid.*, pp. 37–41. Anglo ("Early Tudor Propaganda," pp. 21–22) points out that much of the Arthurian cult of the Tudors was the product of Welsh enthusiasm.

47. Bennett, *Evolution of "The Faerie Queene,"* p. 66. Additional evidence of the renewed faith in Geoffrey is to be found in the publication in 1584 of Humphrey Llwyd's *Historia of Cambria*, a purported "translation" of Caradoc of Llancarvan, a Welsh historian cited by Geoffrey. In 1585 Powel published a condensation of Geoffrey, and Hakluyt's second part of his *Principall Nauigations* in 1589 included a great deal of matter from Geoffrey (*ibid.*, pp. 71–72).

48. Mrs. Bennett (*Evolution of "The Faerie Queene,"* p. 72) claims too much when she speaks of the *Britannia* as demonstrating that "acceptance of much of Arthur's story had become the correct scholarly attitude."

49. Quoted in Howard Maynadier, *The Arthur of the English Poets* (Boston and New York, 1907), p. 279.

50. Bennett, *Evolution of "The Faerie Queene,"* p. 73.

51. *Ibid.*, p. 71.

52. *The Shepheardes Calendar*, iv, 120. This and all subsequent quotations from Spenser are taken from *The Works of Edmund Spenser: A Variorum Edition*, ed. Edwin Greenlaw *et al.* (10 vols.; Baltimore, 1932–1949).

53. See *A Viewe of the Present State of Ireland* in Spenser, *Works, The Prose Works*, pp. 85 and 95; for the rejection of the Brutean settlement, see p. 82. Kendrick (*British Antiquity*, p. 129) argues convincingly that Spenser included in the *Faerie Queene* "signals assuring [his] friends that the British History was in detail such nonsense that almost any liberties could be taken

with it."

54. From the Letter to Raleigh as printed in *Works, FQ*, I, p. 167.

55. *Ibid.*

56. Caspari (*Humanism*, p. 180) observes that while Spenser's conception of the gentleman is very close to that of Castiglione, it also "shows strong traces of the ideals of . . . medieval Christian chivalry."

57. *Ibid.*, p. 184. Caspari's "medieval armor" is perhaps misleading; it may be doubted whether Spenser was conscious of any large difference between medieval armor and that worn in his own day.

58. James Milton Ariail, *Some Immediate English Influences upon Spenser's Faerie Queene, Books I–III* [Abstract of an unpublished doctoral dissertation] in *The University of North Carolina Record*, No. 226 (July, 1925), p. 43. The clearest example of "the glorification of the House of Tudor, and of Elizabeth's Welsh descent," as Jones points out (*King Arthur in History and Legend*, p. 119), is to be found in the reference to the "sparke of fire" that shall be "freshly kindled in the fruitful Ile / Of Mona" (*FQ*, III, iii, st. xlviii).

59. The identification is not to be accepted without qualification; Eleanor Rosenberg justly observes that while Arthur usually stands for no specific hero, he may sometimes "for the moment represent Leicester himself (*Leicester, Patron of Letters* [New York, 1955], p. 345). According to Schulze ("Elizabethan Chivalry," p. 153), Arthur's armor appears to have been based on a well-known set belonging to Leicester. Leicester himself, judging from the entertainment of Elizabeth at Kenilworth in 1575, was interested in the Arthurian story. In the revels, huge imitation trumpeters signified that the man of Arthur's day exceeded modern men. Elizabeth talked with the Lady of the Lake and, by her presence, freed the Lady from the persecutions of Bruse sans Pitee. This and a song of Rience's demand for Arthur's beard make it clear, as Goldman (*Philip Sidney*, p. 189) suggests, that the entertainments were based on Malory. For an account of these festivities as related by an enthusiastic middle-class Londoner, see *Robert Laneham's Letter: Describing a Part of the Entertainment unto Queen Elizabeth at the Castle of Kenilworth in 1575*, ed. F. J. Furnivall (New York and London, 1907), esp. pp. 6–7 and 41.

60. Bennett, *Evolution of "The Faerie Queene,"* p. 24.

61. John Hughes, "Remarks on the Fairy Queen," *The Works of Mr. Edmund Spenser* (1715), quoted in Spenser, *Works, FQ*, I, 315.

62. Thomas Warton, *Observations on the Faerie Queene of Spenser* (London, 1754), p. 5.

63. Richard Hurd, *Hurd's Letters on Chivalry and Romance*, ed. Edith J. Morley (London, 1911), p. 124.

64. W. L. Renwick, *Edmund Spenser, an Essay on Renaissance Poetry* (London, 1925), p. 175. B. E. C. Davis, *Edmund Spenser, A Critical Study* (Cambridge, Eng., 1933), p. 68. Merritt Y. Hughes ("The Arthurs of *The Faerie Queene*," *Études Anglaises*, 6 [Août, 1953], 193–94), after quoting a

number of adverse estimates of Spenser's Arthur, cites only Janet Spens (*Spenser's "Faerie Queene," an Interpretation* [London, 1934]) as an exponent of the view that Arthur's quest of the Faerie Queene is the poem's main theme. C. S. Lewis (*The Allegory of Love: A Study in Medieval Tradition* [London, 1938], p. 337) contents himself with saying that Spenser's "Arthur is inexplicable."

65. But consider Warton's troubled reaction (*Observations*, pp. 12–13): "Though the *Faerie Queene* does not exhibit that oeconomy of plan, and exact arrangment of parts which Epic severity requires, yet we scarcely regret the loss of these, while their place is so amply supplied, by something which more powerfully attracts us, as it engages the affection of the heart, rather than the applause of the head. . . . we are not satisfied as critics, yet we are transported as readers."

66. Merritt Hughes, "The Arthurs of *The Faerie Queene*," p. 194.

67. *FQ*, I, ix. Arthur's mysterious birth and the fact that Igrayne was his mother are found only in the Letter to Raleigh (Spenser, *Works, FQ*, I, 168). In Malory it is Sir Ector who rears Arthur.

68. *FQ*, I, vii and ix. These marvellous weapons are not, it may be added, those traditionally associated with Arthur; cf. Bennett, *Evolution of "The Faerie Queene,"* p. 62.

69. *FQ*, I, viii; II, xi; IV, viii; VI, viii.

70. *FQ*, IV, v; VI, i. Of the Blattant Beast, Spenser remarks that "long time after" he was chased by Lamorack and Pelleas (VI, xii, st. xxxix); perhaps the notion was that Arthur's reign as king was to take place considerably later than his quest of the Fairy Queen, conducted while he was yet only a prince.

71. *FQ*, VI, ii.

72. These lists of omitted characters are based on an examination of Charles Grosvenor Osgood's *Concordance to the Poems of Edmund Spenser* (Washington, 1915) and Charles Huntington Whitman's *Subject Index to the Poems of Edmund Spenser* (New Haven, Conn., 1918).

73. Spenser, *Works, FQ*, I, 168.

74. Warton (*Observations*, pp. 13–15), after admitting Spenser's indebtedness to Ariosto, goes on to say that "the adventures of Spenser's knights are a more exact and immediate copy of those which we meet with in old romances, or books of chivalry," among which Malory is particularly important. This view is carried to extravagant extremes of dubious parallelisms in Marie Walther's *Malorys Einfluss auf Spensers Faerie Queene* (Eisleben, n.d.). The fact is, as Mrs. Bennett (*Evolution of "The Faerie Queene,"* p. 63) demonstrates, clear borrowing from Malory occurs only in the Letter to Raleigh and in Book VI. C. S. Lewis believed "it would be impossible to prove from internal evidence that [Spenser] had read much of Malory" (*Allegory of Love*, p. 305). It has been suggested that Ascham's denunciation of Malory was instrumental in dissuading Spenser from drawing extensively on Malory

(Lilian Winstanley [ed.], *The Faerie Queen, Book I* [Cambridge, Eng., 1915], cited by Millican, *Spenser and the Table Round*, p. 3). Cf. Merritt Hughes, "The Arthurs of *The Faerie Queene*," p. 194. Ariail (*English Influences*, p. 43) suggests that Spenser drew on *King Arthur, Sir Degore, The Squire of Low Degree*, the Gawain cycle, *Sir Perceval de Galles, Sir Lambewell, Sir Orfeo*, and the *Avowynge of Arthur*. The problem of romance sources of *FQ* is also considered in Isabel E. Rathbone's *The Meaning of Spenser's Fairyland* (Columbia University Studies in English and Comparative Literature, No. 131; New York, 1937) and in Margaret Rose Richter's *Spenser's Use of Arthurian Romance* [Abstract of an unpublished dissertation] in *Stanford University Bulletin, Abstracts of Dissertations for the Degree of Doctor of Philosophy* (Stanford University, Calif., 1928), II, 119–24. Both of these latter writers appear to deal largely in rather tenuous analogues.

75. *FQ*, II, x; III, iii.

76. Greenlaw, *Spenser's Historical Allegory*, p. 99. For a thorough study of Spenser's sources for the chronicle, see Carrie A. Harper, *The Sources of the British Chronicle History in Spenser's Faerie Queene* (Philadelphia, 1910). Geoffrey is only one of many sources consulted by Spenser (cf. Bennett, *Evolution of "The Faerie Queene,"* p. 63).

77. William Stanford Webb, "Vergil in Spenser's Epic Theory," *ELH*, 4 (March, 1937), pp. 70–78; cf. Greenlaw, *Spenser's Historical Allegory*, pp. 99–100.

78. In this paragraph I follow Josephine Bennett's theory of the evolution of *The Faerie Queene*. Although I find Mrs. Bennett's reasoning convincing, it must not be forgotten that her explanation is still a hypothesis; it has certainly not been accepted by all Spenserian scholars.

79. Bennett, *Evolution of "The Faerie Queene,"* p. 61.

80. *Ibid.*, pp. 11–15.

81. *Ibid.*, pp. 10 and 79.

82. *Ibid.*, p. 61; the quoted words are, of course, from the Letter to Raleigh.

83. The circumstances of Arthur's birth are not mentioned in the poem itself; in the Letter to Raleigh, Spenser glosses over the matter by saying merely that Arthur was "by Merlin deliuered to Timon to be brought vp, so soone as he was borne of the Lady Igrayne" (Spenser, *Works, FQ*, I, 168).

84. Lord Raglan (*The Hero: A Study in Tradition, Myth, and Drama* [The Thinker's Library, No. 133; London, 1949], p. 193) puts it this way: "The most exciting things happen to our hero at birth, and the most exciting things happen to him as soon as he reaches manhood, but in the meantime nothing happens to him at all." What is true of myth is not always true of romance, in which a great deal is sometimes made of this interim period.

85. Cf. Bennett, *Evolution of "The Faerie Queene,"* pp. 29–30. The view, commonly held in Spenser's time, that the Order of the Garter had originated as an imitation of the Round Table has already been mentioned.

86. MacCallum (*Idylls of the King and Arthurian Story*, p. 132) bases his explanation on the mistaken assumption that Spenser's knights are unmixed moral types. Cf. August J. App, *Lancelot in English Literature: His Rôle and Character* (Washington, 1929), p. 104. Maynadier (*The Arthur of the English Poets*, p. 274) suggests that Spenser's replacement of the old knights by his own creations is due to Spenser's "extreme catholicity of taste and exuberance of imagination."

87. Spenser, *Works*, *FQ*, I, 167–68.

88. Algernon Charles Swinburne, "Short Notes on English Poets," *The Complete Works of Algernon Charles Swinburne*, ed. Sir Edmund Gosse and T. J. Wise (20 vols., Bonchurch Edition; London, 1925–1927), XIV, 102–103.

89. MacCallum, *Idylls of the King and Arthurian Story*, p. 132. I do not mean to imply that moral allegory is incompatible with romance *per se*; on the contrary, the stock motifs and characteristic "sense of undefined significance" of romance may be peculiarly amenable to the allegorist's requirements (Kathleen Williams, "Romance Tradition in *The Faerie Queene*," *Washington State University Research Studies*, 32 [1964], 147–60). My point is simply that specific heroes from romance with well-developed associations are not likely to be suitable for allegorical manipulation.

90. Rathbone, *Spenser's Fairyland*, p. 103. Merritt Hughes ("The Arthurs of *The Faerie Queene*," pp. 205–7) discusses the common Renaissance practice of comparing kings, e.g., Henry VIII to Hercules, and states flatly that Spenser's Arthur is based on Renaissance accounts of Hercules.

91. Thus Tasso says in his *Discourses on the Heroic Poem* that the poet "should refuse materials too dry and arid . . . and above all those that are unpleasant and annoying, and those that end unhappily, as the death of the Paladins and the defeat of Roncesvalles." (Quoted from Allan H. Gilbert, *Literary Criticism: Plato to Dryden* [New York, 1940], p. 488.) A hundred years later, Dryden makes it a major objection against Milton's epic that "his event is not prosperous, like that of all other epic works" ("Discourse Concerning the Original and Progress of Satire," *The Poetical Works of John Dryden*, ed. George R. Noyes [The Cambridge Poets; Boston and New York, 1909], p. 287).

92. Bennett, *Evolution of "The Faerie Queene,"* p. 79.

93. Charles Moorman has felt similar difficulties in regarding *The Faerie Queene* as a chivalric poem: "Spenser's knights have no character or characteristics as knights: they are derived neither from history nor from books; they are figures in an allegory, and they move by the dictates of the allegory. It is impossible, therefore, to place Spenser's knights in relation to any connected history of literary knighthood or to the myth of the hero-knight since they have no definite qualities in themselves" (*A Knyght There Was: The Evolution of the Knight in Literature* [Lexington, 1967], p. 136).

94. The commonly adopted title, *The Misfortunes of Arthur*, is taken from the headnote to the general argument; the words of the actual title page

of the original quarto edition are "Certaine De- / vises and shewes presented to / her MAIESTIE by the Gentlemen of / Grayes-Inne at her Highnesse Court in / Greenewich, the twenty eighth day of / Februarie in the thirtieth yeare of her / MAISTIES most happy / Raigne." This and all subsequent quotations from Hughes are taken from the text of the quarto as given in John W. Cunliffe's *Early English Classical Tragedies* (Oxford, 1912), pp. 217–96. According to various statements in the text (pp. 220, 225, 293–96), Hughes wrote most of the play. Nicholas Trotte wrote the introduction, William Fulbecke wrote speeches to be substituted for the first and last ones spoken by Gorlois, Frauncis Flower wrote additional choruses for the first two acts, and Christopher Yelverton, Frauncis Bacon, John Lancaster, and one Master Penroodocke devised the dumb shows and directed the production at court.

95. Cunliffe, *ibid.*, pp. 224–25.

96. That Hughes took most of his story from Geoffrey seems certain. The death of Uther through poisoning by the Saxons does not occur in Malory at all. So also does Gueneuora's acceptance of Mordred's love come from Geoffrey; in Malory, Guenevere is, of course, indignant at Mordred's usurpation and protects herself from him in the Tower of London. The details of the mutual destruction of Arthur and Mordred may come from Malory as may also Mordred's incestuous begetting, though Hughes omits the vital fact that Arthur was unaware of his sibling relation to Mordred's mother. Cf. Cunliffe, *ibid.*, pp. xc, 326, and 340.

97. The audacity of the Gentlemen of Gray's Inn is also reflected in Nicholas Trotte's Introduction: "Since your sacred Maiestie / In gratious hands the regal Scepter held / All Tragedies are fled from State, to stadge" (Introduction, ll. 131–33)—"a somewhat daring piece of flattery," Cunliffe says (*ibid.*, p. 326), "in the face of the execution of Mary Queen of Scots on Feb. 8, 1587." William A. Armstrong argues, however, that the play was deliberately designed, at least in part, as an "indirect compliment to Queen Elizabeth for not succumbing to [what the Tudor moralists called 'lenity,' or 'indulgency,' or 'wrong pity'] in her dealings with Mary Queen of Scots" ("Elizabethan Themes in *The Misfortunes of Arthur*," *RES*, 7 [1956], 247–48). It is doubtless the proximity of Mary's execution to the presentation of the play that suggested to Evangelia H. Waller ("A Possible Interpretation of *The Misfortunes of Arthur*," *JEGP*, 24 [1925], pp. 219–45) her curiously half-hearted and wholly unconvincing interpretation of the play as a "hidden political allegory" in which Gorlois appears to be Darnley, Arthur is James of Scotland, Gueneuora is Mary Queen of Scots, and Mordred is young Bothwell. Gertrude Reese ("Political Import of *The Misfortunes of Arthur*," *RES*, 21 [April, 1945], 81–91) takes a somewhat more improbable view that the play reflects the circumstances of the death of Mary Queen of Scots, with Mordred standing for Mary and Arthur for Elizabeth.

98. The parallel between the ghost of Tantalus in the *Thyestes* and that

of Gorlois is noted by MacCallum (*Idylls of the King and Arthurian Story*, p. 121) and Cunliffe (*Classical Tragedies*, p. 327).

99. III, iv, 18–27; V, i, 98–105. MacCallum (*Idylls of the King and Arthurian Story*, p. 123) may have overlooked these passages in speaking of "the inexplicable absence of remorse on the part of Arthur for the sin."

100. As Miss Bensel (*Character of King Arthur*, p. 156) correctly points out, both MacCallum and Jones err in attributing the tragic retribution to Arthur's incest. Here, as elsewhere, Mordred is but the instrument of Arthur's fall. In Hughes's play, as the opening and closing speeches of Gorlois should make clear, the retribution is for Uther's sinful seduction of Igerna.

101. Cunliffe's notes (*Classical Tragedies*, pp. 326–42) may be consulted for the full extent of Hughes's borrowings from Seneca. For his wholesale appropriation of the third scene of Act III from Lucan, see J. C. Maxwell, "Lucan's First Translator," *N&Q*, 192 (November 29, 1947), 521–22. Other passages appropriated from Lucan are listed by O. A. W. Dilke, "Thomas Hughes, Plagiarist," *N&Q*, NS 10 (1963), 93–94.

102. Cunliffe, *Classical Tragedies*, p. xci.

103. III, i, 211–34.

104. *Henslowe's Diary*, ed. Walter W. Greg (2 vols.; London, 1904–1908), I, 52–53, 86–87, 112.

105. It may also be suggested that in an age when audiences derived huge merriment from the plight of cuckolds, dramatists might have found the tragically betrayed Arthur a difficult subject for serious treatment. MacCallum (*Idylls of the King and Arthurian Story*, pp. 127–28) argues, rather speciously, it seems to me, that the dramatists neglected Arthurian story because of what he calls its lack of "truth and reality," a lack brought on by the fact that the legend had not been developed by the popular imagination but rather by "the fantastic spirit of foreign chivalrous romance" and was therefore "unfit for common human actuality and fact" and thus unsuitable for "the realistic art of the dramatist." This "explanation" seems to me to raise more questions than it answers. It is difficult to see that there is any more "reality" or "actuality" in *Macbeth* or *The Tempest*, let us say, than is possible in Arthurian story. See also W. Lewis Jones, "Geoffrey of Monmouth and the Legend of Arthur," *Quarterly Review*, 205 (July, 1906), 58–59, for another version of MacCallum's view: "Exploited for the uses of a cosmopolitan culture, the characters and incidents of Arthurian story had become too fantastic and remote for vivid dramatic presentment."

106. MacCallum, *Idylls of the King and Arthurian Story*, p. 125.

107. Thus the song beginning "When Arthur first in court," which Falstaff sings in *II Henry IV* (II, iv, 36), might have been any one of several ballads popular at the time. Justice Shallow's reference to his participation as a youth "in Arthur's show" (*ibid.*, III, ii, 299) tells us that the Justice had been a member of the Fellowship of Prince Arthur's Knights (mentioned earlier).

Of the allusions in *Lear*, one occurs in the Fool's prophecy, of which he says "This prophecy Merlin shall make; for I live before his time" (III, ii, 95); even if the passage is Shakespeare's, it is only a gibe at the popular books of prophecy attributed to Merlin, and widely read by the vulgar. And Kent's wish that he could drive Oswald "cackling home to Camelot" (II, ii, 89–90) scarcely implies a knowledge of Arthurian story past that available in the popular ballads. As for the Hostess's assurance that Falstaff is safe "in Arthur's bosom if ever man went to Arthur's bosom" (*Henry V*, II, iii, 10), it seems likely that the lady has only confused Arthur with Abraham (see Oscar James Campbell [ed.], *The Living Shakespeare* [New York, 1949], p. 483; Hardin Craig [ed.], *The Complete Works of Shakespeare* [Chicago, 1951], p. 746; J. H. Walter [ed.], *King Henry V* [The Arden Edition of the Works of William Shakespeare; Cambridge, Mass., 1954], p. 46).

108. William Edward Mead, "Outlines of the History of the Legend of Merlin," *Merlin, or The Early History of King Arthur*, ed. Henry B. Wheatley (2 vols., EETS, vols. 10, 21, 36, 112; London, 1865–1899), I, lxiii. Mead lists another edition by de Worde in 1529 and a third by John Hawkyns in 1533— evidence of the work's popularity.

109. *Golagrus and Gawain,* a fifteenth-century romance in Scottish dialect, was printed at Edinburgh in 1508 (Mead, ed., *Chinon of England*, p. xliii). The fifteenth-century *Jeaste of Syr Gawayne* was published between 1536– 1554 (*ibid.*, pp. xliii–xliv). Gawain also appears in a number of pieces in the Percy Folio MS (*ca.* 1650): "The Grene Knight" (an abridged and mutilated version of *Gawain and the Green Knight*), "The Turke and Gawain," "The Marriage of Sir Gawain," "Libeaus Desconus" (Libeaus is asserted to be Gawain's son), and "The Carle of Carlile" (*ibid.*, p. xlii). Mead dates all of these in the sixteenth century or earlier (*ibid.*, p. xxxiii). Other Arthurian poems in the MS include "King Arthur and the King of Cornwall," "The Boy and the Mantle," "King Arthur's Death," and a sixty-line ballad on Lancelot's fight with Sir Tarquin (*ibid.*, pp. xxxiii and xli).

110. For a summary of this romance, see Mead, *ibid.*, pp. xlvii–liv. Henslowe mentions in his diary a play called "Chinone of Ingland," first performed January 3, 1595 (*Henslowe's Diary*, ed. R. A. Foakes and R. T. Rickert (Cambridge, Eng., 1961), p. 33.

111. Part I was entered in Stationer's Hall in 1599 as "The history of the souldiour Tom of Lincolne called the Redcrose [*sic*] Knight. surnamed the boast of England." Part II was entered as "The second part of the famous history of Tom a Lincolne the Redd Rose Knight" (*Stat. Reg.*, 24 December 1599 and 20 October 1607). The earliest extant edition is the 6th impression of 1631 (*S.T.C.* 14684). The romance is reprinted in William J. Thoms's *Early English Prose Romances* (2nd ed., 3 vols.; London, 1858), II, 219–361. A relatively detailed summary is available in Mead's edition of *Chinon of England*, pp. xxxiv–xxxvi.

112. The text is available in *Robert Chester's Loves Martyr, or, Rosalins*

Complaint, ed. Rev. Alexander B. Grosart (New Shakespere Society, Series VIII, "Miscellanies," No. 2; London, 1878). According to Nearing (*English Historical Poetry,* p. 110), the source is Robinson's translation of Leland.

113. It is unclear whether this poem with the opening line, "When Arthur first in court began," is the one Falstaff sings in *II Henry IV* (II, iv, 36), or whether Deloney merely borrowed the line from some other ballad. Deloney's poem was entered in the Stationers' Registers in 1603 and appeared with other of his works in *The Garland of Good Will* in 1631. The text is available in *The Works of Thomas Deloney,* ed. Francis Oscar Mann (Oxford, 1912), pp. 323–26.

3. THE DEATH OF A LEGEND: ARTHURIAN STORY IN THE SEVENTEENTH AND EARLY EIGHTEENTH CENTURIES

1. Roberta Florence Brinkley, *Arthurian Legend in the Seventeenth Century* (Johns Hopkins Monographs in Literary History, Vol. III; Baltimore and London, 1932), p. 16. As my notes will indicate, I am much indebted to Miss Brinkley's work at several points in this chapter.

2. *Ibid.,* pp. 7–9. The wholly fanciful derivation of *Britain* from *Brutus* was commonly accepted from the Middle Ages on, but after the advent of humanist scholars in England, it had steadily fallen out of favor among the educated.

3. *Ibid.,* p. 11.

4. *Ibid.,* pp. 9–10.

5. *Ibid.,* pp. 10–11. In the *Speeches* Jonson called the throne "Arthur's seat"; two years later in the *Masque of Oberon* it has become "Arthur's . . . chair."

6. *Ibid.,* pp. 26–29.

7. *Ibid.,* pp. 26 and 40. James I, fearful of the discoveries of the researchers, indicated so much mistrust of the Society of Antiquaries that it was dissolved to avoid prosecution (*ibid.,* pp. 31–32).

8. *Ibid.,* p. 26.

9. *Ibid.*

10. *Ibid.,* pp. viii and 63.

11. *Ibid.,* p. 64. Cf. Homer Nearing, Jr., *English Historical Poetry, 1599–1641* (Philadelphia, 1945), p. 111.

12. Brinkley, *Arthurian Legend,* p. 65.

13. May McKisack, "Samuel Daniel as Historian," *RES,* 23 (July, 1947), 226–36. Other editions of Daniel's *History* appeared in 1617 or 1618, 1621, 1626, 1634, 1636, and 1706.

14. Quoted by McKisack, "Samuel Daniel," p. 237.

15. From Selden's "Illustrations" to Drayton's *Poly-Olbion,* Song IV; I quote from *The Works of Michael Drayton,* ed. J. William Hebel (Tercentenary Edition, 5 vols.; Oxford, 1931–1941), IV, 87.

16. *History of Henry VII*, cited by Brinkley, *Arthurian Legend*, pp. 73–74.

17. Brinkley, *Arthurian Legend*, pp. 72–73.

18. *Ibid.*, p. 76.

19. *Ibid.*, pp. 82–84. In the last lustrum of the century, a more extensive faith in Arthurian story is manifest in the work of a few writers: Crouch, Wynn, and Tyrell; their work, stimulated perhaps by the renewed popularity of the throne under William and Mary, appears to be the death rattle of faith in Geoffrey's account.

20. *History of England* (1695), cited by Brinkley, *Arthurian Legend*, p. 83.

21. Brinkley, *Arthurian Legend*, pp. 40–42.

22. As Miss Brinkley (*Arthurian Legend*, pp. 23–25) points out, the association of Arthur with the Stuart throne declined during James I's reign to a symbolic function, and even this fell into disuse.

23. Brinkley, *Arthurian Legend*, pp. 105–6.

24. Basil Willey, *The Seventeenth Century Background: Studies in the Thought of the Age in Relation to Poetry and Religion* (London, 1950), *passim*.

25. *Ibid.*, p. 88; cf. p. 151.

26. What Willey (*Seventeenth Century Background*, p. 90) says of Descartes's thought—"like all thought which is purely rational and intellectual, [it] was fundamentally unhistorical"—can be applied in a rough way to much of the whole period, it seems to me.

27. See my chap. 1, n. 61.

28. Harrison Ross Steeves, *Learned Societies and English Literary Scholarship in Great Britain and the United States* (New York, 1913), pp. 44–45.

29. Brinkley, *Arthurian Legend*, p. 101.

30. To these causative factors, Steeves (*Learned Societies*, pp. 44–45) adds the preoccupation with scientific study, the decline of nationalism after Elizabeth's death, and the political and religious turmoil of the period.

31. *Poly-Olbion*, Song III, ll. 407–8. This and all subsequent quotations from the poem are taken from *The Works of Michael Drayton*, ed. J. William Hebel (Tercentenary Edition, 5 vols.; Oxford, 1931–1941), IV.

32. Drayton, *Works*, IV, i*.

33. Francis Meres, as cited by Hebel, knew of the plan of the poem in 1598. The First Part was actually published in 1612; a second issue carried the date 1613. The Second Part, consisting of 12 additional Songs appeared in 1622, though it had been finished by 1619. Enough copies of the First Part remained in 1622 to make up whatever complete copies were needed (*ibid.*, IV, viii-x). These facts justify Child's terse comment: "The *magnum opus* fell flat" (Harold H. Child, "Michael Drayton," *The Cambridge History of English Literature*, ed. A. W. Ward and A. R. Waller [15 vols.; New York and Cambridge, 1939], IV, 216). For further information on the poem's re-

ception, see Geoffrey Tillotson, "Contemporary Praise of *Polyolbion*," *RES*, 16 (April 1940), 181–83.

34. *Poly-Olbion*, Song VI, ll. 271–72.

35. *Ibid.*, "To the Generall *Reader*" and "To My Friends, The Cambro-Britans" (Drayton, *Works*, IV, v*-vii*).

36. *Ibid.*, Song IV, ll. 245–322.

37. In addition to Geoffrey, he appears to have drawn on Camden's *Britannia* (1586), Philemon's translation of Camden (1610), Holinshed, and Malory (I. Gourvitch, "Drayton's Debt to Geoffrey of Monmouth," *RES*, 4 [October, 1928], 395–96).

38. *Poly-Olbion*, Song VI, ll. 275–86.

39. *Ibid.*, "From the Author of the Illustrations" (*Works*, IV, x*).

40. Jonson's visit to Drummond took place in 1618–1619. The phrases from the *Conversations* are quoted from *Ben Jonson*, ed. C. H. Herford and Percy Simpson (11 vols.; Oxford, 1925–1952), I, 132 and 136.

41. I, vi, 127–28; I quote from *Ben Jonson*, ed. Herford and Simpson, VI, 422. For the preceding quotation from *Under-Woods*, see VIII, 205.

42. According to Drummond, "Spensers stanzaes pleased him not, nor his matter" (*Ben Jonson*, I, 132).

43. Brinkley, *Arthurian Legend*, p. 125.

44. *An Apology Against a Pamphlet Call'd A Modest Confutation of the Animadversions upon the Remonstrant Against Smectymnuus* [1642], *The Works of John Milton*, ed. Frank Allen Patterson (Columbia University Edition, 18 vols.; New York, 1931–1938), III, Pt. I, pp. 304–5. All subsequent quotations from Milton are taken from this edition. James Holly Hanford (*A Milton Handbook* [3rd ed.; New York, 1944], p. 370) takes the view that in this passage Milton is not thinking of the medieval romances, but rather of Renaissance versions. Such an interpretation does not seem likely to me in light of the references to the reputed immorality of such romances—words that Milton would not have applied to Spenser or Tasso.

45. *An Apology Against a Pamphlet*, *Works*, III, p. 305. Whether Malory was among the romances known to Milton is uncertain; for a possible indebtedness to Malory for a detail in the portrait of Sin in *Paradise Lost*, see Lynette R. Muir, "A Detail in Milton's Description of Sin," *N&Q*, New Series, 3 (1956), 100–1.

46. *Il Penseroso*, ll. 116–20. The passage suggests that Milton probably had Spenser particularly in mind here. Milton's admiration for the "sage and serious Poet *Spenser*" (*Areopagitica*, *Works*, IV, 311) is well known. Among these hints at Milton's youthful interest in chivalric materials also belongs the inclusion of "Kings and Queens and *hero's* old" in the various epic matters listed in the *Vacation Exercise* (l. 47), and an allusion to "those valiant knights of King Arthur" in the *Prolusions*, *Works*, XII, 231.

47. *Paradise Lost*, I, ll. 579–81.

48. *Paradise Regained*, II, ll. 359–61.

49. *Works*, I, 292–93. I have departed from the translation given in this edition in translating "revocabo in carmina" as "I shall recall in song." Charles Knapp renders this as "I shall bring back to my songs."

50. *Ibid.*, pp. 312–13.

51. *Of Reformation Touching Church-Discipline in England, Works*, III, Pt. I, p. 78. What this song "in new and lofty *Measures*" would have been like is the subject of a great deal of ill-tempered and speciously reasoned argument in H. Mutschmann's *Milton's Projected Epic on the Rise and Future Greatness of the Britannic Nation* (Tartu, 1936); at any rate, Arthur, it appears, would have played little part in it.

52. Hanford, *Milton Handbook*, pp. 180–81.

53. Richard Hurd, *Hurd's Letters on Chivalry and Romance*, ed. Edith J. Morley (London, 1911), p. 115. By "fanaticism" Hurd doubtless means Puritanism. As for the supposed effect of Cervantes, there is not much reason to suppose that his influence was great in England by the 1640's; of Shelton's translation (Pt. I, 1612; Pt. II, 1620), no further edition was required until 1652.

54. *Ibid.*, p. 153. The necessity of some sort of "machinery" to an epic was, of course, axiomatic to the Age of Reason: "The pagan Gods and Gothic Faeries were equally out of credit, when Milton wrote. He did well therefore to supply their room with angels and devils" (*ibid.*, p. 144).

55. M. W. MacCallum, *Tennyson's Idylls of the King and Arthurian Story from the XVIth Century* (Glasgow, 1894), p. 140. This reason, which MacCallum offers only as a contributory cause, rests on the very dubious theory that Milton would have taken an allegorical approach to the Arthurian story.

56. The suggestion is made in Verity's Introduction to *Paradise Lost, Books I. and II.*, ed. A. W. Verity (Pitt Press Series; Cambridge, 1924), pp. xxxii–xxxiii.

57. See *The Poems of John Milton*, ed. H. J. C. Grierson (2 vols.; London, 1925), II, xxviii.

58. According to E. M. W. Tillyard (*Milton* [London, 1949], p. 177), Milton gave up the historical plan because he came to feel that the nation's leaders were not "worth celebrating in his own writings any more."

59. James Holly Hanford, "The Chronology of Milton's Private Studies," *PMLA*, 36 (June, 1921), 299.

60. MacCallum, *Idylls of the King and Arthurian Story*, p. 143.

61. Brinkley, *Arthurian Legend*, p. 135. What is here merely asserted, is developed extensively in Miss Brinkley's book, especially chaps. I and II. The position is perhaps to be qualified to some extent by the fact that there was a decline in the political uses of Arthurian and "British" matter with the accession of Charles I—probably because there was no need to bolster Charles' unquestioned right to the throne. Even so, in 1641 Robert Powell, a Stuart supporter, traced the oath of allegiance to King Arthur (*ibid.*, pp. 39–40), and

the "British" past of the nation (as opposed to the Saxon antiquity espoused by the Parliament party), was used several times in royal entertainments in the 1630's.

62. According to Sir Charles Firth ("Milton as an Historian," *Essays Historical and Literary* [Oxford, 1938], pp. 61–64), *The History of Britain, That Part Especially Now Call'd England; From the First Traditional Beginning, Continu'd to the Norman Conquest; Collected out of the Antientest and Best Authours Thereof* was begun after March of 1645. The first two books were probably completed by the end of 1647. By March of 1649 four books were finished; the work was not resumed until 1655. The whole, finally published in 1670, went no further than six books.

63. Putnam Fennell Jones, "Milton and the Epic Subject from British History," *PMLA*, 42 (December, 1927), p. 909.

64. Brinkley, *Arthurian Legend*, p. 135. Firth (*Essays*, pp. 65–69) makes the same point. All of this, of course, is not intended to detract from Milton's undeniable virtues as a historian. There is ample evidence of his scrupulous accuracy, attention to minute points, and careful comparison of sources (see J. Milton French, "Milton's Annotated Copy of Gildas," *Harvard Studies and Notes in Philology and Literature*, 20 [1938], pp. 75–80). On the other hand, there is a palpable absurdity in French's assertion that "Milton's mind . . . was essentially critical rather than creative. He was by sympathy a rationalist, a scientist, a thinker"; his "chief goal is truth—truth of fact—as little obscured by ornament and idle fancy as possible" ("Milton as a Historian," *PMLA*, 50 [June, 1935], pp. 476 and 479). The fact is, as Firth has said, "In Milton's attitude scientific incredulity was reinforced [one might almost say motivated] by Puritanical abhorrence of popery, and by contempt for the triviality of ecclesiastical controversy" (*Essays*, p. 92). Neither "abhorrence" nor "contempt" sort very well with the conception of Milton as a "scientist," though they go very nicely with the controversialist and poet.

65. Brinkley, *Arthurian Legend*, p. 135.

66. *History of Britain, Works*, X, 123. Nennius' "dux bellorum" is obviously the source of Milton's "Cheif General."

67. *Ibid.*, p. 125.

68. *Ibid.*, pp. 127–28.

69. *Ibid.*, pp. 129–31. It seems remarkable that in the *History* Milton omits, as Miss Brinkley points out (*Arthurian Legend*, p. 130), all mention of such obviously fabulous matters as Arthur's mysterious birth and the founding of the Round Table. Were these story elements still too dear to his heart to allow him to use them in mockery?

70. Brinkley, *Arthurian Legend*, pp. 132–34.

71. *Ibid.*, p. 81.

72. *Paradise Lost*, IX, ll. 28–44. Despite this apparently clear rejection of the martial values of chivalric romance, John E. Seaman argues that Milton's

Christ manifests specifically chivalric virtues ("The Chivalric Cast of Milton's Epic Hero," *ES*, 49 [1968], 97–107).

73. *Ibid.*, IV, ll. 763–70. If we may judge at all by Milton's allusions, it seems dubious that the courtly love elements had any large share in his impression of the Arthurian story. While Lancelot is mentioned once and Guenivere is referred to in the *History*, there is no hint of their relationship. Tristram, Iseult, and Mark are not mentioned anywhere. See Frank Allen Patterson and French Rowe Fogle, *An Index to the Columbia Edition of the Works of John Milton* (2 vols.; New York, 1942).

74. Neither the Grail nor its heroes, Galahad and Perceval, are mentioned anywhere in Milton's works. See Patterson and Fogle, *Index.*

75. Willey, *Seventeenth Century Background*, p. 227. While I accept Willey's view of the extent to which notions of "truth" entered into Milton's choice of the subject of *Paradise Lost*, I am unable, for the reasons outlined in my text to follow him in his assertion that Milton's dismissal of the Arthurian subject "constitutes a rejection of 'fiction' by the protestant consciousness, which is strictly comparable with the rejection of scholasticism by the scientific consciousness" (*ibid.*). What is overlooked here, it seems to me, is the fact that the reasons for the rejection of one subject are not by any logical necessity the mere obverse of the reasons for the acceptance of another.

76. *Ibid.*, p. 225.

77. Sir Walter Scott, Introduction to Dryden's *King Arthur* in *The Works of John Dryden*, ed. Sir Walter Scott, rev. George Saintsbury (18 vols.; Edinburgh, 1882–1893), VIII, 125.

78. Miss Brinkley (*Arthurian Legend*, p. 141) takes the view that Milton's recognition that he would have been left without a triumphant hero in the Arthurian story led to his abandonment of the subject. It is scarcely credible that Milton's view of "triumph" was all that naïve; clearly it isn't in *Paradise Lost.*

79. Miss Brinkley (*Arthurian Legend*, pp. 138–41) comes to the conclusion that Milton's interest in such themes could not have found expression in the Arthurian subject. Why, she does not say. That Tennyson used the material for just these purposes did not occur to her, perhaps.

80. How thoroughly the obsession with the epic dominated literary and critical thinking in the seventeenth century is perceptively suggested by Willey (*Seventeenth Century Background*, pp. 220–24). For Dryden's long-cherished hope to write an epic, see Charles E. Ward, *The Life of John Dryden* (Chapel Hill, N.C., 1961), pp. 88, 107–12, 117–18, 258–59, and 283–84.

81. This and the preceding quotations are from Dryden's "Discourse Concerning the Original and Progress of Satire," prefixed to *The Satires of Decimus Junius Juvenalis* (1693), as printed in *The Poetical Works of John Dryden*, ed. George R. Noyes (The Cambridge Poets; Boston and New York, 1909), p. 291. The date, "before 1684," is based on my assumption that the plan that Dryden here discusses doubtless preceded his composition of *King*

Arthur, which, according to his statement, was completed in its first version seven years before the date of its performance in 1691 (see Dryden's "Dedication" to *King Arthur, Dryden: The Dramatic Works*, ed. Montague Summers [6 vols.; London, 1931–1932], VI, 239). It is doubtless this earliest plan via a misreading of an anonymous fictional dialogue in *Fraser's* ("Dialogue Between John Dryden & Henry Purcell, in the Year 1691, on the Subject of their Forthcoming 'Dramatick Opera of *King Arthur*,'" *Fraser's Magazine*, 45 [February, 1852], pp. 196–200) that is responsible for Curdy's assertion that "John Dryden and Henry Purcell also planned an Arthurian epic" (A. E. Curdy, "Arthurian Literature," *RR*, 1 [1910], 266).

82. I suspect that Miss Brinkley (*Arthurian Legend*, p. 142) errs in assuming that the manner of treatment suggested in the last two-thirds of the passage applies to both subjects. The syntax of the passage is troublesome, however.

83. MacCallum, *Idylls of the King and Arthurian Story*, p. 147.

84. See my chap. 2, n. 91.

85. Dryden, "Discourse," *Poetical Works*, ed. Noyes, pp. 289–90. These "guardian angels of . . . kingdoms," Dryden informed Dennis, were not to be used "by every hand"; they required a knowledge of "Platonic philosophy" (Dryden, *Works*, ed. Scott and Saintsbury, XVIII, 115).

86. Dryden, "Discourse," *Poetical Works*, ed. Noyes, p. 291. Scott's explanation is characteristically sentimental:

> "Dryden, in immortal strain,
> Had raised the Table Round again,
> But that a ribald King and Court
> Bade him toil on, to make them sport;
> Demanded for their niggard pay,
> Fit for their souls, a looser lay,
> Licentious satire, song, and play;
> The world defrauded of the high design,
> Profan'd the God-given strength, and marr'd the lofty line."

(*Marmion*, Introduction to Canto I, *The Poetical Works of Sir Walter Scott*, ed. J. Logie Robertson [Oxford Complete Edition; London, 1913], pp. 92–93.)

87. The quotations in this paragraph are drawn from Dryden's "Dedication" of *King Arthur*, in *Dramatic Works*, VI, pp. 239 and 242. For the external evidence that the 1684 version contained political allegory, see Brinkley, *Arthurian Legend*, pp. 143–44. We also have Dryden's comment on how much he had been obliged to alter the play and a few shreds of the allegory remaining in the later version: thus Arthur's magnanimity to the vanquished Saxons and the general depreciation of the Saxons' courage suggest that Arthur was originally identified with Charles, who had at least begun his reign by following conciliatory policies. The Saxons, of course, stood for the Commonwealth or Parliament Party, which had been, at least metaphorically,

conquered by the return of Charles, and which had been in fact identified with the Saxons in the historical controversy in the earlier part of the century.

88. For a cancelled version of these words from the Dedication, see Ward, *Life*, p. 250. The play has had a surprising popularity; under various titles and in various altered forms and abridgements, it was revived in 1701, 1706, 1735/1736, 1740/1741, 1770, 1781, 1784, 1803, 1819, 1827, 1842, and 1928 (Dryden, *Dramatic Works*, VI, 234–38; B. Sprague Allen, *Tides in English Taste (1619–1800): A Background for the Study of Literature* [2 vols.; Cambridge, Mass., 1931], II, 138; *The London Stage: 1660–1800, Part 2: 1700–1729*, ed. Emmett L. Avery [2 vols.; Carbondale, Ill., Southern Illinois University Press, 1960], I, 7, 10, 119, 120; *Part 3: 1729–1741*, ed. Arthur H. Scouten [2 vols.; 1961], I, 537–47, 551–52, 561, 566, 570, 575; II, 602–4, 625–26, 891–92). Ward (*Life*, p. 363) takes the view that Purcell's music accounts for the later popularity of the play. Its publication history, following the editions listed in the British Museum Catalogue, is complicated by alterations in title and content. Dryden's text was first printed in 1691 as *King Arthur: or, The British Worthy. A Dramatick Opera*, which was followed by another edition in 1736. In the same year, it appeared with a new prologue and epilogue as *Merlin: or, The British Inchanter and King Arthur the British Worthy: a Dramatic Opera*, ascribed incorrectly by Curdy ("Arthurian Literature," p. 266) to W. Giffard, a theater manager who spoke the new prologue; see William Cushing (*Anonyms: A Dictionary of Revealed Authorship* [Cambridge, Mass., 1890], p. 423) and Allardyce Nicoll (*A History of Early Eighteenth Century Drama, 1700–1750* [Cambridge, Eng., 1925], p. 332). The shift in title was calculated to capitalize on the publicity which resulted from the satirical controversy then raging around Merlin's Cave, Queen Caroline's recent addition to the royal gardens at Richmond (discussed later in chap. 3). Garrick's alteration of the play was published in 1770 and 1781 under the title *King Arthur: or, the British Worthy, a Masque*, though according to Summers, Garrick's version was acted as *Arthur and Emmeline* (Dryden, *Dramatic Works*, VI, 236). In 1784, another alteration was published as *Arthur and Emmeline, a Dramatic Entertainment in Two Acts Taken from the Masque of King Arthur by Dryden: the Music by Purcel and Arne*.

89. Dryden, *King Arthur, Dramatic Works*, VI, 234 and 281. All quotations from *King Arthur* are drawn from this edition; subsequent references will be given in the text. Dryden was at pains to point out that the Duchess of Monmouth was pleased, doubtless by "the parts of the Airy and Earthy Spirits, and that Fairy kind of writing, which depends only upon the Force of Imagination"; the Queen's approbation was won, he supposed, by "the Praises of Her Native Country; and the Heroick Actions of so famous a Predecessor in the Government of *Great Britain*, as King *Arthur*" (*ibid.*, p. 242).

90. Miss Brinkley (*Arthurian Legend*, p. 176), perhaps through a con-

fusion of Dryden's Merlin with Blackmore's, errs in saying that the former is "portrayed in the rôle of enchanter on the side of the Saxons."

91. Dryden, *Dramatic Works*, VI, 241; Summers asserts (*ibid.*, p. 233) that Tacitus's *Germania* and *Annales* are much likelier sources than Bochart or Bede. He also suggests that Geoffrey was a major source of the play, but there is nothing in *King Arthur* to necessitate or even make likely such a view; cf. Brinkley, *Arthurian Legend*, p. 146.

92. Dryden, *Dramatic Works*, VI, 233; MacCallum, *Idylls of the King and Arthurian Story*, p. 159.

93. E.g., this exchange between Emmeline and Arthur in which that pure maiden gives Arthur her mental image of him:

"*Em.* . . . . . . You have a Face, like mine,
Two Hands, and two round, pretty, rising Breasts,
That heave like mine.
     Arth. But you describe a Woman.
Nor is it sight, but touching with your Hands.
. . . .
. . . I see at distance, where I touch not.
     Em. If you see so far, and yet not touch,
I fear you see my Naked Legs and Feet
Quite through my Cloaths; pray do not see so well" (p. 250).

And this is the play of which Scott said Arthur was "the prince . . . of a beautiful fairy-tale"! (Introduction to *King Arthur* in Dryden, *Works*, ed. Scott and Saintsbury, VIII, 126).

94. Albert Rosenberg, *Sir Richard Blackmore: A Poet and Physician of the Augustan Age* (Lincoln, Neb., 1953), p. 14.

95. This and other quotations in this paragraph are drawn from the unpaginated Preface of Blackmore's *Prince Arthur: An Heroick Poem, in Ten Books* (3rd ed.; London, 1696). So convinced was Blackmore of the moral effects of poetry that he "wish'd that Poets, as Preachers are in some Countries, were paid and licens'd by the State, and that none were suffer'd to write in Prejudice of *Religion* and the *Government*, but that all such Offenders, as *publick Enemies* of Mankind should be silenc'd and duly punish'd" (*ibid.*).

96. Blackmore appears to have taken considerable pride in this off-hand approach to Calliope; in the Preface to *King Arthur, An Heroick Poem, In Twelve Books* (London, 1697), he returns to the subject, saying that *Prince Arthur* was written as "an Innocent Amusement to entertain me in such leisure hours which were usually past away before in Conversation, and unprofitable hearing and telling of News" (p. ix); the actual composition of the poem was carried on "in less than two years time, and by such catches and starts, and in such occasional, uncertain hours, as the Business of my Profession would afford me . . . in Coffee-houses, and in passing up and down the Streets; because I had little leisure elsewhere to apply to it" (p. v). What capital Dryden made of these boasts we shall see later.

97. *Not* twelve books as Miss Brinkley says (*Arthurian Legend*, p. 146). Both British Museum and Library of Congress catalogues show all three editions as having ten books.

98. This curious description and explanation of various meteorological and genetic phenomena has something of the effect of a versified contribution to the Royal Society. It understandably won the admiration of William Molyneux (see Samuel Johnson, *Lives of the English Poets* [2 vols., Everyman's Library, Nos. 770–71; London and New York, 1941], II, 15), and Dr. Johnson subjoined it to his account of Blackmore in *Lives of the English Poets*.

99. The games with which Arthur's men celebrate their victory include, by a curious anachronism, handicapped horse racing: "And those that by their Rules were found too light, / Quilt Lead into their Belts, to give them weight" (Book IX, p. 256).

100. *Not* 1700 as it is dated by Miss Brinkley (*Arthurian Legend*, p. 147).

101. *King Arthur*, Book III, p. 76.

102. In the Preface to *King Arthur* (pp. xi–xii), Blackmore says, "That there was about the end of the Fourth, or the beginning of the Fifth *Century*, a king of *Britain* nam'd *Arthur*; a Prince of extraordinary Qualities, and Famous for his Martial Atchievements, who succeeded his Father *Uter Pendragon*, all our Historians agree; . . . . And tho' . . . *Geofry* of *Monmouth* is indeed a Fabulous Author, yet his authority, especially considering that there was such a warlike Prince as *Arthur*, is a sufficient Foundation for an *Epick Poem*." Blackmore goes on to summarize briefly Arthur's triumphs over the Saxons, Norway, Denmark, and Gallia (*ibid.*, pp. xii–xiii). Miss Brinkley (*Arthurian Legend*, pp. 148–49) suggests a greater indebtedness to Geoffrey than the facts warrant, it seems to me.

103. *Prince Arthur*, Book VII, p. 204.

104. *King Arthur*, p. v.

105. For the most thorough study of Blackmore's sources, see Oskar Liss, *Die Arthurepen des Sir Richard Blackmore* (Strassburg, 1911), p. 24 ff. Miss Brinkley (*Arthurian Legend*, pp. 148–76) also gives extensive treatment to the matter.

106. *Prince Arthur*, Book I, p. 15. According to Miss Brinkley (*Arthurian Legend*, p. 153), the adjective *pious* is applied to Arthur some twenty times. Among the many ingenious parallels with the *Aeneid* that Blackmore managed are the storm, the hospitable reception of the wanderers, the relation of past events, the vision of the future line of kings, and the betrothal of the daughter of the enemy (cf. MacCallum, *Idylls of the King and Arthurian Story*, p. 156). Lest any reader should overlook these borrowings, Blackmore declared in his Preface to *Prince Arthur*, "I have endeavour'd mostly to form myself on *Virgil's Model* . . . . I do not make any *Apology* for my *Imitation* of *Virgil* in so many places of this poem, for the same great Master has imitated *Homer* as frequently and closely."

107. *King Arthur*, p. xiii. In addition to frequent verbal parallels to *Paradise Lost*, Blackmore took over from Milton, virtually in its entirety, his "machinery" in which Lucifer and the fallen angels are arrayed against the heavenly angels who protect Arthur. He thus makes use of Milton's story of the fall of the rebellious angels, Satan's flight through Chaos to the newly created Earth, and the great consultations in Hell. Following the Bible, he modeled Hoel's sudden conversion on that of St. Paul, and on the story of Balaam, he builds Merlin's being forced to speak the truth when he opens his mouth to curse Arthur's forces: "The Heav'nly Fury Merlin did constrain / To Bless, whom he to Curse design'd in vain" (*Prince Arthur*, Book VII, pp. 204–5). The similarity of Book VI of *King Arthur* to *Job* is especially obvious; e.g., God's question to Satan: "Hast thou observ'd my Servant *Arthur's* ways, / That just and perfect Man who still obeys?" and Satan's reply that if Arthur were not always favored by God, he would "curse thee to thy face" (pp. 153–55). Cf. MacCallum, *Idylls of the King and Arthurian Story*, pp. 156–58.

108. Preface, *Prince Arthur*. As Miss Brinkley (*Arthurian Legend*, pp. 151–52) points out, Spenser's uncompleted plan very likely suggested Blackmore's own division of the subject into the periods before and after Arthur was king. Miss Brinkley's view that Blackmore's Arthur was designed to illustrate the various virtues with which Spenser endowed his Prince Arthur (*ibid.*, pp. 152–54) seems less likely to me; Blackmore's Arthur is such a paragon that he is bound to have any virtue that any poet could think of. Both Tasso and Spenser may have had some influence on the Pleasure Garden scene in Book VI of *King Arthur*, but see following note.

109. John Dryden, *Preface to Fables Ancient and Modern* (1700), *Poetical Works*, p. 749. In the same passage Dryden goes on to remark contemptuously, "The guardian angels of kingdoms were machines too ponderous for him to manage; and therefore he rejected them." The *Juvenal* had appeared in 1693, *Prince Arthur* in 1695. In the Preface to *King Arthur* (p. v) Blackmore says that *Prince Arthur* had been written "in less than two years time." Moreover, Blackmore clearly was influenced in his treatment of Arthur's temptation by Fascinia by Dryden's handling of a similar theme in his *King Arthur*. With Blackmore's words,

> "A painful Pleasure seiz'd his beating Heart,
>
> . . . .
>
> The wandering Flame creeps thro' his wounded Veins
>
> . . . .
>
> Amidst such Charms who would not still abide?"
>
> (*King Arthur*, Book VI, p. 173),

compare Dryden's "A Lazie Pleasure trickles through my Veins; / Here could I stay, and well be Couzen'd here" (p. 276). And just as Dryden's Arthur is warned away by the airy spirit Philidel, so Blackmore's Arthur is encouraged to depart by the angel Gabriel. Seeking to cover his tracks, Blackmore asserted in the Preface to *King Arthur* (p. xiii) that he had "in the *Sixth Book* adventur'd on an *Allegory*, finding Homer has done the like in his story of *Circe*." While Fascinia does have the ability to transform men to beasts, Dryden's temptress still remains her immediate source. If more evidence of Blackmore's indebtedness to Dryden were needed, it would quickly reveal itself in the Drydenesque ring of the occasional small felicities that Blackmore achieves in rhetoric or the management of his heroic couplets.

110. Preface, *Prince Arthur*.

111. Preface, *Alfred*, quoted by Brinkley, *Arthurian Legend*, p. 184.

112. *Prince Arthur*, Book VI, p. 173.

113. The peace to this inconclusive war came late in 1697. I am uncertain whether it was Blackmore's fear that events were working out in a manner that would fatally belie his allegory (in which Arthur reduces Paris to submission) or his anxiety to capitalize on the fervor roused by Barclay's conspiracy that caused him to rush into print with *King Arthur*. At any rate, in the Preface to that poem (p. vi) he says he has published in haste for reasons "that the Judicious Reader will soon find in the Poem itself."

114. *Prince Arthur*, Book V. Arthur, learning of Maria's impending fate (Queen Mary died in 1695 before the poem was published), is awakened by his grief. In the dream Blackmore proved himself as quick to revise history as he was to alter tradition; William III follows Elizabeth directly in the succession of British monarchs.

115. For other identifications see Brinkley, *Arthurian Legend*, pp. 176–85, and MacCallum, *Idylls of the King and Arthurian Story*, p. 155.

116. Even Blackmore admitted to some surprise at its success: "The Favour and Approbation it met with, was much greater, and far more universal, even among great Names, and establish'd, uncontested Judges, than I had ever the Vanity to expect" (*King Arthur*, Preface, p. i).

117. The fourth (and last) edition was published by Tonson in 1714. *King Arthur* was not so successful; the edition of 1697 has never been reprinted. Even it did not lack supporters. William Molyneux after reading it wrote to Locke, "All our *English* poets (except *Milton*) have been meer balladmakers, in comparison to him" (quoted by Rosenberg, *Richard Blackmore*, p. 38).

118. See Rosenberg (*Richard Blackmore*, pp. 24–27) for a number of examples of such contemporary estimates. Blackmore himself felt constrained to admit that the *Aeneid* was actually greater, but added that neither Homer nor any of his successors other than Virgil had shown "a more regular Conduct, or a more perfect Model." He admitted that the poem had some faults: the second and third books together with some of the descriptions, digressions, and similes were too long. Such faults sprang partly from "want of Leisure and Retirement, to consider coolly every part of that writing" and partly from "defect of *Judgment* and *Genius* equal to, and sufficient for so great and difficult an Undertaking" (*King Arthur*, Preface, pp. iii–v).

119. William also awarded Blackmore a gold medal and chain to the value of £ 150 (Rosenberg, *Richard Blackmore*, pp. 34–35).

120. *King Arthur*, Preface, p. vi.

121. Johnson, *Lives of the Poets*, II, 22. For the battle of the Wits with Blackmore, see Richard C. Boys, *Sir Richard Blackmore and the Wits: A Study of "Commendatory Verses on the Author of the Two Arthurs and the Satyr Against Wit"* (University of Michigan Contributions in Modern Philology, No. 13; Ann Arbor, Mich., 1949).

122. The words are Blackmore's own (*King Arthur*, Preface, p. ii).

123. Preface to *Fables Ancient and Modern, Poetical Works*, p. 749.

124. *Poetical Works*, p. 899.

125. *The Works of Alexander Pope*, ed. Rev. Whitwell Elwin and William John Courthope (10 vols.; London, 1871–1889), X, 360.

126. I quote from the text edited by James Sutherland (The Twickenham Edition; New York: Oxford University Press, 1943), pp. 131, 137, and 142. This soporific effect, which the reader can easily verify for himself, had earlier been noted in Dr. Kenrick's *A New Session of the Poets* (1700) in which Apollo tells Blackmore, "thy Rhymes a constant Cadence keep, / At once they make us smile, and make us sleep" (quoted by Rosenberg, *Richard Blackmore*, pp. 56–57).

127. Rosenberg, *Richard Blackmore*, p. 65.

128. *Ibid.*, pp. 49–52. Rosenberg identifies many of the authors of these various squibs. Cf. Boys, *Blackmore and the Wits*, pp., 37 ff., 133 ff.

129. Johnson, *Lives of the Poets*, II, 24. Even in Johnson's time, less than a century later, Blackmore's epics were "little read" (*ibid.*, p. 25).

130. It is not unlikely that some of the large sales of *Prince Arthur* rested on the fame that the wits' obloquy brought him. Blackmore looked at the matter more optimistically: his critics "instead of lessening the Credit of the *Poem*, in many Instances . . . very much advanc'd it" (*King Arthur*, Preface, p. iii).

131. Johnson, *Lives of the Poets*, II, 25. MacCallum's estimate of *Prince Arthur* is more succinct: "It is as dull a fabrication as literature has to show" (*Idylls of the King and Arthurian Story*, p. 158).

132. *Prince Arthur*, Preface.

133. *DNB* s.v. "Parker, Martin." The titles given in *DNB* and the British Museum catalogue differ slightly from the version I quote from Miss Brinkley (*Arthurian Legend*, p. 113), whose account of the story I follow.

134. The following examples, which deserve listing for their period interest, are mentioned variously by William Edward Mead ("Outlines of the History of the Legend of Merlin," *Merlin, or The Early History of King Arthur*, ed. Henry B. Wheatley [2 vols., EETS, Vols. 10, 21, 36, 112; London, 1865–1899], I, lxxiv and lxxviii–lxxx), Howard Maynadier (*The Arthur of the English Poets* [Boston and New York, 1907], pp. 303–5), and Brinkley (*Arthurian Legend*, pp. 8 and 76–79): a number of old Scottish prophecies

attributed to Merlin and first printed 1603; two eds. of Merlin's prophecies published by Alanus de Insulis (1603 and 1608); *The Whole Prophecies of Scotland, England, France, and Denmark, Prophecied by Marvellous Merling* (1603, 1615); Thomas Heywood's *The Life of Merlin, Surnamed Ambrosius: His Prophecies and Predictions Interpreted, and Their Truth Made Good by our English Annals: Being a Chronographical History of All the Kings and Memorable Passages of the Kingdom, from Brute to the Reign of King Charles* (1641); *A Prophesie [of Merlin] concerning Hull in Yorkshire* (1642); William Lilly's *Merlinus Anglicus Junior, the English Merlin Reviv'd, or a Mathematicall Prediction upon the Affairs of the English Commonwealth* (1644); *England's Propheticall Merline Foretelling to all Nations of Europe* (n.d., sometime in reign of Charles I); *The Lord Merlin's Prophecy Concerning the King of Scots; Foretelling the Strange and Wonderfull Things that Shall Befall Him in England, As Also the Time and Manner of a Dismal and Fatall Battel* (1651); Partridge's *Merlinus Liberatus* (1680 and annually from 1689 to 1707); *Merlin Reviv'd, or An Old Prophecy Found in a Manuscript in Pontefract Castle in Yorkshire* (1681, 1682); *The Mystery of Ambros Merlins, Standard-bearer, Wolf, and Last Boar of Cornwall, with Sundry Other Misterious Prophecys . . . Unfolded in the Following Treatise on the Signification . . . of that Prodigious Comet Seen . . . Anno 1680, with the Blazing Star, 1682 . . . Written by a Lover of his Countrys Peace* (1683); *Catastrophe Mundi; or Merlin Reviv'd, in a Discourse of Prophecies and Predictions, and Their Remarkable Accomplishment; with Mr. Lilly's Hieroglyphics Exactly Cut, By a Learned Pers[on]* (1683); *Merlin Reviv'd, in a Discourse of Prophecies and Predictions, and Their Remarkable Accomplishment, with Mr. Lilly's Hieroglyphics; Also a Collection of All the Ancient Prophecies, Touching the Grand Revolution Like to Happen in These Latter Ages* (1683); *Merlini Anglici Ephemeris; or, Astrological Judgments for the Year 1685* (1685). For Catholics the use of Merlin's prophecies had been banned by the Church since the Council of Trent in 1545–1563 (Brinkley, *Arthurian Legend*, p. 9). By the Plague of 1664–1665, Merlin had become so identified with prognostication in the popular mind that signs showing the head of Merlin were used, Defoe tells us, to indicate fortune tellers' houses (*A Journal of the Plague Year*, cited by Maynadier, *The Arthur of the English Poets*, p. 304; the passage may be conveniently consulted in the Everyman's Library edition [London and New York, 1943], p. 30).

135. According to William Edward Mead ("Arthurian Story in the Sixteenth Century" in his ed. of Christopher Middleton's *Chinon of England* [EETS, Original Series, No. 165; London, 1925], p. xxxix), this play, first printed in 1662, is to be dated later than 1597. Since the date commonly accepted for Rowley's birth is *ca.* 1585, the proper date must be considerably later than 1597, when Rowley would have been around twelve years old. The claim advanced in the 1662 edition that Shakespeare had a hand in the play is, of course, as Mead says (*ibid.*), merely the publisher's way of advertising.

The play appears to have been staged in 1724, 1736, and possibly 1738 (Allen, *English Taste*, II, 137). In the 1724 production it was titled *Merlin the British Enchanter; or, The Child Has Found His Father* and described as "an excellent new Droll, never acted before" (*The London Stage, Part 2*, ed. Avery, II, 784). In 1736 the words "The Birth of" were restored to the title (*ibid., Part 3*, ed. Scouten, I, 593 and 595). The play also appears to have been the foundation of a puppet show presented in 1710–1711 (*ibid., Part 2*, I, 234). The play presented in 1738 under the title *Merlin, The British Enchanter; or, St. George for England* (*ibid., Part 3*, II, 727) is probably *not* to be identified with Rowley's play.

136. Maynadier, *The Arthur of the English Poets*, p. 308.

137. See *S.T.C.*, 14056. On the basis of the author's initials as given on the title page, the book has been doubtfully assigned to Richard Johnson.

138. Of this poem the British Museum catalogue lists a number of eighteenth-century editions conjecturally dated 1750, 1775, and 1780.

139. Elise Francisca Wilhelmina Maria Van Der Ven-Ten Bensel, *The Character of King Arthur in English Literature* (Amsterdam, 1925), p. 173 n.

140. MacCallum, *Idylls of the King and Arthurian Story*, pp. 166–67.

141. S. Humphreys Gurteen, *The Arthurian Epic: A Comparative Study of the Cambrian, Breton, and Anglo-Norman Versions of the Story and Tennyson's Idylls of the King* (New York and London, 1895), p. 393. Cf. MacCallum, *Idylls of the King and Arthurian Story*, pp. 160–61.

142. *Essay on Criticism* (1711) Part II, ll. 686–92.

143. J. B. Black, *The Art of History: A Study of Four Great Historians of the Eighteenth Century* (London, 1926), p. 17.

144. The phrase from Vico's *Scienza Nuova* (1725–1744) is quoted by Emery Neff, *The Poetry of History* (New York, 1947), p. 86. Iselin (*Philosophical Speculations on the History of Humanity* [1764]) also shows the customary contempt of the philosophical historians for the sources of Medieval history: "It is a recognized principle that in the history of the Middle Ages the judgments of the historians, who were all priests, since no one else could read or write, must not be trusted" (quoted by Neff, *Poetry of History*, p. 20).

145. *Essai sur les moeurs* (1st pirated ed., 1754), quoted by Neff, *Poetry of History*, p. 15.

146. G. P. Gooch, *History and Historians in the Nineteenth Century* (2nd ed.; London, 1935), pp. 8–11. Cf. Black, *Art of History*, p. 73. According to Neff (*Poetry of History*, p. 18), Voltaire's fellow Encyclopaedist d'Alembert shows the same contempt for the Middle Ages in his "Preliminary Discourse."

147. The two volumes of Hume's *History of England* that concern themselves with the Middle Ages appeared in 1761 (O.S.) and doubtless owed something to the encouragements of Hume's publisher; see Thomas Preston Peardon, *The Transition in English Historical Writing* (Studies in History, Economics and Public Law, No. 390; New York, 1933), p. 21. The avian

allusion is cited by Gooch, *History and Historians*, p. 11; the last quotation is from Black, *Art of History*, p. 87.

148. Peardon (*Transition*, p. 30) doubts that these words give a just picture of Gibbon's view of the Middle Ages, and says that Gibbon was more prudent in his judgments than Hume. But consider this comment on the Crusades: "I shall abridge the tedious and uniform narrative of their blind achievements, which were performed by strength and are described by ignorance" (quoted by Neff, *Poetry of History*, p. 80).

149. Gooch, *History and Historians*, pp. 10–13.

150. Black, *Art of History*, pp. 56–57.

151. Basil Willey, *The Eighteenth Century Background: Studies on the Idea of Nature in the Thought of the Period* (London, 1940), p. 44.

152. For an extensive study of eighteenth-century English taste in architecture, see Allen, *English Taste*, esp. I, 19–123. Allen is at considerable pains to demonstrate the persistence of an appreciation and affection for Gothic architecture through the sixteenth, seventeenth, and eighteenth centuries; but as his citations make clear, such feelings were largely nostalgic, and in any event largely confined to antiquarians. Kenneth Clark recognizes the existence of a "tiny brackish stream" of interest in Gothic architecture that "never quite disappears," and even concedes that "from 1600 to 1800 perhaps no year passed which did not see the building of some pointed arch and gabled roof, or the restoration of some crumbling tracery." Nevertheless, the year 1633, when Inigo Jones began the "repairs" on St. Paul's, in the course of which a Renaissance shell was put on a large part of the building, marks the sharp decline in fashionable circles of Gothic; "when the chief Gothic monument of the land was to be given a classical shell, men's vision must have been dominated by new forms" (*The Gothic Revival: an Essay in the History of Taste* [Rev. and enlarged ed.; London, 1950], pp. 13–16).

153. "An Account of the Greatest English Poets" (1694); I quote from *The Works of the Late Right Honorable Joseph Addison, Esq.* (4 vols.; Birmingham, 1761), I, 34–35. These lines do not represent Addison's later opinion of Spenser, partially, perhaps, because, as he later admitted, "when he wrote these lines he had not read Spenser" (Joseph Spence, *Anecdotes* [1820], p. 50, cited by Earl R. Wasserman, *Elizabethan Poetry in the Eighteenth Century* [Illinois Studies in Language and Literature, Vol. XXXII, Nos. 2–3; Urbana, Ill., 1947], p. 17). As Wasserman points out, that Addison had not read the author he so dismisses indicates strongly that his notions "could have been drawn only from current criticism."

154. Quoted from Joseph Stukeley's *Memoirs and Correspondence* by Steeves, *Learned Societies*, p. 67.

155. No. 99, June 23, 1711, of *The Spectator*, ed. George A. Aitkin (6 vols.; London, n.d.), I, 421–22. This satirical summary of the clichés of the chivalric romance is doubtless well taken, but the point is that for Addison, this seems to be all there is to say for the romances. The dominance of such

attitudes toward the chivalry of the romances was not quite absolute, as appears from the recent discovery of the papers of the Order of the Twitcher. The order, complete with a vow involving elements of chivalric romance, a dubbing with a sword, coats of arms for its "knights" and titles for its "damsels," seems to have played a fairly serious part in the fantasy life of a small group of younger members of the lesser landed gentry during the years 1727–1731, though its influence "upon the course of eighteenth-century culture is negligible," as Vedder M. Gilbert observes ("An Early Return to Chivalry in the Eighteenth Century," *N&Q*, 200 [October, 1955], 433–36; for details on one member of the Order, see also Gilbert's "Thomas Edwards as the Wooden Inigo," *N&Q*, 200 [December, 1955], 532–35).

156. "Preface to Shakespeare" (1765); I quote from *Johnson: Prose and Poetry*, ed. Mona Wilson (London, 1950), p. 505. Dr. Johnson's moderation, if we may trust Percy's report to Boswell, may have been conditioned by the fact that, as a boy, Johnson "was immoderately fond of reading romances of chivalry, and he retained his fondness for them through life . . . . Yet I have heard him attribute to these extravagant fictions that unsettled turn of mind which prevented his ever fixing in any profession" (quoted by Mary Patchell in *The Palmerin Romances in Elizabethan Prose Fiction* [Columbia University Studies in English and Comparative Literature, No. 166; New York, 1947], p. 23). No doubt it was to forestall the development of such vacillation that Priestley, who had "a great aversion to plays and romances," seized and threw away a "book of Knight-errantry" that he found his brother Timothy reading (cited by Willey, *Eighteenth Century Background*, p. 185).

157. The publication and acting history of the play is complicated by the fact that Fielding prepared and published three different versions of the text. According to Wilbur L. Cross (*The History of Henry Fielding* [3 vols.; New Haven, 1918], I, 85–101; III, 291–92), the first version in two acts without prologue or epilogue was produced and published in 1730 under the title *Tom Thumb, A Tragedy*. An enlarged version appeared in the same year under the same title, but now provided with a prologue and epilogue, and a preface designed to burlesque Cibber. The immediate success of the play (some forty performances were given within three months) led Fielding to undertake a further revision and enlargement in 1731. This last version, *The Tragedy of Tragedies; or the Life and Death of Tom Thumb the Great*, has three acts, a new preface by "Scriblerus Secundus," and an elaborate apparatus of notes. At least three impressions of the first edition of 1731 are extant and four more editions had appeared by 1776, an indication of the play's popularity. In 1780 Fielding's play was converted by Kane O'Hara into *Tom Thumb, a Burletta*, and, according to John Genest (*Some Account of the English Stage from the Restoration in 1660 to 1830* [10 vols.; Bath, 1832], VI, 186) acted in this form with great success. Genest notes that "the addition of Songs destroys in great degree the original design, as of course there were no Songs in the Tragedies which Fielding meant to ridicule." O'Hara's ambition to cap Fielding led him

to make Tom come out of the cow's mouth at the command of Merlin; the other characters are similarly brought back to life at the finale. O'Hara's adaptation was revived in 1805 and published for the first time.

158. I quote here from the 1731 version of the play as printed in *The Works of Henry Fielding, Esq.*, ed. Leslie Stephen (10 vols.; London, 1882), VIII, 359. Subsequent quotations in this paragraph are from the "Dramatis Personae," pp. 355–56.

159. Fielding, *Works*, VIII, p. 406.

160. Cross (*Henry Fielding*, I, 86) points out that a number of these tragedies were still being acted when Fielding's play was first produced. Dryden's *King Arthur*, it may be added, is among the objects of Fielding's parody.

161. Fielding, *Works*, VIII, p. 351. The ostensible purpose of these parallel passages is to vindicate the justness of the "sentiments of the Author," which, Scriblerus gravely affirms, "are generally the most familiar which I have ever met with" (*ibid.*). The play is also provided with a "Preface" designed to parody the learned scholarship of "Clariss. Bentlium," Dennis, and Burmann the Elder.

162. Fielding's source of the story of Tom Thumb may have been, if the reference is not merely another part of the facetiousness of the Preface, a certain *History of Tom Thumb* "printed by and for Edward M---r, at the Looking-glass on London Bridge" mentioned in the Preface (*ibid.*, p. 349). If not this, it was doubtless some one or other of the numerous chapbooks dealing with Tom Thumb and popular since the early part of the seventeenth century. According to MacCallum (*Idylls of the King and Arthurian Story*, pp. 165–66), who quotes from a number of eighteenth-century chapbooks (*ca.* 1750?), such publications "choose by preference the age of Arthur as the period of their narratives."

163. Fielding, *Works*, VIII, 360. Cross (*Henry Fielding*, I, 103) suggests that the character of Tom was also "a hit at Sir Robert Walpole, the Great Man, as he was called in irony by his enemies. Fielding reduced the Prime Minister to a pigmy, to the delight of the audience, making the little man more powerful than men, giants, and the gods combined."

164. Fielding, *Works*, VIII, 362.

165. *Ibid.*, p. 349.

166. It seems worthy to be recorded that Swift's viewing of the play was one of the two occasions in his life when he laughed, or so Laetitia Pilkington reports (*Memoirs*, 1754, cited by Cross, *Henry Fielding*, I, 87).

167. See above, n. 134.

168. Mead, "Outlines of the History of the Legend of Merlin," in his edition of *Chinon of England*, I, lxxviii–lxxx.

169. Despite the fact that Partridge had died in 1715, an enterprising bookseller brought out *Merlinus Liberatus, An Almanack for the Year of Our Blessed Saviour's Incarnation 1723 . . . by John Partridge*, probably in 1723,

and other publications under the title *Merlinus Liberatus* are recorded in 1753 and 1761 (Mead, ed., *Chinon of England*).

170. With the relatively small number of eighteenth-century examples, compare the more than a dozen such works that appeared in the preceding century (see above, n. 134). Merlin's name was also attached to political satire in *A Prophecy of Ill* in 1762 and to civil engineering in *A Prophecy of Merlin, An Heroic Poem Concerning the Wonderful Success of a Project, Now on Foot, to Make the River from the Severn to Strond Navigable, Translated from the Original Latin, Annexed with Notes Explanatory* (1776). For all of these titles, see Mead, ed., *Chinon of England*.

171. For the history, appearance, and reception of Merlin's Cave, see Allen, *English Taste*, II, 135–38. Allen gives a picture of the structure in Fig. 67, facing p. 136.

172. The revivals of *The Birth of Merlin* took place in 1736 and 1738. Those of Dryden's play in 1735–1736 and 1740–1741 (Allen, *English Taste*, II, 137–38).

173. The Hermitage appears in the first scene, Merlin's Cave in the fourth. The last revival of Dryden's play in 1741 also attracted audiences with a reproduction of the Cave (Allen, *English Taste*, II, p. 38). I am indebted to Allardyce Nicoll (*Eighteenth Century Drama*, p. 349) for the attribution to Edward Phillips. According to Mead (in his edition of *Chinon of England*, p. lxxvii) only a fragment of this play is extant.

174. For Curll's work, see Allen, *English Taste*, II, 136. *Merlin: a Poem* etc. is listed in the British Museum catalogue. There is some reason to suspect that it may be the work of Jane Hughes Brereton; it is subscribed Melissa, a pseudonym used by Mrs. Brereton (William Cushing, *Initials and Pseudonyms: A Dictionary of Literary Disguises* [London, 1886], s.v. "Melissa."

175. I have been unable to find any record of the performance of this operetta. It was first printed from MS in *The Dramatic Works of Aaron Hill, Esq.* (2 vols.; London, 1760), I, 319–50. The date of composition could be no later than 1750 when Hill died. The connection of its inspiration, at least, with Merlin's Cave is suggested by the references to that structure in Hill's theatrical magazine, *The Prompter* (Allen, *English Taste*, II, 136). A date in the 1730's for Hill's "pantomime opera" is also suggested by the fact that Merlin was thus associated with Harlequin in two other pantomimes produced during the decade: *Merlin: or, The British Enchanters* (1731) and *Merlin; or, The Devil of Stone-Henge* (1734) (*The London Stage, Part 3*, ed. Scouten, I, 153 and 440). For Hill's career, see Dorothy Brewster's *Aaron Hill: Poet, Dramatist, Projector* (New York, 1913).

176. Listed by Mead in his edition of *Chinon of England*, I, lxxviii–lxxx.

177. To this account of the uses of Arthurian material in the first half of the eighteenth century may belong works by Maurice McGorman and J. W. Reed, both listed by Curdy, "Arthurian Literature," as either authors or transcribers during the eighteenth century of Arthurian works. Unfortunately, I

have been unable to locate either of these names in any of the standard bibliographies or catalogues.

178. Willey, *Eighteenth Century Background*, p. 10. See also p. 107 for an analysis of the essentially anti-historical nature of satire: the satirist must not allow himself to understand the origins of what he attacks or its reasonableness in the light of its history.

4. ARTHUR STIRS IN AVALON: ARTHURIAN STORY AMONG THE PRE-ROMANTICS

1. In the title of this chapter and at several later points, I have allowed myself the comfortable convenience of the term Pre-Romantic as a generalizing label for such interests during the second half of the eighteenth century; although I sympathize with Northrop Frye's objections to the "anachronism" of the term and its "false teleology" ("Towards Defining an Age of Sensibility," *ELH*, 23 [June, 1956], pp. 144–45), I am not sure that "Age of Sensibility" or "Age of Taste" is a real improvement.

2. Richard Mant's Memoir of Thomas Warton (1791) in *The Poetical Works of the Late Thomas Warton*, ed. Richard Mant (5th ed., 2 vols.; Oxford, 1802), I, cliii.

3. Basil Willey, *The Eighteenth Century Background: Studies on the Idea of Nature in the Thought of the Period* (London, 1940), pp. 9–10.

4. Hoxie Neale Fairchild, *The Romantic Quest* (New York, 1931), p. 8.

5. Cf. Sir Herbert Grierson, *The Background of English Literature, Classical & Romantic, and Other Collected Essays and Addresses* (2nd ed.; London, 1950), pp. 270–72.

6. For Dryden's suggested substitutes for mythology, see chap. 3 of the present study. B. Ifor Evans considers the absence of mythology "the major difficulty in the poetry of the seventeenth century and of the eighteenth" (*Tradition and Romanticism: Studies in English Poetry from Chaucer to W. B. Yeats* [London, 1940], p. 45).

7. W. P. Ker ("The Literary Influence of the Middle Ages," *The Cambridge History of English Literature*, ed. A. W. Ward and A. R. Waller [15 vols.; New York and Cambridge, Eng., 1939], X, 245) takes the view that Gothic architecture was more influential in the Medieval Revival than the study of medieval literature. Something of the same view is taken by a more recent writer: "Those who participated in the Medieval Revival did not model their works on Chaucer or Gower or Malory, but made literary capital of an enthusiasm for the castles and cathedrals, the superstitions, and the chivalry of their day" (Earl R. Wasserman, *Elizabethan Poetry in the Eighteenth Century* [Urbana, Ill., 1947], p. 192).

8. Kenneth Clark, *The Gothic Revival: An Essay in the History of Taste* (rev. ed.; London, 1950), p. 14; cf. p. 40. For the continuousness of the interest in Gothic, see B. Sprague Allen, *Tides in English Taste (1619–1800): A Back-*

ground for the Study of Literature (2 vols.; Cambridge, Mass., 1937), II, 44–68.

9. Allen, *Tides in English Taste*, II, 69.

10. Clark, *Gothic Revival*, pp. 61–63.

11. The growing interest in earlier literature in the eighteenth century is admirably surveyed in René Wellek's *The Rise of English Literary History* (Chapel Hill, N.C., 1941).

12. For the place of ballad literature in these books, see Albert B. Friedman's *The Ballad Revival: Studies in the Influence of Popular on Sophisticated Poetry* (Chicago, 1961), pp. 114–29.

13. *Ibid.*, pp. 86–87, 132, 183–84.

14. No. 70, May 21, 1711, of *The Spectator*, ed. George A. Aitkin (6 vols.; London, n.d.), I, 300.

15. No. 74, May 25, 1711, *The Spectator*, I, 322.

16. I am much indebted to Friedman (*Ballad Revival*, pp. 90–112) for this interpretation of Addison's purposes. Addison's prestige was not the only operative factor in the revival of the ballad, of course; the writing of ballads by "the political and literary great," increasing interest in "bardism" and the "Homeric question," and the general cult of simplicity all played their part (pp. 157 and 167).

17. I have been unable to examine a copy of this collection. The British Museum catalogue lists a 2nd edition in 3 parts (Edinburgh: James Watson, 1713–1719) and another copy in which parts 2 and 3 are from the 1st edition and dated respectively 1709 and 1711. That the date of the first part of the 1st edition was 1706 may be deduced from Scott's reference to a collection of Scots poetry published by James Watson in Edinburgh in 1706 (*Minstrelsy of the Scottish Border*, ed. T. F. Henderson [4 vols.; Edinburgh, 1932], I, 24).

18. *A Collection of Old Ballads, Corrected from the Best and Most Ancient Copies Extant, with Introductions Historical, Critical, or Humorous* (3 vols.; London, 1723–1725). The book reached a third edition in 1727. Friedman (*Ballad Revival*, p. 147) considers the ascription to Philips very doubtful.

19. *The Tea-Table Miscellany: A Collection of Choice Songs, Scots & English* (2 vols.) received steady additions of earlier poetry in the host of new editions called for during the century. A unique copy of Vol. I at Yale bears the date 1723 (Friedman, *Ballad Revival*, p. 140 n.). The most convenient modern edition (Glasgow, 1871) is a reprint from the 14th edition. *The Ever Green: A Collection of Scots Poems Wrote by the Ingenious Before 1600* (2 vols.) does not appear to have been so popular. I quote below from the modern reprint (Glasgow, 1875) of the first edition.

20. Parnell's "A Fairy Tale in the Ancient English Style" was written sometime before 1718, the year of his death. He introduces his recounting of an old Irish fairy tale thus: "In Britain's isle, and Arthur's days, / When midnight faeries daunc'd the maze," lines adapted from the opening of Chaucer's *Wife of Bath's Tale*. Parnell, who also wrote a "Night Piece on Death"

and a "Hymn to Contentment," shows an early clustering of the interests associated with Pre-Romanticism.

21. Printed under the misleading title "The Noble Acts of King Arthur and the Knights of the Round Table; with the Valiant Atchievements of Sir Lancelot du Lake" in *A Collection of Old Ballads* (ed. cited) II, 18–24. It is the ballad usually assigned to Deloney.

22. Ramsay (ed.), *The Ever Green*, I, pp. vii and ix.

23. The task of the ballad editors was generally simplified by a determination to please the public at all costs; difficulties in their manuscripts were resolved with a stroke of the pen—a stroke that usually supplied a standard English word or a Neo-Classical phrase or stanza for the offending term or passage. Whole poems were rewritten along such lines and others partially conflated and partially filled out by supplied stanzas. Modern ballad students are still struggling with the wreckage.

24. This is not to say, of course, that individual lives in the first half of the eighteenth century were necessarily more tranquil than they are today or than they have ever been. The point is that what may be called the "official" ideal of the good life was a life of ordered tranquillity. It may be added that the chances to achieve this ideal for individuals in the middle and upper ranks of society were probably greater than they have ever been, before or since.

25. Cf. Clark, *Gothic Revival*, p. 63. Sir Kenneth makes something of the same point I am developing, but illustrates it with an unfortunate conflation of Addison's *Spectator* papers on the "Ballad of Chevy-Chase" and Jane Austen's *Northanger Abbey*. See also Ernest Bernbaum, *Guide Through the Romantic Movement* (2nd ed.; New York, 1949), p. 12.

26. Cf. Fairchild, *Romantic Quest*, p. 12.

27. For the development of Shaftesbury's theory of man's natural "moral sense" and the school of Sensibility, see the summary in Bernbaum, *Romantic Movement*, pp. 9–26. Shaftesbury's influence on eighteenth-century poetry and ethical thought is particularly well treated in Cecil A. Moore's *Backgrounds of English Literature, 1700–1760* (Minneapolis, 1953), pp. 3–52.

28. Fairchild, *Romantic Quest*, p. 238.

29. Sir Kenneth Clark (*Gothic Revival*, p. 60) puts the first "gothicising" of Strawberry Hill in 1750. Additions were made as late as 1776.

30. Wasserman, *Elizabethan Poetry*, p. 192; this conflation of the Renaissance and the Middle Ages was probably a result of the fact that to eighteenth-century readers the most noticeable qualities of the Elizabethans best known to them, Shakespeare and Spenser, were "scenes of horror and terror," the absence of classical form, and, in Spenser, chivalric elements. Thus the Augustans tended to see the Renaissance "as only a later segment of the Gothic period" (p. 199).

31. Wellek, *English Literary History*, p. 102; see also pp. 95, 109–111.

32. Wasserman gives an extensive list of these eighteenth-century poems influenced by *The Faerie Queene* (*Elizabethan Poetry*, pp. 260–68). For his

analysis of these works and of the various attitudes toward Spenser in the century, see pp. 92–152. In general Spenser was mostly admired during the first part of the period for his imagery, didacticism, and allegory. The imitators used him as a model for poetic allegories demonstrating everything from the notion that the "Whigs are the defenders of liberty" to the proposition that "the city of Birmingham was founded by the offspring of Industry and Genius" (p. 116). As Wasserman notes, it was only from Beattie's *Minstrel* (1771) on that the imitators began to exploit the medievalist associations of *The Faerie Queene*; thus Spenser's stanza was a natural choice for T. D. Fosbrooke's *The Economy of Monastic Life . . . A Poem, with Philosophical, and Archaeological Illustrations from Lyndwood, Dugdale, etc.* (1796) (p. 137). But with all this, it is interesting to note that the age was not always satisfied with Spenser "in the original," judging from the several verse and prose paraphrases of *The Faerie Queene* published during the century. The author of one of these, Alexander Bicknell (*Prince Arthur: An Allegorical Romance* [1779]), is incorrectly listed as the author of an independent Arthurian treatment in A. E. Curdy's "Arthurian Literature," *RR*, I (1910), 125–39, 265–78.

33. Clark, *Gothic Revival*, p. 91.

34. Arthur Johnston's *Enchanted Ground: The Study of Medieval Romance in the Eighteenth Century* (London, 1964) would have saved me a great deal of labor had it come to my attention before the completion of the present chapter. I am gratified to find that my brief account is not in significant conflict with Johnston's far more detailed work.

35. Hughes's *Remarks on the Faerie Queene* appeared in 1715. Cf. Bernbaum, *Romantic Movement*, pp. 11 and 17. Hughes's demand that Spenser be tried by his own rules is in England, as Wellek says, "one of the very earliest statements of the contrast between classical unity and 'romantic diversity'" (*English Literary History*, p. 102).

36. "Though the Faerie Queene does not exhibit that oeconomy of plan, and exact arrangement of parts which Epic severity requires, yet we scarcely regret the loss of these, while their place is so amply supplied, by something which more powerfully attracts us, as it engages the affection of the heart, rather than the applause of the head; we are not satisfied as critics, yet we are transported as readers" (Thomas Warton, *Observations on The Faerie Queene of Spenser* [London, 1754], pp. 12–13). There are considerable differences between the first edition and the second (1762); in the latter Warton urges that Spenser should not be judged by rules that he had had no intention of following (Wellek, *English Literary History*, pp. 167–68). In the course of the *Observations*, as Raymond D. Havens has demonstrated, Warton takes up three mutually inconsistent attitudes toward *The Faerie Queene* and holds all three: "first, that it lacks plan; second, that it has plan but not that of classic epic; third, that it is without plan and is better so"; in all this Warton is "thoroughly typical of the unsettled, transitional age to which he belonged"

("Thomas Warton and the Eighteenth-Century Dilemma," *SP*, 25 [January, 1928], 38–43).

37. Warton, *Observations*, p. 217. Nevertheless, some readers and critics continued to object to what Warton had sought to vindicate by his historical method—Spenser's allegory. Even John Pinkerton, a noted editor of collections of older poetry, was capable of contempt for Spenser on this ground: "A short allegory . . . is a most delicious treat: but a long allegory is always dull: witness Spenser, whom nobody can read, and yet he is thought a good poet" (Preface, *Ancient Scotish Poems, Never Before in Print* [2 vols.; London, 1786], I, ix).

38. Letter to Warton, dated July 16, 1754, quoted from Mant's Memoir in Warton, *Poetical Works*, I, xxvii.

39. Warton, *Observations*, pp. 1 and 3. In the second edition of the *Observations*, Warton is kinder toward medieval institutions (Wellek, *English Literary History*, p. 170).

40. Although Hurd has often been considered a conscious rebel against Neo-Classicism, Hoyt Trowbridge has demonstrated lucidly that Hurd's critical methods are both internally consistent and externally reconcilable with Neo-Classical critical theory ("Bishop Hurd: A Reinterpretation," *PMLA*, 58 [June, 1943], 450–65). The ultimate effect of Hurd's arguments is, of course, a different matter. How well Hurd's *Letters* pleased his contemporaries may be gauged from the fact that a second edition appeared in 1765, and this was reprinted in 1771, 1776, and 1788.

41. *Hurd's Letters on Chivalry and Romance*, ed. Edith J. Morley (London, 1911), p. 81. Subsequent references to this edition appear in my text. A facsimile reproduction of the *Letters on Chivalry and Romance*, ed. Hoyt Trowbridge, was issued by the Augustan Reprint Society (Los Angeles, 1963).

42. Trowbridge ("Bishop Hurd," p. 463) points out that Hurd does not mean to argue that a poem should be judged by its "own" laws; his contention is that it must be judged by the rules that apply to its specific kind or genre.

43. Ker, "Literary Influence," X, 272. Indeed, Hurd even speaks on occasion of the actual medieval romancers as "bad writers" and observes that the real genius of the English Middle Ages, Chaucer, had employed his talents against Gothic manners (*Letters*, ed. Morley, pp. 145–46).

44. *Fragments of Ancient Poetry Collected in the Highlands of Scotland, and Translated from the Gaelic or Erse Language* (1760) was followed in 1762 by *Fingal, an Ancient Epic Poem, by Ossian the Son of Fingal, Translated from the Gaelic* and by *Temora, an Ancient Epic Poem* (1763).

45. For an excellent study of Macpherson's literary methods, see Derick S. Thomson, *The Gaelic Sources of Macpherson's 'Ossian'* (Edinburgh and London, [1951]). It appears that Macpherson did collect a considerable amount of authentic material and made very loose use of a number of genuine Gaelic poems. But the final result was an incongruous mixture of incidents

and notions from many sources with conceptions fashionable in Macpherson's own time.

46. Bernbaum, *Romantic Movement*, p. 19.

47. *Ibid.*, p. 22. Chatterton's immediate effect was indirect, and he died before Tyrwhitt published the first collection of his poetry together with an exposure of the fraud in 1777–1778. "Forgery" and "imposture" are perhaps excessively harsh terms to use of the Ossianic and Rowley poems; as Frye observes, they were "not simple hoaxes: they were pseudepigrapha[;] they take what is psychologically primitive, the oracular process of composition, and project it as something historically primitive" ("Defining an Age," p. 149).

48. Malcolm Laing's edition of Macpherson's works (1805) was instrumental in revealing the imposture, but in some quarters the issue lived on during much of the nineteenth century. It should be added that Johnson was not, of course, the only contemporary of Macpherson to doubt the authenticity of Ossian.

49. Cf. Thomas Preston Peardon, *The Transition in English Historical Writing*, Studies in History, Economics and Public Law, No. 390 (New York, 1933), pp. 107–110. It is perhaps mostly to the nationalist movement in history and literature that the study of Scandinavian antiquities owed its impetus, although the fact that Percy was the translator of *Five Pieces of Runic Poetry* (1763) and *Northern Antiquities* (1770, from the French of Paul Henri Mallet) indicates the strong general alliances between the interest in early Scandinavian literature and other "Pre-Romantic" interests. The melancholy and mythology of northern literature had attracted interest in England as early as the appearance in 1703 of George Hickes's *Linguarum Veterum Septentrionalium Thesaurus*. During the eighteenth century, English Scandinavian studies occupied a number of scholars: Mathias, Downman, Johnstone, Jerningham, Sterling, Hole, Sayers, and Amos and Joseph Cottle. The *Poetic Edda* was finally translated in 1787 (Bernbaum, *Romantic Movement*, pp. 11–12, 20–22). The interest of Gray in this material represents its most important impact on eighteenth-century poetry.

50. Ker, "Literary Influence," X, 269.

51. After Evan Evans' *Specimens* (London, 1764), several other collections containing early Welsh materials in translation appeared during the rest of the century: Nicholas Owen's *British Remains: or a Collection of Antiquities Relating to the Britons* (London, 1777), Edward Jones's *Musical and Poetical Relics of the Welsh Bards, Preserved by Traditional and Authentic Manuscripts Never Before Published* (2 vols.; London, 1784), Walter Davies' *The Celtic Remains, Originally Collected by the Late Lewis Morris* (London, 1793), and William Owen's *The Works of Taliesin, a Bard of the Sixth Century* (London, 1793). For these titles I am indebted to William Rowlands' *Cambrian Bibliography*, ed. D. Silvan Evans (Llanidloes, 1869).

52. Friedman, *Ballad Revival*, p. 185; see pp. 185–232 for a survey of Percy's work. The best modern edition of the *Reliques*, following the text of

Percy's 4th edition, is edited by Henry B. Wheatley (3 vols.; London, 1886); subsequent references in my text are to this edition.

53. Wordsworth, "Essay, Supplementary to the Preface," *Poems* (1815), *The Poetical Works of William Wordsworth*, ed. E. de Selincourt (5 vols.; Oxford, 1940–1949), II, 425. In later years Scott recalled his first reading of the *Reliques* thus: "The summer day sped onward so fast, that, notwithstanding the sharp appetite of thirteen, I forgot the hour of dinner, was sought for with anxiety, and was still found entranced in my intellectual banquet" (*Minstrelsy of the Scottish Border*, I, x). For the way in which Scott's bankruptcy was the product of his incurable itch to realize physically at Abbotsford his fantasy world of baronial mansion and feudal splendor, see Herbert Grierson, *Sir Walter Scott, Bart.: A New Life Supplementary to, and Corrective of, Lockhart's Biography* (London, 1938), *passim*, esp. pp. 258–59. The influence of the *Reliques* on Wordsworth, Coleridge, and Scott is briefly surveyed in John L. Mahoney's "Some Antiquarian and Literary Influences of Percy's *Reliques*," *CLA Journal*, 7 (1964), 240–46.

54. Cf. Friedman, *Ballad Revival*, pp. 204–9; M. L. MacKenzie, "Ballad Collectors in the Eighteenth Century," *Humanities Association Bulletin* (Canada), 17 (1966), 33–45.

55. Shenstone claimed to have suggested the project to him; at any rate it is clear that Percy was at work on it as early as 1761 (*Reliques*, I, lxxv). Percy's other "Pre-Romantic" publications include translations of Scandinavian antiquities (see n. 49 above) and Oriental fiction.

56. Cf. Percy's justification for publishing the *Reliques*: such poetry, he asserts, will afford his readers an opportunity "to survey the progress of life and manners, and to inquire by what gradations barbarity was civilized, grossness refined, and ignorance instructed" (I, 2).

57. The letter is dated August 26, 1762. Quoted from Leah Dennis, "The Text of the Percy-Warton Letters," *PMLA*, 46 (December, 1931), 1175.

58. Howard Maynadier, *The Arthur of the English Poets* (Boston, 1907), p. 329.

59. These four ballads are grouped together at the beginning of Percy's third volume (Percy, *Reliques*, III, 3–43).

60. "King Ryence's Challenge" is printed with the four Arthurian ballads previously mentioned (Percy, *Reliques*, III, 24–27). "Sir Lancelot du Lake" is in volume I, pp. 204–9. Deloney's ballad had already been reprinted in *A Collection of Old Ballads* (1723–1725).

61. Percy, *Reliques*, III, 339–76. The essay originally prefaced the third volume.

62. Percy seems to have used the 1634 edition of Malory, which in one place (I, 204) he dates correctly and in another cites as published in 1632 (III, 4–5). He also knew of earlier editions, and was aware that the arrangement into books varied between the early and late editions (I, 204). The first

edition he dates in 1484 (III, 4). I have been unable to determine how rare copies of Malory were by this time.

63. With this approach contrast Philips' (?) headnote to "The Noble Acts of King Arthur etc." in the *Collection of Old Ballads* (1723). The summary of the events of Arthur's career there given (II, 18) is taken from the historian Speed.

64. Percy incorporated various changes into this second edition of 1767 and in the subsequent editions of 1775 and 1794. The number of editions fails to indicate properly the enormous reputation of Percy's work during the century following its first publication.

65. The following list is doubtless incomplete: David Herd (ed.), *The Ancient & Modern Scots Songs, Heroic Ballads, &c. Now First Collected into One Body, From the Various Miscellanies Wherein They Formerly Lay Dispersed* (Edinburgh, 1769); of this work an expanded edition in two volumes appeared in 1776 and another in 1791. T. Evans (ed.), *Old Ballads, Historical and Narrative, with Some of Modern Date* (2 vols.; [London], 1777); a second edition enlarged to four volumes appeared in 1784. John Pinkerton (ed.), *Scottish Tragic Ballads* (London, 1781). Pinkerton (ed.), *Select Scotish Ballads* (2 vols.; London, 1783); volume II of this publication is "The Second Edition, Corrected and Enlarged" of Pinkerton's earlier *Scottish Tragic Ballads*. Joseph Ritson (ed.), *A Select Collection of English Songs* (3 vols.; London, 1783). Pinkerton (ed.), *Ancient Scotish Poems, Never Before in Print* (2 vols.; London, 1786). George Ellis (ed.), *Specimens of the Early English Poets* (London, 1790); this work appears in its first edition to have been restricted to the sixteenth and seventeenth centuries; in a later and much expanded three-volume form, it reached a fourth edition in 1811. Ritson (ed.), *Ancient Songs, from the Time of King Henry the Third, to the Revolution* (London, 1790). Ritson (ed.), *Pieces of Ancient Popular Poetry: From Authentic Manuscripts and Old Printed Copies* (London, 1791). Pinkerton (ed.), *Scotish Poems, Reprinted from Scarce Editions* (3 vols.; London, 1792). Ritson (ed.), *Scotish Songs* (2 vols.; London, 1794). Ritson (ed.), *Robin Hood; A Collection of All the Ancient Poems, Songs, and Ballads, Now Extant, Relative to That Celebrated Outlaw* (2 vols.; London, 1795).

66. [Joseph Ritson (ed.)], *A Select Collection of English Songs* (3 vols.; London: Printed for J. Johnson, 1783), II, 291–96. This was the third time the ballad had been printed in the century (see n. 60 above). Ritson's impressively learned *Life of King Arthur* is examined in my chap. 5.

67. Pierre Jean Baptiste Le Grand d'Aussy's *Fabliaux* is a very much mixed collection of medieval narrative materials including some of Marie de France's *lais* and a considerable number of actual *fabliaux* in the modern scholarly sense of the term. All have been considerably altered in his translations from the medieval originals. The book was first translated into English prose by John Williamson, whose text appeared in the following editions: *Tales of the Twelfth and Thirteenth Centuries, From the French of Mr.*

Le Grand (London, 1789 and 1790); *Tales of the Minstrels . . . Fourth Edition* (London, 1800); *The Feudal Period: Illustrated by a Series of Tales Romantic and Humorous*, ed. W. C. Hazlitt (London, 1873). Much more influential was the translation into English verse by Gregory Lewis Way: *Fabliaux or Tales, Abridged from French Manuscripts of the XIIth and XIIIth Centuries, by M. Le Grand, Selected and Translated into English* (2 vols.; London, 1796–1800). The fact that Le Grand d'Aussy's book had been twice translated and published in five editions by 1800 suggests a popularity that I am at a loss to explain, nor have I been able to locate any evidence of its having influenced writers in the eighteenth century. In the next century, Way's translation is frequently cited and appears to have been well known. It appeared in a new and corrected edition with preface, notes, and appendix by G. Ellis (3 vols.; London, 1815). The Arthurian matter in Way's translation includes *The Mantle Made Amiss, The Mule Without a Bridle, The Knight and the Sword, The Vale of False Lovers*, and two of Marie's *lais, The Lay of Sir Lanval* and *The Lay of Sir Gugemar*.

68. For Ritson's strictures on Percy, see especially his notes in *A Select Collection of English Songs, passim*. Pinkerton was excoriated for the inclusion of such forgeries as *Hardyknute* in his *Select Scotish Ballads* (1783).

69. John Pinkerton (ed.), *Scotish Poems, Reprinted from Scarce Editions* (3 vols.; London: Printed by and for John Nichols, 1792), III, 65–126 and 195–226.

70. *Ibid.*, I, xxx.

71. Recognition that the glories of medieval literature were not to be found in its lyrics and ballads, but rather in its longer works may be inferred from Ritson's Advertisement to his *English Anthology* (3 vols.; London, 1793–1794), I, v: "It were, perhaps, to be wished, that the collection could have commenced at an earlier period; but . . . no composition of moderate length is to be found prior to the year 1500, which would be thought to deserve a place in these volumes."

72. "Written in a Blank Leaf of Dugdale's Monasticon," in Warton, *Poetical Works*, II, 150. Mant in his Memoir in *Poetical Works* says that Warton kept a record of the various Gothic buildings he visited (I, xxx-xxxi). See also his note on the subject affixed to the 1762 edition of *Observations on the Faerie Queene*.

73. Warton, *Poetical Works*, I, cxlv.

74. Thomas Warton, *The History of English Poetry, from the Close of the Eleventh to the Commencement of the Eighteenth Century* (3 vols.; London, 1774–1781); subsequent references in my text are to this edition. A fragment of the fourth volume was written before Warton's death. For a thorough analysis of Warton's *History* and its achievement, see Wellek, *English Literary History*, pp. 170–201. Although recognizing that the work was "first of all, an accumulation of materials, a bibliography and anthology, and only secondarily a history," Professor Wellek justly declares that "Warton was the

first historian of English literature in the full sense of the term, . . . and his achievement, imperfect as it was, made genuine literary history in England possible" (pp. 174 and 201). See also David Nichol Smith's "Warton's History of English Poetry," *Proceedings of the British Academy* (1929) (London, 1929), pp. 73–99. Warton's lack of interest in English literature prior to the twelfth century is dealt with in A. M. Kingshorn's "Warton's *History* and Early English Poetry," *ES*, 44 (1963), 197–204.

75. For Scott's opinion and Ker's more balanced estimate, see Ker, "Literary Influence," X, 270–71. B. Ifor Evans (*Tradition and Romanticism*, pp. 91–92), having stipulated that Warton's "influence on the development of the art of poetry has often been exaggerated," goes on to say that Warton was the first to produce "a history of English poetry, which, whatever its short-comings, . . . first laid the foundations for studying the continuity of our poetry. . . . Through his scholarship he opened up the ways to that 'gothic' literature in which the eighteenth century became so widely interested."

76. It is important, however, not to exaggerate Warton's enthusiasm. As D. Nichol Smith says, his "interest in the old romances was largely induced by the pleasure of escape from the beaten road of the classics. The *History* offers no proof that he was consistently fonder of the one class of poetry than the other" ("Warton's History," p. 99).

77. Cf. M. W. MacCallum's observation: "When Arthurian story is recognized to be fiction, and yet has its dignity and worth acknowledged, a new period in its development is come" (*Tennyson's Idylls of the King and Arthurian Story from the XVIth Century* [Glasgow, 1894], p. 178). The phrasing seems to me to overstate the matter to some degree, and to ignore the ambiguities in Warton's attitudes.

78. B. Ifor Evans, *Tradition and Romanticism*, p. 92. Havens wisely suggests that Warton "may have regarded Gothic architecture and medieval literature as his hobbies, possibly even his weaknesses" ("Eighteenth-Century Dilemma," p. 44); much as Warton admired Gothic architecture, the evidence of many of his poems suggests that he thought—or thought he ought to think—classical design superior. D. Nichol Smith says tersely that the *History* is "not the manifesto of a school, nor a document in a controversy" ("Warton's History," p. 99); cf. Wellek, *English Literary History*, pp. 185–88.

79. Writing as late as 1833, Scott makes substantially the same case for the study of early literature; see Scott, *Minstrelsy of the Scottish Border*, I, 67. Frances Schouler Miller observes that Warton's approach to earlier literature is "essentially antiquarian" and for the most part simply unconcerned with aesthetic matters ("The Historic Sense of Thomas Warton, Junior," *ELH*, 5 [March, 1938], 71–92); cf. Havens, "Eighteenth-Century Dilemma," p. 43.

80. [Joseph Ritson], *Pieces of Ancient Popular Poetry: From Authentic Manuscripts and Old Printed Copies* (London, 1791). I quote from the 2nd edition (London, 1833), p. viii.

81. Ritson, *The English Anthology*, I, v. Ritson, whose name was gen-

erally absent from the title pages of his collections, and who had wielded the
critical lash mercilessly, goes on to say "Nor will any person be forward to
rescue such things from oblivion, while the attempt exposes him to the malig-
nant and ruffian-like attacks of some hackney scribbler or personal enemy,
through the medium of one or other of two periodical publications, in which
the most illiberal abuse is vented under colour of impartial criticism, and both
the literary and moral character of every man who wishes to make his peculiar
studies contribute to the information or amusement of society are at the mercy
of a conceited pedant, or dark and cowardly assassin." Chaucer, it may be
observed, was excluded from the proscription.

82. [John Pinkerton (ed.)], *Select Scotish Ballads* (2 vols.; London,
1783), I, xxv. Subsequent references in my text are to this edition.

83. Emery Neff, *The Poetry of History* (New York, 1947), p. 29.

84. Hurd, *Letters*, ed. Morley, *passim*, esp. pp. 94–103.

85. While Warton's view here is not logically inconsistent with his comments on the "transitions from barbarism to civility," the shift in emphasis is
obvious. To some degree, this may have been based on rhetorical considerations. The earlier passage occurs in the Introductory material to the first
volume of the *History of English Poetry*; the bold assertion of the superior
poetic qualities of the Middle Ages occurs in the conclusion to the second
volume. Warton may have supposed that any reader still with him by that
time was sympathetically inclined. So far as I know, no one has commented
on the clear indebtedness of the latter passage to Hurd's *Letters on Chivalry*.

86. Peardon (*English Historical Writing*, p. 66) generalizes thus on the
state of medieval historical studies in the last quarter of the eighteenth century: "The nascent literary Romanticism was beginning to influence the out-
look of historians, but in general history lagged far behind literature in doing
justice to the Middle Ages."

87. Evan Evans (trans. and ed.), *Some Specimens of the Poetry of the
Antient Welsh Bards* (London, 1764), p. i.

88. G. P. Gooch, *History and Historians in the Nineteenth Century* (2nd
ed.; London, 1935), p. 9.

89. Peardon, *English Historical Writing*, p. 28; cf. J. B. Black, *The Art of
History: A Study of Four Great Historians of the Eighteenth Century* (London, 1926), pp. 121 and 129.

90. Lyttelton's *History of the Life of King Henry the Second* appeared
in 1767–1771; Robert Henry's *History of Great Britain on a New Plan* (1771–
1793) had reached a fourth edition by 1805–1806. Russell's *History of Modern
Europe from the Fall of the Roman Empire to 1763* (1779–1784) was widely
used by students for nearly a century. For discussions of all these historians,
see Peardon, *English Historical Writing*, pp. 36–38, 65–66, 127–29.

91. The phrase is Lyttelton's; quoted by Peardon, *ibid.*, p. 128.

92. Quoted from Russell by Peardon, *ibid.*, p. 66.

93. Gilbert Stuart's *Historical Dissertation Concerning the Antiquity of*

the English Constitution (1768) traced English institutions to Germanic tribes and the Germanic tribes to the Celts. John Whitaker's *History of Manchester* (1771–1775) pictured an ancient Britain with a parliament, popular liberty, and pre-Norman feudalism. John Smith's *Galic Antiquities* (1780) argued for a perfected Celtic society that had even instructed the Greeks. For discussion of these and other primitivist historians, see Peardon, *English Historical Writing*, pp. 104–115, 130–37.

94. Strutt's work had reached the times of Henry VIII by 1774–1775. See Peardon, *English Historical Writing*, p. 157.

95. Fairchild, *Romantic Quest*, p. 242.

96. Edmund Burke, *Reflections on the French Revolution*, Everyman's Library, No. 460 (London and New York, 1910, reprinted 1953), p. 73.

97. Geoffrey of Monmouth's *Historia* was also available. One translation by Aaron Thompson, published in 1718, appears to be the source of Curdy's confusing listing of Aaron Thompson as the author of an eighteenth-century Arthurian treatment.

98. I have been unable to find an occurrence of any Arthurian name in John Neve's *A Concordance to the Poetical Works of William Cowper* (London, 1887) or in J. B. Reid's *A Complete Word and Phrase Concordance to the Poems and Songs of Robert Burns* (Glasgow, 1889). The one allusion to Arthur listed in Albert S. Cook's *A Concordance to the English Poems of Thomas Gray* (Boston, 1908) is to be found in *The Bard* III, 1, 109. The same poem (I, 3, 33) also contains a reference to a Modred "whose magic song / Made huge Plinlimmon bow his cloud-top'd head," a figure not to be equated, apparently, with Arthur's treacherous nephew. I quote here from *The Works of Thomas Gray in Prose and Verse*, ed. Edmund Gosse (4 vols., rev. ed.; London, 1902), I, 43.

99. Warton, *Poetical Works*, I, clxi. Subsequent references to this edition are inserted in my text.

100. It is characteristic of the age that Warton regards Spenser's verse as the guarantee of the immortality of Arthur and his "Chiefs."

101. MacCallum (*Idylls of the King and Arthurian Story*, p. 177) suggests Selden's notes to Drayton's *Poly-Olbion* as a possible source, and parallels the structural idea of Warton's poem with the characteristic Elizabethan distinction between the Arthur of history and the Arthur of the romances. It is difficult to imagine just what Maynadier (*Arthur of the English Poets*, p. 329) had in mind when he asserted that "in these [Arthurian] pieces of Thomas Warton, the legends for the first time since the Commonwealth inspire whole poems which treat them with reverence and fidelity. This means that the Arthurian stories, substantially unchanged from their medieval forms, are again recognized as proper material for poets to work with." Only one of the poems concerns itself centrally with the "legends" and that poem introduces the legend, as we shall see, only to refute it.

102. In the Advertisement prefixed to the poem, Warton relates the

tradition that Henry's diggers found Arthur's bones under a huge slab at a depth of some twenty feet.

103. MacCallum, *Idylls of the King and Arthurian Story*, p. 176. For another favorable estimate, see Miller, "Historic Sense," p. 87.

104. I have been unable to find Hilton's name in the standard reference works of the period; the British Museum Catalogue falls back on a *floruit* date derived from Hilton's two publications. From his assertion of 1759 as the completion date of his *Arthur*, it seems likely that he could not have been born much after *ca.* 1740; he was still alive in 1776 when the second volume of his poetry was published.

105. William Hilton, *The Poetical Works of William Hilton* (2 vols.; Newcastle upon Tyne, 1775–1776). Subsequent references are inserted in my text. *Arthur* is printed in Volume II, 169–251. I have discovered no other editions. Hilton's Preface states that the play was never performed.

106. It is not impossible, of course, that the date November 29, 1759, which Hilton attaches to the play, may be a cover for political allusions to later events, but if the play contains any such references, I have been unable to find them. At any rate, the parallel of the attitudes in the play to those current in 1759 argues convincingly for the validity of the 1759 date.

107. For a brief account of the events and feelings of the time, see Basil Williams, *The Whig Supremacy, 1714–1760*, Oxford History of England, Vol. XI (Oxford, 1952), pp. 333–52.

108. Hilton, *Poetical Works*, II, 171, 173, and 175–76. Pitt's near-egalitarianism in respect to his military commanders must have lent special flavor in 1759 to Galvan's view that "as a *Briton*, 'tis my part to rise, / By gen'rous deeds, and gen'rous deeds alone!" (II, 188). For the determination of Pitt, the "Great Commoner," "that officers may be convinced that neither high birth nor great employments" were to be operative factors in judging their conduct, see Williams, *Whig Supremacy*, p. 341.

109. I may add that it is just this unsuitability of Arthur to effusions of national patriotism that may explain the curious fact, so often noted, that a British hero was adopted with such ease by the various European countries, even to the point of supplanting in France interest in a truly national hero, Charlemagne. The question of practical success or a happy issue seems to have been a common element of epic theory from the beginning, and may point to a useful nonformal distinction between epic and tragedy.

110. A few examples from *Arthur, Monarch of the Britons* will suffice to demonstrate the quality of Hilton's verse and sensibility. Here is Guinever lamenting her guilt:

"How gloomy all, when innocence is gone!
Not the dire horrors of the martial feuds,
Nor wars intestine, that destroy the realm,
Nor fate of *Britons*, can in *Arthur's* soul
A torment raise, equal to mine" (II, 180).

And here is Arthur dilating on Nature:
> "Lo the magnificence of rural scenes!
> Not more attractive to the curious eye,
> Than pleasing to the heart. The soul, convinc'd,
> Wonders and believes. Wonders at the works
> Of perfect nature, variously display'd,
> And wisdom tracing, in her God believes" (II, 198–99).

Not even the villainous Molus can fall without falling into moral platitude:
> "A Providence there is: I own it now:
> And all who act as infamy controuls,
> Sooner, or late, eternal vengeance find.
> I have been wrong in ev'ry scene of life;
> False to my country! Now too late to change.
> O had I been on patriot virtue's side!" (II, 238).

111. Richard Hole, *Arthur: or, The Northern Enchantment. A Poetical Romance in Seven Books* (London, 1789). Subsequent references to this edition are inserted in my text.

112. Hole was born in 1746 and died in 1803. For details of his life, see *DNB*, s.v. "Hole, Richard." Hole's *Poetical Translation of Fingal* appeared in 1772.

113. It is, of course, possible that Hole thought he was paralleling the couplets of the metrical romances, but whatever the formal similarities, the dissimilarity of manner is absolute.

114. Of the heroes of his "imitation of the old metrical Romance," Hole observes that they are "rather those of Ariosto than of Homer" (p. iv). The confusion of Renaissance and medieval romance was almost universal in the period, as we have seen.

115. Hole was not so bold as to assert a preference for the "desultory wildness" of romance to the "correct fancy" of Homer. But since it was impossible to equal or surpass Homer, and tedious merely to imitate him, he turned to "the old Gothic fables" since they exhibit "a peculiarity of manners and situation, which, if not from their intrinsic excellence, may, from their being less hackneyed, afford more materials for the writer's imagination, and contribute more to the reader's entertainment" (p. iv).

116. The pseudohistorians and historians place Hengist's death well before that of Uther, and thus well before Arthur's time of battles with the Saxons.

117. It is difficult to tell to what extent Hole drew on genuine medieval romance for these and other romance motifs. Doubtless many of them were inspired by Tasso, Ariosto, Boiardo, and Spenser. Such an episode as the death of Lionel's beloved, Guendolen, as a result of her following Lionel into battle disguised (Book VI), seems far more Renaissance in tone than medieval.

118. The parallel goes as far as placing the revelation of antecedent action in the second book as in the *Aeneid*. One wonders if Hole's division of the

poem into the number of seven books (there seems to be no particular structural reason for it) may not have been done to give the poem a "romantic" irregularity.

119. In this assertion of the identity of Northern and chivalric manners, Hole follows a misconception frequent in his time, and beloved of speculative historians who traced English virtues back to Teutonic sources. Elsewhere Hole gives more cautious expression to the view when he describes chivalry as "a singular institution, that is thought to have existed in an imperfect state amidst the forests of Germany before the Christian aera." He then goes on to give an account more completely characteristic of his time: "In the middle ages, during the night of ignorance and barbarism, it arose to splendor and magnificence; and, like the Aurora borealis, a phenomenon no less strange than beautiful, gilded the darkness which enveloped the northern hemisphere; inspired an elevation of sentiment and refinement of manners, unknown to the philosophy and religion of the times; and in spite of its absurdities, still commands our respect and admiration" (pp. vii–viii).

120. The "soft compassion" which swells in the breast of Ivar, prince of Ebuda (one of the Happy Isles) when he sees Arthur thrown upon the shore by a billow, and his prolonged tears when he is not allowed to accompany Arthur, reflect Macpherson's sentimentalized third-century Celts. By 1789, as the phrasing indicates, Hole was beginning to have his doubts about the authenticity of the Ossianic poems, though he was still disposed to believe that they were genuine for the most part.

121. The phrase "horror visible" occurs, quite appropriately, in the description of the Northern underworld. For Satan's spear, cf. *Paradise Lost*, I, ll. 292–94.

122. For Hole's faith in Arthur's historicity, see p. iii. In relation to Hole's primitivism, see also his conviction of the superiority of the lot of the "wild Arabs" to those who live amid the "tasteless pleasures of a court": "To think, speak, act, by no harsh laws confin'd, / Is theirs—the charter of the free-born mind!" (pp. 188–89). The grief of a family of noble rustics at Arthur's departure after passing a night with them suggests the edifying comment that "More strongly speaks the feelings [*sic*] of the heart, / Than studied eloquence can ever reach / With all the labour'd pomp, and grace of speech" (p. 219). Towards filial duty, though, the conservatism of Hole's attitude would have satisfied Clarissa Harlowe's father:

"Ye beauteous maids, who Britain's coast adorn,
Warn'd by the luckless fair, reject with scorn
The fraudful vow, th' insidious plea, addrest
To counteract a father's wise behest;
Tho' seemingly severe, 'tis yours to know,
From love parental it alone could flow" (p. 194).

123. Domesticity is another tender value capable of exciting sentimental tears in Hole's medieval warriors; thus Valdemar, thinking about his family:

"in spight of manly pride,
From his swoll'n eyes forth gush'd the genial tide.
Th' endearing joys that crown domestic life,
The smiling offspring and the faithful wife
Rise on his soul" (p. 170).

124. B. Ifor Evans, *Tradition and Romanticism*, p. 85. Arthurian literature has its example of literary forgery during the period: William Henry Ireland's *Vortigern*, a Shakespearean forgery first presented in 1796 and first printed in 1799. I have eliminated discussion of the play because its connection with the central Arthurian story is very slight. Ireland's career is surveyed in Bernard Grebanier's *The Great Shakespeare Forgery* (New York, 1965). For a somewhat more sympathetic discussion of the poetic problems and achievements of the latter half of the eighteenth century, see Frye, "Age of Sensibility," pp. 144–52.

5. THE PAST RESTORED: ROMANTIC MEDIEVALISM AS PREPARATION FOR ARTHUR'S RETURN

1. F. L. Lucas, *The Decline and Fall of the Romantic Ideal* (2nd ed.; Cambridge, Eng., 1948), p. 135.

2. Lucas views admiration for children, primitives, and the Middle Ages as variants of the same central impulse: "There are two main lines of escape from over-civilized life—back to Nature and the Noble Savage . . . or back to the Middle Ages" (*ibid.*, p. 98). And elsewhere (p. 110): "The childishness of the Middle Ages or the childishness of the nursery—both alike are refuges from the present." The words "escape" and "refuge" are reflections of Lucas' thesis that Romanticism is a rejection of "reality."

3. William Paton Ker (*The Art of Poetry: Seven Lectures, 1920–1922* [Oxford, 1923], p. 80) observes—perhaps incautiously—that " 'Romantic' implies reminiscence . . . . Hence the romantic schools have always depended more or less on the past."

4. Lucas, *Romantic Ideal*, p. 10.

5. Cf. Kenneth Clark, *The Gothic Revival: an Essay in History of Taste* (rev. ed.; London, 1950), p. 87; Alice Chandler, "The Quarrel of the Ancients and Moderns: Peacock and the Medieval Revival," *Bucknell Review*, 13, iii (1965), 39–50. This is not to say, of course, that a number of Romantic poets did not make use of themes drawn from classical antiquity, but it is instructive to note that even so such themes are generally mythical or fabulous—rarely merely historical. The Rome of Addison's *Cato* is the Rome of the Senate and the Forum; the Corinth of Keats's *Lamia* is centered around a mysterious palace reared by magic. It must also be observed that medievalism is far from universal among the English romantics. In fact, as Hoxie Neale Fairchild (*The Romantic Quest* [New York, 1931], pp. 21 and 240) has pointed out, Medievalism seems as far back as Burke to have appealed largely to those of conservative, even Tory temper: Scott, the older Wordsworth, Coleridge, and

Southey, and to the politically indifferent like Keats. For political liberals like Byron and Shelley, Medievalism had little interest. The closest thing to Medievalism in Byron is the Ossianism of his early work, although he had laid abortive plans in 1807 for making a collection of "Erse" traditions and poems. Mrs. Shelley explained her husband's lack of interest in Medievalism by saying that he had not read the "romances and chivalry of the middle ages" but rather German horror tales, which thus left an impress of pseudomedievalism on some of his work (*ibid.*, pp. 302–4). Professor Fairchild's view of the affinities of medievalism and conservatism requires some qualification in the case of Coleridge, who was still a political radical of sorts in 1797–1798 when "The Ancient Mariner" and part of "Christabel" were written. But even so, "France, an Ode" (1798) shows already his drift toward conservatism.

6. Lucas, *Romantic Ideal*, p. 46.

7. *Ibid.*, p. 15, and Fairchild, *Romantic Quest*, pp. 1 and 141. I hasten to say that neither I nor the critics cited are attempting a complete definition of Romanticism in these phrases. Perhaps I should add that in this and the following chapter the limitation of the terms Romantic and Romanticism to the period covering roughly the first third of the nineteenth century is purely a matter of convenience. That Romanticism continued as a major force throughout the nineteenth and on into the twentieth century has been made amply clear: see, for example, John Bayley, *The Romantic Survival: A Study in Poetic Evolution* (London, 1957); Frank Kermode, *Romantic Image* (London, 1957); and R. A. Foakes, *The Romantic Assertion: A Study in the Language of Nineteenth Century Poetry* (New Haven, 1958).

8. Lucas, *Romantic Ideal*, p. 46.

9. Sir Herbert Grierson, *The Background of English Literature, Classical & Romantic, and Other Collected Essays and Addresses* (2nd ed.; London, 1950), pp. 278–79.

10. Lucas, *Romantic Ideal*, pp. 76–78.

11. Lascelles Abercrombie, *Romanticism* (London, 1926), p. 165. For brief surveys of the Medievalism of Wordsworth, Coleridge, and Keats, see Fairchild, *Romantic Quest*, pp. 270–79, 290–99, 306–11.

12. Wordsworth's early plans for the use of Arthurian materials are discussed in my chap. 6, along with his "Egyptian Maid."

13. B. Ifor Evans, *Tradition and Romanticism: Studies in English Poetry from Chaucer to W. B. Yeats* (London, 1940), p. 85; cf. p. 109. For Scott's own handling of Arthurian story, see my chap. 6, where it is considered alongside other Romantic treatments of the legend.

14. The full title is *Minstrelsy of the Scottish Border Consisting of Historical and Romantic Ballads Collected in the Southern Counties of Scotland: With a Few of Modern Date, Founded upon Local Tradition*. The first two volumes appeared in 1802 with a third following in the next year. The final edition prepared by Lockhart in 1833 contained four volumes. The best mod-

ern edition is that rev. and ed. by T. F. Henderson (4 vols.; Edinburgh, 1932 [originally published 1902]).

15. To this publication, edited from the Auchinleck MS, the date 1805 is mistakenly assigned by M. W. MacCallum, *Tennyson's Idylls of the King and Arthurian Story from the XVIth Century* (Glasgow, 1894), p. 182. Evidently the work enjoyed a fair popularity, since it reached a third edition as early as 1811.

16. Cf. Maurice Halperin, *Le Roman de Tristan et Iseut dans la littérature anglo-américaine au XIXe et XXe siècles* (Paris, 1931), pp. 16–17.

17. "The Journal of Sir Walter Scott," *The Complete Works of Algernon Charles Swinburne*, ed. Sir Edmund Gosse and T. J. Wise (20 vols., Bonchurch Edition; London, 1925–1927), XV, 238. Even so, Swinburne's general estimate was that Scott "if not an ideal was a very passable editor."

18. Margaret Rose Grennan, *William Morris: Medievalist and Revolutionary* (New York, 1945), p. 3.

19. Swinburne, "A Note on Charlotte Bronte," *Complete Works of . . . Swinburne*, XIV, 8.

20. Thomas Preston Peardon, *The Transition in English Historical Writing* (Studies in History, Economics and Public Law, No. 390; New York, 1933), p. 216.

21. Fairchild, *Romantic Quest*, p. 263.

22. Headnote to *The Lay of the Last Minstrel, The Poetical Works of Sir Walter Scott*, ed. J. Logie Robertson (Oxford Complete Edition; London, 1913), p. 1. In the Introduction to the First Edition of *Marmion* (*Poetical Works*, p. 171), Scott describes *Marmion* as "an attempt to paint the manners of the feudal times." The same intention of historical reconstruction is evident throughout Scott's historical novels.

23. For the influence on Scott of German medievalism—or more accurately, pseudomedievalism, see Fairchild, *Romantic Quest*, pp. 259–66. Emery Neff (*The Poetry of History* [New York, 1947], p. 48) suggests that Scott's youthful translation of Goethe's *Götz von Berlichingen* provided him with the initial inspiration for his historical novels.

24. Neff, *Poetry of History*, p. 118. The alliance of political conservatism, chivalry, and medievalism has been touched on above, n. 5. See also Alice Chandler, "Sir Walter Scott and the Medieval Revival," *Nineteenth-Century Fiction*, 19 (1965), 315–32.

25. But I hasten to add that what motivated Scott's readers ought not to be confused with what motivated Scott himself. Lucas' view (*Romantic Ideal*, p. 136) that "Scott and Morris call up an imaginary world to redress the drab balance of the real," is doubtless true of Morris, but much more dubious in regard to the bluff Sir Walter, whose "love of the romantic past was not," as Fairchild (*Romantic Quest*, p. 257) puts it perceptively, "the result of a deliberate philosophy," but was instead "native and instinctive."

26. "Sir Walter Scott" in Thomas Carlyle's *Critical and Miscellaneous Essays* (3 vols.; London, n.d.), III, 214.

27. Cf. Fairchild's assertion that Scott's novels are thus "related to the essentially romantic program of making the strange real and the real strange" (*Romantic Quest*, p. 264). In the present century Scott's encyclopedic knowledge of the past has been commended by no less an expert than R. S. Rait (Peardon, *English Historical Writing*, p. 214).

28. Clark, *Gothic Revival*, pp. 76 and 115–22. For a full account of the Gothic Revival in architecture during the first third of the nineteenth century, see pp. 97–159, whence I have drawn the details of my summary of the development.

29. *Auch eine Philosophie der Geschichte zur Bildung der Menschheit* was published anonymously in 1774. *Ideen zur Philosophie der Geschichte der Menschheit* (1784–1791) was translated into English in 1800 as *Outlines of the Philosophy of the History of Man*. On Herder's conception of historiography and the Middle Ages, see Neff, *Poetry of History*, pp. 21–24 and 47–77.

30. Neff, *Poetry of History*, p. 88.

31. Quoted from the Preface to Luden's *Geschichte des deutschen Volkes* (1825–1837) by G. P. Gooch (*History and Historians in the Nineteenth Century* [2nd ed.; London, 1935], p. 72). My summary of developments in German historiography during the first third of the nineteenth century is based on Gooch's work, pp. 54–74 and 535–57.

32. Of Scott, Thierry later said, "My admiration for this great writer was profound; it grew as I contrasted his wonderful comprehension of the past with the petty erudition of the most celebrated modern historians" (quoted by Gooch, *History and Historians*, p. 170). For the French romantic historians here discussed, see pp. 161–74. Michelet's work, which belongs to the second third of the century, lies outside our period.

33. Quoted from Herford's *The Age of Wordsworth* by Peardon, *English Historical Writing*, p. 214. In the following survey of English historiography of the Middle Ages during the first third of the nineteenth century, I am indebted largely to Peardon, esp. pp. 218–76, and Gooch, *History and Historians*, pp. 282–84.

34. Peardon, *English Historical Writing*, p. 216.

35. *Ibid.*, pp. 218 and 225. For Turner's place in the history of Arthurian scholarship, see Roger S. Loomis, "Pioneers in Arthurian Scholarship," *BBSIA*, 16 (1964), 95–97.

36. Lingard, a Catholic priest, took great pride in the fact that his religious beliefs could not be deduced from his histories.

37. Peardon, *English Historical Writing*, p. 271.

38. *Ibid.*, p. 274.

39. Quoted in Gooch, *History and Historians*, p. 283.

40. *Past and Present*, Bk. II, Chap. 1; I quote from *The Works of Thomas Carlyle* (Centenary Edition, 30 vols.; London, 1897–1899), X, 39.

41. Cobbett's central concern was not so much the truth of the Middle Ages as it was the breaking up of prejudices that threatened the various Catholic Emancipation bills, a process he hoped to accomplish by tracing England's economic ills to the Reformation. Cobbett's and Southey's medieval sympathies are admirably surveyed by Miss Grennan (*William Morris*, esp. pp. 7-12).

42. Robert Southey, *Sir Thomas More: or, Colloquies on the Progress and Prospects of Society* (2 vols.; London, 1829), II, 246–47. Southey is here speaking through Sir Thomas' mouth; More does not, however, have it all his own way in the dialogue.

43. *Ibid.*, p. 12.

44. Kenelm Henry Digby's name does not even appear in the *Cambridge Bibliography of English Literature*. The importance of Digby's work to Young England is justly described by Charles Whibley: "If one book were chosen as the breviary of Young England, that book would be Kenelm Digby's . . . 'The Broadstone of Honour' " (*Lord John Manners and His Friends* [2 vols.; Edinburgh and London, 1925], I, 133).

45. The title alludes to the Rhine fortress of Ehrenbreitstein, which, according to Digby, "appears to represent, as it were, knightly perfection, being lofty and free from the infection of a base world" (*The Broad Stone of Honour: The True Sense and Practice of Chivalry* [Volume I], *Godefridus* [London, 1844], p. 5). In 1826–1827 the book was revised, enlarged, and published in four volumes bearing the individual titles *Godefridus*, *Tancredus*, *Morus*, and *Orlandus*. There were numerous subsequent editions and impressions. An edition published in the 1840's, of which I have seen the first, second, and third volumes, dated 1844, 1846, and 1848 respectively, bore the subtitle *The True Sense and Practice of Chivalry*. A five-volume edition was published in 1876–1877. Judging from the preface to *Morus* (I quote from the 1826 edition [London, 1826], pp. v–vii), Digby intended further additions on "Arturus" as "at least the ideal model of excellence" and thus suitable for the patron spirit of a study of the virtues proper to chivalry. There were also to be volumes entitled "Alfredus" and "Bayardus." Digby's other literary work includes *Mores Catholici* (1831–1840).

46. The first statement of Digby's intentions is taken from *Godefridus*, p. 9; the second quotation is from the Preface to *Morus*, p. v.

47. Digby, *The Broad Stone of Honour* [Volume II], *Tancredus* (London, 1848), pp. v–vii.

48. E.g., "I have often had the advantage of hearing some of the most noble *clerks* of the world dispute on questions of this kind" (*Broad Stone of Honour* [Volume III], *Morus* [London, 1848], p. 5).

49. Quoted by Amy Cruse, *The Victorians and Their Books* (London, 1935), p. 141.

50. Cf. Grennan, *William Morris*, p. 28. Amy Cruse (*Victorians*, p. 141) asserts that Digby's influence on Young England outweighed that of Newman,

Carlyle, and Disraeli: "The high romantic tone of the book captured the imaginations of these young idealists, and they were as eager, at its bidding to restore medievalism in the State as they had been, at the call of Newman, to restore medievalism in the Church." See also Charles H. Kegel, "Lord John Manners and the Young England Movement: Romanticism in Politics," *Western Political Quarterly*, 14 (1961), 691–97.

51. One of the best ways to catch the spirit of the new medieval scholarship in the first third of the century is to read through Scott's voluminous correspondence with such men as Ritson, George Ellis, David Laing, Richard Heber, Skene, and Leyden. See *The Letters of Sir Walter Scott*, ed. Sir Herbert Grierson (12 vols.; The Centenary Edition; London, 1932–1937), esp. XII, 155–371.

52. I quote from the Advertisement to the first edition (1822) of Laing's *Select Remains of the Ancient Popular Poetry of Scotland* as reprinted in the 2nd edition: *Select Remains of the Ancient Popular and Romance Poetry of Scotland*, re-edited with additions by John Small (Edinburgh and London, 1885), pp. xxxi–xxxii.

53. [E. V. Utterson (ed.)], *Select Pieces of Early Popular Poetry* (2 vols.; London, 1817), I, vi.

54. *Ibid.*

55. Of the five such organizations founded before Victoria came to the throne, the Roxburghe Club (1814) and the Surtees Society (1834) continued publication throughout the century. The Bannatyne Club (1823–1861), the Maitland Club (1828–1859), and the Abbotsford Club (1834–1866) were also responsible for a number of valuable publications. For the history of such clubs and societies see Bernard Quaritch, *Account of the Great Learned Societies and Associations, and of the Chief Printing Clubs of Great Britain and Ireland* ("Sette of Odde Volumes, Miscellanies," No. 14; London, 1886); Harrison Ross Steeves, *Learned Societies and English Literary Scholarship in Great Britain and the United States* (New York, 1913); and Harold Williams, *Book Clubs and Printing Societies of Great Britain and Ireland* (London, 1929).

56. Joseph Ritson, *Ancient Engleish Metrical Romanceës* (3 vols.; London, 1802). In the same year Ritson also produced his *Bibliographica Poetica: A Catalogue of Engleish Poets, of the Twelfth, Thirteenth, Fourteenth, Fifteenth, and Sixteenth, Centurys* (London, 1802). Ritson's interest in spelling reform accounts for the orthographical peculiarities.

57. *Metrical Romances of the Thirteenth, Fourteenth, and Fifteenth Centuries: Published from Ancient Manuscripts* (3 vols.; Edinburgh, 1810).

58. See above, n. 52, for the first two editions of the *Select Remains*. The *Early Metrical Tales* was issued in a new edition as *Early Scottish Metrical Tales* (London and Glasgow, 1889). Both of Laing's books were finally amalgamated into *Early Popular Poetry of Scotland and the Northern Border*,

re-arranged and revised with additions by W. Carew Hazlitt (Library of Old Authors, 2 vols.; London, 1895).

59. Swinburne's reference to Hartshorne's *Ancient Metrical Tales* (London, 1829) as "the most execrably misedited book that ever . . . disgraced the press—. . . Hartshorne's *Metrical Romances*" ("The Journal of Sir Walter Scott," *Complete Works of . . . Swinburne*, XV, 238) with its curious mangling of Hartshorne's title says a great deal more about Swinburne's congenital intemperance than Hartshorne's editorial methods.

60. A 2nd edition, enlarged, appeared as *Early English Prose Romances* (3 vols.; London, 1858). Another edition revised by Morley *et al.* appeared as late as 1907. See the Prefatory Notice to the 2nd edition (I, v) for Thoms's disappointment.

61. The 1st edition of this work had appeared in one volume in 1790, but contained no material previous to the sixteenth century. The 2nd edition, radically enlarged, appeared as *Specimens of the Early English Poets, To Which is Prefixed an Historical Sketch of the Rise and Progress of the English Poetry and Language* (3 vols.; London, 1801). Further editions appeared in 1803, 1811, 1845, and 1851. Rudolph Willard says that Ellis' book was the first to present Laȝamon "primarily as literature, and set before the reader a sizable selection from the *Brut* itself" ("Laȝamon in the Seventeenth and Eighteenth Centuries," [Texas] *Studies in English*, 27 [1948], 269).

62. The work reached a 2nd edition in 1811.

63. Ed. Owen Jones, E. Williams, and W. Owen Pughe. Among other materials, the book included a number of the Triads dealing with Arthur.

64. I give the titles adopted by modern scholarship. Ellis has *Merlin*, Part I (drawn largely from Lincoln's Inn MS 150); *Merlin*, Part II (Auchinleck MS); and *Morte Arthur* (Harley MS 2252).

65. Dunlop's book enjoyed considerable popularity. A 2nd edition in 3 vols. appeared in 1816; a 3rd edition in one volume in 1845; another edition in two volumes in 1896 when the title was altered to *History of Prose Fiction*; and yet another edition in 1906. An American edition was published in 1842 and a German translation in 1851. Dunlop, it may be observed, did not content himself with borrowing Ellis' method—he also borrowed Ellis' words when he could—without quotation marks or indication of source. Compare the treatment of Lancelot's origin in George Ellis' *Specimens of the Early English Metrical Romances* (2nd ed., 3 vols.; London, 1811), I, 325–27, with John Dunlop's *The History of Fiction: Being a Critical Account of the Most Celebrated Prose Works of Fiction from the Earliest Greek Romances to the Novels of the Present Age* (3rd ed.; London, 1845), pp. 78–79.

66. I have been unable to discover any reliable evidence to support Maurice Halperin's contention that Dunlop's book played a considerable part in the renaissance of the Tristram story in the nineteenth century (*Roman de Tristan et Iseut*, p. 16).

67. Fairchild, *Romantic Quest*, p. 262.

68. For the quoted phrase and its use, see Mrs. Amelia Heber, *The Life of Reginald Heber, D. D., Lord Bishop of Calcutta* (2 vols.; New York, 1830), I, 323, where it is drawn from a friend's account of young Reginald Heber's improvisations of early romances. For Heber's indebtedness to Ellis' résumé of Arthurian story, see my chap. 6.

69. Walter Scott (ed.), *Sir Tristrem; a Metrical Romance of the Thirteenth Century; by Thomas of Erceldoune, Called the Rhymer* (3rd ed.; Edinburgh, 1811), p. lxxx.

70. The rarity of copies of Malory is suggested by the tone of Scott's reference to the book in his introduction to *Sir Tristrem*—a tone that indicates that he expected most of his readers to be unacquainted with Malory. In 1807 Scott believed that Caxton's edition was no longer extant (Scott, *Letters*, XII, 296), although he was aware that Stansby's edition presented a thoroughly expurgated text. Southey was so little acquainted with other editions of Malory that he did not know even that much (*The Life and Correspondence of Robert Southey*, ed. Charles Cuthbert Southey [New York, 1855], p. 262). In the Advertisement to the Wilks edition of 1816, a total of seven copies of the 1485, 1498, 1529, and 1557 editions are listed as extant, and the Earl of Spenser is reported to have paid £325 for his copy of the 1485 edition in 1816. Of East's edition (1578?), "a fair copy . . . is worth about 40 guineas," and of the 1634 edition "an indifferent copy is worth from eight to ten guineas" (*La Mort d'Arthur: The Most Ancient History of the Renowned Prince Arthur and the Knights of the Round Table* [3 vols.; London: R. Wilks, 1816], I, i–iii). But with this, contrast the prices (tipped into the catalogue by hand) realized at the sale of the great library of Richard Heber in 1834–1835 at which a copy of East's folio brought 5/15/6 and Copland's folio only 2/18/0 (*Bibliotheca Heberiana: Catalogue of the Library of the Late Richard Heber, Esq.* [London: Sotheby and Son, 1834–1835], Pt. IV, p. 27). I am unable to supply any certain explanation for these prices.

71. Ellis, *Specimens of the Early English Metrical Romances*, I, 407–8. Oddly enough, Ellis mistakenly assigns the speech to "Sir Bohort" (Bors).

72. Scott (ed.), *Sir Tristrem*, p. lxxx.

73. Scott, Notes to *Marmion* in *Poetical Works*, p. 173.

74. *Ibid.*

75. Scott, *Letters*, XII, 269 n. In offering the publication rights to Millar, Scott admitted that the preface he intended to write for the Malory would cost him little trouble, but he still thought the sixty guineas he might expect for it not excessive for the use of his reputation. Writing to Southey in November of 1807, he gives as his motive a desire "merely to preserve that ancient record of English chivalry" (*ibid.*, I, 390).

76. Southey, *Selections from the Letters of Robert Southey*, ed. John Wood Warter (4 vols.; London, 1856), II, 27. In a slightly earlier letter to Longmans (November 13, 1807), Southey had said, "Morte d'Arthur is a book which I shall edit with peculiar pleasure, because it has been my delight

since I was a school-boy." His view of his editorial responsibilities is suggested by his direction to Longmans to turn over a copy of the book to the printers as soon as one could be found (Southey, *Life and Correspondence*, p. 226). This letter suggests that the project had just been put on foot, as does the fact that other letters of Southey's dealing with the edition are dated after November 13. Nevertheless, Southey in telling Scott of his project (after Scott had told Southey he was planning an edition) speaks under the date December 8, 1807, of "my long-projected edition of Morte d'Arthur" (*ibid.*, p. 230).

77. Scott's last reference to the project seems to be in a letter to Southey dated December 29, 1810: "The only thing which delays my motions is that I am desirous to collate the ordinary edition Stansby with the only *Caxton* known to exist and which belongs to Lady Jersey" (Scott, *Letters*, II, 417). For the details of all the negotiations about these two projected editions, see *ibid.*, I, 390, 401; II, 23, 236, 417; and XII, 296, 296 n., and 297; Southey, *Life and Correspondence*, 226–27, 230–31, 261–62; and Southey, *Selections from the Letters*, II, 27, 32, 34, 39, 43.

78. The full title was *The History of the Renowned Prince Arthur, King of Britain; with His Life and Death, and All His Glorious Battles. Likewise, the Noble Acts and Heroic Deeds of His Valiant Knights of the Round Table* (2 vols.; London: Walker & Edwards, 1816). Although the edition is said to be an "exact reprint" (I, vi) of the 1634 edition, as Wright points out, "the editor, or printer, has taken . . . great liberties with [the text] in various ways, especially in altering phrases when he did not understand them" (Thomas Wright [ed.], *La Mort d'Arthure, The History of King Arthur and of the Knights of the Round Table* [3 vols.; London, 1865], I, xiii). The editor also failed to remedy the hiatus arising from Stansby's edition having been printed from a copy of East's folio edition lacking a leaf. Sommer errs in describing the Walker and Edwards edition as 12mo. (it is in fact 24mo.) and in failing to list it as the first nineteenth-century edition (H. Oskar Sommer [ed.], *Le Morte Darthur* [3 vols.; London, 1889–1891], II, 2). The priority of the Walker and Edwards edition is established by the fact that the comments of the editor of the Wilks edition show a full acquaintance with the published form of the Walker and Edwards edition.

79. *La Mort d'Arthur: The Most Ancient History of the Renowned Prince Arthur and the Knights of the Round Table* (3 vols.; London: R. Wilks, 1816), I, iv–v. Even Haslewood's text appears to have been too libertine for some past owner of the Columbia Library copy, in which further expurgation has been accomplished with a heavy black pencil—so thankless is the labor of the censor! On the defects of the text, see Wright (ed.), *La Mort d'Arthure*, I, xii. The hiatus in the 1634 text was remedied. Like the Walker and Edwards edition, the Wilks print is 24mo. rather than 12mo. as Sommer asserts (Sommer [ed.], *Le Morte Darthur*, II, 2).

80. The full title of Southey's edition was *The Byrth, Lyf, and Actes of King Arthur: of his Noble Knyghtes of the Round Table, Theyr Merveyllous*

Enquestes and Aduentures, Thachyeuyng of the Sanc Greal; and in the End Le Morte Darthur, with the Dolorous Deth and Departyng out of this Worlde of Them Al (2 vols.; London, 1817). Southey's attempt to replace Caxton's erroneous title *Le Morte Darthur* had no lasting effect. Even he himself continued to refer to the book as "Morte Arthur" in later years (Southey, *Selections from the Letters*, III, 427). It is, by the way, an altogether fitting conclusion to the history of Southey's dealings with Longmans in regard to *Le Morte Darthur* to note that even when he finally did prepare an edition for the firm, it was only because another editor had "left the book and the booksellers in the lurch for the sake of decamping with another man's wife" (*ibid.*, III, 426).

81. For Southey's labors in preparing his Preface and Notes, see Southey, *Letters and Correspondence*, III, 47–49.

82. Wright (ed.), *La Mort d'Arthure*, I, xiii–xiv.

83. Southey himself, as he was at pains to point out, had nothing to do with editing the text (Southey [ed.], *Byrth, Lyf, and Actes of King Arthur*, I, lviii). For various strictures on its accuracy, see Sir Edward Strachey (ed.), *Morte D'Arthur* (The Globe Edition; London, 1868), pp. xv–xvii.

84. The fact that all but the last of the editions printed before the nineteenth century were in folio is clear evidence that they were directed to an aristocratic or, at any rate, wealthy audience. In the nineteenth century it was almost exclusively through the cheaper 1816 editions that poets such as Wordsworth, Keats, and Tennyson made their acquaintance with Malory and the Arthurian story.

85. It is possible, of course, that both accident and commercial zeal played some part in the appearance of the three editions so close together. The Advertisement to the Wilks print (I, iii) manifests considerable irritation at having been forestalled by the Walker and Edwards edition, and asserts that Wilks's edition was far advanced when it was discovered that another edition was being printed. But with so much advance notice as Longmans had, it does not seem likely that the firm would have pushed the Southey edition to completion unless at least a fair sale had still seemed likely. That the three editions saturated the market for some time is suggested by the fact that another edition did not appear until Wright's edition of 1858 over forty years later. At that time, according to Wright, the two 1816 editions had "become rare, and the want of a good edition of [*Le Morte Darthur* had] been felt generally" (Wright [ed.], *La Mort d'Arthure*, I, xiv).

86. On July 2, 1803, Ritson informed Scott that he had put the MS in the publisher's hands; six days later he wrote that it had been refused. Ritson died September 23, 1803, before he could seek out another publisher. See Bertrand H. Bronson's admirable biography, *Joseph Ritson: Scholar at Arms* (2 vols.; Berkeley, Calif., 1938), II, 282–83.

87. *Ibid.*, II, 286.

88. Joseph Ritson, *The Life of King Arthur: From Ancient Historians and Authentic Documents* (London, 1825), pp. i and xxi.

89. Annette B. Hopkins, "Ritson's Life of King Arthur," *PMLA*, 93 (March, 1928), 252 and 286. Cf. Loomis, "Pioneers in Arthurian Scholarship," pp. 98–102.

90. Cf. the comment of the editor of the Walker and Edwards edition of *The History of the Renowned Prince Arthur* (I, vii): "The modern reader . . . need not be told, that the Arthur of *history*, and the Arthur of *romance*, are very different personages."

91. Margaret J. C. Reid's explanation of the relative failure of the Romantics to employ the Arthurian theme is that the Romantics were in revolt against marriage as "too narrow a vessel for the seething potion of romantic passion. Yet no marriage could have contained more restricting rules than the chivalric code. This is perhaps why [the Romantic poets] found more appropriate subjects . . . in the myths and legends of Greece and Italy. Chivalric love, especially as represented in Malory, is too conventional and literary a theme" (*The Arthurian Legend: Comparison of Treatment in Modern and Medieval Literature: A Study in the Literary Value of Myth and Legend* [Edinburgh, n.d.], p. 10). It is difficult to imagine *ad hoc* reasoning being carried further.

92. Northrop Frye, *Fearful Symmetry: A Study of William Blake* ([Princeton, N.J.], 1947), p. 172; cf. p. 303. Blake did, it is true, assert in his discussion of his picture "Three Ancient Britons" that "the stories of Arthur are the acts of Albion, applied to a Prince of the fifth century," but this seems insufficient ground for calling Arthurian myth "integral" to his symbolism.

93. Cf. Frye, *Fearful Symmetry*, p. 373. Edward B. Hungerford (*Shores of Darkness* [New York, 1941], pp. 35–61) and Ruthven Todd (*Tracks in the Snow: Studies in English Science and Art* [London, 1946], pp. 29–60) discuss Blake's mythological theories at length and trace them very convincingly to the works of a number of contemporary and near-contemporary mythographers and antiquarians. Blake probably had much of his Arthurian information from the Welsh antiquarian William Owen Pughe, whose *Cambrian Biography* (1803) includes some of the notions Blake mentions. In lumping all mythology together, Blake is probably following the lead of Jacob Bryant's *A New System, or, An Analysis of Ancient Mythology: Wherein an Attempt is Made to Divest Tradition of Fable; and to Reduce the Truth to Its Original Purity* (1774–1776).

94. The works were, of course, not frescoes at all, but rather a species of water-color painting on a ground made of gessoed wood or canvas. Despite his claims of greater permanency for his new method, such examples as have survived exhibit an abnormally high degree of darkening. For details of Blake's method, together with the text of the various advertisements and the *Descriptive Catalogue of Pictures, Poetical and Historical Inventions* . . . that Blake prepared for this exhibition, see *The Complete Writings of William*

Blake with All the Variant Readings, ed. Geoffrey Keynes (London, 1957), pp. 560–86, and 913 n. The "Welch Triades" on which the picture is based are given thus by Blake (p. 560):

"In the last battle that Arthur fought, the most Beautiful was one
That return'd, and the most Strong another: with them also return'd
The most Ugly, and no other beside return'd from the bloody Field.
The most Beautiful, the Roman warriors trembled before and
  worshipped:
The most Strong, they melted before him and dissolved in his
  presence:
The most Ugly they fled with outcries and contortion of their Limbs."

Blake's own account of his sources (pp. 577–78) is appended: "The British Antiquities are now in the Artist's hands; all his visionary contemplations, relating to his own country and its ancient glory, when it was, as it again shall be, the source of learning and inspiration. Arthur was a name for the constellation Arcturus, or Boötes, the keeper of the North Pole. And all the fables of Arthur and his round table; of the warlike naked Britons; of Merlin; of Arthur's conquest of the whole world; of his death, or sleep, and promise to return again; of the Druid monuments or temples; of the pavement of Watling-street; of the caverns in Cornwall, Wales, Derbyshire, and Scotland; of the Giants of Ireland and Britain; of the elemental beings called by us by the general name of fairies; and of these three who escaped, namely Beauty, Strength, and Ugliness. Mr. B. has in his hands poems of the highest antiquity. Adam was a Druid, and Noah; also Abraham was called to succeed the Druidical age, which began to turn allegoric and mental signification into corporal command, whereby human sacrifice would have depopulated the earth. All these things are written in Eden. The artist is an inhabitant of that happy country; and if everything goes on as it has begun, the world of vegetation and generation may expect to be opened again to Heaven, through Eden, as it was in the beginning." According to Keynes (p. 913 n.), "this picture has for many years been entirely lost to sight. Seymour Kirkup, who visited Blake's exhibition and afterward wrote his memories of it for Swinburne, regarded this painting as Blake's masterpiece. Kirkup made a sketch of it for Swinburne, but this too has been lost." For another of Kirkup's letters on the subject, see William Michael Rossetti (ed.), *Rossetti Papers: 1862 to 1870* (New York, 1903), p. 170.

95. These and all succeeding quotations are drawn from Blake's *Descriptive Catalogue,* in *Complete Writings,* pp. 577–80.

96. See Hungerford, *Shores of Darkness,* pp. 3–34, for a survey and analysis of the speculative mythographers. Their influence on Blake is fully discussed on pp. 35–61.

97. For Bryant, see n. 93 above.

98. "Essay, Supplementary to the Preface," *Poems* (1815), in *The Poetical*

Works of William Wordsworth, ed. E. de Selincourt (5 vols.; Oxford, 1940–1949), II, 425.

99. For Wordsworth's lone Arthurian poem, see my chap. 6.

100. This assertion is based on an examination of Sister Eugenia Logan's *Concordance to the Poetry of Samuel Taylor Coleridge* (Saint Mary of the Woods, Indiana, 1940). The allusion to Merlin occurs in "The Pang More Sharp Than All," l. 39. According to Henry Alford ("The Idylls of the King," *Contemporary Review*, 13 [January, 1870], 104), "Coleridge many years ago pronounced the Arthurian legends a profitable source for a great national epic." I have been unable to locate this recommendation in Coleridge's work. What Coleridge did say in the *Table Talk* (September 4, 1833) was "As to Arthur you could not by any means make a poem on him national to Englishmen. What have *we* to do with him?" (*Specimens of the Table Talk of Samuel Taylor Coleridge* [Edinburgh, 1905], p. 292).

101. Southey (ed.), *Byrth, Lyf, and Actes of King Arthu*r, I, xxviii.

102. MacCallum, *Idylls of the King and Arthurian Story*, pp. 199–202. The work of Ariosto appears to have been Southey's *beau ideal* of chivalric romance: "Undoubtedly it is true that no poem of any lasting popularity has been produced upon a Round Table Story; and that in its kind the Orlando Furioso will hardly be equalled, and cannot be surpassed" (Southey [ed.], *Byrth, Lyf, and Actes of King Arthur*, I, vii).

103. The passage occurs in Part I, Section XI ("The Gorsedd"); I quote from *The Poetical Works of Robert Southey* (10 vols. in 5; Boston, 1880), V, 94–95.

104. Scott's *Bridal of Triermain* is discussed in my chap. 6.

105. For Frere's poem, see my chap. 6.

106. See above, n. 5.

107. My assertion is based on an examination of F. S. Ellis' *A Lexical Concordance to the Poetical Works of Percy Bysshe Shelley* (London, 1892). For the Merlin allusion, see the fragmentary historical drama *Charles the First* (I, 370).

108. Fairchild, *Romantic Quest*, pp. 306–7.

109. The inventory of Keats's library drawn up by Charles Brown in 1821 contains this entry: "Hist. of K. Arthur (2d lost) 18mo—1 vol" (Hyder Edward Rollins [ed.], *The Keats Circle; Letters and Papers 1816–1878* [2 vols.; Cambridge, Mass., 1948], I, 259). Both title and the fact that Brown seems to have believed the full set consisted of two volumes indicate that this was the Walker and Edwards edition of Malory (1816).

110. See the letter to Thomas Keats dated July 17 and postmarked July 30, 1818, in *The Letters of John Keats: 1814—1821*, ed. Hyder Edward Rollins (2 vols.; Cambridge, Mass., 1958), I, 333–34.

111. These lines, the last two of st. 19, have occasioned a number of comments by editors. Forman, after observing that Hunt was unable to explain the passage, says that "the monstrous debt was his [i.e., Merlin's] existence,

which he owed to a demon and repaid when he died or disappeared through the working of one of his own spells by Viviane," and suggests that the words "never on such a night" refer to some tradition of a storm over Broceliande the night of Merlin's entombment. As a source, Forman suggests Dunlop's *History of Fiction* (*The Complete Works of John Keats*, ed. H. Buxton Forman [5 vols.; Glasgow, 1900–1901], II, 74 n.). De Selincourt agrees with Forman's interpretation, but questions Dunlop as a source since Dunlop does not mention a storm (*The Poems of John Keats*, ed. E. de Selincourt [2d ed.; New York, 1909], p. 468). Recently Walter Jackson Bate has explained the allusion with the following note: "the magician Merlin, who owed his life to a devil, and paid for it by committing evil deeds" ("John Keats," *Major British Writers*, ed. G. B. Harrison [2 vols.; enlarged ed.; New York, 1959], II, 338 n.). If the "monstrous debt" meant is Merlin's demonic paternity, either Dunlop's *History of Fiction* or Ellis' *Specimens of Early English Metrical Romances* would be convenient possible sources. And if "paid his Demon" is a reference to Merlin's magical entombment, either Dunlop or Malory could have supplied Keats with the motif. But the fact is that the allusion is so brief that both of these explanations deserve no more than the title of speculation. As for the "storm," it seems not to have been noticed by either Forman or de Selincourt that none has been mentioned by Keats at this point in the poem, nor is a storm mentioned until much later (st. 36 ff.) after the lovers have, it appears, slept. The "such a night" that Keats has reference to is much more likely a night of magic and enchantment such as has not been since Merlin's magical powers left the world. The two lines that immediately precede the reference to Merlin are in favor of this reading: "While legioned faeries paced the coverlet, / And pale enchantment held her sleepy-eyed." Such an explanation, at any rate, makes the allusion to Merlin significantly functional in the poem as a reinforcement of the atmosphere of the magic love and troth plighted on the mystic Eve of St. Agnes. One other allusion to Merlin, a quite insignificant use of his name, occurs in the *Epistle to John Hamilton Reynolds* (l. 34). An examination of Dane Lewis Baldwin *et al.*, *A Concordance to the Poems of John Keats* (Washington, D. C., 1917), reveals no other Arthurian allusions in Keats's work.

6. ARTHUR WAKES IN AVALON: ARTHURIAN LITERATURE OF THE ROMANTIC PERIOD

1. An opponent of all oaths and even promises, Thelwall early espoused radical opinions and became a member of the Corresponding Society formed by Thomas Hardy. After his indictment for sedition in 1794, he was confined with Hardy and Horne Tooke until his acquittal. He seems to have been known to and admired by such men as Southey, Hazlitt, Coleridge, and Lamb. See *DNB*, s.v. "Thelwall, John."

2. The play was first published in Thelwall's *Poems Chiefly Written in Retirement* (Hereford, 1801). According to the author, it was originally

intended for stage production, but, he goes on, "since the prospect of stage representation has been abandoned, the dialogue and mythological allusions, in several of the scenes, have been considerably lengthened; by which, tho its bulk may have been rendered somewhat extra-theatrical, it is hoped, that in point of interest, in the closet, it has not been injured" (*ibid.*, p. xlvii n.).

3. *Ibid.*, p. 2.

4. See Nennius' *Historia Britonum*, sections 31–49. Geoffrey omits the incestuous relationship between Vortigern and his daughter.

5. Thelwall, *Poems*, p. 207.

6. *Ibid.* In his notes to the play, Thelwall cites a fair variety of authorities on Northern mythology and archaeology. The source of his "Cambrian superstitions" is less clear. Possibly the presentation of Tristram as a bibulous low-comedy figure derives from some Welsh tradition that he may have picked up during his stay in "the obscure and romantic village of Llys-Wen."

7. In his younger days Frere (1769–1846) contributed along with Canning and Ellis to the *Anti-Jacobin*. Later he was appointed Envoy and Plenipotentiary to the Spanish Central Junta, but retired from public life after the failure of Moore's campaign, an event which was attributed, not altogether justly, to Frere's mistaken advice. Literary pursuits occupied the rest of his life. See the summary of Frere's life in John Hookham Frere, *The Monks and the Giants*, ed. R. D. Waller (Publications of the University of Manchester, No. 172, English Series No. 14; Manchester, 1926). Cf. J. Steven Watson, *The Reign of George III, 1760–1815* (Oxford History of England, Vol. XII; Oxford, 1960), pp. 460–61.

8. Cantos I and II appeared in 1817, III and IV in 1818, both editions under the title of *Prospectus and Specimen* etc. A 2nd edition of I and II also appeared in 1818 followed by a 3rd edition in the same year. Apparently copies of the 2nd edition of I and II were combined by the binder with copies of the 1st edition of III and IV—such is the case in both the British Museum and Columbia University copies. In 1821 all four cantos appeared in what are described as 3rd and 4th editions, although the 4th is nothing but this 3rd edition with a new title page. The title *The Monks and the Giants* appeared for the first time in this "4th" edition. The number of editions gives a misleading look of popularity to the poem; as late as June of 1818 Murray was complaining that the book was not a success and that it had not then sold five hundred copies. A further edition was not called for until 1842. For a discussion of these bibliographical problems see *The Monks and the Giants*, ed. Waller, pp. 61–62.

9. *The Works of the Right Honorable John Hookham Frere in Verse and Prose* with a Memoir by Sir Bartle Frere, ed. W. E. Frere (2nd ed., 3 vols.; London, 1874), I, 166.

10. [J. H. Frere], *Prospectus and Specimen of an Intended National Work, by William and Robert Whistlecraft, of Stow-Market, in Suffolk, Harness and Collar-makers, Intended to Comprise the Most Interesting Par-*

ticulars Relating to King Arthur and His Round Table (2nd ed.; London, 1818), Proem, st. 9. Subsequent quotations from this edition are cited by canto and stanza number in the text.

11. Another canto was begun by Frere, who "for sometime after the work was first published . . . was very fond of pursuing the idea, and used to finish a couple of stanzas every day" (Frere, *Works*, I, 167). These additional stanzas concern a young giant who was healed of a broken leg and as far as possible converted to Christianity by the monks. Such a development had already been foreshadowed in the concluding lines of Canto II, st. 59.

12. "You can't go on joking with people who won't be joked with. . . . so I thought it was no use offering my jokes to people who would not understand them" (Frere, *Works*, I, 166–67). Frere's other reason for abandoning the poem—"the sort of stigma which at first attached to the metre after the publication of 'Don Juan'" (*ibid.*, I, 167)—is surely one of the more unusual examples in literary history of guilt by association. It is curious that Frere does not mention the relatively slow sale of the poem among his reasons for stopping work on it. Southey, writing to Landor in 1820, accepted Frere's disavowels of topically satirical intent at face value, and explained the poem's lack of popularity on that ground; the poem, was, he said, "too good in itself, and too inoffensive, to become popular; for it attacked nothing and nobody" (quoted in Frere, *Works*, I, 165).

13. *Ibid.*, I, 166–67.

14. The Peninsular War is surveyed by Watson, *Reign of George III*, p. 459 ff. For Wellington's complaints about the lack of discipline in both officers and troops, see Elie Halévy, *A History of the English People in the Nineteenth Century* (2nd ed., 6 vols.; London, 1949–1952), I, 83 ff. Tristram's strange victory may very well glance specifically at the taking of the fortress of Badajoz in 1812 when for reasons never satisfactorily explained a mere diversionary force managed to seize the fortress at the very moment when the main attacking force was driven off. Other references to Tristram make topical application a most intriguing possibility:

"His schemes of war were sudden, unforeseen,
  Inexplicable both to friend and foe;
It seem'd as if some momentary spleen
  Inspired the project and impell'd the blow" (I, 21).

Or this allusion to Gawain, who "serv'd his friend, but watch'd his opportunity" (I, 25):

". . . his success in war was strangely various;
  In executing schemes that others plann'd,
    He seem'd a very Caesar or a Marius;
  Take his own plans, and place him in command,
    Your prospect of success became precarious:
His plans were good, but Launcelot succeeded
And realized them better far than He did" (I, 26).

15. Frere, *The Monks and the Giants*, ed. Waller, p. 34; cf. Frere, *Works*, I, 164. The imaginary "Morgan's Chronicle" that, in true romance fashion, "Whistlecraft" gravely claims to follow, may have been suggested by the title of Pulci's romance.

16. As an Eton schoolboy, Frere composed a metrical version of an Anglo-Saxon Ode on Athelstan's Victory, which he contributed to Ellis' *Specimens of the Early English Poets* (Frere, *Works*, I, 175). The possibility that Frere had begun work on *The Monks and the Giants* as early as 1813 (Frere, *The Monks and the Giants*, ed. Waller, p. 33) need not eliminate Malory as a likely source; it is not probable that a friend of George Ellis' would have been obliged to wait until 1816 for the new publication of *Le Morte Darthur* to see a copy of that work.

17. In 1817 Byron wrote to Murray, "I have written a poem [*Beppo*] in or after the excellent manner of Whistlecraft (whom I take to be Frere)." In the following year he wrote again of *Beppo*, "The style is not English, it is Italian;—Berni is the original of *all*; Whistlecraft was my immediate model" (quoted in Frere, *Works*, I, 163–64 and 164 n.).

18. The full text is reprinted in *The Works of Thomas Love Peacock*, ed. H. F. B. Brett-Smith and C. E. Jones (8 vols., The Halliford Edition; London and New York, 1924–1934), V, 261–76. Although the first edition bore the date 1814, the book had appeared at the end of 1813. It ran through five illustrated editions in as many years and was printed once more in the middle of the century (*ibid.*, I, lii–liii).

19. Printed in Peacock, *Works*, VI, 315–34. For the passage quoted see p. 317.

20. *Ibid.*, VI, 321. For Peacock's attitudes toward the Middle Ages, see Alice Chandler, "The Quarrel of the Ancients and Moderns: Peacock and the Medieval Revival," *Bucknell Review*, 13 (1965), 39–50.

21. Portions of *Calidore* were first printed by Richard Garnett in *Calidore and Miscellanea* (1892). The entire MS is printed in Peacock, *Works*, VIII, 301–41. An earlier MS fragment of an attempt of the same subject and bearing the title *Satyrane: or The Stranger in England* is also printed in Peacock, *Works*, VIII, 295–99. The date of composition of *Calidore* appears to have been 1816 (*ibid.*, I, lxvii).

22. Peacock, *Works*, VIII, 324.

23. *Ibid.*, I, cxxxvii. A more recent critic takes the opposite view, and asserts that the fact that Peacock "interrupted his story with long and tedious adaptations of bardic songs can only be explained by his liking for displaying recondite knowledge, . . . his penchant for third-rate poetry[, and] his incurable tendency to indulge himself in versifying" (Olwen W. Campbell, *Thomas Love Peacock* [The English Novelists; London, 1953], p. 64).

24. Peacock, *Works*, I, cxxxviii–cxxxix. See also Herbert Wright, "The Associations of Thomas Love Peacock with Wales," *Essays and Studies by Members of the English Association*, 12 (1926), pp. 24–46, and David Gallon,

"Thomas Love Peacock and Wales: Some Suggestions," *Anglo-Welsh Review,* 17 (1968), 125–34.

25. Peacock, *Works,* I, cxxxix.

26. I follow the text printed in Peacock's *Works,* IV, 1–152. The present quotation is found on p. 79.

27. M. W. MacCallum, *Tennyson's Idylls of the King and Arthurian Story from the XVIth Century* (Glasgow, 1894), p. 204.

28. Opinion varies widely as to the seriousness of Peacock's antiquarianism. MacCallum (*ibid.,* pp. 204–5) and Campbell (*Thomas Love Peacock,* p. 65) take the position that he was at considerable pains to achieve archaeological accuracy. Brett-Smith (Peacock, *Works,* I, cxxxvii–cxxxviii) expresses doubts and notes that in Peacock's treatment of the theme, he "allowed himself a latitude and levity very unlike the spirit of respectful scholarship in which he approached a classical theme."

29. Peacock, *Works,* IV, 15–16. Seithenyn's speech is usually considered a parody of Canning's famous speech of 1825 against reform, but Brett-Smith suggests Wellington's speeches on the same subject as more probable models (*ibid.,* I, cxxxvi).

30. For a much more sympathetic view of the novel, see MacCallum, *Idylls of the King and Arthurian Story,* pp. 207–8. MacCallum's view that Peacock demonstrated that the old materials might be successfully filled with new meaning for a new day is doubtless true in theory; in practice there is not any evidence that any subsequent writer made this discovery from reading Peacock. And anyhow the meaning that Peacock gave it is too arbitrary to be significant.

31. The best proof of the book's failure to attract readers is the fact that remainders were still available forty years after publication (Peacock, *Works,* I, cxl–cxlii).

32. For a full account of Leyden's career, see the "Life of John Leyden" by Tom Brown in *The Poetical Works of Dr. John Leyden* (London and Edinburgh, 1875), pp. ix–xcv.

33. Tom Brown's description of the poem gives a concise summary of Leyden's plan: "The plan of the poem is simple and complete. It carries the reader to the tiny 'burn' which emerges from the Cheviot Hills, and widens into a foaming river, under the name of Teviot. [Leyden] mentions the various places of interest that lie in its basin, or along the course of its tributaries. These are interwoven with a great variety of allusions to the customs, legends, and heroes of his own and other lands, events that lie beyond the pale of history, and those that agitated the stirring period in which he lived." Brown's concluding estimate of the poem has more piety than judgment: "It is altogether a poem of a very high class, and needs only to become better known and more accessible in order to be more read" (*ibid.,* p. lv).

34. John Leyden, *Scenes of Infancy: Descriptive of Teviotdale* (2nd ed.; Edinburgh, 1811), pp. 6–7.

35. The Caledonian Merlin, or Merlin the Wild, is traditionally supposed to have been trained in bardic art by Taliesin. Following a fit of madness brought on by his killing of his own nephew, he was given an apple orchard by a prince, and later prophesied the return of Arthur *and* Modred for another battle at Camlann. Leyden seems to have drawn at least some of these traditions from Geoffrey's *Vita Merlini Caledonii* (cf. Leyden, *Scenes of Infancy*, pp. 151–54).

36. *Ibid.*, p. 76.

37. *Ibid.*, pp. 75–76. In this passage Leyden glances at the tradition that after the battle of Camlann Arthur and his knights were laid asleep in Eildon hill to be awakened in some latter day need of England.

38. Introduction to Canto I of *Marmion, The Poetical Works of Sir Walter Scott*, ed. J. Logie Robertson (Oxford Complete Edition; London, 1913), pp. 92–93.

39. The first fragment of the poem was published as "The Vision of Triermain" along with imitations of Crabbe and Moore, all three accompanied by a preface entitled *The Inferno of Altesidora* and first printed in the *Edinburgh Annual Register* for 1809 (published 1811). For the details of this publication and of the hoax designed to have the poem attributed to Erskine, see J. G. Lockhart, *The Life of Sir Walter Scott* (Everyman's Library, No. 55; London and New York, 1937), pp. 220, 231–39. For the 1813 edition Erskine himself rewrote Scott's MS version of the *Preface* and was thus able to include references to Scott as "the master" of "romantic poetry;—the popularity of which has been revived in the present day under the auspices, and by the unparalleled success, of one individual [i.e., Scott]" ([Walter Scott], *The Bridal of Triermain, or The Vale of St. John* [Edinburgh, 1813], p. viii).

40. The phrase "systematic mystification" is Lockhart's (*Life of Sir Walter Scott*, p. 220). It is just possible that one motive for the hoax was a desire to compete with Byron without doing so under the name by which Scott had won fame for another kind of verse narrative. As Karl Kroeber has observed, Scott did not "surrender narrative poetry without a fight. *The Bridal of Triermain* shows him trying unsuccessfully to transform the mood and purpose of his verse stories. In this poem he aims for imaginatively sensuous effects and relies little upon naturalistic detail or direct narrative" (*Romantic Narrative Art* [Madison, Wis., 1960], p. 177).

41. Scott, *Bridal of Triermain*, Introduction to Canto I, st. viii. Subsequent quotations are cited in my text by canto and stanza number.

42. Lockhart, *Life of Sir Walter Scott*, p. 238. Both Scott and Lockhart (*ibid.*, pp. 231 and 238) seem to hint, though in a very ambiguous manner, that the introductory passages were, at least in part, an accessory to the hoax, the character and experiences of the minstrel Arthur supposedly having been drawn after those of William Erskine. But, as we shall see, this can scarcely be so. Not only do these passages involve reminiscences of Scott's own courtship days, but they also portray a wooing that could scarcely reflect Erskine's

courtship. The Euphemia Robinson who became Erskine's wife was the daughter of an Edinburgh Professor of Natural History, and thus not a likely candidate for prototype of the wealthy, socially superior Lucy of the poem. For the available details of the life of Erskine, later Lord Kinneder, see Florence McCunn, *Sir Walter Scott's Friends* (2nd impression; Edinburgh and London, 1909), pp. 48–54. The best that can be said for the structure of *The Bridal of Triermain* has been urged by Kroeber: "Surprisingly, Scott manipulates this difficult structure with skill and tact. The Arthur-Lucy sections are light-hearted, realistic, and edged with satire. The story of Sir Roland is presented in the manner of a Spenserian allegory. Lyulph's story of King Arthur is Ariostan, impossible, immoral, charming" (*Romantic Narrative*, p. 178). But despite the perceptiveness of these distinctions, the question of the artistic or thematic functions of the tripartite structure remains unresolved.

43. Una Pope-Hennessy, *Sir Walter Scott* (The English Novelists; London, 1948), p. 53. Even Roland de Vaux's title, Baron of Triermain, was inspired by Triermain Castle, which is in the neighborhood of Gilsland. Herbert Grierson (*Sir Walter Scott, Bart.: A New Life Supplementary to, and Corrective of, Lockhart's Biography* [London, 1938], pp. 54 and 106) confirms the associations of the Introductions with Gilsland.

44. For Charlotte's antecedents and the courtship, see Grierson, *Sir Walter Scott, Bart.*, pp. 45–62.

45. *Ibid.*, p. 28. See pp. 28–44 for details of Scott's abortive wooing of Williamina. According to Grierson (p. 42), yet another Lucy (in *The Bride of Lammermoor*) may reflect qualities of Williamina Belsches.

46. *Ibid.*, p. 28. As late as 1808 Scott spoke of the rejection as a "never to be forgotten experience" (p. 31).

47. Scott here made use of an actual physical phenomenon, a pile of jumbled rocks in the Vale of St. John in the Lake country. From a distance these rocks have the form of a Gothic castle, but on a nearer approach the spectator discovers that the resemblance disappears. See Scott, *Bridal of Triermain*, pp. 211–12.

48. It was a favorite moral with Scott. Quentin Durward, it may be observed, did a little better for himself—at the end of his history, his "sense, firmness, and gallantry . . . put him in possession of WEALTH, RANK, and BEAUTY!" But then Scott had learned about money by then. Morality of this sort may be explained away partially by the tastes of the time, but the fact that the Scottian treatment of chivalry was to become the fixed type of such fiction for boys' magazines suggests the essential immaturity of much of Scott's work. The novels of Scottish life are, of course, quite another matter.

49. Cf. MacCallum (*Idylls of the King and Arthurian Story*, pp. 194–95), who develops the notion of the unsuitability of Arthurian material for historical reconstruction at some length.

50. The real heir of Scott's poem is Browning's non-Arthurian "Childe Roland to the Dark Tower Came." The mystery of how this superb poem

could have been inspired by the jumbled nursery rhyme in "Edgar's Song in 'Lear' " becomes somewhat less mysterious when the presence of the same line used as a title by Browning is noted in *The Bridal of Triermain* (Introduction to Canto III, st. vi), where it introduces a quest involving many elements paralleled in Browning's poem. Like the quest of the Dark Tower pursued by Childe Roland and his fellows, the quest of Gyneth is an adventure "perilous to knightly worth" (I, ix); it attracts many and requires much preparation; few have even attained the castle, and none have returned. In the end the quest is only to be attained by one who has resisted various moral temptations, the other knights having failed through some one lapse. One of the most terrifying moments in "Childe Roland"—"came a click / As when a trap shuts—you're inside the den!" (ll. 173–74)—seems clearly to have been suggested by the mysterious closing of the doors of Gyneth's castle on Scott's Roland—"Now closed is the gin and the prey within" (III, xvii). There are a number of other resemblances between the two poems, such as the striking similarity between the locations of Gyneth's castle and the Dark Tower in valleys and the generally romantic, dreamlike atmosphere of both poems. The difference is, of course, that the dream in Scott is on the whole a rather pleasant wish-fulfillment, while in Browning it is a terrifying nightmare deriving its energy from a strange kind of agonized moral realism. The many parallels between the two works seem to have been noticed first by Irene Hardy ("Browning's 'Childe Roland,' a Literary Parallel—and Something More," *Poet Lore*, 24 [1913], 53–58). Queried by Miss Hardy, Browning disclaimed any acquaintance with Scott's poem—a response which must surely be laid to a lapse of memory.

Of the dramatizations based on *The Bridal of Triermain*, an operetta entitled *Triermain* by Ellerton appeared in 1831 (Allardyce Nicoll, *A History of English Drama, 1660–1900* [4th ed., 6 vols.; Cambridge, Eng., 1952–1959], IV, 92 n.). Scott's poem was also used as the basis of Isaac Pocock's *King Arthur and the Knights of the Round Table: A New Grand Chivalric Entertainment, in Three Acts* (London, 1834). Of this "Christmas equestrian spectacle" (*DNB*, s.v. "Pocock, Isaac"), the author declares Scott's poem to have been the inspiration "as affording a more connected story" than the excessively "voluminous" and episodic Malory, but later he asserts that "every fact—if such a term can be applied to matter so fabulous—the names and indications of character from King Arthur, down to the giant Cormoran and the goblin dwarf, have emanated from the *veritable* history of those times (as given by Sir John [!] Malory, Knt.) when, about the year 540, Arthur is said to have flourished" (Pocock, *King Arthur*, pp. iii–v). The only action in this extravaganza of scenic effects, pageants, songs, and dances seems to have been Roland de Vaux's quest, which is apparently made contemporary with Arthur's reign. Pocock's estimate of his own contribution was modest enough: "The manufacturer of a holiday piece can pretend to little merit but that of contriving a frame-work on which the talents of the various artists concerned in its completion may be exhibited to the best possible advantage—a matter of no small difficulty when it is considered how extensive a variety of material must be brought into action to give effect to a subject of so splendid a character as the title imports, and which would have been impracticable but for the unlimited expence with which the Lessee [i.e., of the Theatre Royal, Drury Lane] has sanctioned its production" (*ibid.*, p. iii).

51. Introduction to Canto I of *Marmion*, Scott, *Poetical Works*, p. 93.

52. For Wordsworth's medievalism, see Hoxie Neale Fairchild, *The Romantic Quest* (New York, 1931), pp. 270–80. Fairchild's assertion (p. 279) that "certainly the *Lyrical Ballads* would never have been written except for the revival of interest in the past" seems excessive to me.

53. William Wordsworth, Preface, *Lyrical Ballads* (2nd ed.; 1800).

54. Basil Willey, *The Seventeenth Century Background* (London, 1950), pp. 298, 305–6. Cf. B. Ifor Evans, *Tradition and Romanticism: Studies in English Poetry from Chaucer to W. B. Yeats* (London, 1940), pp. 122–25.

55. *The Prelude*, Book I, ll. 166–85. In this and all succeeding quotations from Wordsworth, I follow the text of *The Poetical Works of William Wordsworth*, ed. Thomas Hutchinson (Oxford Edition; London, 1910). According to Hutchinson (p. xxvi), Book I was probably finished before the end of 1800. The whole poem in its earlier state was completed in 1805, but was much later drastically revised for its first publication in 1850. Of the passage which I quote, ll. 175–85 with their strong note of ethical Christianity have no counterpart in the original text. See *The Prelude, or Growth of a Poet's Mind*, ed. Ernest de Selincourt (2nd ed., rev., Helen Darbishire; Oxford, 1959) for the text of the earlier version.

56. *Prelude*, I, 228–29.

57. *Ibid.*, I, 161–65.

58. B. Ifor Evans, *Tradition and Romanticism*, p. 123.

59. *Artegal and Elidure*, ll. 49–56.

60. "Struggle of the Britons Against the Barbarians," number 10 of the *Ecclesiastical Sonnets*, 1st series. The allusion seems to be to the Mt. Badon battle in which, according to Geoffrey, Arthur carried an image of the Virgin on his shield.

61. The following allusions have been compiled from Lane Cooper's *A Concordance to the Poems of William Wordsworth* (London, 1911). The Lady of the Lake is referred to in the fourth of the *Poems on the Naming of Places*. "Arimathean Joseph's wattled cells" are mentioned in "Dissolution of the Monasteries," number 21 of the *Ecclesiastical Sonnets*, 2nd series. The allusions to Merlin are found in the sonnet beginning "With how sad steps, O Moon" (number 23 of the *Miscellaneous Sonnets*) and in *The Prelude* (VII, 713) where the term "Merlin" is used as a generic name for fortune-tellers and astrologers. The association of Merlin with such gentry was perpetuated in the first quarter of the nineteenth century through a number of catchpenny publications: *Merlinus Liberatus. An Almanack* "by John Partridge" (pub-

lished from 1819 up to 1864); *The Philosophical Merlin: Being the Translation of a Valuable Manuscript, Formerly in the Possession of Napoleon Buonaparte . . . Enabling the Reader to Cast the Nativity of Himself . . . Without the Aid of Tables . . . or Calculations* (1822); *Urania; or the Astrologers Chronicle and Mystical Magazine,* ed. "Merlinus Anglicus, jun." [R. C. Smith] (1825) (William Edward Mead, "Outlines of the History of the Legend of Merlin," *Merlin, or The Early History of King Arthur,* ed. Henry B. Wheatley [EETS, Vols. 10, 21, 36, 112, 2 vols.; London, 1865–1899], I, LXXVIII–LXXX).

62. The composition of the poem clearly dates back to 1828; in a letter to Edward Quillinan, dated in November of that year by de Selincourt, Wordsworth wrote, "the poem Mrs. W-- mentions is a sort of Romance—with no more solid foundation than the word—Waterlily" (*The Letters of William and Dorothy Wordsworth: The Later Years,* ed. Ernest de Selincourt [3 vols.; Oxford, 1939], I, 323).

63. "The Egyptian Maid," l. 66. Subsequent quotations from this poem are cited by line numbers indicated parenthetically in my text.

64. In the headnote to the poem, Wordsworth says, "For the names and persons in the following poem see the 'History of the renowned Prince Arthur and his Knights of the Round Table'; for the rest the Author is answerable" (*Poetical Works,* p. 369). The title indicates that he probably used the Walker and Edwards edition in which the spellings "Ninine" and "Nineve" may have suggested his "Nina." He was also acquainted with Geoffrey of Monmouth and possibly with some of the later chronicles from which he may have had (if he did not, as seems most likely, simply invent it for himself) the motif of Arthur's having conquered Egypt. The description of the storm, especially lines 47–48, seems to have been adapted from Sir T. Herbert's *Discription of the Persian Monarchy or a Relation of Some yeares Travaile begunne Anno 1626 into Afrique etc.* (see E. de Selincourt [ed.], *The Poetical Works of William Wordsworth* [5 vols.; Oxford, 1940–1949], III, 502 n.).

65. MacCallum's view that the poem is "an allegory of the power of purity" (*Idylls of the King and Arthurian Story,* p. 212) ignores, it seems to me, practically the entire action of the poem, and is moreover not really responsive to the moralizing song of the angels which Wordsworth tacked on to the end of the poem. For an unconvincing attempt to relate the poem to the Annette Vallon affair, see Donald Hayden's psychologizing *After Conflict, Quiet: A Study of Wordsworth's Poetry in Relation to His Life and Letters* (New York, 1951), p. 202.

66. "Mechanist" is here a key word. Of the two senses of the term listed by *Webster's New International Dictionary* (2nd ed., unabridged), the first, "a maker of machines; one skilled in mechanics," is inapplicable. The second, "one who regards the phenomena of nature as the effects of forces merely mechanical," fits both the poem and Wordsworth's notions perfectly.

67. In the Fenwick notes (dictated in 1843) Wordsworth observed that

the poem "rose out of a few words casually used in conversation by my nephew Henry Hutchinson. He was describing with great spirit the appearance and movement of a vessel which he seemed to admire more than any other he had ever seen, and said her name was the 'Water Lily.' This plant has been my delight from boyhood, as I have seen it floating on the lake; and that conversation put me upon constructing and composing the poem. Had I not heard those words it would never have been written." That the poem was not the result of deliberate planning is suggested by his comment on the stanza form as being "perhaps not well suited to narrative, and certainly [it] would not have been trusted to had I thought at the beginning that the poem would have gone to such length" (quoted to E. de Selincourt [ed.], *Poetical Works of William Wordsworth*, III, 502 n.). Cf. n. 62 above. How important the ship was to him in the poem may be judged from his assignment of its name to the subtitle: "The Romance of the Water Lily."

68. Wordsworth, *Poetical Works*, p. 369. The sculpture that impressed itself so deeply on Wordsworth's imagination was probably the remarkably beautiful Augustan portrait bust, which formerly was called "Isis" or "Clytie" and which has been supposed to be possibly a portrait of Mark Antony's daughter Antonia. See A. H. Smith, *A Catalogue of Sculpture in the Department of Greek and Roman Antiquities, British Museum* (3 vols.; London, 1892–1904), III, 147–49 and Pl. XIV. For this identification I am indebted to my wife, Mira Merriman.

69. This distinction between classical calm and later anxiety seems to go back, at least in part, to Winckelmann.

70. The description of the ship as "to Christ devoted" does not contravene the interpretation of the ship as a symbol of the nonmoral instinctual life; the phrase means only, as Nina makes clear in an earlier declaration, that "on Christian service this frail Bark / Sailed . . . / Though on her prow a sign of heathen power / Was carved" (ll. 73–76). That Christian service performed by the old heathen ship was the carrying of the Maiden.

71. From the letter to Quillinan quoted earlier, n. 65 above.

72. For a rarely intelligent and sympathetic treatment of Wordsworth's religious attitudes, see Edith C. Batho, *The Later Wordsworth* (New York and Cambridge, 1933), pp. 234–311. Of course High Church is here to be understood in the high and dry eighteenth-century sense, rather than in terms of the liturgical enthusiasms of the later High Church of the Victorians.

73. For Heber's life see Mrs. Amelia Heber, *The Life of Reginald Heber, D.D., Lord Bishop of Calcutta* (2 vols.; New York, 1830) and Arthur Montefiore, *Reginald Heber, Bishop of Calcutta, Scholar and Evangelist* (New York, Chicago, and Toronto, n.d.), largely based on Mrs. Heber's *Life*.

74. Amelia Heber, *Life of Reginald Heber*, I, 323. See also I, 8 and 20 for other evidences of Heber's affection for earlier literature.

75. One version of this fragmentary poem is printed by Amelia Heber in the *Life* (I, 324–27). A slightly different version with a completion was later

printed in a limited edition of thirty copies: *The Lay of The Purple Falcon: Now First Printed from the Original Manuscript, in the Possession of the Hon. Robert Curzon* (London, 1847). Of the four cantos in this edition, only the first and a part of the second were written by "Reginaldus Episcopus C——" (*ibid.*, p. iii). The completion was supplied by Curzon (see *DNB*, s.v. "Curzon, Robert, fourteenth Baron Zouche [or de la Zouche] of Harringworth").

76. The fragment seems to have been first published in 1830 by Amelia Heber, *Life of Reginald Heber*, II, 485–525. In 1841 it appeared in a collected edition of Heber's *Poetical Works*. In my quotations from the poem (cited parenthetically by canto and stanza numbers in my text) I follow the text of *The Poetical Works of Reginald Heber, Late Lord Bishop of Calcutta* (Philadelphia, 1859). Mrs. Heber (*Life of Reginald Heber*, I, 353) appears to be responsible for the assignment of the beginning of the poem to 1812, but a reference in a letter of 1810 to a "poem, which . . . will be longer than any of my preceding ones" (*ibid.*, I, 347), suggests the possibility of 1810 as the date for the poem's commencement. By June of 1812 at least one canto had been finished (*ibid.*, I, 357). Before he finally abandoned the poem sometime between 1815 when he was still at work on it and 1819 when he sadly noted he had given it up (*ibid.*, I, 404, 476), he had completed a first canto of fifty-six Spenserian stanzas, a second of sixty-one, and an unfinished third of forty-two.

77. The notes to the poem supplied by Mrs. Heber (*ibid.*, II, 571–72) include illustrations from a "Hist. of Prince Arthur," but whether this was the 1634 edition or one of the 1816 editions is uncertain. At any rate Heber could not have used the latter when he began the poem between 1810 and 1812. He may have borrowed a Malory from his half-brother Richard, whose library may have already included one or both of the early editions of Malory that it contained at his death in 1833 (see my chap. 5, n. 70).

78. For the motif of the hind, see Malory, Book III, ch. 5 ff. Heber adds the hind's flight to Ganora for protection. He also alters the Balin story: in Malory, after Balin has drawn the sword, he rudely refuses the maiden's request to return it and rides off alone; in Heber's poem the damsel and Balin go off together on the best of terms.

79. See [P. J. Baptiste] Le Grand [d'Aussy], *Fabliaux or Tales, Abridged from French Manuscripts of the XIIth and XIIIth Centuries*, trans. G. L. Way, notes by G. Ellis (New ed., 3 vols.; London, 1815), I, 198.

80. The description of Merlin's battle banner (III, xxiii) is derived from Ellis' abstract of the Auchinleck MS *Merlin* (George Ellis [ed.], *Specimens of Early English Metrical Romances* [2nd ed., 3 vols.; London, 1811], I, 283). The *enfance* of Lancelot (III, xxxvi–xl) is based on Ellis' account of one of the French *Lancelots* (*ibid.*, I, 325–26).

81. Amelia Heber, *Life of Reginald Heber*, I, 476. Other evidences of epic intention are to be found in the opening *in medias res*, the marking of the

passage of time by descriptions of the coming of morning, the catalogue of the amusements at Carduel, and the frequent extended similes, often doubled.

82. In view of the poem's unfinished state, this may seem an over-confident assertion, but there is some positive evidence to support it. In eliminating Arthur's incestuous fathering of Modred and in making Arthur's guilt the result of the much less heinous killing of his sister's seducer, Heber probably envisioned an Arthur about whose origins there was no mystery. Again the description of Morgue as "Uther's child" (II, xiv) seems to indicate that the mysterious birth of Arthur played no part in his plans.

83. The fact that the Grail is on such everyday, unceremonious display indicates that its spiritual significance had largely escaped Heber. But his description of it suggests that he had plans for its use later in the poem:

". . . that gracious implement
      Of heavenly love, the three-times hallow'd Grayle
To Britain's realm awhile in mercy lent,
Till sin defiled the land, and lust incontinent" (III, xv).

84. The focus on Ganora is established early in the poem by Heber's injunction to the modern lady who reads his story to remember that "Fair was her face as thine, her heart as warm, / Whose antique story marks my simple page; / Yet luckless youth was hers, and sorrowful old age" (I, iv).

85. In a letter of June 10, 1812, he had ominously remarked, "King Arthur has made pretty considerable progress in another canto, which is to be much fuller of moralization than the former" (Amelia Heber, *Life of Reginald Heber*, I, 357).

86. This anxiety for archaeological accuracy is best illustrated by the point-blank assertion that "antique times were rude and homely all; / And ill might Arthur's nuptial banquet vie" with modern feasts (I, xxi).

87. For Heber's Neo-Classicist manner, consider the second stanza of the first canto:

"Say, can the silken bed refreshment bring,
      When from the restless spirit sleep retires?
Or, the sharp fever of the serpent's sting,
      Pains it less shrewdly for his burnish'd spires?
      Oh, worthless is the bliss the world admires,
And helpless whom the vulgar mightiest deem:
      Tasteless fruition, impotent desires,
Pomp, pleasure, pride, how valueless ye seem
When the poor soul awakes, and finds its life a dream!"

The Miltonic echoes hang most thickly around the evil Morgue, who seems to have more than a little of the Satan of *Paradise Lost* in her makeup. Her moment of remorse when she gazes on the sleeping king and queen (II, vi–vii) strongly suggests Satan's emotions in Eden under similar circumstances. Musing on the defeat of her evil plans by Merlin's magic, she asks, "What yet remains?—to blast with mutter'd spell / The budding promise" (II, xi). Later she flies with "slope flight" through the heavens (II, xiv), and boasts that nothing "can tame my steadfast will. All, Modred, is not lost!" (II, xx), and still later she declares that "to delude / The force we cannot stem is triumph still, / And from reluctant fate t'extort our good or ill" (II, xxxii).

88. Amelia Heber, *Life of Reginald Heber*, I, 476.

89. First printed in 1830, *ibid.*, I, 425–34. Also printed in the 1841 *Poetical Works*. My quotations are taken from the text in Reginald Heber, *Poetical Works* (1859).

90. Summarized by Ellis in his *Specimens of Early English Metrical Romances*; see esp. I, 77. The association of Merlin with demonic powers is commonplace, but it is developed with particular emphasis in Ellis' summaries.

91. Amelia Heber, *Life of Reginald Heber*, I, 425. In Chaucer the hero of the episode is nameless, and he is out to save his own neck. Chaucer also cleverly relates the return of the wife's beauty to the husband's granting her just what she has told him women most desire—full domination. In Percy's version, Gawain is specified by name, and he seeks the answer to save another man (in this case, Arthur). The device of an evil spell that Gawain releases accidentally by the kiss and the sign of the cross appears to be Heber's addition from some other source.

92. Cf. MacCallum, *Idylls of the King and Arthurian Story*, pp. 202–3. MacCallum suggests that this antiquarian impulse accounts for the popularity of the Welsh materials at this time, since they, presumably, were closer to the actual historical and topographical facts.

93. Ernest Renan, *Ethical and Critical Essays* (1859), quoted by Emery Neff, *The Poetry of History* (New York, 1947), p. 161.

94. *Essay on Chivalry*, first published in the *Encyclopaedia Britannica* in 1814. Quoted by F. J. C. Hearnshaw, "Chivalry and Its Place in History," *Chivalry: A Series of Studies to Illustrate Its Historical Significance and Civilizing Influence*, ed. Edgar Prestage (London, 1928), pp. 29–30.

95. Cf. Hearnshaw, "Chivalry," p. 29.

96. Quoted by Hearnshaw, *ibid.*, p. 30.

97. Halévy, *English People*, II, 175. Canning's reversal in Commons in 1823 of Burke's lament would have been but one more evidence for the young followers of Digby that Lord Grey was right in thinking Canning "no gentleman" (Watson, *Reign of George III*, p. 445).

98. G[eorgiana] B[urne]-J[ones], *Memorials of Edward Burne-Jones* (2 vols.; London, 1906), II, 56.

99. The assumptions that underlay the administration of pre-Industrial England are admirably summarized by Watson, *Reign of George III*, pp. 36–66. For the dominance of the plutocracy in the nineteenth century, see Halévy, *English People*, I, 167.

100. Quoted by Halévy, *English People*, I, 192.

101. *Ibid.*, I, 15 and 425.

102. *Ibid.*, I, 5.

103. *Ibid.,* I, 196.

104. The history of the idea of the gentleman is extraordinarily confused. For a brief survey of the development and the conflicting definitions of the idea, see A. W. Reed, "Chivalry and the Idea of a Gentleman," in *Chivalry,* ed. Prestage.

105. Ernest Bernbaum, *Guide Through the Romantic Movement* (2nd ed.; New York, 1949), p. 304.

Bibliography

Abercrombie, Lascelles. *Romanticism*. London: Martin Secker, 1926.

Ackerman, Robert W. Review of R. W. Barber's *Arthur of Albion*. *College English*, 23 (1962), 512.

Addison, Joseph. *The Works of the Late Right Honorable Joseph Addison, Esq.* 4 vols. Birmingham: Printed by John Baskerville, for J. and R. Tonson, 1761.

Alford, Henry. "The Idylls of the King," *Contemporary Review*, 13 (1870), 104–25.

Allen, B. Sprague. *Tides in English Taste (1619–1800): A Background for the Study of Literature*. 2 vols. Cambridge, Mass.: Harvard University Press, 1937.

Andreas Capellanus. *The Art of Courtly Love*. Translated with an introduction by John Jay Parry. (Records of Civilization: Sources and Studies, No. 33.) New York: Columbia University Press, 1941.

Anglo, Sydney. "The *British History* in Early Tudor Propaganda," *Bulletin of the John Rylands Library*, 44 (1961), 17–48.

App, August J. *Lancelot in English Literature: His Rôle and Character*. Washington: Catholic University of America, 1929.

Ariail, James Milton. "Some Immediate English Influences upon Spenser's *Faerie Queene*, Books I–III" [abstract of an unpublished doctoral dissertation], *The University of North Carolina Record*, No. 226 (1925), 42–44.

Armstrong, William A. "Elizabethan Themes in *The Misfortunes of Arthur*," *Review of English Studies*, NS 7 (1956), 238–49.

Arnold, Matthew. *The Study of Celtic Literature*. Edited by Alfred Nutt. [London]: David Nutt, 1910.

Baldwin, Dane Lewis, *et al*. *A Concordance to the Poems of John Keats*. Washington: The Carnegie Institution of Washington, 1917.

Barber, R. W. *Arthur of Albion: An Introduction to the Arthurian Literature and Legends of England*. London: Barrie and Rockliff with Pall Mall Press, 1961.

Batho, Edith C. *The Later Wordsworth*. New York: The Macmillan Company; Cambridge, Eng.: At the University Press, 1933.

271

Baugh, Albert C., *et al. A Literary History of England.* Edited by Albert C. Baugh. New York and London: Appleton-Century-Crofts, Inc., 1948.

Bayley, John. *The Romantic Survival: A Study in Poetic Evolution.* London: Constable, 1957.

Bennett, J. A. W. (ed.). *Essays on Malory.* Oxford: Clarendon Press, 1963.

————. Review of *The Works of Sir Thomas Malory,* ed. Eugène Vinaver (1947). *Review of English Studies,* 25 (1949), 161–67.

Bennett, Josephine Waters. *The Evolution of "The Faerie Queene."* Chicago: University of Chicago Press, 1942.

Bensel, Elise Francisca Wilhelmina Maria Van Der Ven-Ten. *The Character of King Arthur in English Literature.* Amsterdam: H. J. Paris, 1925.

Benton, John F. "The Court of Champagne as a Literary Center," *Speculum,* 36 (1961), 551–91.

Bernbaum, Ernest. *Guide Through the Romantic Movement.* 2d ed. revised and enlarged. New York: The Ronald Press Company, 1949.

Bibliotheca Heberiana: Catalogue of the Library of the Late Richard Heber, Esq. 5 pts. [London]: Sotheby and Son, 1834–1835.

Black, J. B. *The Art of History: A Study of Four Great Historians of the Eighteenth Century.* London: Methuen & Co. Ltd., 1926.

Blackmore, Richard. *Prince Arthur: An Heroick Poem, in Ten Books.* 3d ed. corrected. London: Printed for Awnsham and John Churchil at the Black Swan in Pater-Noster-Row, 1696.

————. *King Arthur: An Heroick Poem, in Twelve Books.* London: Printed for Awnsham and John Churchil at the Black Swan in Pater-Noster-Row, and Jacob Tonson at the Judges Head near the Inner-Temple-gate in Fleet-street, 1697.

Blake, William. *The Complete Writings of William Blake with All the Variant Readings.* Edited by Geoffrey Keynes. London: The Nonesuch Press, 1957.

Bodkin, Maud. *Archetypal Patterns in Poetry: Psychological Studies of Imagination.* New York: Vintage Books, 1958.

Boys, Richard C. *Sir Richard Blackmore and the Wits: A Study of "Commendatory Verses on the Author of the Two Arthurs and the Satyr against Wit" (1700).* (University of Michigan Contributions in Modern Philology, No. 13.) Ann Arbor: The University of Michigan Press, 1949.

Brewer, D. S. "Form in the *Morte Darthur,*" *Medium Ævum,* 21 (1952), 14–24.

————. Review of Eugène Vinaver's ed. of *The Tale of the Death of King Arthur* and R. M. Lumiansky's "The Question of Unity in Malory's *Morte Darthur.*" *Medium Ævum,* 25 (1956), 22–26.

————. Review of Charles Moorman's *The Book of Kyng Arthur. Modern Language Review,* 62 (1967), 109.

Brewster, Dorothy. *Aaron Hill: Poet, Dramatist, Projector.* (Columbia University Studies in English and Comparative Literature, No. 45.) New York: Columbia University Press, 1913.

Brinkley, Roberta Florence. *Arthurian Legend in the Seventeenth Century.* (Johns Hopkins Monographs in Literary History, Vol. III.) Baltimore: The Johns Hopkins Press; London: Humphrey Milford, Oxford University Press, 1932.

Bronson, Bertrand H. *Joseph Ritson: Scholar-at-Arms.* 2 vols. Berkeley: University of California Press, 1938.

Brown, Paul A. "The Arthurian Legends: Supplement to Northup and Parry's Annotated Bibliography," *Journal of English and Germanic Philology*, 49 (1950), 208-13.

Bruce, James Douglas. *The Evolution of Arthurian Romance from the Beginnings Down to the Year 1300.* (*Hesperia*, "Ergänzungsreihe: Schriften zur englischen Philologie," Hefte VIII–IX.) 2 vols. Göttingen: Vandenboeck & Ruprecht; Baltimore: The Johns Hopkins Press, 1923.

Bulletin Bibliographique de la Société Internationale Arthurienne: Bibliographical Bulletin of the International Arthurian Society. Issued annually since 1949. Beginning with vol. 19 (1967), title changed to *Bibliographical Bulletin of the International Arthurian Society: Bulletin Bibliographique de la Société Internationale Arthurienne.* Vols. 1–18 edited by Jean Frappier; thereafter by Lewis Thorpe.

Burke, Edmund. *Reflections on the French Revolution.* Everyman's Library, No. 460. London: J. M. Dent & Sons Ltd.; New York: E. P. Dutton & Co. Inc., 1910.

B[urne]-J[ones], G[eorgiana]. *Memorials of Edward Burne-Jones.* 2 vols. London: Macmillan and Co. Limited, 1906.

Campbell, Olwen W. *Thomas Love Peacock.* The English Novelists. London: Arthur Barker Ltd., 1953.

Campbell, Oscar James (ed.). *The Living Shakespeare.* New York: The Macmillan Company, 1949.

Carlyle, Thomas. *Critical and Miscellaneous Essays.* 3 vols. London: Chapman and Hall, n.d.

————. *The Works of Thomas Carlyle.* Centenary Edition. 30 vols. London: Chapman and Hall Limited, 1897–1899.

Caspari, Fritz. *Humanism and the Social Order in Tudor England.* Chicago: The University of Chicago Press, 1954.

Chambers, E. K. *Arthur of Britain.* London: Sidgwick & Jackson, Ltd., 1927.

————. *English Literature at the Close of the Middle Ages.* Oxford History of English Literature, Vol. II, Pt. 2. Oxford: At the Clarendon Press, 1945.

Chandler, Alice. "The Quarrel of the Ancients and Moderns: Peacock and the Medieval Revival," *Bucknell Review*, 13, No. 3 (1965), 39–50.

————. "Sir Walter Scott and the Medieval Revival," *Nineteenth-Century Fiction*, 19 (1965), 315–32.

Chester, Robert. *Robert Chester's Loves Martyr, or, Rosalins Complaint.* Edited by the Rev. Alexander B. Grosart. New Shakespere Society, Series VIII, Miscellanies, No. 2. London, 1878.

Child, Harold H. "Michael Drayton," *The Cambridge History of English Literature.* Edited by A. W. Ward and A. R. Waller. 15 vols. New York: The Macmillan Company; Cambridge, Eng.: At the University Press, 1939. IV, 193–224.

Clark, Kenneth. *The Gothic Revival: An Essay in the History of Taste.* Revised and enlarged ed. London: Constable, 1950.

Cook, Albert S. (ed.). *A Concordance to the English Poems of Thomas Gray.* Boston: Houghton Mifflin Company, 1908.

Cooper, Lane. *A Concordance to the Poems of William Wordsworth.* Edited for The Concordance Society. London: Smith, Elder and Co., 1911.

Craig, Hardin (ed.). *The Complete Works of Shakespeare.* Chicago: Scott, Foresman and Company, 1951.

Crane, Ronald S. *The Vogue of Medieval Chivalric Romance During the English Renaissance.* Menasha, Wis.: The Collegiate Press, George Banta Publishing Company, 1919.

Cross, Tom Peete, and Nitze, William A. *Lancelot and Guenevere: A Study on the Origins of Courtly Love.* Modern Philology Monographs of the University of Chicago. Chicago: The University of Chicago Press, 1930.

Cross, Wilbur L. *The History of Henry Fielding.* 3 vols. New Haven: Yale University Press, 1918.

Cruse, Amy. *The Victorians and Their Books.* London: George Allen & Unwin Ltd., 1935.

Cunliffe, John W. (ed.). *Early English Classical Tragedies.* Oxford: At the Clarendon Press, 1912.

Curdy, A. E. "Arthurian Literature," *Romanic Review,* 1 (1910), 125–39, 265–78.

Cushing, William. *Anonyms: A Dictionary of Revealed Authorship.* Cambridge, Mass.: William Cushing, 1890.

———. *Initials and Pseudonyms: A Dictionary of Literary Disguises.* London: Sampson Low, Marston, Searle & Rivington, 1886.

Davies, R. T. Review of R. W. Barber's *Arthur of Albion. Review of English Studies,* NS 13 (1962), 399–400.

———. Review of Charles Moorman's *The Book of Kyng Arthur. Review of English Studies,* NS 17 (1966), 428–30.

Davis, B. E. C. *Edmund Spenser: A Critical Study.* Cambridge, Eng.: At the University Press, 1933.

Davis, Gilbert R. "Malory's 'Tale of Sir Lancelot' and the Question of Unity in the *Morte Darthur,*" *Papers of the Michigan Academy of Science, Arts, and Letters,* 49 (1964), 523–30.

Defoe, Daniel. *A Journal of the Plague Year.* Everyman's Library, No. 289.

London: J. M. Dent & Sons Ltd.; New York: E. P. Dutton & Co. Inc., 1943.

Deloney, Thomas. *The Works of Thomas Deloney.* Edited by Francis Oscar Mann. Oxford: Clarendon Press, 1912.

Dennis, Leah. "The Text of the Percy-Warton Letters," *PMLA,* 46 (1931), 1166–1201.

"Dialogue Between John Dryden & Henry Purcell, in the Year 1691, on the Subject of Their Forthcoming 'Dramatick Opera of *King Arthur,*'" *Fraser's Magazine,* 45 (1852), 196–200.

Dichmann, Mary E. "Characterization in Malory's *Tale of Arthur and Lucius,*" *PMLA,* 65 (1950), 877–95.

Digby, Kenelm Henry. *The Broad Stone of Honour: or The True Sense and Practice of Chivalry.* 4 vols. as follows: [Vol. I], *Godefridus.* London: Edward Lumley, 1844. [Vol. II], *Tancredus.* London: Edward Lumley, 1846. [Vol. III], *Morus.* London: Edward Lumley, 1848. Vol. IV, *Orlandus.* London: Sold by Joseph Booker, 1829.

———. *Morus.* London: Sold by Longman, Rees, Orme, Brown, & Green, 1826.

Drayton, Michael. *The Works of Michael Drayton.* Edited by J. William Hebel. Tercentenary Edition. 5 vols. Oxford: Printed at the Shakespeare Head Press & Published for the Press by Basil Blackwell, 1931–1941.

Dryden, John. *Dryden: The Dramatic Works.* Edited by Montague Summers. 6 vols. London: The Nonesuch Press, 1931–1932.

———. *The Poetical Works of John Dryden.* Edited by George R. Noyes. The Cambridge Poets. Boston and New York: Houghton Mifflin Company, 1909.

———. *The Works of John Dryden.* Edited by Sir Walter Scott, revised by George Saintsbury. 18 vols. Edinburgh: William Paterson, 1882–1893.

Dilke, O. A. W. "Thomas Hughes, Plagiarist," *Notes and Queries,* NS 10 (1963), 93–94.

Ditmas, E. M. R. "King Arthur in Literature," *Books,* No. 331 (1960), 159–64.

Dunlop, John. *The History of Fiction: Being a Critical Account of the Most Celebrated Prose Works of Fiction from the Earliest Greek Romances to the Novels of the Present Age.* 3d ed. London: Longman, Brown, Green, and Longmans, 1845.

Edelman, Nathan. *Attitudes of Seventeenth-Century France toward the Middle Ages.* New York: King's Crown Press, 1946.

Ehrentreich, Alfred. "Tristan und Isolde in der neueren englischen Literatur," *Englische Studien,* 49 (1934), 220–36.

Ellis, F. S. *A Lexical Concordance to the Poetical Works of Percy Bysshe Shelley.* London: Bernard Quaritch, 1892.

Ellis, George (ed.). *Specimens of Early English Metrical Romances.* 2d ed. 3 vols. London: Longman, Hurst, Rees, Orme, and Brown, 1811.

———— (ed.). *Specimens of the Early English Poets, to Which is Prefixed an Historical Sketch of the Rise and Progress of the English Poetry and Language.* 3 vols. London: Printed by W. Bulmer and Co. for G. and W. Nicol . . . and J. Wright, 1801.

[Elyot, Thomas]. *Bibliotheca Eliotae: Eliotis Librarie.* N.p.: n. pub., 1548.

Erskine, John. *The Delight of Great Books.* Indianapolis: Bobbs-Merrill Company, 1928.

Evans, B. Ifor. *Tradition and Romanticism: Studies in English Poetry from Chaucer to W. B. Yeats.* London: Methuen & Co. Ltd., 1940.

Evans, Evan (trans. and ed.). *Some Specimens of the Poetry of the Antient Welsh Bards.* London: Printed for R. and J. Dodsley in Pall-Mall, 1764.

Fairchild, Hoxie Neale. *The Romantic Quest.* New York: Columbia University Press, 1931.

Ferguson, Arthur B. *The Indian Summer of English Chivalry: Studies in the Decline and Transformation of Chivalric Idealism.* Durham: Duke University Press, 1960.

Fielding, Henry. *The Works of Henry Fielding, Esq.* Edited by Leslie Stephen. 10 vols. London: Smith, Elder, & Co., 1882.

Firth, Sir Charles. "Milton as an Historian," *Essays Historical and Literary.* Oxford: The Clarendon Press, 1938. Pp. 61–102.

Fletcher, Robert Huntington. *The Arthurian Material in the Chronicles.* New York: Burt Franklin, 1958. (Originally published as Vol. X of [Harvard] Studies and Notes in Philology and Literature, Boston, 1906.)

Foakes, R. A. *The Romantic Assertion: A Study in the Language of Nineteenth Century Poetry.* New Haven: Yale University Press, 1958.

French, J. Milton. "Milton as a Historian," *PMLA*, 50 (1935), 469–79.

————. "Milton's Annotated Copy of Gildas," *Harvard Studies and Notes in Philology and Literature*, 20 (1938), 75–80.

Frere, John Hookham. *The Monks and the Giants.* Edited with notes and introduction by R. D. Waller. (Publications of the University of Manchester, No. CLXXII, English Series No. XIV.) Manchester: The University Press, 1926.

————. *Prospectus and Specimen of an Intended National Work, by William and Robert Whistlecraft, of Stow-Market, in Suffolk, Harness and Collarmakers, Intended to Comprise the Most Interesting Particulars Relating to King Arthur and His Round Table.* 2d ed. London: John Murray, 1818.

————. *The Works of the Right Honourable John Hookham Frere in Verse and Prose.* Edited by W. E. Frere with a memoir by Sir Bartle Frere. 2d ed. revised with additions. 3 vols. London: Basil Montagu Pickering, 1874.

Friedman, Albert B. *The Ballad Revival: Studies in the Influence of Popular on Sophisticated Poetry.* Chicago: The University of Chicago Press, 1961.

————. "The First Draft of Percy's *Reliques*," *PMLA*, 69 (1954), 1233–49.

Frye, Northrop. *Fearful Symmetry: A Study of William Blake.* Princeton: Princeton University Press, 1947.

———. "Towards Defining an Age of Sensibility," *ELH*, 23 (1956), 144–52.

Gallon, David. "Thomas Love Peacock and Wales: Some Suggestions," *Anglo-Welsh Review*, 17 (1968), 125–34.

[Genest, John]. *Some Account of the English Stage from the Restoration in 1660 to 1830.* 10 vols. Bath: Printed by H. E. Carrington, Sold by Thomas Rodd, 1832.

Geoffrey of Monmouth. *The Historia Regum Britanniae of Geoffrey of Monmouth with Contributions to the Study of Its Place in Early British History.* Edited by Acton Griscom. London, New York, and Toronto: Longmans, Green and Co., 1929.

———. *Histories of the Kings of Britain.* Translated by Sebastian Evans. Everyman's Library, No. 577. London: J. M. Dent & Sons, Ltd.; New York: E. P. Dutton & Co., Inc., 1912.

———. *The History of the Kings of Britain.* Translated with an introduction by Lewis Thorpe. The Penguin Classics, No. L170. Baltimore: Penguin Books, 1966.

Gilbert, Allan H. *Literary Criticism: Plato to Dryden.* New York: American Book Company, 1940.

Gilbert, Vedder M. "An Early Return to Chivalry in the Eighteenth Century," *Notes and Queries*, 200 (1955), 433–36.

———. "Thomas Edwards as the Wooden Inigo," *Notes and Queries*, 200 (1955), 532–35.

Goldman, Marcus Selden. *Sir Philip Sidney and the Arcadia.* (Illinois Studies in Language and Literature, Vol. XVII, Nos. 1–2.) Urbana: University of Illinois, 1934–1935.

Golther, Wolfgang. *Parzival und der Gral in der Dichtung des Mittelalters und der Neuzeit.* Stuttgart: J. B. Metzlersche Verlagsbuchhandlung, 1925.

———. *Tristan und Isolde in den Dichtungen des Mittelalters und der neuen Zeit.* Leipzig: Verlag von s. Hirzel, 1907.

Gooch, G. P. *History and Historians in the Nineteenth Century.* 2d ed. London: Longmans, Green and Co., 1935.

Gourvitch, I. "Drayton's Debt to Geoffrey of Monmouth," *Review of English Studies*, 4 (1928), 394–403.

Gray, Thomas. *The Works of Thomas Gray in Prose and Verse.* Edited by Edmund Gosse. Revised ed. 4 vols. London: Macmillan and Co., Limited, 1912.

Grebanier, Bernard. *The Great Shakespeare Forgery.* New York: Norton; London: Heinemann, 1965.

Greene, Richard Leighton. Review of *Malory's Originality*, ed. R. M. Lumiansky. *Journal of English and Germanic Philology*, 66 (1967), 120–24.

Greenlaw, Edwin. *Studies in Spenser's Historical Allegory.* (Johns Hopkins

Monographs in Literary History, Vol. II.) Baltimore: The Johns Hopkins Press; London: Humphrey Milford, Oxford University Press, 1932.

Grennan, Margaret Rose. *William Morris: Medievalist and Revolutionary.* New York: King's Crown Press, 1945.

Grierson, Sir Herbert. *The Background of English Literature, Classical & Romantic, and Other Collected Essays and Addresses.* 2d ed. London: Chatto and Windus, 1950.

————. *Sir Walter Scott, Bart.: A New Life Supplementary to, and Corrective of, Lockhart's Biography.* London: Constable & Co. Ltd., 1938.

Gurteen, S. Humphreys. *The Arthurian Epic: A Comparative Study of the Cambrian, Breton, and Anglo-Norman Versions of the Story and Tennyson's Idylls of the King.* New York and London: G. P. Putnam's Sons, 1895.

Gutbier, Elisabeth. *Psychologisch-ästhetische Studien zu Tristandichtungen der neueren englischen Literatur.* Erlangen: Karl Döres, 1932.

Halévy, Elie. *A History of the English People in the Nineteenth Century.* Translated by E. I. Watkin and D. A. Barker. 2d ed. revised. 6 vols. London: Ernest Benn Limited, 1949–1952.

Halperin, Maurice. *Le roman de Tristan et Iseut dans la littérature anglo-américaine au XIX*e *et XX*e *siècles.* Paris: Jouve et Cie., 1931.

Hanford, James Holly. "The Chronology of Milton's Private Studies," *PMLA,* 36 (1921), 251–314.

————. *A Milton Handbook.* 3d ed. New York: F. S. Crofts & Co., 1944.

Hardy, Irene. "Browning's 'Childe Roland,' a Literary Parallel—and Something More," *Poet Lore,* 24 (1913), 53–58.

Harper, Carrie A. *The Sources of the British Chronicle History in Spenser's Faerie Queene.* Philadelphia: Bryn Mawr, 1910.

Harrison, G. B. (ed.). *Major British Writers.* Enlarged ed. 2 vols. New York: Harcourt, Brace and Company, 1959.

Hartshorne, Charles Henry (ed.). *Ancient Metrical Tales.* London: William Pickering, 1829.

Havens, Raymond D. "Thomas Warton and the Eighteenth-Century Dilemma," *Studies in Philology,* 25 (1928), 36–50.

Hay, Denys. *Polydore Vergil: Renaissance Historian and Man of Letters.* Oxford: At the Clarendon Press, 1952.

Hayden, Donald E. *After Conflict, Quiet: A Study of Wordsworth's Poetry in Relation to His Life and Letters.* New York: Exposition Press, 1951.

Hearnshaw, F. J. C. "Chivalry and Its Place in History," *Chivalry: A Series of Studies to Illustrate Its Historical Significance and Civilizing Influence.* Edited by Edgar Prestage. London: Kegan Paul, Trench, Trubner & Co., Ltd., 1928. Pp. 1–35.

Heber, Amelia. *The Life of Reginald Heber, D.D., Lord Bishop of Calcutta.* 2 vols. New York: Protestant Episcopal Press, 1830.

Heber, Reginald. *The Poetical Works of Reginald Heber, Late Lord Bishop of Calcutta.* Philadelphia: E. H. Butler & Co., 1859.

[Heber, Reginald, and Curzon, Robert]. *The Lay of the Purple Falcon: A Metrical Romance, Now First Printed from the Original Manuscript, in the Possession of the Hon. Robert Curzon.* London: Printed by William Nicol, Shakspeare Press, 1847.

Henslowe, Philip. *Henslowe's Diary.* Edited by R. A. Foakes and R. T. Rickert. Cambridge, Eng.: At the University Press, 1961.

———. *Henslowe's Diary.* Edited by Walter W. Greg. 2 vols. London: A. H. Bullen, 1904–1908.

Hill, Aaron. *The Dramatic Works of Aaron Hill, Esq.* 2 vols. London: Printed for T. Lownds, 1760.

Hilton, William. *The Poetical Works of William Hilton.* 2 vols. as follows: Vol. I, New Castle upon Tyne: Printed by Angus and Robson, 1775; Vol. II, Newcastle upon Tyne: Printed by T. Saint, 1776.

Hirsch, E. D., Jr. *Validity in Interpretation.* New Haven and London: Yale University Press, 1967.

Hole, Richard. *Arthur: or, The Northern Enchantment, A Poetical Romance in Seven Books.* London: Printed for G. G. J. and J. Robinson in Paternoster Row, 1789.

Hopkins, Annette B. "Ritson's Life of King Arthur," *PMLA*, 43 (1928), 251–87.

Hughes, Merritt Y. "The Arthurs of *The Faerie Queene*," *Études Anglaises*, 6 (1953), 193–213.

Huizinga, J. *The Waning of the Middle Ages: A Study of the Forms of Life, Thought and Art in France and the Netherlands in the XIVth and XVth Centuries.* Translated by F. Hopman. London: Edward Arnold & Co., 1952.

Hungerford, Edward B. *Shores of Darkness.* New York: Columbia University Press, 1941.

Hurd, Richard. *Hurd's Letters on Chivalry and Romance.* Edited by Edith J. Morley. London: Henry Frowde, 1911.

———. *Letters on Chivalry and Romance.* Edited by Hoyt Trowbridge. The Augustan Reprint Society, No. 101–102. Los Angeles: William Andrews Clark Memorial Library, University of California, 1963.

Ireland, William Henry. *Vortigern: An Historical Play.* London: Joseph Thomas, 1832.

Jackson, W. T. H. "The *De Amore* of Andreas Capellanus and the Practice of Love at Court," *Romanic Review*, 49 (1958), 243–51.

———. *The Literature of the Middle Ages.* New York: Columbia University Press, 1960.

Johnson, Samuel. *Johnson: Prose and Poetry.* Edited by Mona Wilson. London: Rupert Hart-Davis, 1950.

———. *Lives of the English Poets.* Everyman's Library, Nos. 770–71. 2 vols. London: J. M. Dent & Sons Ltd.; New York: E. P. Dutton & Co. Inc., 1941.

Johnston, Arthur. *Enchanted Ground: The Study of Medieval Romance in the Eighteenth Century*. London: University of London, Athlone Press, 1964.

Jones, David. "The Myth of Arthur," *For Hilaire Belloc: Essays in Honour of His 72nd Birthday*. Edited by Douglas Woodruff. London: Sheed & Ward, 1942. Pp. 174–214.

Jones, Putnam Fennell. "Milton and the Epic Subject from British History," *PMLA*, 42 (1927), 901–909.

Jones, W. Lewis. "Geoffrey of Monmouth and the Legend of Arthur," *Quarterly Review*, 205 (1906), 54–78.

————. *King Arthur in History and Legend*. The Cambridge Manuals of Science and Literature. 2d ed. Cambridge, Eng.: Cambridge University Press, 1914.

Jonson, Ben. *Ben Jonson*. Edited by C. H. Herford and Percy Simpson. 11 vols. Oxford: At the Clarendon Press, 1925–1952.

Keats, John. *The Complete Works of John Keats*. Edited by H. Buxton Forman. 5 vols. Glasgow: Gowans & Gray, 1900–1901.

————. *The Letters of John Keats*. Edited by Maurice Buxton Forman. 4th ed. revised. London, New York, Toronto: Geoffrey Cumberlege, Oxford University Press, 1952.

————. *The Letters of John Keats: 1814–1821*. Edited by Hyder Edward Rollins. 2 vols. Cambridge, Mass.: Harvard University Press, 1958.

————. *The Poems of John Keats*. Edited with an introduction and notes by E. de Selincourt. 2d ed. revised. New York: Dodd, Mead & Co., 1909.

Kegel, Charles H. "Lord John Manners and the Young England Movement: Romanticism in Politics," *Western Political Quarterly*, 14 (1961), 691–97.

Kelso, Ruth. *The Doctrine of the English Gentleman in the Sixteenth Century*. (University of Illinois Studies in Language and Literature, Vol. XIV.) Urbana: University of Illinois Press, 1929.

Kendrick, T. D. *British Antiquity*. London: Methuen & Co., Ltd., 1950.

Ker, William Paton. *The Art of Poetry: Seven Lectures, 1920–1922*. Oxford: At the Clarendon Press, 1923.

————. "The Literary Influence of the Middle Ages," *The Cambridge History of English Literature*. Edited by A. W. Ward and A. R. Waller. 15 vols. New York: The Macmillan Company; Cambridge, Eng.: At the University Press, 1939. X, 245–73.

Kermode, Frank. *Romantic Image*. London: Routledge and Kegan Paul, 1957.

Kinghorn, A. M. "Warton's *History* and Early English Poetry," *English Studies*, 44 (1963), 197–204.

Klenke, Sister M. Amelia, O.P. "Some Mediaeval Concepts of King Arthur," *Kentucky Foreign Language Quarterly*, 5 (1958), 191–98.

Knight, Stephen. *The Structure of Sir Thomas Malory's Arthuriad*. (Australian Humanities Research Council Monographs, No. 14.) Sydney: Sydney University Press, 1969.

Kroeber, Karl. *Romantic Narrative Art.* Madison: The University of Wisconsin Press, 1960.

Laing, David (ed.). *Early Popular Poetry of Scotland and the Northern Border.* Re-arranged and revised with additions and a glossary by W. Carew Hazlitt. Library of Old Authors. 2 vols. London: Reeves and Turner, 1895.

———— (ed.). *Early Scottish Metrical Tales.* New ed. London: Hamilton, Adams & Co.; Glasgow: Thomas D. Morison, 1889.

———— (ed.). *Select Remains of the Ancient Popular and Romance Poetry of Scotland.* Re-edited with additions by John Small. Edinburgh and London: William Blackwood and Sons, 1885.

Laneham, Robert. *Robert Laneham's Letter: Describing a Part of the Entertainment unto Queen Elizabeth at the Castle of Kenilworth in 1575.* Edited by F. J. Furnivall. New York: Duffield & Company; London: Chatto & Windus, 1907.

Le Grand [d'Aussy], [P. J. Baptiste]. *Fabliaux or Tales, Abridged from French Manuscripts of the XIIth and XIIIth Centuries.* Translated by G. L. Way; preface, notes, and appendix by G. Ellis. New ed. corrected. 3 vols. London: Printed for J. Rodwell, 1815.

Levin, Harry. "Some Meanings of Myth," *Myth and Mythmaking.* Edited by Henry A. Murray. New York: George Braziller, 1960. Pp. 103–114.

Lewis, C. S. *The Allegory of Love: A Study in Medieval Tradition.* London: Oxford University Press, Geoffrey Cumberlege, 1938.

Leyden, John. *The Poetical Works of Dr. John Leyden.* With a "Life of John Leyden" by Tom Brown. London and Edinburgh: William P. Nimmo, 1875.

————. *Scenes of Infancy: Descriptive of Teviotdale.* 2d ed. Edinburgh: Printed by James Ballantyne and Co. for Longman, Hurst, Rees, Orme, and Brown, 1811.

Liss, Oskar. *Die Arthurepen des Sir Richard Blackmore.* Strassburg: Druck von M. DuMont Schauberg, 1911.

Lockhart, J. G. *The Life of Sir Walter Scott.* Everyman's Library, No. 55. London: J. M. Dent & Sons Ltd.; New York: E. P. Dutton & Co. Inc., 1937.

Logan, Sister Eugenia. *Concordance to the Poetry of Samuel Taylor Coleridge.* Saint Mary of the Woods, Indiana: Privately printed, 1940.

The London Stage: 1660–1800. Part 2: 1700–1729. Edited by Emmett L. Avery. 2 vols. *Part 3: 1729–1747.* Edited by Arthur H. Scouten. 2 vols. Carbondale: Southern Illinois University Press, 1960–1961.

Loomis, Roger Sherman (ed.). *Arthurian Literature in the Middle Ages: A Collaborative History.* Oxford: At the Clarendon Press, 1959.

————. *Celtic Myth and Arthurian Romance.* New York: Columbia University Press, 1927.

————. "Chivalric and Dramatic Imitations of Arthurian Romance," *Medi-*

eval Studies in Memory of A. Kingsley Porter. 2 vols. Cambridge, Mass.: Harvard University Press, 1939. I, 79–97.

———. *The Development of Arthurian Romance.* Hutchinson University Library. London: Hutchinson & Co., 1963.

———. *The Grail: From Celtic Myth to Christian Symbol.* Cardiff: University of Wales Press; New York: Columbia University Press, 1963.

———. "Pioneers in Arthurian Scholarship," *Bulletin Bibliographique de la Société Internationale Arthurienne,* 16 (1964), 95–106.

Lucas, F. L. *The Decline and Fall of the Romantic Ideal.* 2d ed. Cambridge, Eng.: At the University Press, 1948.

Lumiansky, R. M. "Gawain's Miraculous Strength: Malory's Use of *Le Morte Arthur* and *Mort Artu,*" *Études Anglaises,* 10 (1957), 97–108.

——— (ed.). *Malory's Originality: A Critical Study of Le Morte Darthur.* Baltimore: The Johns Hopkins Press, 1964.

———. "Malory's Steadfast Bors," *Tulane Studies in English,* 8 (1958), 5–20.

———. "Malory's 'Tale of Lancelot and Guenevere' as Suspense," *Mediaeval Studies,* 19 (1957), 108–22.

———. "The Question of Unity in Malory's *Morte Darthur,*" *Tulane Studies in English,* 5 (1955), 29–39.

———. "The Relationship of Lancelot and Guenevere in Malory's 'Tale of Lancelot,' " *Modern Language Notes,* 68 (1953), 86–91.

———. "Two Notes on Malory's *Morte Darthur*: Sir Urry in England [and] Lancelot's Burial Vow," *Neuphilologische Mitteilungen,* 58 (1957), 148–53.

———. Review of *Essays on Malory,* ed. J. A. W. Bennett. *Modern Philology,* 62 (1964), 158–59.

MacCallum, M. W. *Tennyson's Idylls of the King and Arthurian Story from the XVIth Century.* Glasgow: James Maclehose and Sons, 1894.

McCunn, Florence. *Sir Walter Scott's Friends.* Edinburgh and London: William Blackwood and Sons, 1909.

McKisack, May. "Samuel Daniel as Historian," *Review of English Studies,* 23 (1947), 226–43.

MacKenzie, M. L. "Ballad Collectors in the Eighteenth Century," *Humanities Association Bulletin* (Canada), 17 (1966), 33–45.

McShane, Mother Edith E. *Tudor Opinions of the Chivalrous Romance: An Essay in the History of Criticism.* Micro-card. Washington: The Catholic University of America Press, 1950.

Mahoney, John L. "Some Antiquarian and Literary Influences of Percy's *Reliques,*" *CLA Journal,* 7 (1964), 240–46.

Malory, Thomas. *The Byrth, Lyf, and Actes of King Arthur: of His Noble Knyghtes of the Round Table, Theyr Merveyllous Enquestes and Aduentures, Thachyeuyng of the Sanc Greal; and in the End Le Morte Darthur, with the Dolorous Deth and Departyng out of this Worlde of Them Al.* Edited with introduction and notes by Robert Southey. 2 vols. London: Longman, Hurst, Rees, Orme, and Brown, 1817.

————. *The History of the Renowned Prince Arthur, King of Britain.* 2 vols. London: Printed for Walker & Edwards, 1816.

————. *King Arthur and His Knights.* Edited by Eugène Vinaver. Boston: Houghton Mifflin, 1956.

————. *La Mort d'Arthur: The Most Ancient History of the Renowned Prince Arthur and the Knights of the Round Table.* 3 vols. London: R. Wilks, 1816.

————. *La Mort d'Arthure: The History of King Arthur and of the Knights of the Round Table.* Edited with an introduction and notes by Thomas Wright. 3 vols. London: John Russell Smith, 1865.

————. *Le Morte Darthur.* Edited with an introduction and glossary by H. Oskar Sommer, and an essay on Malory's style by Andrew Lang. 3 vols. London: David Nutt, 1889–1891.

————. *Le Morte D'Arthur.* Everyman's Library, Nos. 45–46. 2 vols. London: J. M. Dent and Sons Ltd.; New York: E. P. Dutton & Co., Inc., 1906.

————. *Morte D'Arthur.* Edited with an introduction by Sir Edward Strachey. The Globe Edition. London: Macmillan and Co., 1868.

————. *Le Morte Darthur.* Edited with a revised introduction by Sir Edward Strachey. London: Macmillan and Co., Limited, 1901.

————. *The Tale of the Death of Arthur.* Edited by Eugène Vinaver. London: Oxford University Press, 1955.

————. *The Works of Sir Thomas Malory.* Edited with an introduction by Eugène Vinaver. 3 vols. Oxford: Clarendon Press, 1947.

————. *The Works of Sir Thomas Malory.* Edited with an introduction by Eugène Vinaver. 2d ed., revised. 3 vols. Oxford: Clarendon Press, 1967.

————. *The Works of Sir Thomas Malory.* Edited by Eugène Vinaver. 1 vol. London: Oxford University Press, 1954.

Matthews, William. Review of *Malory's Originality*, ed. R. M. Lumiansky. *Speculum*, 41 (1966), 155–59.

Maxwell, J. C. "Lucan's First Translator," *Notes and Queries*, 192 (1947), 521–22.

Maynadier, Howard. *The Arthur of the English Poets.* Boston and New York: Houghton Mifflin, 1907.

Mead, William Edward. "Arthurian Story in the Sixteenth Century," in his edition of Christopher Middleton's *Chinon of England.* Early English Text Society, Original Series No. 165. London: Humphrey Milford, Oxford University Press, 1925. Pp. xxv–xlvi.

————. "Outlines of the History of the Legend of Merlin," in *Merlin, or The Early History of King Arthur.* Edited by Henry B. Wheatley. Early English Text Society, Nos. 10, 21, 36, and 112. 2 vols. London, 1865–1899. I, v–cclvi.

Miller, Frances Schouler. "The Historic Sense of Thomas Warton, Junior," *ELH*, 5 (1938), 71–92.

Millican, Charles Bowie. "Spenser and the Arthurian Legend," *Review of English Studies*, 6 (1930), 167–74.

——. *Spenser and the Table Round: A Study in the Contemporaneous Background for Spenser's Use of the Arthurian Legend*. (Harvard Studies in Comparative Literature, Vol. VIII.) Cambridge, Mass.: Harvard University Press, 1932.

Milton, John. *Paradise Lost, Books I. and II*. Edited by A. W. Verity. Pitt Press Series. Cambridge, Eng.: At the University Press, 1924.

——. *The Poems of John Milton*. Edited by H. J. C. Grierson. 2 vols. London: Chatto & Windus, 1925.

——. *The Works of John Milton*. Columbia University Edition, Frank Allen Patterson, general editor. 18 vols. New York: Columbia University Press, 1931–1938.

Montefiore, Arthur. *Reginald Heber, Bishop of Calcutta, Scholar and Evangelist*. New York, Chicago, and Toronto: Fleming H. Revell Company, n.d.

Moore, Cecil A. *Backgrounds of English Literature, 1700–1760*. Minneapolis: The University of Minnesota Press, 1953.

Moore, T. Sturge. "The Story of Tristram and Isolt in Modern Poetry," *The Criterion*, 1 (1922–1923), 34–49, 171–87.

Moorman, Charles. *Arthurian Triptych: Mythic Materials in Charles Williams, C. S. Lewis, and T. S. Eliot* (Perspectives in Criticism, No. 5.) Berkeley and Los Angeles: University of California Press, 1960.

——. *The Book of Kyng Arthur: The Unity of Malory's Morte Darthur*. [Lexington]: University of Kentucky Press, 1965.

——. "Courtly Love in Malory," *ELH*, 27 (1960), 163–76.

——. "The First Knights," *Southern Quarterly*, 1 (1962), 13–26.

——. "Internal Chronology in Malory's *Morte Darthur*," *Journal of English and Germanic Philology*, 60 (1961), 240–49.

——. "King Arthur and the English National Character," *New York Folklore Quarterly*, 24 (1968), 103–12.

——. *A Knyght There Was: The Evolution of the Knight in Literature*. Lexington: University of Kentucky Press, 1967.

——. "Lot and Pellinore: The Failure of Loyalty in Malory's 'Morte Darthur,'" *Mediaeval Studies*, 25 (1963), 83–92.

——. "Malory's Tragic Knights," *Mediaeval Studies*, 27 (1965), 117–27.

——. "Malory's Treatment of the Sankgreall," *PMLA*, 71 (1956), 496–509.

——. "Myth and Mediaeval Literature: *Sir Gawain and the Green Knight*," *Mediaeval Studies*, 18 (1956), 158–72.

——. "The Relation of Books I and III of Malory's 'Morte Darthur,'" *Mediaeval Studies*, 22 (1960), 361–66.

Morgan, Sister Mary Louise. *Galahad in English Literature*. Washington: Catholic University of America, 1932.

Morton, A. L. "The Matter of Britain: the Arthurian Cycle and the Development of Feudal Society," *Zeitschrift für Anglistik und Amerikanistik*, 8 (1960), 5–28.

Muir, L. "A Detail in Milton's Description of Sin," *Notes and Queries*, NS 3 (1956), 100–101.

Mutschmann, H. *Milton's Projected Epic on the Rise and Future Greatness of the Britannic Nation*. Tartu: J. G. Kruger, Ltd., 1936.

Nearing, Homer, Jr. *English Historical Poetry, 1599–1641*. Philadelphia: University of Pennsylvania, 1945.

Neff, Emery. *The Poetry of History*. New York: Columbia University Press, 1947.

Neve, John. *A Concordance to the Poetical Works of William Cowper*. London: Sampson Low, Marston, Searle, & Rivington, 1887.

Newstead, Helaine. Review of R. W. Barber's *Arthur of Albion*. *Speculum*, 37 (1962), 600–601.

———. Review of *Essays on Malory*, ed. J. A. W. Bennett. *Medium Ævum*, 33 (1964), 233–40.

Nicoll, Allardyce. *A History of Early Eighteenth Century Drama, 1700–1750*. Cambridge, Eng.: At the University Press, 1925.

———. *A History of English Drama, 1660–1900*. 4th ed. 6 vols. Cambridge, Eng.: At the University Press, 1952–1959.

Nitze, William A. "Arthurian Problems," *Bulletin Bibliographique de la Société Internationale Arthurienne*, 5 (1953), 69–84.

———. *Arthurian Romance and Modern Poetry and Music*. Chicago: University of Chicago Press, 1940.

Northup, Clark S. "King Arthur, the Christ, and Some Others," *Studies in English Philology: A Miscellany in Honor of Frederick Klaeber*. Edited by Kemp Malone and Martin B. Ruud. Minneapolis: University of Minneapolis Press, 1929. Pp. 309–19.

Northup, Clark S. and Parry, John J. "The Arthurian Legends: Modern Retellings of the Old Stories: An Annotated Bibliography," *Journal of English and Germanic Philology*, 43 (1944), 173–221.

Oehninger, Ludwig. *Die Verbreitung der Königssagen der Historia Regum Britanniae von Geoffrey of Monmouth in der poetischen Elisabethanischen Literatur*. Kitzingen a/M: Druck von Meschett & Hissiger, 1905.

Osgood, Charles Grosvenor (ed.). *A Concordance to the Poems of Edmund Spenser*. Washington: The Carnegie Institution of Washington, 1915.

Parry, John J. *A Bibliography of Critical Arthurian Literature for the Years 1922–1929*. New York: The Modern Language Association, 1931.

——— and Schlauch, Margaret. *A Bibliography of Critical Arthurian Literature for the Years 1930–1935*. New York: The Modern Language Association, 1936.

———. "A Bibliography of Critical Arthurian Literature for the Years 1936–1939," *Modern Language Quarterly*, 1 (1940), 129–74. (Continued annually through 1963 in *Modern Language Quarterly*; edited by Paul A. Brown from 1955 through 1963.)

Parry, John J. "Editor's Supplement" [to Northup and Parry's "The Arthurian Legends: Modern Retellings of the Old Stories: An Annotated Bibliography"], *Journal of English and Germanic Philology*, 49 (1950), 213–16.
———. "The Historical Arthur," *Journal of English and Germanic Philology*, 58 (1959), 365–79.

Patchell, Mary. *The Palmerin Romances in Elizabethan Prose Fiction*. (Columbia University Studies in English and Comparative Literature, No. 166.) New York: Columbia University Press, 1947.

Patterson, Frank Allen, assisted by Fogle, French Rowe. *An Index to the Columbia Edition of the Works of John Milton*. 2 vols. New York: Columbia University Press, 1942.

Peacock, Thomas Love. *The Works of Thomas Love Peacock*. Edited by H. F. B. Brett-Smith and C. E. Jones. The Halliford Edition. 8 vols. London: Constable & Co. Ltd.; New York: Gabriel Wells, 1924–1934.

Peardon, Thomas Preston. *The Transition in English Historical Writing*. (Studies in History, Economics and Public Law, No. 390.) New York: Columbia University Press, 1933.

Percy, Thomas (ed.). *Reliques of Ancient English Poetry, Consisting of Old Heroic Ballads, Songs, and Other Pieces of Our Earlier Poets, Together with Some Few of Later Date*. Edited by Henry B. Wheatley. 3 vols. London: Swan Sonnenschein, Lebas, & Lowrey, 1886.

Pevsner, Nikolaus. *An Outline of European Architecture*. Pelican Books, No. A109. 5th ed. revised and enlarged. Harmondsworth: Penguin Books, 1957.

[Philips, Ambrose] (supposed ed.). *A Collection of Old Ballads, Corrected from the Best and Most Ancient Copies Extant, with Introductions Historical, Critical, or Humorous*. 3 vols. London: Printed for J. Roberts; and sold by J. Brotherton in Cornhill; A. Bettesworth in Pater-Noster-Row; J. Pemberton in Fleet Street; J. Woodman in Bow Street, Covent Garden; and J. Stag in Westminster-Hall, 1723–1725. (Vols. II and III show variations in the list of booksellers.)

Pinkerton, John (ed.). *Ancient Scotish Poems, Never Before in Print*. 2 vols. London: Printed for Charles Dilly and for William Creech at Edinburgh, 1786.

——— (ed.). *Scotish Poems, Reprinted from Scarce Editions*. 3 vols. London: Printed by and for John Nichols, 1792.

——— (ed.). *Select Scotish Ballads*. 2 vols. London: Printed by and for J. Nichols, 1783.

Plesner, K. F. *Engelsk Arthur-Digtning*. (Studier fra Sprog-og Oldtidsforskning, Nr. 136). Copenhagen: V. Pios Boghandel-Povl Branner Nørregade, 1925.

Pochoda, Elizabeth T. *Arthurian Propaganda: Le Morte Darthur as an Historical Ideal of Life*. Chapel Hill: The University of North Carolina Press, 1971.

[Pocock, Isaac]. *King Arthur and the Knights of the Round Table: A New Grand Chivalric Entertainment, in Three Acts.* London: John Miller, 1834.

Pope, Alexander. *The Dunciad.* Edited by James Sutherland. The Twickenham Edition. New York: Oxford University Press, 1943.

——. *The Works of Alexander Pope.* Edited by Rev. Whitwell Elwin and William John Courthope. 10 vols. London: John Murray, 1871–1889.

Pope-Hennessy, Una. *Sir Walter Scott.* The English Novelists. London: Home & Van Thal Ltd., 1948.

Previté-Orton, C. W. *The Shorter Cambridge Medieval History.* 2 vols. Cambridge, Eng.: At the University Press, 1952.

Quaritch, Bernard. *Account of the Great Learned Societies and Associations, and of the Chief Printing Clubs of Great Britain and Ireland.* Sette of Odde Volumes, Miscellanies, No. 14. London, 1886.

Raglan, Lord [FitzRoy Richard Somerset]. *The Hero: A Study in Tradition, Myth, and Drama.* The Thinker's Library, No. 133. London: Watts & Co., 1949.

Ramsay, Allan (ed.). *The Ever Green: A Collection of Scots Poems Wrote by the Ingenious Before 1600.* 2 vols. Reprinted from the original edition of 1724. Glasgow: Robert Forrester, 1875.

—— (ed.). *The Tea-Table Miscellany: A Collection of Choice Songs, Scots & English.* 2 vols. Reprinted from the 14th ed. Glasgow: John Crum, 1871.

Rank, Otto. "The Myth of the Birth of the Hero: A Psychological Interpretation of Mythology," *The Myth of the Birth of the Hero and Other Writings.* New York: Vintage Books, 1959. Pp. 1–96.

Rathbone, Isabel E. *The Meaning of Spenser's Fairyland.* (Columbia University Studies in English and Comparative Literature, No. 131.) New York: Columbia University Press, 1937.

Ray, B. K. *The Character of Gawain.* (Dacca University Bulletin, No. XI.) London: Published for the University of Dacca by the Oxford University Press, 1926.

Reed, A. W. "Chivalry and the Idea of a Gentleman," *Chivalry: A Series of Studies to Illustrate Its Historical Significance and Civilizing Influence.* Edited by Edgar Prestage. London: Kegan Paul, Trench, Trubner & Co., Ltd., 1928.

Reese, Gertrude. "Political Import of *The Misfortunes of Arthur*," *Review of English Studies,* 21 (1945), 81–91.

Reid, J. B. *A Complete Word and Phrase Concordance to the Poems and Songs of Robert Burns.* Glasgow: Kerr & Richardson, 1889.

Reid, Margaret J. C. *The Arthurian Legend: Comparison of Treatment in Modern and Medieval Literature: A Study in the Literary Value of Myth and Legend.* Edinburgh: Oliver and Boyd, [1938].

Reiss, Edmund. *Sir Thomas Malory.* Twayne's English Authors Series, No. 35. New York: Twayne Publishers, Inc., 1966.

Renwick, W. L. *Edmund Spenser: An Essay on Renaissance Poetry.* London: Edward Arnold Ltd., 1925.

Rhys, Ernest. *Gwenevere: A Lyric Play, Written for Music: The Music by Vincent Thomas.* London: J. M. Dent & Company, 1905.

Richter, Margaret Rose. "Spenser's Use of Arthurian Romance" [abstract of an unpublished doctoral dissertation], *Stanford University Bulletin,* 2 (1928), 119–24.

Rigaud, Louis. "Le graal au service de la morale victorienne," *Lumière du Graal.* Edited by René Nelli. Paris: Les Cahiers du Sud, [1951]. Pp. 282–88.

Ritson, Joseph (ed.). *Ancient Engleish Metrical Romanceës.* 3 vols. London: Printed by W. Bulmer and Company . . . for G. and W. Nicol, 1802.

—— (ed.). *Ancient Songs, from the Time of King Henry the Third, to the Revolution.* London: Printed for J. Johnson, in St. Pauls Church Yard, 1790.

——. *Bibliographica Poetica: A Catalogue of Engleish Poets, of the Twelfth, Thirteenth, Fourteenth, Fifteenth, and Sixteenth, Centurys.* London: Printed by C. Roworth, Hudsons-Court, for G. and W. Nicol, Bookselers to his Majesty, Pel-Mel, 1802.

—— (ed.). *The English Anthology.* 3 vols. London: Printed by C. Clarke, for T. and J. Egerton, Whitehall, 1793–1794.

——. *The Life of King Arthur: From Ancient Historians and Authentic Documents.* London: Printed for Payne and Foss . . . and Harding, Triphook, and Lepard, 1825.

—— (ed.). *Pieces of Ancient Popular Poetry: From Authentic Manuscripts and Old Printed Copies.* London: Printed by C. Clarke, for T. and J. Egerton, 1791.

—— (ed.). *Pieces of Ancient Popular Poetry: From Authentic Manuscripts and Old Printed Copies.* 2d ed. London: William Pickering, 1833.

—— (ed.). *A Select Collection of English Songs.* 3 vols. London: Printed for J. Johnson, 1783.

Robertson, D. W., Jr. "The Subject of the *De Amore* of Andreas Capellanus," *Modern Philology,* 50 (1953), 145–61.

Rollins, Hyder Edward (ed.). *The Keats Circle: Letters and Papers 1816–1878.* 2 vols. Cambridge, Mass.: Harvard University Press, 1948.

Rosenberg, Albert. *Sir Richard Blackmore: A Poet and Physician of the Augustan Age.* Lincoln: University of Nebraska Press, 1953.

Rosenberg, Eleanor. *Leicester, Patron of Letters.* New York: Columbia University Press, 1955.

Rossetti, William Michael (ed.). *Rossetti Papers: 1862–1870.* New York: Charles Scribner's Sons, 1903.

Rowlands, William. *Cambrian Bibliography.* Edited by D. Silvan Evans. Llanidloes: Printed and published by John Pryse, 1869.

Rumble, Thomas C. "The First *Explicit* in Malory's *Morte Darthur,*" *Modern Language Notes,* 71 (1956), 564–66.

————. "Malory's *Balin* and the Question of Unity in the *Morte Darthur*," *Speculum*, 41 (1966), 68–85.

————. "Malory's *Works* and Vinaver's Comments: Some Inconsistencies Resolved," *Journal of English and Germanic Philology*, 59 (1960), 59–69.

Schlauch, Margaret. Review of *The Works of Sir Thomas Malory*, ed. Eugène Vinaver. *New York Times Book Review* (September 12, 1948), p. 28.

Schüler, Meier. *Sir Thomas Malorys 'Le Morte D'Arthur' und die Arthurdichtung des XIX. Jahrhunderts*. Strassburg: Josef Singer, 1900.

Schulze, Ivan L. "Notes on Elizabethan Chivalry and 'The Faerie Queene,'" *Studies in Philology*, 30 (1933), 148–59.

Scott, Sir Walter. *The Bridal of Triermain, or The Vale of St. John*. Edinburgh: Printed by James Ballantyne and Co. for John Ballantyne and Co., Hanover-Street; and for Longman, Hurst, Rees, Orme, and Brown; and Gale, Curtis, and Fenner; London, 1813.

————. *The Letters of Sir Walter Scott*. Edited by Sir Herbert Grierson. Centenary Edition. 12 vols. London: Constable & Co. Ltd., 1932–1937.

———— (ed.). *Minstrelsy of the Scottish Border*. Revised and edited by T. F. Henderson. 4 vols. Edinburgh: Oliver and Boyd, 1932.

————. *The Poetical Works of Sir Walter Scott*. Edited by J. Logie Robertson. Oxford Complete Edition. London: Henry Frowde, 1913.

———— (ed.). *Sir Tristrem: a Metrical Romance of the Thirteenth Century: by Thomas of Erceldoune, Called the Rhymer*. 3d ed. Edinburgh: Archibald Constable and Company and Longman, Hurst, Rees, Orme, and Brown, 1811.

Seaman, John E. "The Chivalric Cast of Milton's Epic Hero," *English Studies*, 49 (1968), 97–107.

Smith, A. H. *A Catalogue of Sculpture in the Department of Greek and Roman Antiquities, British Museum*. 3 vols. London: Printed by Order of the Trustees, 1892–1904.

Smith, David Nichol. "Warton's History of English Poetry," *Proceedings of the British Academy* (1929). London: Humphrey Milford, Oxford University Press, 1929. Pp. 73–99.

Southey, Robert. *The Life and Correspondence of Robert Southey*. Edited by the Rev. Charles Cuthbert Southey. New York: Harper & Brothers, Publishers, 1855.

————. *The Poetical Works of Robert Southey*. 10 vols. in 5. Boston: Houghton, Osgood and Company, 1880.

————. *Selections from the Letters of Robert Southey*. Edited by John Wood Warter. 4 vols. London: Longman, Brown, Green, and Longmans, 1856.

————. *Sir Thomas More: or, Colloquies on the Progress and Prospects of Society*. 2 vols. London: John Murray, 1829.

The Spectator. Edited by George A. Aitkin. 6 vols. London: George Routledge & Sons, Ltd., n.d.

Spenser, Edmund. *The Works of Edmund Spenser: A Variorum Edition*.

Edited by Edwin Greenlaw *et al.* 10 vols. Baltimore: The Johns Hopkins Press, 1932–1949.

Spindler, Robert. "Die Arthursage in der Viktorianischen Dichtung," *Britannica: Max Förster zum sechzigsten Geburtstage.* Leipzig: Bernhard Tauchnitz, 1929. Pp. 249–66.

Starr, Nathan Comfort. *King Arthur Today: The Arthurian Legend in English and American Literature 1901–1953.* Gainesville: University of Florida Press, 1954.

——. Review of R. W. Barber's *Arthur of Albion. Modern Language Quarterly*, 23 (1962), 401–402.

Steeves, Harrison Ross. *Learned Societies and English Literary Scholarship in Great Britain and the United States.* New York: Columbia University Press, 1913.

Swinburne, Algernon Charles. *The Complete Works of Algernon Charles Swinburne.* Edited by Sir Edmund Gosse and T. J. Wise. Bonchurch Edition. 20 vols. London: Heinemann, 1925–1927.

Tatlock, J. S. P. *The Legendary History of Britain: Geoffrey of Monmouth's Historia Regum Britanniae and Its Early Vernacular Versions.* Berkeley and Los Angeles: University of California Press, 1950.

Thelwall, John. *Poems Chiefly Written in Retirement. The Fairy of the Lake, a Dramatic Romance; Effusions of Relative and Social Feeling: and Specimens of The Hope of Albion; or, Edwin of Northumbria: an Epic Poem* . . . *With a Prefatory Memoir of the Life of the Author; and Notes and Illustrations of Runic Mythology.* Hereford: Printed by W. H. Parker, 1801.

Thoms, William J. (ed.). *Early English Prose Romances.* 2d ed. enlarged. 3 vols. London: Nattali and Bond, 1858.

Thomson, Derick S. *The Gaelic Sources of Macpherson's 'Ossian.'* (Aberdeen University Studies, No. 130.) Edinburgh and London: Oliver and Boyd, [1951].

Tillotson, Geoffrey. "Contemporary Praise of *Polyolbion*," *Review of English Studies*, 16 (1940), 181–83.

Tillyard, E. M. W. *Milton.* 4th impression. London: Chatto & Windus, 1949.

Todd, Ruthven. *Tracks in the Snow: Studies in English Science and Art.* London: The Grey Walls Press, 1946.

Trowbridge, Hoyt. "Bishop Hurd: A Reinterpretation," *PMLA*, 58 (1943), 450–65.

Tucker, P. E. "The Place of the 'Quest of the Holy Grail' in the 'Morte Darthur,'" *Modern Language Review*, 48 (1953), 391–97.

Tunison, J. S. *The Graal Problem from Walter Map to Richard Wagner.* Cincinnati: The Robert Clarke Company, 1904.

[Utterson, E. V.] (ed.). *Select Pieces of Early Popular Poetry.* 2 vols. London: Printed by T. Davison for Longman, Hurst, Rees, Orme, and Brown, 1817.

Valency, Maurice. *In Praise of Love: An Introduction to the Love-Poetry of the Renaissance.* New York: The Macmillan Company, 1958.

Vettermann, Ella. *Die Balen-Dichtungen und ihre Quellen.* (Beiheft zur Zeitschrift für romanische Philologie, Vol. LX.) Halle: Niemeyer, 1918.

Vinaver, Eugène. *Malory.* Oxford: Clarendon Press, 1929.

————. "Le Manuscrit de Winchester," *Bulletin Bibliographique de la Société Internationale Arthurienne,* 3 (1951), 75–82.

V[inaver], E[ugène]. Review of Margaret J. C. Reid's *The Arthurian Legend. Review of English Studies,* 16 (1940), 331–32.

Waller, Evangelia H. "A Possible Interpretation of *The Misfortunes of Arthur,*" *Journal of English and Germanic Philology,* 24 (1925), 219–45.

Walter, J. H. (ed.). *King Henry V.* The Arden Edition of the Works of William Shakespeare. Cambridge, Mass.: Harvard University Press, 1954.

Walther, Marie. *Malory's Einfluss auf Spenser's Faerie Queene.* Eisleben: Druck von August Klöppel, n.d.

Wangelin, Anna-Marie. *Die Liebe in den Tristandichtungen der Viktorianischen Zeit.* Tübingen: Buchdruckerei Bolzle, 1937.

Ward, Charles E. *The Life of John Dryden.* Chapel Hill: The University of North Carolina Press, 1961.

Warton, Thomas. *The History of English Poetry, from the Close of the Eleventh to the Commencement of the Eighteenth Century.* 3 vols. London: Printed for, and sold by J. Dodsley, J. Walter, T. Becket, J. Robson, G. Robinson, and J. Bew, and Messrs. Fletcher, 1774–1781.

————. *Observations on the Faerie Queene of Spenser.* London: Printed for R. and J. Dodsley; and J. Fletcher, in the Turl, Oxford, 1754.

————. *The Poetical Works of the Late Thomas Warton.* Edited with a memoir by Richard Mant. 5th ed. corrected and enlarged. 2 vols. Oxford: At the University Press, for W. Hanwell and J. Parker; and F. and C. Rivington, London, 1802.

Wasserman, Earl R. *Elizabethan Poetry in the Eighteenth Century.* (Illinois Studies in Language and Literature, Vol. XXXII, Nos. 2–3.) Urbana: The University of Illinois Press, 1947.

Watson, J. Stephen. *The Reign of George III, 1760–1815.* The Oxford History of England, Vol. XII. Oxford: At the Clarendon Press, 1960.

Webb, William Stanford. "Vergil in Spenser's Epic Theory," *ELH,* 4 (1937), 62–84.

Weber, Henry (ed.). *Metrical Romances of the Thirteenth, Fourteenth, and Fifteenth Centuries: Published from Ancient Manuscripts.* 3 vols. Edinburgh: Printed for Archibald Constable and Co., 1810.

Wellek, René. *The Rise of English Literary History.* Chapel Hill: The University of North Carolina Press, 1941.

Whibley, Charles. *Lord John Manners and His Friends.* 2 vols. Edinburgh and London: William Blackwood and Sons, 1925.

White, Alison. Review of *Malory's Originality*, ed. R. M. Lumiansky. *Humanities Association Bulletin*, 15 (1964), 68–69.

Whitman, Charles Huntington. *A Subject-Index to the Poems of Edmund Spenser*. Published under the Auspices of The Connecticut Academy of Arts and Sciences. New Haven: Yale University Press, 1918.

Willard, Rudolph. "Laȝamon in the Seventeenth and Eighteenth Centuries," [Texas] *Studies in English*, 27 (1948), 239–78.

Willey, Basil. *The Eighteenth Century Background: Studies on the Idea of Nature in the Thought of the Period*. London: Chatto & Windus, 1940.

———. *The Seventeenth Century Background: Studies in the Thought of the Age in Relation to Poetry and Religion*. London: Chatto & Windus, 1950.

Williams, Basil. *The Whig Supremacy, 1714–1760*. Oxford History of England, Vol. XI. Oxford: At the Clarendon Press, 1952.

Williams, Harold. *Book Clubs and Printing Societies of Great Britain and Ireland*. London: First Editions Club, 1929.

Williams, Kathleen. "Romance Tradition in *The Faerie Queene*," *Washington State University Research Studies*, 32 (1964), 147–60.

Williams, Mary. "King Arthur in History and Legend," *Folklore*, 73 (1962), 73–88.

Wilson, R. H. "How Many Books Did Malory Write?" [Texas] *Studies in English*, 30 (1951), 1–23.

———. "The Prose *Lancelot* in Malory," [Texas] *Studies in English*, 32 (1953), 1–13.

———. Review of *The Works of Sir Thomas Malory*, ed. Eugène Vinaver. *Modern Philology*, 46 (1948), 136–38.

———. Review of *Essays on Malory*, ed. J. A. W. Bennett. *Criticism*, 6 (1964), 92–95.

Winstanley, Lilian. "The Arthurian Empire in the Elizabethan Poets," *Aberystwyth Studies*, 4 (1922), 59–66.

Wolff, Lucien. "Tristan et Iseult dans la poésie anglaise au XIXᵉ siècle," *Annales de Bretagne*, 40 (1932), 113–52.

Wordsworth, William. *The Poetical Works of William Wordsworth*. Edited by Thomas Hutchinson. Oxford Edition. London: Henry Frowde, Oxford University Press, 1910.

———. *The Poetical Works of William Wordsworth*. Edited by E. de Selincourt. 5 vols. Oxford: At the Clarendon Press, 1940–1949.

———. *The Prelude, or Growth of a Poet's Mind*. Edited by Ernest de Selincourt. 2d ed. revised by Helen Darbishire. Oxford: At the Clarendon Press, 1959.

——— and Wordsworth, Dorothy. *The Letters of William and Dorothy Wordsworth: The Later Years*. Edited by Ernest de Selincourt. 3 vols. Oxford: At the Clarendon Press, 1939.

Wright, Herbert. "The Associations of Thomas Love Peacock with Wales,"

Essays and Studies by Members of the English Association, 12 (1926), 24–46.

Wright, Louis B. *Middle-Class Culture in Elizabethan England*. Ithaca, N. Y.: Published for the Folger Shakespeare Library by Cornell University Press, 1958.

Wülker, Richard Paul. *Die Arthursage in der englischen Literatur*. Leipzig: A. Edelmann, 1895.

Index